LANDSCAPES OF HOPE

LANDSCAPES *of* HOPE

Nature and the Great Migration in Chicago

BRIAN MCCAMMACK

Harvard University Press

Cambridge, Massachusetts
London, England

First Harvard University Press paperback edition, 2021
First printing

Library of Congress Cataloging-in-Publication Data
Names: McCammack, Brian, 1981– author.
Title: Landscapes of hope : nature and the Great Migration in Chicago /
Brian McCammack.
Description: Cambridge, Massachusetts : Harvard University Press, 2017. |
Includes bibliographical references and index.
Identifiers: LCCN 2017007311 | ISBN 9780674976375 (cloth : alk. paper) |
ISBN 9780674260375 (pbk.)
Subjects: LCSH: African Americans—Migrations—History—20th century. | African
Americans—Illinois—Chicago—History—20th century. | African Americans—
Illinois—Chicago—Social conditions—20th century. | Human geography—Illinois—
Chicago—History—20th century. | Recreation areas—Illinois—History—20th century. |
Recreation areas—Michigan—History—20th century.
Classification: LCC F548.9.N4 M325 2017 | DDC 305.896/0730773110904—dc23
LC record available at https://lccn.loc.gov/2017007311

For Laura and Catherine Louise

Contents

LANDSCAPES OF HOPE

Introduction

KINSHIP WITH THE SOIL

I N 1941 the author Richard Wright reflected on the Southern landscapes where African Americans lived and toiled for centuries,
writing, "The land we till is beautiful, with red and black and brown
clay, with fresh and hungry smells, with pine trees and palm trees, with
rolling hills and swampy delta—an unbelievably fertile land." And yet,
Wright continued, "We stand and look out over the green, rolling fields
and wonder why it is that living here is so hard. Everything seems
to whisper of the possibility of happiness, of satisfying experiences; but
somehow happiness and satisfaction never come into our lives. The land
upon which we live holds a promise, but the promise fades with the
passing seasons."[1]

In search of happiness, satisfaction, and promises fulfilled, black
Southerners—migrants from places like New Orleans, Atlanta, Memphis, Birmingham, Jackson, Macon, and hundreds of small towns and
thousands of sharecropping plantations in between—had poured
into the North in the decades before Wright penned those words. Over
that time, the Black Belts of cities like Chicago, New York, Detroit, and
Pittsburgh grew by leaps and bounds as a result of what became known
as the Great Migration. In Chicago, the city that in many ways became
symbolic of the migration and to which Wright himself migrated in
1927, the African American population more than sextupled between

1910 and 1940, from just over 44,000 to nearly 280,000.[2] All told, an estimated 1.6 million African Americans left the South in those three decades, bound for the North that migrants sometimes referred to as "the Promised Land" or "the Land of Hope." Contrasting his adopted home with the South he left behind, Wright wrote that "there in that great iron city, that impersonal, mechanical city, amid the steam, the smoke, the snowy winds, the blistering suns; there in that self-conscious city, that city so deadly dramatic and stimulating, we caught whispers of the meanings that life could have, and we were pushed and pounded by facts much too big for us."[3]

The land itself contributed to the many "whispers of the meanings that life could have" for migrants in the Land of Hope, adding to the promise of political and social equality, economic opportunity, and freedom from racial prejudice and violence. If Southern landscapes evoked bittersweet reminiscences of broken promises from migrants such as Wright, the North offered the possibility of promises realized: more rewarding relationships with nature in landscapes of hope. When black Chicagoans sought out, fought for, built, and enjoyed these natural and landscaped environments in and around the city, they were seeking out, fighting for, building, and enjoying the promise of the Great Migration itself.[4]

Appreciating the many ways that these natural and landscaped environments held meaning for black Chicagoans yields a deeper, richer, and more complex account of African American life during the first wave of the Great Migration, presenting a fresh perspective on what it meant for Southern migrants to adapt to urban metropolises. Black Chicagoans fostered relationships with nature in a wide range of sometimes unexpected places, often well beyond the commonly understood historical and cultural geography of the city's Black Belt: from the South Side's 371-acre Washington Park designed by Frederick Law Olmsted and Calvert Vaux to the 10-acre Madden Park constructed with New Deal funding; from beaches along Lake Michigan at 31st Street and Jackson Park to lakes at African American resort towns such as Idlewild and at youth camps like the YMCA's Camp Wabash, both in rural Michigan; from the Cook County Forest Preserves on Chicago's outskirts to Civilian Conservation Corps camps across the rural Midwest's marshes, farmlands, and forests.[5]

These natural and landscaped environments dotting the Midwestern landscape were every bit as symbolic of the opportunities and possibilities that urban modernity held for African Americans as the Stroll, black Chicago's South Side entertainment district that featured a variety of theaters, clubs, and restaurants. Yet they were the negative image of the Stroll, offering a stark contrast with most of modern urban life.[6] They were greener and more alive—with plants and animals, if not with the people and excitement that the Stroll boasted. They smelled different, and they were often quieter and cooler on hot summer evenings than the South Side's built environment. They were places where changing seasons meant more than just the Midwest's heavy, humid air in summer or winter's snow and bone-chilling cold. They were more spacious and less densely built and populated. For many migrants, all of these features would have made those spaces reminiscent of the "unbelievably fertile land" they had left behind in the South. However, whereas those Southern landscapes were irreparably tainted with race discrimination past and present, these Northern landscapes were imbued with the same hopefulness that drove the Great Migration itself.

The Great Migration that led black Chicagoans to these landscapes of hope was part of a much broader, longer story about the transition away from rural agricultural economies and toward modern industrial economies that forever altered Americans' relationships with nature. Between 1910 and 1940, for instance, more than 3.3 million whites migrated out of the South, mostly in search of the same economic opportunities that drew African Americans to the North's cities.[7] Reflecting on these historical trends that stretched back decades and even centuries, Richard Wright put it this way: "The advent of machine production altered [humans'] relationship to the earth," and with "their kinship with the soil altered, men became atoms crowding great industrial cities." The consequences of mechanization and industrialization were so profound, he argued, that they constituted "a dilemma more acidly corroding than even that of slavery."[8]

Wright may have been correct, but thousands of black Southerners gladly traded one dilemma for another in the half-century following Emancipation: as "acidly corroding" as mass industrialization may have been, it simultaneously helped loosen and sometimes break the bonds of African Americans' ties to exploitative agricultural economies that dated back to slavery. Black Southerners became more mobile, and migration to slowly industrializing Southern cities and towns was already underway well before the Great Migration to the North began. Booker T. Washington's infamous Atlanta Compromise speech in 1895, which urged black Southerners to "cast down your bucket where you are," was in large part a futile response to these black migratory patterns that amounted to a roiling upheaval in search of economic and social opportunity one historian has described as "a gradual weaning from the land."[9] Although data are frustratingly sparse, it seems that these trends meant that many if not most migrants had significant urban experience before moving north, undertaking a step migration from the rural South to the urban South before making the leap to cities in the North.[10] Even if a migrant was born an Alabama sharecropper near Washington's Tuskegee Institute, she or he could have taken up a job washing clothes in Atlanta or pouring molten iron in one of Birmingham's steel mills before venturing north—distinctions that could make a world of difference when contemplating how and why migrants forged new hybrid environmental cultures in and around Chicago.

But even if many—perhaps most—migrants had some sort of urban experience before migrating to the Land of Hope, what would "urban" actually have meant to these future Chicagoans? In the early twentieth century, the United States Census Bureau defined "urban" as a city or town with a population larger than 2,500. In 1910, just before the Great Migration began, less than half of the U.S. population lived in such places, and only fifty cities had populations of 100,000 or more. Southern hubs such as Atlanta, Memphis, and Birmingham all had populations smaller than 200,000 (New Orleans was an outlier with nearly 350,000 residents), and more than 9 percent of the nation's population lived in the only three cities with more than one million inhabitants: New York, Chicago, and Philadelphia. By 1940, after millions of Southerners had migrated north, Chicago was still the nation's second largest city (behind New York) with a population that neared 3.4 million, almost four times the size of Atlanta, Memphis, and Birmingham combined. Only eleven cities (five of them in the North) had African American populations larger than 100,000—and Chicago, New York, and Philadelphia were the only ones with African American populations surpassing 200,000.[11]

It is difficult to grasp the particulars of urban life based on those numbers alone, but with a population in the millions Chicago clearly created a vastly different environmental experience than even a sizable Southern town. The boundaries between rural Southern agricultural life and urban life remained quite fluid well into the twentieth century, and even black Southerners who lived in large cities tended to reside in places that retained rural characteristics. Nothing could have been further from the truth for African Americans in Chicago, where rapid industrialization had long ago turned it into the "impersonal, mechanical city" that Wright saw in 1927, its connections to the surrounding rural hinterlands all but completely obscured for most migrants. At that time, city life in the South was undoubtedly more removed from daily contact with nature than was Southern rural agricultural life, but it was still a far cry from life in a place like Chicago's South Side.[12]

Some migrants seemed to sense that a move to a city like Chicago would represent a significant—and unwelcome—departure from nature as they knew it. One real estate developer noted that some "recent arrivals from the South" who chose to build small communities just outside Chicago were often "rural people [who] wanted homes out in the country" that afforded elements of nature scarcely attainable in the city: they built homes on deep lots with "plenty of space for gardens," sometimes cultivating vegetables on nearby vacant lots.[13] These small communities were the exception to the overwhelming rule, however, claiming only a few thousand black residents at a time when Chicago's African American population had already surpassed 200,000. The vast majority of black migrants to Chicago settled in the heart of Wright's "great iron city."[14]

Broader urbanization and modernization trends meant that for most Chicagoans—regardless of race, ethnicity, gender, or age—natural and landscaped environments became spaces for leisure rather than labor. The contours of urban life meant that kinships with the soil that had been forged through labor *and* leisure in the South were now mainly nurtured through leisure alone: as Richard Wright put it, the Great Migration meant that for African Americans, in particular, "no longer do our lives depend upon the soil, the sun, the rain, or the wind; we live by the grace of jobs and brutal logic of jobs."[15] But although nature no longer factored into most migrants' working lives as directly as it once did, it remained integral to their culture, both recalling a way of life left behind and offering a complement to modern urban conditions. City parks and beaches, forest preserves, rural resorts, youth camps, and countless other public and private leisure spaces in and around Chicago promised respite from industrial areas, commercial centers, and densely built neighborhoods that swelled with ever more people. It was no accident, in other words, that Idlewild, the African American resort town in rural Michigan, and the Cook County Forest Preserves surrounding Chicago can each trace their origins to 1916: both were created by Chicagoans who sought a temporary reprieve from city life.

When the Great Depression began in 1929, it profoundly disrupted these urbanization and industrialization trends, and it significantly slowed black migration to the city.[16] Ultimately the 1930s only represented an eddy in those stronger historical currents, however, and the Depression decade largely reaffirmed nature's importance for urban dwellers in many ways. Washington Park's green expanse simultaneously helped catalyze eviction protests and offered common ground for a community in chaos, New Deal investments reinforced reformers' ideas about the role of urban green space and applied them to public housing ventures, and nature in rural retreats from Idlewild to the YMCA's Camp Wabash continued to provide respite for thousands of black Chicagoans, who now sought refuge from urban ills that had only multiplied. Even the Civilian Conservation Corps, a New Deal agency that put millions of working-class Americans (including hundreds of thousands of African Americans) to work performing manual labor in rural environments during the Great Depression, promoted leisure in nature and intended to prepare young men for the city's "brutal logic of jobs" once the economy recovered.

Although black and white perspectives on nature in and around Chicago overlapped significantly and emerged concurrently as a response to modern urban life between World Wars I and II, race—and racism—caused them to diverge. This was in part what Wright meant when he said that migrants like himself "were pushed and pounded by facts much too big for us": black Chicagoans were forced to confront new forms of racial discrimination no less hostile, vicious, insidious, and destructive than what they left behind in the South. Along with the lasting legacy of slavery and sharecropping that migrants could never completely shake, this discrimination made black Chicagoans' landscapes of hope that much more fraught than those of white city dwellers. It also made them much more fragile: they could all too easily fall prey to the same forces that had made the South a land of broken promises. Nearly every one of

Chicago's public parks and beaches was fiercely and violently contested until whites simply decided to spend their leisure time elsewhere, redrawing the city's de facto racial boundaries. Whether tainted by race violence or not, nearly all of the rural Midwest's natural and landscaped environments were similarly segregated. Faced with segregation uncomfortably akin to that in the Jim Crow South, African Americans fought for integration while also forging racially homogeneous environmental cultures that blended elements of South and North. When the Great Depression threw the thriving Black Metropolis and its landscapes of hope into turmoil, the federal government's myriad New Deal programs proved a mixed blessing, simultaneously facilitating African Americans' connections to nature while perpetuating and even intensifying inequalities and segregation trends that would continue in the years after World War II.

Largely because such persistent and varied forms of racial discrimination in the North usually exposed African Americans to the worst urban environmental conditions, the standard picture of Chicago's South Side tends toward rat-filled tenements and unsanitary kitchenettes, hazardous steel mills and bloody slaughterhouses, or smoky skies and polluted creeks. These are the sorts of urban environments that the famous Chicago School of Sociology analyzed and that in turn created and imprisoned Bigger Thomas in *Native Son,* Richard Wright's novel that came to define the South Side in the popular imagination.[17] Those places remain critical to understanding the environmental inequalities that confronted black Chicago, but they only appear at the margins of this book for two reasons. First and most importantly, they were landscapes of despair, not landscapes of hope: virtually devoid of nature as migrants understood it, they were the places that drove black Chicagoans to seek out, think about, dream of, and value natural and landscaped environments.[18] Second, a story that begins and ends with environmental inequalities and battles over urban space fails to fully account for how and why black Chicagoans experienced, perceived, talked about, valued, and shaped natural and landscaped environments in diverse ways on a daily basis.

Nature was never merely a political proxy for racial inequalities: it was a good in and of itself, freighted with multifaceted cultural significance that reveals black Chicagoans' modern urban lives to be more varied—and more complex—than is typically understood. Domestic workers lived in cramped, unsanitary tenements and went to Olivet

Baptist Church with their families, but they also took their children to play in Madden Park and sent them to camp in rural Michigan. Stockyards laborers frequented the Stroll's clubs and theaters, but they also played baseball and strolled with lovers in Washington Park. Jesse Binga founded a bank that became a community pillar before the Great Depression shuttered it, but he also lived across the street from Washington Park and regularly retreated to a vacation home in rural Idlewild, Michigan.

The complexity and variation in black Chicagoans' modern urban lives also mean that it is impossible to generalize about a single, coherent culture that African Americans forged in these natural and landscaped environments.[19] Indeed, this book explores how and why intraracial conflicts over nature sometimes emerged in and around the city. Perhaps most notably, class status shaped black Chicagoans' environmental cultures: nature often meant something different for a working-class domestic worker or stockyards laborer than it did for a member of the black cultural elite like Jesse Binga.[20] Low-paying jobs and racially discriminatory housing policies had the effect of clustering black Chicago's working classes in the most impoverished and segregated neighborhoods, so building connections with nature in their own private green spaces was virtually out of the question. At the same time, the public parks and beaches most easily accessible to them were small, ill equipped, and even hazardous—landscapes that could inspire more disillusionment than hope. When working-class migrants ventured to larger, more well-equipped public parks and beaches in less segregated areas of the city, they became more vulnerable to race violence. But they were also subject to fellow African Americans' critiques of their Southern-inflected behaviors, which many in the city's black cultural elite worried would confirm whites' racist assumptions about African Americans. Yet despite that intraracial paternalism that could be alienating, the black cultural elite's commitment to fostering connections with nature yielded improved parks and beaches in the working-class Black Belt and afforded thousands of girls and boys opportunities to attend youth camps across the rural Midwest. By developing these privately owned and segregated youth camps in environments similar to what they enjoyed in resort towns like Idlewild, the black cultural elite attempted to shape the values and behaviors of the working classes in places that embodied the ideal landscape of hope: more pristine versions of nature that were largely free from race discrimination.[21]

Class status could be quite fluid within the average migrant's lifetime, but for the vast majority of black Chicagoans, race and their Southern heritage were immutable features that shaped their relationships with nature. Clarice Durham and Charles Davis, siblings who migrated to Chicago from Chattanooga, Tennessee, for instance, grew up "dirt poor" on the South Side during the Depression before going on to build solidly middle- to upper-class careers: Clarice became a schoolteacher and social justice activist, while Charles became an editor at the *Chicago Defender* (the city's and arguably the nation's premier African American newspaper) and, later, a public relations entrepreneur. When they arrived in Chicago in 1931, they joined a community that was already staggeringly Southern in its origins because of the Great Migration. At that time, more than 80 percent of African Americans living in Chicago had been born in the South; in 1930, a black Chicagoan was as likely to have been born in Mississippi as anywhere in the North.[22] That shared background meant that the environmental culture that black migrants such as Clarice and Charles forged in Chicago was, despite its rich variety that sometimes fueled intraracial conflict, almost always a hybrid that blended Southern folkways and responses to urban modernity in the North.[23]

Left orphaned when both their parents succumbed to tuberculosis within a year, Clarice and Charles were only eleven and eight years old, respectively, when their grandfather brought them to Chicago to live with extended family members who had migrated decades earlier to find work in the city's stockyards, laundries, and storefront churches. In Chattanooga they had lived between Lookout Mountain and Missionary Ridge, and Charles remembers wandering off to Missionary Ridge to gather wild nuts. Sometimes they took excursions with adults to Lookout Mountain or even to the banks of the Tennessee River. In the city proper, Clarice and Charles remember Chattanooga having "houses that were spaced apart so that you had that feeling of air, and freedom." And with all of that open space came "a lot of freedom to just be outdoors" where, unless you were downwind of a local tannery, "you smelled the flowers and the fresh air, and you know it was very pleasant." Even in a city of nearly 120,000, then, much of Clarice's and Charles's early environmental consciousness was shaped by the same elements of nature that, for Richard Wright, "seem[ed] to whisper of the possibility of happiness."

When they arrived on Chicago's South Side and settled in the heart of a black community seven times larger than Chattanooga's, Clarice and Charles were greeted with inches of accumulated snow—something that they, like most migrants from the South, had rarely if ever experienced. Like so many others in a city of nearly 3.4 million, Clarice and Charles remember that they first "lived in a row house on a narrow street [with] traffic" and became integrated into "a kind of dense urban community where the street was the playground." In their new home at 36th Street and Vincennes Avenue, just blocks from Madden Park and scarcely a ten-minute walk east of the fictional home of Richard Wright's Bigger Thomas in *Native Son*, they were immersed in the city that Wright described as "huge, roaring, dirty, noisy, raw, stark, brutal; a city of extremes: torrid summers and sub-zero winters . . . a city whose black smoke clouds shut out the sunshine for seven months of the year; a city in which, on a fine balmy May morning, one can sniff the stench of the stockyards."[24] Not only did the stockyard stench pervade their new neighborhood, but Clarice remembered that unlike Chattanooga, "in Chicago, there was not that smell of nature. You'd smell, you know, the horse leavings, the exhaust from cars, and that sort of thing. But not the pleasant smells."[25] The Chicago that Clarice and Charles knew, and the Chicago that Richard Wright immortalized, was a city much further from nature— bigger, more crowded, more industrial—than most migrants from the South had ever seen.

But Clarice and Charles also knew a different Chicago. Like thousands of other migrants, they forged a hybrid environmental culture in Chicago's landscapes of hope that not only worked to counter the urban industrial city that Wright described but also evoked elements of nature left behind in the South. They both visited Washington Park, where they could take a rowboat out on the lagoons with a date, picnic with friends, smell the conservatory's flowers, watch the more affluent ride horses on the bridle paths, or listen to soapbox orators decry the poverty of the Depression. Clarice retreated to a camp that Good Shepherd Church owned in rural Michigan near Idlewild, where she enjoyed bathing in a trout stream, discovered how difficult learning to swim can be, and got lost on a hike until enrollees from a nearby Civilian Conservation Corps company guided her back to camp. Charles, meanwhile, joined the Boy Scouts and with other boys in Mohawk Patrol explored the Forest Preserves surrounding the city on overnight hikes and spent part of his summer at rural Michigan's Camp Belnap.

Robert Abbott's *Chicago Defender* famously proclaimed May 15, 1917, the "Great Northern Migration Day," celebrating and further stoking the wave of migration that eventually drew Clarice and Charles to Chicago, and that irrevocably changed America's cultural geography. A century later, the natural and landscaped environments that Clarice and Charles recall so vividly—and countless others that thousands of migrants sought out, fought for, and enjoyed—make it clear that the way we understand the Great Migration and black Chicago's environment must change as well. As the chapters that follow reveal, migrants' "kinship with the soil" was never completely severed in Chicago. Instead, relationships with nature were actively reshaped, recast, and reimagined in the city's landscapes of hope.

PART I

THE MIGRATION YEARS,
1915–1929

"Booker T." Washington Park and Chicago's Racial Landscapes

W HEN BUDDING AUTHOR Richard Wright arrived in Chicago in 1927, fresh from rural Mississippi by way of Memphis, he was struck by the urban built environment's sheer dominance over nature. Recalling his first impressions of the city to which he would become so tightly linked, he reflected, "There were no curves here, no trees; only angles, lines, squares, bricks and copper wires."[1] To a migrant from the South, Chicago's dense urban landscape must have indeed been something of a shock. But although much of the South Side was as Wright described it, his account (and most others of black Chicago since) conspicuously failed to fully appreciate at least one significant exception that had plenty of curves and trees: the landscape of hope that, by the time of his arrival, lay directly adjacent to the Black Belt. Washington Park, an enormous public park with pastoral green lawns, lagoons, wooded paths, and curving roads, represented a marked contrast to the urban grid that characterized Midwestern cities like Chicago. In fact, its sprawling meadow-like lawn had been designed by famed landscape architects Frederick Law Olmsted and Calvert Vaux in 1871 as the most important element of Chicago's entire South Park system, creating an "antithesis to [the city's] bustling, paved, rectangular, walled-in streets."[2] Although the park was just as constructed as the city around it, Olmsted and Vaux had hoped to obscure the human influence in their design to create a pastoral antidote to the supposed physical, mental, and spiritual ills of urban life. Once completed, Washington Park and the lakefront Jackson Park (the two were designed as a whole, linked through the Midway Plaisance) had more combined acreage than Olmsted and Vaux's Central Park in New York City and represented an ambitious reshaping of marshy area south of the city that many had considered wasteland.[3]

The marshy area was still six miles from Chicago's rapidly expanding city center in the late nineteenth century; Olmsted and Vaux saw its development as an opportunity to create an urban oasis that would offer a striking and beneficial contrast not only to the city but also to the "flat and treeless prairie and limitless expanse of lake [that] are such prominent characteristics" of the region.[4] Bounded by South Parkway on the west and Cottage Grove Avenue on the east (a distance of a half-mile, or four city blocks), Washington Park stretched more than a mile north and south, all the way from 51st Street south to 60th Street; it could easily take a full hour to walk its perimeter. By the time African American migrants settled on the South Side, the character of Washington Park's 371 acres—an area of roughly thirty-six city blocks—had stood largely unchanged for nearly a half-century, more or less as Olmsted and Vaux had envisioned it. Washington Park was a multisensory experience with sights, sounds, and smells that varied at different locations in the park, as well as with the time of day, the day of the week, and the seasons. This particular landscape of hope was an amalgamation of different micro-geographies, environmentally and experientially distinct leisure spaces that each in its own unique way countered the rigid spatial and temporal boundaries of the bustling city outside its perimeter. While the park's micro-geographies stood (and continue to stand) largely unchanged, many of the surrounding neighborhoods—and consequently the park's visitors—changed a great deal during the Great Migration years.[5]

African Americans began frequenting Washington Park in ever-larger numbers in the late 1910s and became its primary visitors by the late 1920s in large part as the result of Chicago's evolving residential geography that was shaped by racially discriminatory real estate practices and violence. City planners certainly had not had African Americans in mind when the park was commissioned and built in the 1870s in a district that by the end of the century featured some of the city's best housing and the University of Chicago. Instead, it was intended as—and quickly became—a leisure space mostly for wealthy whites who lived nearby.[6] Even by 1920, the Black Belt's southernmost extension was only in a narrow swath west of State Street to nearly 60th Street, still several blocks west of Washington Park. By 1930, however, it had expanded a half-mile to the east, all the way to the north and west boundaries of Washington Park (see Figure 1.1). The years of the African American Great Migration marked a period of rapid transition in the Washington Park neighborhood, which stretched the park's entire length and extended about a half-mile from South Parkway west to the Rock Island & Pacific Railroad tracks. In 1920, the neighborhood had 38,000 residents, only 15 percent of whom were black. By 1930, the equation had completely changed: of 44,000 residents, nearly 92 percent were black. Indeed, the white novelist James T. Farrell, who grew up in the Washington Park neighborhood, recalled that by "about 1927 the neighborhood around 58th Street just west of Washington Park, was considerably and noticeably black."[7] Hemmed in by racially restrictive residential covenants and white violence, African Americans were largely confined to limited sections of the city, and the housing near Washington Park was among the best quality available to them. During the migration years, then, Washington Park was becoming many African Americans' neighborhood park, located just a few steps away from the homes of the black cultural elite. Although only 2,700 black Chicagoans enjoyed Washington Park daily according to one 1922 estimate, they still accounted for 10 percent of the park's visitors (more than double the percentage of Chicagoans who were African American), and by the end of the decade African Americans made up the majority of park visitors.[8]

For Chicago's African American population, which was more than 80 percent Southern-born by 1930, Washington Park's landscape of hope was as close as most of them could get to the more pastoral landscapes many of them had left behind, and they developed hybrid leisure practices there that blended elements of South and North. Indeed, when African Americans, whether migrants or "old settlers," spent their leisure time in the Olmsted and Vaux-designed South Side parks, they did so in a space for which landscape architects hoped that certain elements would create "a combination of the fresh and healthy nature of the North with the restful, dreamy nature of the South."[9] Used primarily by African Americans by the late 1920s, Washington Park perhaps evoked the "restful, dreamy nature of the South" in a way Olmsted and Vaux

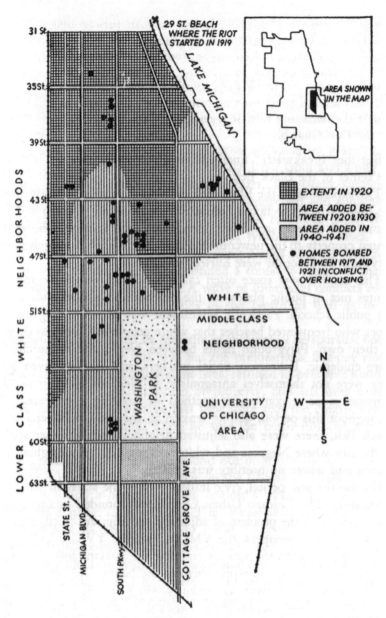

Figure 1.1. Chicago's South Side Black Belt. Note the location of Washington Park in relation to the expanding Black Belt. Jackson Park is just southeast of the "University of Chicago area." Map from *Black Metropolis: A Study of Negro Life In a Northern City* by St. Clair Drake and Horace R. Cayton. Copyright 1945 by St. Clair Drake and Horace R. Cayton. Copyright © Renewed 1973 by St. Clair Drake and Susan Woodson. Reprinted by permission of Houghton Mifflin Harcourt Publishing Company. All rights reserved.

could have scarcely imagined when they penned those words—because distant locales were evoked not only by the landscaped environment they had so carefully designed but also by the culture of the people who used it. Especially for those black Chicagoans who migrated from more rural environments, escaping to Washington Park also would have meant the ability to, in some small way, reconnect to the texture, flow, and sensory experience of lives and folkways they had left behind in the South —but now only temporarily, in the context of modern urban life that buzzed outside and permeated the park's borders. There is little doubt that the meticulously shaped and maintained park landscape was more constructed and urbanized than many rural leisure spaces African American migrants had frequented in the South, and here in the North they were subject to sometimes opaque racial boundaries and class expectations that tended to denigrate Southern folkways. But at the same time, Washington Park's sheer expansiveness could afford the geographical and cultural space such that park goers might easily lose sight of the myriad buildings and miles of roads and paths crisscrossing the green space, perhaps even briefly finding refuge from the city's complex racial and class antagonisms.[10]

Yet although some migrants were no doubt nostalgic for Southern landscapes as they adjusted to their new Northern homes, neither environment was nearly as "restful" and "dreamy" or "fresh and healthy" for African Americans as Olmsted and Vaux's ideal. The Southern pastoral ideal was irreparably rendered bittersweet by an ongoing history of racial discrimination and violence that most black Chicagoans had experienced personally and that made the North's landscapes of hope all the more potent for migrants.[11] But for the African Americans who streamed into northern cities such as Chicago, the urban environments they confronted were anything but "fresh and healthy." Racial discrimination tended to force black Chicagoans to live in cramped and often unsanitary tenements, predominantly funneling them into unskilled manual labor in stockyards, steel mills, and the service and cleaning industries that often threatened their health. For many working-class black Chicagoans who simply sought a leisure escape from the environmental injustices that confronted them at home and at work—and the vast majority of black Chicago was working class—public recreational spaces such as Washington Park promised a low- or no-cost, family-friendly way to temporarily step away from the ills of modern urban life that were disproportionately visited on African Americans. They should have been oases in the urban desert. All too often, however, the racial discrimination and violence that plagued African Americans in the South's natural and landscaped environments were replicated in the North's.[12]

When black Chicagoans sought out these public pastorals, in large part to counter unhealthy and discriminatory conditions at home and on the job, instead they often confronted race violence at the city's parks and beaches. In one way or another, race discrimination wormed its way into nearly every city space, public and private. Racist whites who resented the influx of black migrants targeted African Americans in public green spaces, particularly those used by both races and adjacent to neighborhoods undergoing racial transitions. Chicago's infamous 1919 race riot began at a beach that was ever nearer to the growing Black Belt, for example, and the ensuing violence raged throughout the South Side, much of it only a stone's throw away from Washington Park, where sheep grazed on the meadow. But the rash of race violence in and around Washington Park throughout the late 1910s and early 1920s did not have the intended effect of deterring African Americans from using the park or living near it—far from it. In fact, white resistance, violent and otherwise, seemingly only stiffened the resolve of black Chicagoans determined to enjoy their leisure time in the city's public landscapes of hope, and little could stem the flow of migrants to the city, each trainload of which helped push the residential Black Belt closer and closer to the park. But when race violence finally abated in Washington Park by the late 1920s, it was a somewhat hollow victory for black Chicagoans that was achieved only after whites informally redrew the boundaries of segregated public environments in the city. Racial antagonism had simply changed addresses, moving a mile and a half east from what was now the predominantly African-American–used Washington Park to its lakefront sister, Jackson Park, where many white Chicagoans were determined to maintain exclusive use of its long, spacious beaches.

Washington Park's tree-lined meadow and its shimmering lagoon were not only violent interracial battlegrounds in the Great Migration era but also intraracial social battlegrounds where black Chicagoans clashed over the contours of the new, hybrid leisure culture they were forging there. Many migrants played baseball and tennis, picnicked, played music, rowed, and appreciated their surroundings in their own

Southern-inflected ways, often challenging black reformers' ideas about respectability and race uplift that were informed in part by Northern sensibilities and prejudices. These reformers in the black cultural elite (who tended to live in the much better housing stock nearest the park, on the vanguard of the expanding Black Belt) somewhat paternalistically policed behavioral boundaries and promoted what they saw as public health among working-class migrants in public places such as Washington Park. In doing so, they both acted in response to ideas that saw African Americans as a "primitive" race and built on a long history of beliefs about how green spaces were vital in producing healthy—and respectable—citizens, particularly in the rapidly urbanizing North. In addition to fighting racial inequalities, both sets of ideas were primary reasons why black reformers fought for the creation of smaller parks and playgrounds in the most poverty-stricken areas of the Black Belt that had few nearby recreational spaces of any size, let alone the size of Washington Park. In the mid-1920s, black reformers acting with the broad support of the community finally managed to convince the city to construct the tiny ten-acre Madden Park, roughly twenty blocks north of Washington Park. It was an effort that closely resembled those of the city's white Progressive reformers dating back to the late nineteenth century; the settlement house worker Jane Addams, for example, had long promoted the virtues of playgrounds and parks for the working classes.[13]   ·

In the Great Migration era, black Chicagoans contributed to an already complex and often fraught array of ideas concerning culture, class, and morals that were inscribed in the city's natural and landscaped environments. They grafted not only race but also a cultural geography of North and South onto spatial and ideological boundaries that had been drawn and challenged by diverse groups of white park goers dating back at least to the decade following the Civil War—indeed, these ideas were central to the very design and creation of Washington Park in the 1870s. But the stakes of this battle over the city's natural and landscaped environments were higher for African Americans because they consistently faced greater environmental inequalities and systemic discrimination than any other racial or ethnic group, and they had to wage their intraracial battles over just how they should use the city's green spaces before whites' judgmental eyes. Yet although these battles were often pitched and the stakes were high, their fraught nature would not always have been so apparent to the average African American migrant who spent a Sunday afternoon in Washington Park. For all black Chicagoans, the city's public landscapes of hope still offered them the possibility of coming together as a community and realizing the full potential of the Great Migration. Throughout the year, they could enjoy leisure time outdoors amidst green grass, stately oak trees, and blue lagoons—elements of nature markedly different from the bulk of the South Side's built environment.

Everyday Park Use in Olmsted and Vaux's Landscaped Environment

For African American migrants in particular, myriad activities in Washington Park's various micro-geographies represented a hybrid experience, combining elements of leisure widely practiced in the urban North with reminders of leisure practices and experiences left behind in the South. Entering from the northwest corner of the park at South Parkway and 51st Street nearest the heart of the Black Belt and walking south, perhaps the first thing a migrant would have noticed was that Chicago's streets, straight as arrows outside the park, became long tree-lined arcs within it. Of course it was all by design; streets aside, no matter how natural this landscape might have seemed to African American migrants who were adjusting to urban life, none of it had been there prior to Olmsted and Vaux's dramatic reshaping of the land (see Figure 1.2). Indeed, when the two landscape architects had taken special note of large oak tree groves growing at the northwest corner of what would become Washington Park, it was because "not one of these has a character which would be of high value in a park. Most of them are evidently struggling for mere existence, and the largest are nearly all decrepid [sic]." More generally, they told Chicago officials, "park-like great trees [were] hardly more natural to your conditions than hills, crags, or dashing streams."[14] To remedy this situation, year after year park officials planted trees and shrubs by the thousands. The list of hardwood and softwood timber selected looked like an index of North American forest stock, regardless of nativity to the Chicago area: ash, alder, birch, dogwood, elm, hackberry, larch, linden, maple, oak, pine, poplar, spruce, sycamore, walnut. As the South Park Commission's general superintendent described the tree-planting effort, it was a meticulous, labor-intensive process: the various plantings "must be placed, cared for, watched, thinned out, thickened up, modified in many ways, as it develops, reaching its perfection only after many, many years."[15] But when she or he saw dead trees or shrubs, a park visitor may have become dimly aware that control of the landscape was not completely in human hands. The park's horticulturists battled evergreen-killing droughts, cottony maple scale and tussock moth infestations, and, most commonly and consistently, Chicago's inhospitable climate. By 1922, the same year a white resident suggested that Washington Park be renamed "Booker T. Washington Park" because of its increased use by the city's burgeoning African American population, a South Park Commission report noted with frustration, "Maintaining trees, shrubs and flowers is becoming more difficult every year, owing to the atmospheric conditions of Chicago. . . . Some of the most attractive shrubs . . . will not thrive. Trees such as the Norway Maple, Sugar Maple, Horse Chestnut Birches [sic] in variety, cannot be grown successfully any more."[16] So although Washington Park's broad outlines still adhered to Olmsted and Vaux's design, park officials had nearly as much success maintaining a constant landscaped environment there as did nearby white residents in stemming the flow of African Americans into their neighborhood and the adjacent green leisure space—very little.

Nevertheless, by the time African American migrants arrived in Chicago and were strolling the grounds, Washington Park's remaining original plantings had reached full maturity, or "perfection" as the general superintendent put it, and landscapers' persistent work had produced a thick canopy of cool shade over the roads, sidewalks, and paths that wound around its northern half. A visitor in early May would have seen blooming hawthorn trees that dropped their small white flowers on the grass and roadways and heard the return of thousands of noisy, chirping purple martins to Washington Park's birdhouses—a stark contrast to the clang of city streetcars or the music and conversation on the Stroll. Migrating north with warmer weather in search of insects, these large black or steely-blue swallows signaled the beginning of spring after a long winter—sights and sounds that a migrant from Mississippi or Alabama would have experienced as early as January or February down South. Nestled among the trees near Washington Park's northwest corner, a first-time visitor might have been surprised to come across

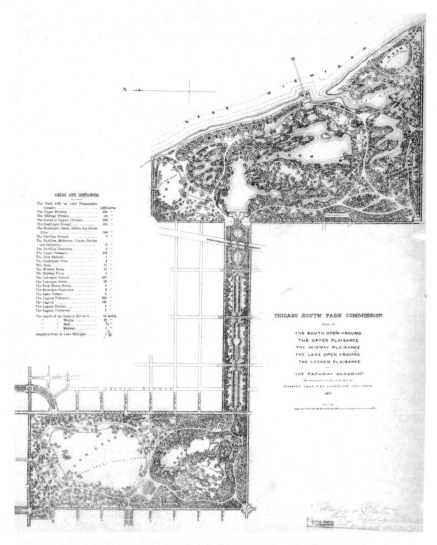

Figure 1.2a. Original Olmsted and Vaux plan for Washington (*bottom left*) and Jackson (*top right*) Parks. North is to the left. At this time, the former was called the Upper Division, and the latter the Lower Division. By permission and courtesy of the Chicago Park District Special Collections.

a shallow pond that played host to ducks and children alike, both cooling off in the hot summer months. For a visitor in October, Washington Park's borders would have offered an exceptional vantage point for the changing fall colors as temperatures gradually dropped to lows unknown to those born and raised in the South.[17]

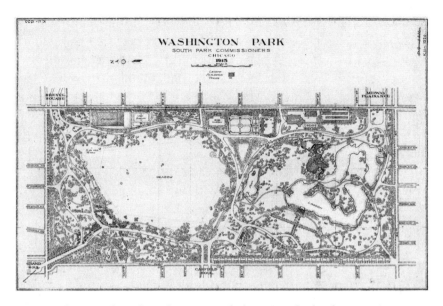

Figure 1.2b. 1913 plan of Washington Park depicting the landscape migrants would have encountered. North is to the left. Although it generally adheres to Olmsted and Vaux's original design, note that differences include a larger lagoon on the southern half, several buildings along Cottage Grove Avenue (including the proposed armory which was eventually built), tennis courts along South Parkway (which Jesse Binga's home in the 5900 block faced), and the duck pond along South Parkway just north of 53rd Street. The darkly shaded area at the northwest border of the lagoon is the boathouse that became the site of considerable racial conflict. By permission and courtesy of the Chicago Park District Special Collections.

Once across the boulevard and through the ring of trees at the park's northwest corner that had long ago replaced the original scrub oaks, Washington Park's African American visitors would have been greeted by a vast open meadow of about one hundred acres, stretching more than two city blocks on each side. Olmsted and Vaux had considered the South Park's "first obvious defect" its flatness, though they went on to note that this was actually an advantage when creating the huge lawn that would eventually entertain thousands of park goers simultaneously.[18] On a weekday afternoon with most of black Chicago hard at work, though, the meadow would have likely been quiet—maybe mothers strolling with their children, the elderly chatting on nearby benches—a marked difference from the bustle of nearby business districts. In winter, the sheer flat expanse of white on the 100-acre meadow after a fresh snowfall would have been unrivaled elsewhere on the South Side; no other public green space—and certainly no other city block—had as much wide open, unbroken space as Washington Park. To an African American migrant experiencing his or her first snowfall, the meadow would have offered a winter experience wholly different from the harsh city winter outside, where snow quickly piled up and became dirty with city grime. In the warmer months, however, the meadow could be bustling with activity.

On an evening or weekend from early spring to late fall, a migrant would have seen the meadow alive with the din of perhaps a dozen simultaneous games of baseball or cricket, both of which had long been popular in Washington Park. The international flavor of cricket games between the International Cricket Club—made up of men from the West Indies—and other city squads would have likely been somewhat foreign to African American migrants, but countless Southerners played baseball and it would have been a familiar reminder of home for many. As one study put it, "baseball is the most popular sport in these communities [in the South]. Even in the isolated rural sections of Alabama, the Saturday baseball game is the most popular form of diversion."[19] Although Chicago's climate inevitably reduced the number of months in which baseball could be played outdoors—especially compared to the South—park officials made sure to keep the diamonds in playing condition "from early in the spring until the end of the calendar year" for the most popular park sport.[20] Baseball in the park was played on a scale and with a level of interracial interaction that migrants were unlikely to have experienced before. Even before African Americans began using Washington Park in any significant way, there was "nowhere near room enough to accommodate all of those who would like to play ball in the parks on Saturdays and Sundays," despite more than two dozen diamonds in use simultaneously.[21] In 1914, two years before grazing sheep were reintroduced to the park, a group of African American churches began a Sunday School Baseball League in Washington Park and other city parks that grew over the years from a dozen to twenty teams, each representing a different congregation. By the late 1920s, the "Industrial League" that featured both black and white teams played baseball in Washington Park and drew tens of thousands of spectators over the course of a summer. It had begun in 1917 when Chicago's meatpacking plants "sought the help of the [city's segregated black] Y.M.C.A. in ori-

enting rural Negroes who flocked to their plants during the war migration" and eventually included employees from a range of companies
including Sears, Roebuck & Company and the Illinois Central Railroad,
the same train line that thousands of migrants rode north.[22] Some migrants may have been quite familiar with these sorts of company-
sponsored teams even before they came north; the steel industry in
Birmingham, Alabama, for instance, had begun a league in 1916 and
fielded at least a half-dozen teams by 1919.[23]

Traveling farther south, beyond the meadow, a park visitor would
have crossed 55th Street, the park's curving main east-west thoroughfare, and entered the southern half of Washington Park that was dominated by the manmade lagoon, bridle paths, and denser planting. Indeed,
Olmsted and Vaux's vision for the park explicitly planned for different
park uses in different places, crafting various micro-geographies within
the broader design that tended to encourage more active, athletic park
use in the northern half's open space and more passive, reflective park
use in the southern half. Exceptions to this rule were the picnic grounds
and tennis courts along the southern half's western edge. Numerous African American churches held Sunday school picnics there—community
events and popular respites from labor that many migrants would have
transplanted from the South—when they were not held in the meadow.
Beyond the picnic grounds were more than two dozen tennis courts
along the length of the park's western edge from 55th all the way to 60th
Street, directly across from the homes of some of the most well-to-do
black Chicagoans, including banker and real estate magnate Jesse Binga.
Certainly less familiar to the average working-class migrant than baseball, both tennis and horseback riding in Washington Park (the latter of
which attracted members of the black cultural elite such as Mrs. Robert
Abbott, wife of the *Defender* publisher, and Mrs. Herbert Turner, wife of
the Chicago NAACP president and medical doctor) had the potential to
be alienating for those without the money or social capital to seamlessly
pick up new activities. But the smells of the stables where horses were
kept on the park's eastern border—and the mere presence of the animals themselves, in a city where they were rapidly being replaced by
automobiles—could have been a reminder for some migrants of Southern
farms left behind.[24]

For a newly minted black Chicagoan still adjusting to a city with few
bodies of water on the South Side other than the lakefront, the extensive

manmade lagoon was easily the most striking landscape feature of Washington Park's southern half. Dug out of the flat earth and filled with water and aquatic plants in the 1870s, the lagoon was surrounded by trees that were planted to achieve the "character of rather dense natural woods," which Olmsted and Vaux had hoped would "[afford] an agreeable change from the Open Ground" of the meadow that dominated the park's northern half.[25] Despite a setting that could be conducive to solitary contemplation, the lagoon also played host to more communal activities. In the winter, ice skating no doubt would have been new to migrants unused to temperatures cold enough to freeze ponds or lakes. A *Defender* editorial from 1912 echoed Olmsted and Vaux's view of the park as a healthy place and noted that African Americans were beginning to take advantage of ice skating in Washington Park, encouraging its readers to take part in the sport that was "getting to be quite a fad" because of "the benefits derived from filling your lungs with fresh, pure air."[26] Ice skating may have been out of reach for the vast majority of working-class black Chicagoans who lacked the disposable income to purchase ice skates, but the sport nevertheless remained a fixture of African Americans' enjoyment of Washington Park in the frigid Chicago winters for decades, drawing as many as 500 to "enjoy themselves any clear winter's day."[27] Competitive ice skating was often touted as a model interracial endeavor possible only in the North, and one that migrants could certainly watch if not participate in; the *Defender* proudly noted, "In all parts of the city skaters of both races will be seen participating in championship meets. They enjoy it. Could this be done below the Mason and Dixon line?"[28] Especially for a migrant (or prospective migrant reading the *Defender* in the South), the answer was obvious—both for racial and climatic reasons.

Ice skating on Washington Park's frozen lagoon may have been foreign to working-class migrants newly arrived to Chicago from the South, but they would have found some familiarity in the way the lagoon hosted both fishermen and rowers in the busier warmer months. Indeed, the lagoon itself would have been reminiscent of small lakes or ponds in the South where fishing and boating were popular leisure activities, even in and around urbanized areas. One study found that in the South, fishing had been a primary leisure activity for those who eventually migrated; another noted that, "in Macon County, Alabama, fishing was regarded next in importance to baseball."[29] In Washington Park, of course, migrants found both those leisure activities in one place. Here, though, fishing was a decidedly more regulated and managed enterprise than in much of the South: the South Park Commission stocked the man-made lagoon with fish and scrupulously kept the water clear of seaweed, restricting the fishing season to a few weeks in autumn. Although the South Park Commission prohibited swimming there, another regulated leisure activity it promoted on the lagoon was boating. Whereas a rural Southerner might have had his or her own boat for fishing or other leisure activities, in Chicago they were available for rent on an hourly basis and thus accessible to working-class migrants who might spend the same amount on a movie or a concert on the Stroll. Timuel Black, a migrant whose family came to Chicago from Birmingham in 1919 before he was even a year old, recalled, "We'd rent a boat, go up and down the lagoon and just have a good time."[30]

The ability to take advantage of Washington Park's myriad micro-geographies was particularly welcome for African American migrants because they were more free, open, and accessible than many Southern landscapes, which were increasingly segregated and privatized. As one study at the time put it, in the Jim Crow South, "Negroes are not admitted to the commercial amusement park, which has taken the place of the old picnic ground. They are turned away from the bathing beach which was once a free-for-all swimming place. . . . Negroes are not admitted to the private game reserve which occupied the old fishing and hunting grounds, and they cannot have any parties on the placid lake where they once rowed their canoes without fear of disturbance."[31] With more freedom in the North, African Americans could lay claim to equal access to Washington Park's—and the city's—public green spaces in a way they could not in the Jim Crow South.

Laying claim to those equal rights in the migration years, however, came at a price. Racial violence around the lagoon had largely dissipated by the late 1920s when Timuel Black enjoyed rowing there, but the boat-house situated at the northwest corner had been the scene of some of the ugliest race violence in the early migration years. George Arthur, the YMCA executive secretary, "described the condition in the vicinity of the boathouse . . . as 'fierce'" in the early 1920s, noting, "There were fights there every Sunday."[32] Rendered faithfully as a "long, low, open structure, bounded on two sides by shrubbery" in James T. Farrell's novel *The Young Manhood of Studs Lonigan*, it was also a place that the fictional Studs and his friends complain "stunk with niggers" and was "so bad that a decent girl can't walk alone here any more for fear a nigger might rape her. They ruin the park." Later, giving voice to a commonly held sentiment among white South Side residents, Studs comments, "Niggers didn't have any right in a white man's park."[33] In reality, it was most often African Americans, not whites, who stood to be beaten or raped by gangs of young white men in Washington Park; even couples simply sitting on park benches together were targeted, victims of racist whites who resented the park's racial transition in the Great Migration era. Despite the *Defender*'s sometimes rosy view of race relations in Chicago as compared to the South, for many migrants the sort of race violence they encountered in the city's public natural and landscaped environments would have been an unwelcome reminder of the racist and exclusionary society they had tried to leave behind.

Race Violence in Washington Park and Beyond

Washington Park was but one of many of Chicago's public landscapes of hope where African Americans were the targets of white violence during the Great Migration years. Indeed, white gangs attacked African Americans in South Side parks as early as 1913 in attempts to deny them access to what had been exclusively white spaces; it was a trend that continued into the early 1920s and well beyond, even as it slowly abated.[34] It would have been a depressingly familiar situation for black migrants with any experience of the urban Jim Crow South from Richmond to Atlanta to Birmingham to Houston to Nashville, where African Americans had long been prohibited from enjoying the most well-equipped public parks (if they had access to any at all, which was rare).[35] When the poet Langston Hughes visited the South in 1927, he was prepared for Jim Crow in public spaces, but still expressed surprise at the fact that "in Nashville there were certain parks Negroes could not enter or cross. If a park lay between you and your destination, you could not walk through the park as a white person might do. Being colored, you had to go *around* the park" or risk an attack. He continued, "About such subtleties as parks, I was ignorant."[36] He probably should not have been. Hughes had spent time in Chicago in the midst of this rash of race violence in the city's parks and was well aware of how urban space—in the North and the South alike—was violently patrolled by whites, having himself been beaten for unknowingly crossing a dividing road into a white neighborhood. Migrants could perhaps take solace in the fact that there were no officially segregated public green spaces in Chicago as there were in the South, and community advocates like the *Defender* fought de facto segregation at every turn. But black Chicagoans citywide still had to contend with whites—some of them city and park police—who were intent on keeping the races separate by any means necessary, by and large relegating African Americans to inferior, ill-equipped recreational spaces. Indeed, Washington Park's prized environmental amenities and its unmatched expanse of open space were in part what made it such a fiercely contested space in the Great Migration years. One could say the same of Chicago's lakefront, which was one of the few places where urban dwellers could cool off in the hot summer months.[37]

The city's simmering race violence came to a head at the lakefront in the summer of 1919, but it could have just as easily erupted in Washington Park. Both parks and beaches in the North were unique places of virtually unprecedented race and class mingling—particularly on Sundays when much of the city was free from work—that made them likely points of conflict. As one study of Chicago later noted, "On the beaches and in the parks there is less isolation and greater intermingling. People meet and brush elbows who have only remote and fleeting contact with one another in other respects."[38] In the weeks before the riot that would roil Chicago, white gangs clashed with African Americans in Washington Park and posted signs throughout the grounds (and elsewhere on the South Side) that threatened, "We will get you July 4." There was little question as to whom the "you" referred; for years, black Chicagoans had held picnics in Washington Park on Independence Day, a holiday whose celebration of national independence held special significance for African Americans still struggling for freedom.[39] Such threats prompted some churches to relocate planned picnics from Washington Park more than thirty blocks north to Douglas Park and other park goers to carry weapons in their picnic baskets. Although no violent encounters were reported over the holiday, the *Defender*, long a promoter of the freedoms the North offered to prospective migrants, stepped in to condemn the race violence in the South Side's green spaces as tensions continued to mount that July. Condemning the "gangs of young hoodlums from the district west of Wentworth avenue [who] have been making it a practice of attacking our people under cover of darkness" and calling on park police to make the "breathing spots" of parks "a safe retreat for all," the *Defender* pointed out that African American tax dollars helped pay for maintenance and upkeep in the parks.[40]

The *Defender*'s pleas for more police protection in public recreational space citywide apparently went unheeded, and the spark that touched off the powder keg of escalating race violence that summer was an African American boy's death along Chicago's segregated lakeshore. African American writer Alden Bland set the scene in his fairly accurate fictionalization of the riot in his migration novel, *Behold a Cry:* "White and colored went swimming," he wrote, "Separating them was a line, years old and imaginary, crossing the beach and reaching far out into the even surface of the lake. Imaginary it was, but as solid as a wall and as unyielding. It was held inviolate."[41] On Sunday, July 27, 1919, that imaginary, inviolate line was perhaps unwittingly crossed when Chicagoans of all races flocked to Lake Michigan to cool off as temperatures soared into the nineties. A group of African Americans, chafing at the segregation and discrimination that plagued the race both South and North, asserted their right to enjoy leisure time in any Chicago landscape by attempting to enter the lake at the 29th Street beach, which whites claimed as their own. Apparently unaware of the conflict brewing on shore, another group of young African American boys floated south on a homemade raft from a point between the black beach at 25th Street and the white beach at 29th Street. One of the boys, seventeen-year-old Eugene Williams, drowned when he was struck in the head by a rock thrown by a white man after crossing the invisible racial barrier that extended from the beach out into the lake. Police refused to arrest the offender (arresting a black protestor instead), and the conflict erupted into five days of rioting in which African Americans were targets of roving bands of white gangs. The violence was so bad that *The Broad Ax,* another of Chicago's African American newspapers, declared, "The south side had been transformed into a slaughter house."[42] At a time when roughly 4 percent of Chicago's population was African American, 38 people were killed (23 black and 15 white) and more than 500 sustained injuries (roughly twice as many black as white).[43]

Although the white-on-black violence spread far from its origins at the 29th Street beach, it was mostly contained to the South Side, in and around African American neighborhoods. James T. Farrell's fictionalized account of the riot in *The Young Manhood of Studs Lonigan* accurately captures the bloodthirsty lynch mobs reminiscent of the South that roamed Chicago streets that July. When Studs and his working-class Irish friends first hear that the riot began, they proclaim, "The niggers were never going to forget the month of July, 1919," and "they ought to hang every nigger in the city to the telephone poles, and let them swing there in the breeze."[44] Agitating for a fight due west of Washington Park (between 55th and 59th Streets), Studs and his friends largely fail to encounter any African American victims save a ten-year-old boy they terrorize and humiliate; in 1919, this area was still well south of the heart of Chicago's Black Belt.[45] Indeed, no African American deaths and only a smattering of injuries were reported south of 51st Street (Washington Park's northern border), and no violence whatsoever was reported in the park itself, probably because few if any African Americans dared to go there during the riot. But in the wake of the riot, the *Chicago Whip*, another African American newspaper in Chicago, was quick to point out that "open demonstrations of violence in Jackson and Washington Parks against Colored people had a most important part in creating a culture medium for MOB psychology" that Farrell would so accurately fictionalize.[46] For the Juvenile Protective Association of Chicago (a predominantly white Progressive reform organization with a history of some black involvement), the riot belied the city's promotional signage that announced, "Chicago Leads the World in Parks, Playgrounds and Beaches," noting that such claims clearly did not apply equally to all citizens. Lamenting Eugene Williams's death that had ignited the riot, the association's annual report went on to state that the city had "turned on a harmless boy, who had gone out for a natural pleasure on the open shore, and cast him out and betrayed him in a crime that rightly degraded her throughout the nation."[47] The race riot undoubtedly and justifiably cast a shadow over black Chicago's relationship with outdoor recreational space for generations; one South Side resident who was born the year after the riot recalled that, for his parents who refused to swim after that day in 1919, the "blue lake always had a tinge of red from the blood of that young black boy."[48]

Racial violence in Washington Park remained enough of a problem in the months after the riot to prompt George Arthur, executive secretary of the segregated African American YMCA branch, to express concern "that a riot might occur in Washington Park any Sunday afternoon."[49] A front-page *Defender* article similarly noted in 1922 that the park was "one of the few such places that people of the Race seek to enter and there they are made the pry [sic] of white hoodlums." This violence, the author wrote, was Washington Park's "permanent blister."[50] Predictably, it did have at least a small tangible effect on park patronage: the city's 1922 race relations report released in the wake of the riot noted, "The use of the parks by Negroes is determined almost entirely by the degree of antagonism in the neighborhood, and Negroes are afraid to make use of the parks where the neighborhood sentiment is hostile." Rather than risk an attack in Washington Park, some African Americans in the early 1920s apparently preferred to travel to a much smaller park nearly three miles southwest of Washington Park and farther from the Black Belt.[51]

But despite the race violence, most African Americans continued to spend their leisure time at Washington Park, picnicking, playing baseball, boating on the lagoon—and they made it clear they would physically fight for that right if necessary. The white gangs, intending to scare the black population away from the park and almost always outnumbering isolated African Americans, would not succeed. Concluding on a note that echoed the insistence and confidence that were emerging among "New Negroes" nationwide, the *Defender* article that spoke of Washington Park's "permanent blister" somewhat ominously alluded to imminent retaliation: African American park-goers "are not going to stay out," but instead "are going in larger numbers and then there will be a sad story to tell."[52] The self-assured threat must have been music to the ears of many migrants who would not have dared make such a bold declaration in the Jim Crow South—or perhaps even in the North—as they continued to adjust to the city's often opaque racial codes.

White-on-black violence plagued not only Washington Park's public green space in the early years of the Great Migration but also the nearby residential neighborhoods that were increasingly housing black Chicago's professional classes. Because these neighborhoods were on the fringes of the expanding Black Belt that were undergoing a rapid racial transition, settling in Chicago's best African American neighborhoods did not guarantee any safety and security. In fact, it made targets of the city's "Talented Tenth," a term coined by W. E. B. Du Bois to refer to race leaders.[53] There were fifty-eight bombings of African American homes on the South Side between 1917 and 1921 as violence peaked in the early years of the migration, only ebbing significantly by 1925 (see Figure 1.1). Perhaps the most prominent victims of this white violence were Oscar De Priest, former Chicago alderman and future U.S. congressman, and Jesse Binga, the Black Belt's preeminent banker and real estate magnate. De Priest's home near 38th Street and South Parkway sustained $2,000 in damages when it was bombed in April 1921, and Binga's home overlooking the southwest corner of Washington Park, near 59th Street and South Parkway, was bombed multiple times throughout the late 1910s and early 1920s when the area was still overwhelmingly white; one bombing is even fictionalized in Farrell's *The Young Manhood of Studs Lonigan.*[54] Several months after De Priest's home was bombed in 1921, and after his own home was bombed for the seventh time, Binga declared that he had "just as much right . . . to enjoy [his] home at Washington Park as anyone else to go there and play tennis or baseball or enjoy other advantages of the district."[55] In his steadfastness, Binga was representative: the bombings ultimately failed to prevent the black cultural elite who had the means to live near Washington Park from moving there, just as race violence failed to deter black Chicagoans from enjoying the park. With each passing year, African American neighborhoods inched closer and closer to the South Side's Olmsted- and Vaux-designed pastoral landscape. The geography of black leisure was inextricably changing along with black residential geography on the South Side, and violent attacks in both public and private spaces were only one of several methods that resentful white residents employed in an attempt to slow the inevitable. Many white neighborhoods also drew up racially restrictive covenants to prevent African Americans from renting or buying homes.

Although the *Defender* regularly blamed race violence in and around Washington Park on the white working classes, restrictive racial covenants in nearby middle-class white neighborhoods made it clear that racial animosity toward African Americans in Chicago transcended class lines and manifested itself in countless ways. The city's riot commission report euphemistically noted in 1922, "Among [white] visitors to Washington Park the real estate problem in the residence districts near the park seemed to be the primary cause of ill feeling," and one white property owner complained "that the park ought to be rechristened 'Booker T. Washington Park,'" invoking the Tuskegee Institute's founder to reference the park's racial transition.[56] But by the late 1920s, these neighborhoods immediately north and west of Washington Park had nearly completely transitioned racially, and that transition had spurred the middle-class neighborhoods of Hyde Park to the east and the Washington Park subdivision to the south to draft restrictive covenants that prevented African Americans from renting or buying homes there. The neighborhood popularly known as the "white island" in this period stayed white because, as the sociologist Gunnar Myrdal described it in his landmark study *An American Dilemma,* the neighborhood improvement association "shifted its function from planting shrubbery and cleaning the streets to preventing Negroes from getting into the neighborhood, when the Black Belt began to expand in the direction of this community."[57] That turn away from neighborhood beautification was even more sadly ironic, given that the black Chicagoans these "improvement associations" were so desperately trying to keep out were themselves actively working to beautify their own neighborhoods in virtually identical ways: community organizations like the South Side's segregated YMCA initiated spring cleanup campaigns that brought citizens together to pick up rubbish and plant grass, flowers, and gardens.[58]

The Shifting Geography of Leisure in Nature on the South Side

Almost exactly a decade after the 1919 riot, another weekend of racial violence along Chicago's lakefront illustrated just how much the city's racial geography of leisure in public natural and landscaped environments had evolved in the Great Migration years. Racial tensions were running as high as record temperatures in late July 1929 when the heat drew record crowds of South Siders to Chicago's beaches, forcing tens of thousands into close bodily contact with one another. On Friday, July 26, 1929, a group of white teenage boys threatened and threw rocks at a group of twenty-three black Girl Scouts and their adult leaders at Jackson Park beach near 63rd Street, and one of the adults was so "paralyzed from shock and fear" that she was admitted to Cook County Hospital.[59] Later that weekend, a group of white men and boys at Jackson Park beach targeted two black couples, "giving them five minutes in which to 'clear out'" or face a violent confrontation. A witness to the incident credited the "coolness of the Negroes" on a hot summer day; their decision to leave and report the incident to police "prevented any serious consequences."[60] Both incidents were unwelcome reminders to black Chicagoans—many of whom had migrated to the city after the 1919 riot—that public green spaces could be dangerous places. Had a rock thrown at the Girl Scouts in 1929 seriously injured one of them (as did the rock that ultimately drowned Eugene Williams in Lake Michigan in 1919), perhaps Chicago would have been plunged into another race riot. This time, however, bloodshed was averted and the beach confrontations led instead to a flurry of letters to the editors of the *Defender* and *Tribune* (the city's most prominent daily and self-proclaimed "World's Greatest Newspaper"), editorials in both newspapers, as well as promises from city officials of improved beach facilities for African Americans—all of which offered a window into just how much had changed and how much had remained the same since 1919.

For all their differences, many Chicagoans naturally drew parallels, both explicitly and implicitly, between 1929's unrest and 1919's bloodshed in the city's landscapes of hope. Indeed, one of the black victims of the 1929 attack on the Girl Scouts warned the perpetrators "that as they have sown they shall also reap. They will suffer for their acts. There is no escape. We pay, and pay dearly, for all the wrong we do." She went on to write, "None of us have forgotten the horrors of the last race riot," and speculated that "had [the Scout] troop been composed of boys instead of girls, we would have had a different story."[61] Similarly, another emboldened black writer warned, "The whites who are causing these conflicts should bear in mind that Negroes will fight back when it is a matter of self-defense. Moreover, there are bigger and better Negroes and a greater number in Chicago now than there were 10 years ago."[62] This statement was a similar, if not even more self-confident, declaration to that of the 1922 *Defender* letter writer who warned that there would be a "sad story to tell" if white-on-black violence continued at Washington Park. Meanwhile, white letter writers warned of the growing "mob spirit" incited by "colored people mixing with the whites at Jackson park beach" and that "trouble more serious than that of a few years ago" lay ahead.[63] The parallel was not lost on the *Tribune* either; four days after the initial letter to the editor appeared, it published an editorial on the situation that referenced "the race riots of a decade ago" stemming from similar conflict at the beaches.[64] If the *Tribune* intended to calm the situation with its editorial, however, it failed miserably. Instead, it fanned the flames, prompting one reader to suggest, "If the Chicago Tribune wishes to incite another clash of the races it could not begin in a livelier manner."[65]

So what did the *Tribune* editorial say that was so inflammatory? It began by affirming that "there is no question of the legal right of colored citizens to bathe at any public beach in Chicago" and went on to assert that it was the duty of park police to "preserve order" when "confronted by the threat of race conflict at the beach." With that perfunctory nod to equal rights out of the way, however, the *Tribune* moved on to the crux of its argument, stating that "there is a good deal more involved in these incidents than mere legalisms" because for "a very large section of the white population the presence of a Negro, however well behaved, among white bathers is an irritation." To appease the white population and avoid any such irritations, the *Tribune* suggested that a "voluntary waiver of the right to bathe at the Jackson Park beach would seem . . . to be a small price to pay for peace between the races, particularly after proper facilities have been provided for them elsewhere." The *Tribune* went on to argue that the right to enjoy leisure activities was a step below rights to own property and to an education, and that such a voluntary waiver represented "a recognition, founded upon mutual respect, of the right of Negroes to certain beaches and of whites to others." To facilitate this separation, the *Tribune* argued that the South Park Commission should "provide adequate bathing facilities along the miles of beach between Roosevelt road [12th Street] and Pershing road [39th Street] which Negroes now may use and do use without hindrance."[66] One could scarcely dream up a more striking illustration of the way de facto segregation could operate in the North during the era of "separate but equal" de jure segregation in the Jim Crow South: migrants had escaped the latter only to be confronted with the former.

In addition to the obviously racist, segregationist nature of the *Tribune*'s suggestions (it would have hardly been surprising to African Americans who long knew the *Tribune* was a newspaper hostile to their interests, after all), they also reveal the significant ways in which Chicago's geography of black leisure in public green spaces had evolved after a decade of massive migration and profound residential transition. Although the violent confrontations in 1919 and 1929 along the Lake Michigan shore both exposed the environmental inequalities that black Chicagoans continually faced during the Great Migration era, they took place in radically different contexts, bookending a decade in which the arrival of tens of thousands of black migrants helped more than double the city's African American population. During this decade, the primary locus of interracial contact—and violence—had moved more than four miles south along Lake Michigan's shore, leaving in its wake a stretch of shoreline increasingly used almost exclusively by African Americans. In 1919, Eugene Williams drowned after being assaulted by white rock throwers because he strayed too close to 29th Street beach, which was then used nearly exclusively by whites. But by the summer of 1929— just two days before the Girl Scout troop was assaulted at Jackson Park beach—it was a twenty-one-year-old African American man who hit a white boy near the old 29th Street Beach that, in the intervening decade, had become nearly exclusively used by African Americans. It was a rare instance of black-on-white violence at public recreational facilities, and the man's arrest by park police narrowly averted a "probable race riot," at least in the *Defender*'s estimation.[67] Now in the overwhelming racial majority in nearby neighborhoods, generally speaking African Americans were no longer on the receiving end of racial violence at beaches that far north. By 1929, Jackson Park beach at 63rd Street was effectively the new 29th Street beach—the place where African Americans found themselves in the racial minority, fighting for their right to enjoy public recreational space free of intimidation, harassment, and violence.[68]

The conflict over public recreational space in 1929 also revealed how parks, beaches, and playground facilities nearest the poorest and oldest portions of the Black Belt were not only few and far between but also were quite small and often poorly maintained or supplied in comparison to facilities serving the city's white populations. The *Tribune*'s call for "adequate bathing facilities" between 12th Street and 39th Street— which was seconded by several white letter writers—implicitly confirmed just how inadequate those facilities actually were. Indeed, 31st Street beach, adjacent to ground zero of the 1919 riot, was clearly inferior to predominantly white-used beaches (see Figure 1.3). Black Chicagoans roundly denounced the small, rocky beach as a disgrace—well short of the potential of landscapes of hope such as Washington Park or Jackson Park beach. Described as a "stone quarry dumped on the lake front" that was little more than a breakwater protecting the adjacent railroad lines and shore road, 31st Street beach also had a dressing room that was an "eyesore" resembling a "farmer's smokehouse."[69] Other citizens considered the beach "a farce" ultimately "fit only for dogs—or, rather, for seals," a place where "breakwater rats [were] swimming with you."[70] The *Defender* warned that the water was deep and the train lines running just west of the beach were dangerous too: "if the waves don't get you the railroad will; you'll be killed in either case."[71] City officials were well aware of the black community's dissatisfaction with the facilities; earlier that summer, president of the South Park Board (and future mayor) Edward Kelly had met with the *Defender* to discuss "the prospect of better beach facilities and playgrounds for Chicago's children."[72]

Despite a small minority of Chicago's South Side residents who simply wished for better quality beaches at and around 31st Street—a sentiment not that different from some white readers' suggestions—the African American community's priority was maintaining their right to have access to *any* public facility anywhere. The dominant approach simultaneously argued for both the right to access primarily white-used facilities and for improved facilities in predominantly African American neighborhoods, even though many worried that such improvements would only encourage further segregation. To settle for anything less would make Chicago's public green spaces even more uncomfortably like those in the South, and the Chicago chapter of the NAACP staunchly supported equal rights, stating in part that "the colored people will continue to bathe at all beaches that are supported by their taxes."[73] Along the same lines, in response to the *Tribune* editorial, one *Defender* letter writer noted that "it is only in the South that they can set aside portions of God's earth and water for the exclusive use of Negroes" and that, as taxpayers, African Americans should be guaranteed equal use of public facilities.[74] It would have been a poignant comparison for readers who had themselves suffered the indignities of the Jim Crow South. The same day, the *Defender* published a front-page editorial cartoon titled "The Foolish Question Hovering over Lake Michigan" that featured a giant

Figure 1.3a. Women and men enjoying 31st Street beach in 1931. Note the relatively small sandy beach frontage that gives way to a rocky breakwater near the dressing room at left, as well as the South Side's industrial skyline in the background. Chicago History Museum, DN-0096102; *Chicago Daily News*, photographer.

Figure 1.3b. Men diving off the pier at 31st Street beach in 1931. Chicago History Museum, DN-0096103; *Chicago Daily News*, photographer.

question mark hovering over the lake and Chicago's skyline in the background. Written in the question mark was the foolish question itself: "What color should people be to bathe at a public beach?"[75]

Not only did proposals to provide better segregated bathing facilities north of 39th Street ignore African American claims to equal access citywide but they also exhibited a distinct unwillingness to recognize just how much the Black Belt had expanded in the past decade toward Washington and Jackson Parks and, in particular, the fact that the black cultural elite constituted the southernmost vanguard of that expansion. For these black professionals with at least some small measure of sway in local politics, Jackson Park beach was not only much better equipped than beaches farther north but also much nearer their homes. By 1920 the Black Belt already nearly reached 39th Street; by 1930 it stretched south nearly to 47th Street along the lake and all the way past 63rd Street farther inland, little more than a mile due west of Jackson Park. In other words, by the time the *Tribune* suggested there be better facilities north of 39th Street, the Black Belt already bordered the lake for nearly a full mile farther south. Even for those African Americans living inland, it was a much closer trip to Jackson Park beach at 63rd Street than to the 31st Street beach. A black Chicagoan living near the intersection of 60th Street and Michigan Avenue (likely to have been a professional in the black cultural elite, given the neighborhood) could travel about three miles east to Jackson Park beach—a short drive or streetcar trip, or perhaps a leisurely hour-long walk. Traveling north to 31st Street beach, by contrast, would have been a journey of four and a half miles.[76]

The *Defender*'s scorching editorial response to the *Tribune* affirmed the black cultural elite's values and confirmed the ways that the geography of black leisure in Chicago's public landscapes of hope had changed in the intervening decade. Its title, "The *Tribune* Speaks," suggested a response that was half outrage and half bemused annoyance from a newspaper accustomed to dealing with the racism that permeated Chicago's most widely read daily. Mocking the *Tribune*'s suggestion of a voluntary waiver of the right to use certain beaches and likening white Chicagoans to Southern antebellum plantation owners, the *Defender* pointed out that "out of deference to [their] white lords and masters and mistresses who resent our presence," African Americans already stayed away from Clarendon, Oak Street, and Lincoln Park beaches—all beaches on the city's North Side, far from the South Side Black Belt. By contrast, the *Defender* noted, "A public beach within a few blocks of most of our homes is the logical place for us to seek the recreation we need as badly as the whitest foreigner who objects to our presence there," and went on to write that "Jackson Park beach . . . is the one we can reach most easily—and we intend to reach it."[77]

Of course, the *Defender*'s perspective on leisure spaces' proximity could hardly be said to be universal in Chicago's black community, given that its editorial pages generally served as the bully pulpit of the black cultural elite in this period. One *Defender* reader agreed with the paper, pointedly wondering "why should Negroes who live in the very entrance of Jackson Park be expected to drive as far north as 39th St. to use the beach simply to satisfy a group of white hoodlums who doubtless live far west of Wentworth Ave. or Halsted St.?"[78] But another African American who wrote to the *Tribune* said that he "live[d] just three blocks from the Thirty-first beach [*sic*], and would much rather go there, as thousands of others would, but the condition there is an outrage."[79] Clearly, when the *Defender* said that Jackson Park beach was nearest "most of our homes," it really meant most homes owned or rented by the black cultural elite. Geographically speaking, 31st Street beach was still closer to the vast majority of black residential neighborhoods, many of which were exceedingly poor; Jackson Park was far enough south that it would have been closer only for those living south of about 47th Street, an area that, by the late 1920s, was emerging as the new social and cultural capital of the Black Belt.

Even closer to the black cultural elite's neighborhoods than Jackson Park beach, of course, was Washington Park. Indeed, the 1929 conflict over Jackson Park beach prompted another letter writer—almost certainly the writer James T. Farrell, whose family had just moved from their Washington Park home the year before and who was beginning to write his first *Studs Lonigan* novel that summer—to suggest that because "Washington park has been conceded to the Negroes by the whites, . . . why not install a swimming pool for them there? If a lake beach is desired, then build the Negroes one, under Negro management."[80] The *Tribune* also framed the fraught racial transition in such public green spaces in terms of whites' ostensibly benevolent deeds for African Americans. An editorial argued that African Americans had "inherited two of Chicago's finest boulevards, and the presence of colored people in Washington park, one of the largest, most beautiful, and best equipped in the city, is not resented."[81] The idea of Chicago's African Americans somehow "inheriting" boulevards and parks as some sort of generational gift from whites who ceded such public property, supposedly free of resentment, would have been particularly galling to those who had experienced the regular violence associated with interracial contact in those spaces earlier in the decade. But at the same time, the *Tribune* had clearly hit on some version of the truth. By 1929 Washington Park was unquestionably and overwhelmingly used by African Americans, and race violence that the *Defender* had called its "permanent blister" in 1922 had all but disappeared in just seven years. Even when violence still raged in the park, some South Siders unsuccessfully advocated erecting a monument to famed black abolitionist Frederick Douglass there, but by the onset of the Great Depression evidence abounded that African Americans certainly had come to see Washington Park as their park.[82] Black YMCA industrial league baseball games were moved twenty blocks south to Washington Park in 1927, for instance, and a 1928 proposal to build an armory on the park's eastern border elicited a letter to the *Defender* warning that the project's elimination of recreational space would "be a menace to the whole Race."[83] Obviously such changes were not due to increased racial tolerance or understanding; instead, whites gradually ceased using Washington Park as they moved away from adjoining neighborhoods, creating yet another de facto segregated public green space much like they had along the lakefront.

Declarations that a threat to Washington Park's green space represented a threat to all of black Chicago locked in an interracial battle for the city's natural and landscaped environments were not entirely inaccurate, but they obscured persistent intraracial class tensions about precisely who had access to these public spaces and how they should behave in them. The same day the *Defender* published its editorial blasting the *Tribune*'s treatment of racial conflict at Jackson Park beach in 1929, it published another editorial—directly adjacent—with the rosy title "This Is Progress." While the situation at Jackson Park beach simmered just a few miles away, the *Defender* lauded an interracial tennis tournament "unlike anything ever attempted before in America" just completed in Washington Park. The tournament, organized by an African American and with a trophy donated by the Illinois governor, featured black, white, and Hispanic competitors, both male and female, adult and youth. Hinting at the long history of race conflict in Chicago's parks, the *Defender* breathlessly praised the tournament's success, proclaiming, "Twenty, ten years ago this scene could not have taken place," and marveling that "this took place in a public park in Chicago!" Arguably even more revealing, though, was the way the editorial described the tournament itself: held "on grass courts, in the most beautiful setting conceivable," where competitors "fought for supremacy in the age-old game—the sport of kings—tennis."[84] It hinted at the fact that tennis was largely the domain of members of the black cultural elite who were taking up the "sport of kings," and it conspicuously ignored the ways the sport—and the Washington Park courts in particular—had become an intraracial battleground over class politics and appropriate behavior in the Great Migration years.

Leisure Culture and Intraracial Class Politics in the Black Belt's Green Spaces

Perhaps no two spaces in Washington Park invited intraracial class conflict as much as the tennis courts and the baseball diamonds. In both places, working-class African American migrants forged hybrid leisure cultures that blended Southern cultures with Northern environments in ways that often upset and embarrassed the black cultural elite. As the voice of the black cultural elite's values in this era, the *Defender* admonished its readers in 1922 that "tennis is strictly a gentleman's game" in which "no gentleman of any breeding will appear on any tennis court without a top shirt" or in work clothes. The *Defender* specifically targeted postal workers and dining-car waiters—both highly sought-after and respected working-class jobs for migrants—who had come "directly from work" and played in their uniforms, because these blue clothes "look[ed] at a distance like overalls and jumpers," attire that could easily be mistaken for the sorts of clothes worn by stockyard laborers, steel mill workers, or even Southern sharecroppers. More explicit markers of working-class status and Southernness also came under fire from the *Defender*, as black Chicagoans who played "ragtime songs that belong in a cabaret" were implored to "keep your ukuleles at home."[85] Two years later, the tennis courts were still a point of conflict in the black community. A *Defender* editorial again complained that African Americans should not "play ukeleles [*sic*], dance jigs, sing and perform generally" near the tennis courts, this time calling the gatherings "open-air performances of minstrelsy" that disturbed the Sunday morning sleep of Jesse Binga and other well-heeled South Siders who lived across the street.[86]

Of course, what the *Defender* considered embarrassing "open-air performances of minstrelsy" in this landscape of hope were, to many migrants, simply continuations of working-class folk cultural practices that bound together Southern black communities in public green space. Gospel singer Mahalia Jackson (who migrated to Chicago in 1928 at the age of sixteen), for instance, recalled that when she was growing up just outside New Orleans, the Mississippi River "levee was high and grassy, and it was our playground. We used to sit out there and sing songs with ukuleles and bake sweet potatoes in fires made from driftwood and catch all the fish and shrimp and crabs we wanted."[87] Had she attempted to adapt that communal experience to Chicago's parks or beaches, there is little doubt that many in the city's black cultural elite would have objected. Migrants were also criticized by the *Defender* in 1924 when a South Side congregation used Lake Michigan at the 29th Street beach as a baptismal pool, following a folk cultural tradition widespread across the South dating back centuries that used lakes, ponds, streams, and rivers as sites for one of the most important rituals in the Baptist faith (which accounted for roughly half of black Chicago's congregations in the migration years).[88] The *Defender* urged the pastor to "desist from this primitive form of religious conduct" at the same beach where the race riot had begun just five years earlier, noting that the "Churches of Chicago have never disgraced themselves by staging a Sunday circus on the lake front."[89] To the *Defender*, such practices at a beach that too closely resembled the rural Jim Crow South with its "farmer's smokehouse" of a changing station added insult to injury, perhaps worryingly confirming racist whites' prejudices against migrants.

Just as the sacred religious rituals that migrants adapted to Chicago's public green spaces were not safe from comparisons to minstrelsy, the Sunday School Baseball League games played in the park's northern half were also fraught with the potential for intraracial discord. Given that baseball was already widely popular in the South in the early twentieth century, many of the players on Washington Park's meadow no doubt would have been working-class migrants who were adapting their love of the sport to new environmental and social contexts. In the minds of Chicago's black professionals, games that could under ideal circumstances foster healthful physical activity and exhibit respectable behavior and values in front of white spectators could just as easily devolve into what many in the black cultural elite believed was an embarrassing reflection on the race. After witnessing heated arguments break out and nearly erupt in fistfights at the Sunday School Baseball League, a 1924 *Defender* article declared that this behavior was "humiliating to both Colored and white fans."[90] Three years later, an editorial lamented that Sunday School Baseball League games were getting increasingly heated thanks to players who amounted to "a gang of roughnecks," declaring that "the good the Sunday School league has done for the past ten years has been undone" by a disgraceful and unchristian fight that broke out during the game and caused "women and children [to run] screaming." The writer warned, "Churches lose their hold on the layman. They lose their hold on the Christian. They lose their hold on the sinner, too, when they allow men to wear the uniforms and perform like hoodlums."[91]

Whether on or off the baseball diamonds, the black cultural elite's concerns about behavior in Washington Park had been percolating for years and often centered on the younger generation's supposed potential for delinquency. In 1913, before the Great Migration was even underway in earnest, the *Defender* noted, "During the past few years the conduct of both girls and boys of color at Washington Park has been so very raw at times that some of the best people of the race shun it, especially on Sundays, when the youthful crowd comes out after Sunday school." Rather than entertain boys in public places like parks, the author said, girls would do well to remember that "home is the best place."[92] This was similar to the behavioral criticism the *Defender* leveled against the loud and "boisterous" crowds and young African Americans "in the shadow of the boathouse, indulging in 'petting parties,' publicly encouraging and acknowledging advances," as well as against "boys who should have learned something from their home training" who instead insulted couples as they walked past and dropped rocks off lagoon bridges to splash row-boating couples below.[93] The newspaper implored people of both races to condemn the lascivious "lip slobbering," "lip-biting," and "spooning" in Black Belt parks and on the grassy, tree-lined median of South Parkway. The author suggested that police should intervene on "behalf of the respectable members of the Race on the South Side" and went on to write that he supposed whites were "annoyed by these same sort of pests." Co-opting racist white descriptions of African Americans, the editorial concluded by condemning the "band of monkeys of both races."[94]

When African Americans began using Washington Park in ever-larger numbers during the Great Migration years, these intraracial conflicts grafted a layer of race onto competing and evolving class-based notions about the appropriate use of park space that had roots dating back to the late nineteenth century and the design of the park itself. Whether in these public parks and beaches or in private dance halls and theaters of the Stroll, it was largely the behavior of the working classes and the younger generation that reformers of all races and ethnicities perceived as a threat. African American reformers, for instance, would have agreed with the assertion of the Juvenile Protective Association of Chicago that supervision of children at recreational spaces such as parks, beaches, and playgrounds was "no less important" than policing dance halls and roadhouses for illicit behavior.[95] In particular, the Stroll's dance halls, theaters, and restaurants represented the excitement and possibilities of modern urban life, as well as the moral filth and vice that reformers were desperately trying to eliminate. Reformers tended to see the city's public green spaces as pastoral antidotes to urban vice, but in many ways, Washington Park and the Stroll were simply two sides of the same coin. In both spaces, migrants forged a hybrid leisure culture that blended elements of North and South and stirred controversy among African Americans, all while making claims to social equality and building a community. And all too often in the eyes of reformers in the black cultural elite, in both spaces African Americans were not behaving like the "good citizens [who] are the stars you should hitch your wagon to."[96]

Beyond the affront to their own behavioral sensibilities, what was particularly vexing to many black reformers was that these "performances of minstrelsy" on the tennis courts and baseball games ruined by "a gang of roughnecks" threatened to confirm racist stereotypes in part because they occurred in front of whites in a park that was undergoing a racial transition.[97] This was one key difference between reformers' concerns about behavior in public green spaces and on the Stroll. Even though the Stroll entertained a relatively small group of white patrons who sought out that nightlife, its theaters, restaurants, and dance halls were privately owned spaces that entertained a more exclusively African American clientele in the 1910s and 1920s—and these spaces were, in a sense, expected to invite illicit behavior. Washington Park, in contrast, was frequented by both races and all classes in this transitional period, and the behavioral expectations in such places were radically different in part because reformers (and the park's designers) believed they should counter those supposedly destructive behavioral tendencies to which the Stroll catered. Upset about behavior in Washington Park, the *Defender* reminded its readers that "all other races realize the better element take up tennis," and that even if those playing in such disgraceful clothes had been "follow[ing] after the fashion of some whites," that "bad example . . . is not the correct thing for us to follow." In addition to those who might be watching from the park grounds, tennis players were in "full view of thousands of motorists" along South Parkway, the majority of whom would have been white.[98] At a time when Jesse Binga was perhaps the only black resident who lived on South Parkway across from Washington Park, another *Defender* article was even more explicit, warning that the behavior in the park was the reason why "people who live on the west side of South Park Av. [*sic*], opposite the park . . . forming opinions about us that affect us in all our dealings with them in all other walks of life." The article went on to invoke the history of class politics in the park and alluded to the newfound upward mobility that city life sometimes facilitated for migrants, encouraging readers to remember that, "at all times . . . we are being watched closely by those who are quick to see our faults and magnify them. Let us try to emulate the best of those whose privilege it was to use the parks, play tennis and row long before we had time for such amusements."[99]

Some reformers in the black cultural elite feared that such behavior would not only confirm prejudices and stereotypes but also aggravate the race violence plaguing Washington Park. Though there was little evidence to prove the connection, one *Defender* editorialist even suggested that white violence was in part invited by African American behavior in the park. He exhorted his readers, "above all, let us not forget that trouble is the easiest thing in life to acquire and hardest to get rid of, and in our own peculiar positions, we have enough of it as it is."[100] In other words, many black reformers had faith that if black Chicagoans acted more respectably in public, equal treatment would follow and race prejudice would eventually dissipate. But when it came to race preju- dice in Great Migration-era Chicago, it was exceedingly difficult if not impossible to disentangle cause and effect, and it remains highly de- batable whether behavior—and the stereotypes and prejudices that many in the black cultural elite believed it confirmed—had much to do with the racist treatment experienced by black Chicagoans of all classes, backgrounds, and ages in the city's public natural and land- scaped environments. If anything, as the multiple bombings of Jesse Binga's home illustrate, the members of the successful black cultural elite who were on the vanguard of the expanding Black Belt could be more vulnerable to white racism and violence than the working classes. Indeed, one could argue that reformers' quest to win the respect of whites was largely a fool's errand that sowed intraracial class strife while accomplishing little to combat either race violence or prejudice, because, at the end of the day, African Americans could not change their skin color. As James T. Farrell put it with respect to the conflict at Jackson Park beach in 1929, "the whites will never tolerate mixed bathing at any beach."[101] Or, as *Tribune* editorialists argued that same summer, for "a very large section of the white population the presence of a Negro, *however well behaved* [emphasis added], among white bathers is an irritation."[102]

Fighting for Working-Class Green Space in the Black Belt

In small pockets of the South Side, black Chicagoans succeeded in carving out landscapes of hope in both private and public green spaces: a neighborhood a half-mile west of Washington Park, for instance, was described in the late 1920s as having "green lawns, trees, neat and brightly painted cottages," and beautification efforts included a "common flower fund" that paid for flower boxes along the parkways.[103] Most mi- grants initially settled in the northernmost reaches of Chicago's Black Belt, however, in an area that had exceedingly poor housing stock, but that was not as densely built as many other parts of the city. In some ways, then, African Americans had more access to open space and sun- light than some Chicagoans; as one study noted, "there is a considerable amount of vacant space in the lots which occasionally have fairly large back yards" that supported "occasional attempts at vegetable gardens" and small livestock like chickens or goats.[104] More often, however, these spaces were "disfigured by shacks and rubbish heaps" that made "any attempt to utilize the unoccupied portions of the lot for garden plots . . . extremely difficult," and "trees, shrubbery, grass, and flowers are not seen in the tenement districts" because the black Chicagoans who lived there "work[ed] hard and [had] little money to spend on the things that are beautiful but not necessary."[105] The open space was practically unusable for anything other than disposing of waste and was certainly far from reformers' aesthetic rather than utilitarian ideals of nature.

Because the South Side Black Belt so sorely lacked functional and uplifting private green spaces, then, public green spaces became even more important for reformers. As the *Defender* would put it in the midst of its campaign for a new South Side park, "Nature never intended that this vast number of people should live confined in such small space without any touch of nature and clear sunshine. We need and must have sunning places and spots where our children may enjoy the blessings of nature as provided by flowers, grass, air and sunshine. There is more to life than the splendor of brick and stone structures that go to make up the life of this city."[106] So although African American reformers' convictions about the importance of respectable behavior in extant city parks and beaches could be alienating for working-class migrants and hopelessly paternalistic, their beliefs about the myriad individual and social benefits of urban green space could also help the working classes when these reformers turned their sights more directly on the impoverished heart of the Black Belt that had precious few green spaces. Here, too, these reformers did not have to worry about behavioral judgments from whites: the area was populated nearly exclusively by African Americans, most of whom were working class. For better or worse, then, new neighborhood playgrounds or parks would almost inevitably become unofficially segregated, just like 31st Street beach.

This far north in the Black Belt, working-class black Chicagoans were two miles from the racially transitioning Washington Park, which hardly could have been considered a neighborhood park. As the *Defender* put it in one of its many columns vehemently supporting the creation of a new park in the heart of the Black Belt, "Washington and Jackson parks are far from the center of our community activities and are inadequate to handle the number of families that seek the fresh air and sunshine. We must have a park which will care for the children that seek the outdoors and green grass. We must have the beauty of flowers and pools of clear water."[107] From the outset, at least some city planners had known that Washington and Jackson Parks' location and size threatened to leave the near South Side with inadequate public green space. Considering the parks' geographical history, one of the five original South Park Commissioners who had been deeply involved in implementing Olmsted and Vaux's design reflected on debates about the distribution of the city's green space in the nineteenth century. He recalled that at one point he had "suggested the advisability of reducing the area of Jackson Park by about 120 acres off the south end, and in its place add a number of small parks west and northwest of Washington Park" because there was no parkland easily accessible to people living in those areas. Although the proposal gained some support, plans for constructing Washington and Jackson Parks following the broad outlines of Olmsted and Vaux's design were already too far advanced, and city leaders decided that the green space of boulevards would have to suffice for those residents' recreational needs.[108]

As a result of that fateful decision, the neighborhoods west and north of Washington Park—not entirely coincidentally the very neighborhoods that would make up the Black Belt in the Great Migration years—were repeatedly identified over the next several decades as having a deficit of adequate recreational facilities. One migrant's comments included in the Chicago Commission on Race Relations 1922 report (released in the wake of the riot) approvingly noted that in Chicago as compared to the South, there were "more places to go, parks and playgrounds for children." Yet this statement reflected more on the dearth of landscapes of hope in the South than on their bounty on the South Side.[109] Indeed, in the same report South Park officials "strongly deprecated the lack of recreation centers within the Negro area" and identified the area between 30th and 47th Streets as a stretch particularly in need of additional recreational facilities; another assessment estimated that African Americans in these neighborhoods had "less than 1–16 of the park and playground space available to the average resident of Chicago."[110] Likely inspired by the report's findings, later that year Oscar De Priest ambitiously campaigned for the establishment of "a park like

Jackson Park, with playgrounds and bathing beach, between 31st and 39th streets and from Cottage Grove avenue to the lake" that would, in effect, right the wrong of the South Park Commissioners committed a half-century earlier.[111] But as the ensuing years would reveal, even much smaller additions to the near South Side's impoverished public green space would be difficult to realize.

Indeed, black Chicagoans' near constant fight for more playgrounds and parks across the South Side throughout the 1920s yielded only mixed success. Cheaper to construct and maintain than either landscaped parks or indoor community centers, playgrounds were, in a sense, the bare minimum tool in reformers' fight against delinquency. The fact that much less privately owned land needed to be purchased or condemned, and that maintenance and staffing costs were only a few thousand dollars per year—as compared to large parks like Washington and Jackson that cost several hundred thousand dollars per year to operate—made it much easier for reformers to press city officials for additional playgrounds. It was no surprise then that the Chicago Commission's 1922 report noted that the few existing recreational facilities in the Black Belt were playgrounds—which often consisted of treeless open space and scant facilities that were arguably little better than the vacant lots adjacent to working-class homes, but for the fact that they were staffed by officials who organized athletic competitions and directed play.[112] Despite their shortcomings, community leaders still had to fight tooth and nail for new playgrounds on the South Side, and their creation was cause for celebration. Dedicated in October 1926 and named after the black alderman who spearheaded its construction, Jackson Playground at 37th Street and Rhodes Avenue marked a notable, if still small victory for an underserved community; indeed, Alderman Jackson cited that playground and another school playground as the top two reasons to support his reelection campaign in 1927 (see Figure 1.4).[113] Yet Jackson and other community leaders set their sights even higher, hoping to convince city officials to establish a larger, more well-equipped neighborhood park with indoor facilities.

For reformers in the black cultural elite who believed that green recreational spaces could serve as an anchor of health and morality in a community, places like Jackson Playground—although better than nothing at all—were often woefully inadequate for at least two reasons. First, they were small, unimproved spaces that could not accommodate

Figure 1.4. Jackson Playground, circa 1930. Although little more than a dirt baseball field and swing sets, it would soon grow and evolve into the more well-equipped Madden Park. By permission and courtesy of the Chicago Park District Special Collections.

very many people, lacking the size and natural landscaping of places like Washington Park, which reformers still believed provided a healthful contrast to city life. Just months after Jackson Playground was dedicated, for example, the *Defender* made it clear that this new community resource would be insufficient: "Playgrounds cannot take the place of green grass and flowers," the newspaper declared. "We want a place where our families may rest each evening after contributing to the work of the city."[114] Second, as the *Defender*'s plea for serving entire families hinted and as the Commission's 1922 report astutely noted, playgrounds were "intended for the use of young children and [had] practically nothing to attract older children and adults, except sometimes a baseball or athletic field."[115] Because reformers saw adolescents and adults as the primary populations threatened by the lure of the Stroll's vice and nightlife, playgrounds mainly benefiting young children fell far short of comprehensively addressing the community's needs. Instead, reformers hoped to bring to the underserved Black Belt a small park with outdoor and indoor facilities for children and adults alike. At a cost of tens of thousands of dollars per year, such facilities represented a middle ground between large, expensive parks like Washington Park and small, inexpensive playgrounds.

Although reformers in the black cultural elite led the fight for a small park in the heart of the Black Belt, it garnered support from the entire community, which saw it as an opportunity to replicate the ostensibly beneficial effects of Washington Park on a smaller scale. Both black and white reformers had considered the area in desperate need of a full-fledged park for years: African American community leaders had appeared in front of the South Park Commissioners requesting a park as early as 1917 (and again in 1919 in the months before the riot), but the slow gears of a bureaucracy that did not appear terribly interested in responding to the community's desires did not even begin turning until 1923. Even then, so little happened over the course of the next two years that in 1925, the Chicago Urban League's T. Arnold Hill—with the backing of community organizations as diverse as the NAACP, Marcus Garvey's Universal Negro Improvement Association (UNIA), the Chicago Woman's Club, the Second Ward Branch of the Woman's City Club, and "other civic organizations, prominent ministers and individuals"—presented a petition signed by property owners in the neighborhood that noted that "the long delay in locating a small park in this district presents a distressful situation."[116] Two months later, a community meeting at Wendell Phillips High School expressed broad support for the plan, but still the South Park Commissioners dithered. The park plan did not gain traction until 1926, when a group including the aging titan of anti-lynching reform, Ida B. Wells (on behalf of the Chicago Federation of Women's Organizations), presented them with "a petition signed by fifty property owners . . . declaring their willingness to sell their holdings for the purposes of establishing a small park."[117] As spring turned to summer, "twenty civic organizations identified with colored people" including the Urban League, once again voiced support for the effort, finally leading to the South Park Commissioners' investigation of land values to determine the feasibility of buying a continuous stretch of land large enough to establish a new park.[118]

When city officials had agreed to create Jackson Playground at 37th Street and Rhodes Avenue in 1926, they may have conceived it as a stopgap solution to address ongoing community protests, but the movement for a more well-equipped park continued to gather steam in the winter of 1926–1927. There was still a question of exactly where the park should be established, and the South Park Commissioners ultimately decided to let the community itself decide. The commissioners were apparently "deluged with suggestions from all sides as to likely locations," and they recommended that the *Defender* "conduct a campaign to feel the pulse of the people and ascertain the site most popular with them."[119] Easily the most widely read publication in Chicago's black community, if the *Defender* could not reach the masses, nothing could. A few weeks later, the *Defender* initiated its campaign under the headline "Do You Want a Park?" and attempted to put a positive spin on the continued delays by eliciting responses from its readers to the "rare opportunity to have a park of their own making upon a site which they can select."[120] Now without a doubt, the push for a park was more than a movement organized and directed by reformers and civic-minded citizens; it involved the average black Chicagoan. One reader worried that the proposed park would be a "grave insult to the entire South side community" because proponents were essentially "advocating segregation" by building a park in the heart of the Black Belt that would be, for all practical purposes, "for colored only."[121] The concerns echoed those surrounding the improvement of nearby 31st Street beach, which by this time was surrounded by black neighborhoods and used nearly exclusively by African Americans. Similarly, even in the early 1920s the neighborhoods surrounding the proposed park were nearly all more than 80 percent black; as the decade wore on, the percentage of black residents edged closer to 90 percent in many areas. Instead, the reader suggested that the community should use Washington and Lincoln Parks in greater numbers—located near more mixed-race neighborhoods and still frequented by at least some whites—because African American citizens were "justly entitled" to them yet failing to take full advantage of them.[122] The *Defender* contended, in contrast, that "Jackson and Washington parks [were] far inadequate to meet the needs of people" who lived in the Black Belt's more impoverished northern portion. "The new park is not to be a Jim Crow affair," the paper assured readers, even though its beneficiaries would almost certainly be overwhelmingly African American.[123]

Much like the campaign for lakeshore access that was a two-pronged effort to build and improve public beaches serving overwhelmingly black bathers while also asserting an equal right to access those enjoyed by both races, black Chicagoans fought both for better facilities and equal access to park space across the South Side, regardless of whether or not neighborhood demographics and leisure patterns meant that a given park would likely cater almost exclusively to African Americans. In May 1927, after more than two years of focused protest, a group of community leaders including Alderman Jackson, the Urban League's A. L. Foster, and white settlement house worker Mary McDowell spurred the South Park Commissioners to finally begin making land purchases on the same block where Jackson Playground had been dedicated just six months earlier. In the end, then, it was decided to upgrade the playground to a park. The *Defender*'s front page triumphantly declared its own "relentless" campaign a success—"*Defender* Wins Fight for Recreation Spot," the subheadline read—and that "the winning of this fight is only an incentive for the gaining of many other public conveniences and rights that the citizens need and must have."[124]

Although the *Defender* declared victory, the transition from playground to park would prove much messier and more frustrating for South Siders than was then apparent, threatening to turn a landscape of hope into one of disillusionment. Land purchases were well underway as 1927 drew to a close, but by this point the South Park District was in exceedingly poor financial shape and the Depression would soon wreck city finances even more. Condemnations and property acquisition dragged out over the next four years, and what was eventually named Madden Park (after Congressman Martin B. Madden) amounted to less than ten acres between 37th and 39th Streets just east of South Parkway, on the very same block where Oscar De Priest's home had been bombed in 1921. In that time, the space remained largely unimproved and retained many of the buildings the South Park Commission had yet to demolish or repurpose. But black Chicagoans did gain a larger community space that eventually offered far more than vacant lots or even Jackson Playground could. Indeed, Madden Park's creation would be an especially important victory for those working-classes who lived nearby;

all ages, whether children, the elderly, or black Chicago's toiling masses, now had much easier access to public green space than the first migrants to the city had. As the *Defender* described it in midst of the long battle to establish the park, "our tired workers need and must have a place in which to sit in the sunshine and rest and breathe the clean fresh air, as nature meant them to do." A park was absolutely necessary because in the Black Belt, the "supposedly fresh air that blew off the house tops and dirty streets" was the norm, rather than the restorative fresh air attendant with green space.[125]

Well before Madden Park was established in the heart of the Black Belt and began serving the South Side's working classes, *Defender* columnist Dr. A. Wilberforce Williams similarly emphasized the value of green space, both inside the city and outside it. For those working classes who "cannot possibly go to the country, even for a day on the trolley cars," he wrote, there were Chicago's "beautiful and spacious parks [that] are splendid breathing places and are beautiful bits of God's country brought right into the city for the benefit of those who dwell in sections where air, sun and elbow room are hard to get." Writing in 1913, just before the Great Migration began in earnest, Williams scarcely could have realized just how difficult getting "air, sun and elbow room" would soon become for tens of thousands of African Americans who streamed into Chicago's South Side—or just how long the fight would be to establish a "breathing place" in the heart of the Black Belt where migrants often lived in cramped, run-down tenements and worked in the city's enormous stockyards and steel mills.

Like many reformers in the black cultural elite, Williams believed that mental, physical, and spiritual health sprang not just from the supposed absence of material and moral filth in the city's public green spaces, but also from the presence of nature there. While Williams suggested that public natural and landscaped environments like the 371-acre Washington Park (and, had it existed at the time, the 10-acre Madden Park) were restorative for urban dwellers, he also believed that pastoral green spaces far from the city were even better options for offering true health and wellness. Here, Williams advised, "close communication with birds and trees and flowers and . . . breathing the clean, fresh country air" would be especially beneficial to children, who would learn "from the greatest of all teachers, Nature."[126] Whether consciously or not, diverse groups of African Americans followed Williams's advice during the Great Migration years to a perhaps surprising degree, sometimes retreating to rural and even wild landscapes of hope—many but not all of them privately owned by African Americans and hence mostly free from white racism and violence—to find nature at fledgling resorts, youth camps, and the newly established Cook County Forest Preserves.

Black Chicagoans in Unexpected Places

O N THE NIGHT of August 25, 1921, a bomb tore through Jesse Binga's home directly across from Washington Park, causing serious damage to his property. It was only pure luck that no one was injured or killed. But it marked the seventh bombing that Binga and his family had endured in the space of just two years, and the racially motivated violence had apparently become so commonplace that the *Chicago Tribune* casually reported, "As usual, the pillars of the front porch were blown out of place and scores of window panes in the neighborhood were shattered."[1] This time, the only person home that late summer night was Binga's maid. Binga and his wife were vacationing with Oscar De Priest—perhaps the most prominent of Chicago's black citizens, whose own home had been bombed just months earlier—at an African American resort in rural Michigan called Idlewild, where word of the bombing reached Binga by telegram hours later and prompted him to rush back to the city. One of the very first African Americans to live in the overwhelmingly white middle- to upper-class neighborhood located in such close proximity to the Olmsted and Vaux-designed park, the banker and real estate magnate—a blockbusting symbol of black entrepreneurial success on the South Side—no doubt was the target of a disproportionate amount of white anger, resentment, and hostility in the years following the 1919 race riot. The bombings not only threw into sharper relief the race prejudice that virtually all black Chicagoans faced on a near-daily basis but they also revealed the stakes of escaping to relatively isolated, most often privately owned landscapes of hope outside the city.[2]

The regular summer excursions that Binga and his wife took in the 1920s to Idlewild, by then already a premier African American resort town, show how and why many black Chicagoans valued nature beyond the city in the Great Migration years—as well as the fact that some had much easier access to those rural and wild landscapes than others. Just weeks before Binga's home was bombed for the seventh time in 1921, W. E. B. Du Bois had lauded Idlewild's virtues in the pages of the *Crisis*, the official national publication of the NAACP, articulating some of the reasons why many black Chicagoans such as Binga and De Priest sought out the resort and others like it. Accompanied by a full page containing eight photographs featuring canoeing on Lake Idlewild, Du Bois led with the romantic and hyperbolic: "For sheer physical beauty—for sheen of water and golden air, for nobleness of tree and flower of shrub, for shining river and song of bird and the low, moving whisper of sun, moon and star, it is the beautifulest stretch I have seen for twenty years." Du Bois's flowery prose went on, describing his experience at this rural Michigan resort:

> I have seen the moon rising above purple waters against the velvet background of tall and silent trees. I have seen the stars mirrored in the depths of the mystic bosom of the lake. I have seen the sun sink gloriously to rest with no roar of noise or rage of heartbeat, but filmed and crowned and kissed by the music of a million waving leaves and the song of many waters. I have seen the mystery of Dawn, the filmy mists that swathed the light limbs of the world, the hush of dreamless sleep, the chill of conquered death and then—the wide, wild thunder of the rising sun.[3]

Du Bois's eagerness to promote a resort town in which he himself owned a lot—despite never building a home on the land, he named the parcel "Bois Du Bois," or Du Bois's woods—may seem a bit much. But his prose simply reflected and expanded on the general tendency of promoters and visitors to refer to the natural splendor of the resort town they invariably called "Beautiful Idlewild."[4]

Many early twentieth-century Americans—both white and black— valued both rural and even more remote, relatively untouched "wilderness" landscapes for the same reasons: these were places that offered a contrast to urban industrial places that were increasingly believed to contribute to poor physical, mental, and spiritual health. Massive urban green spaces such as Washington and Jackson Parks could offer a salve for those ills, but they still lay within the city and were vulnerable to the modern, urban ills from which one might seek escape. Certainly, public parks and beaches were oases in the urban desert, but both their constructedness and proximity to the city's vices led many to seek out a more authentic experience of nature, most often in privately owned places far from the city. Even though Idlewild was far from "wild" compared to landscapes that environmentalists like John Muir were busy trying to protect from development, a large part of its attraction was its marked contrast from metropolises like Chicago, which was then the nation's second largest city. In language strikingly similar to Richard Wright's recollection of his first impressions of Chicago just six years later, Du Bois began his praise of Idlewild by reflecting on the city he departed from, which was still recovering from the race riot two summers earlier: "Chicago scares me: the crowd at State and Madison, the ruthless raggedness and grime of the blazing streets, the brute might of the Thing. And the colored folk are fighting today just as they fought in the Battle of the Riot, with heads bloody but unbowed, triumphant, fearless, wild."[5] At least for the most well-off black Chicagoans, the spoils of those battles were, in part, landscapes of hope like Idlewild. African American resort towns across the North were effectively built with black urban wealth created by the Great Migration. Without the "brute might" of Chicago's built environment and the millions who lived there, Idlewild would never have existed, nor would there have been a need for it to exist. The toxic environmental and social urban context that many like Du Bois sought to temporarily escape in the Great Migration years was a byproduct of the same Northern industrial giant that gave most African Americans vastly expanded economic and social opportunities compared to the South.

Indeed, Idlewild and other black resort towns across the North were symbols of just how modern the Great Migration had made urban-dwelling African Americans, contesting broader cultural expectations about how a supposedly "primitive" race should interact with nature and acting on environmental values that many believed were universally human, not racially unique. Simply put, black primitivist ideology, which was common currency during the migration years, was a school of thought that posited African Americans were inherently, biologically "uncivilized" and thus "closer to nature" than other races. It was a deterministic view that rationalized exploitative sharecropping culture and racial subjugation more generally, explaining everything from ostensibly "authentic" black cultural expression to the supposedly morally deficient urban entertainment districts such as the Stroll that were frequented by black migrants thought to be ill suited to the urban environment. Indeed, these ideas were in large part what drove the black cultural elite's anxieties about migrant behavior in Washington Park: they worried that migrants were confirming whites' worst racist assumptions.

Revolving around the twin geographies of rural labor spaces in the South and urban leisure spaces in the North, black primitivist thought simply did not have a vocabulary to understand the black cultural elite's leisure in the rural North's landscapes of hope: these were black Chicagoans in unexpected places.[6] One doubts, for instance, that those behind the repeated bombings of Binga's home would have expected him to be hundreds of miles away, at a leisure resort in rural Michigan, when they attacked. Despite their self-segregation, then, Idlewild and other black resort towns represented a subversive play for racial equality, turning racist ideas about African Americans' supposed proximity to nature on their head and reformulating a relationship with the natural environment that had been fractured by the legacy of more than two centuries of forced labor on the land. In doing so, Idlewilders laid claim to a growing impulse among rapidly modernizing and urbanizing populations in the early twentieth century: to take part in healthy and restorative leisure activity in natural and landscaped environments outside the city.

Although the development of rural retreats for African Americans was consistent with broader social and cultural trends in this era, these rural Northern landscapes of hope held special significance for black Chicagoans in the Great Migration era in ways that similar resorts for whites did not. These resorts were hybrid spaces that blended environmental and social elements of the more rural, agricultural South and the more urban, industrial North. With roots in the former and new lives in the latter, many Idlewilders forged new relationships with nature. For one, despite ecologies and climates that differed greatly from those in the South, these rural landscapes no doubt reminded many resort goers of the rural environments in the South they had traded for the promise of advancement in the urban North. They were a version of a home left behind, transplanted and transformed into a landscape of hope, ideally devoid of the racial violence that plagued both the rural South and many green spaces in the urban North. Here in the rural North, these environments were no longer Booker T. Washington's Southern landscapes of labor, laden with a long, brutal history of racial violence; instead, they served as Northern landscapes of leisure, mostly for those in W. E. B. Du Bois's Talented Tenth. In his 1901 autobiography, *Up from Slavery,* a book consistent with his philosophy in its devotion to the uplifting potential of manual labor on the land (often agricultural), Washington used language strikingly similar to that Du Bois would use to praise Idlewild two decades later. He effusively lauded leisure time spent with his family in "the woods, where we can live for a while near the heart of nature, where no one can disturb or vex us, surrounded by pure air, the trees, the shrubbery, the flowers, and the sweet fragrance that springs from a hundred plants, enjoying the chirp of the crickets and the songs of the birds."[7]

Indeed, the solitude offered by the "heart of nature" was precisely the type of escape from city life sought by early visitors to Idlewild. When *Defender* founder and Hampton Institute alumnus Robert Abbott said after a visit to Idlewild in 1926 that it "will be the most beautiful resort in America. People will make no mistake in lowering their buckets at Idlewild," he was clearly invoking Washington's landmark 1895 Atlanta Exposition speech that controversially encouraged African Americans to pursue economic prosperity in the South rather than demand social and political equality or migrate in search of a better life.[8] Abbott, an admirer of Washington's, was hardly alone; his reference would have been hard to miss for Idlewilders who had hung a portrait of Booker T. Washington in the resort's clubhouse. But Abbott was effectively turning Washington's exhortation to "cast down your bucket where you are" on its head, encouraging the settlement of a rural leisure resort in the North and addressing a Northern audience that had already long ago rejected Washington's rationale for remaining in the agricultural South. Idlewilders were largely black professionals who had not settled for Washington's particular brand of accommodationism, and there was perhaps no more central figure in that rejection than Abbott himself, whose *Defender* helped spur the Great Migration that ultimately generated the wealth that made places like Idlewild possible. Idlewild's landscape of leisure, far from the South's landscapes of labor, was the quintessential landscape of hope, emblematic of the accomplishments of the Talented Tenth.[9]

From the very beginning, therefore, Idlewild and other black resort towns represented a hybrid of Du Bois's and Washington's ideas about nature and race. If the black Chicagoans who vacationed in Idlewild were in many ways an example of Du Bois's well-educated Talented Tenth, many joined Abbott in their deep indebtedness to a version of Booker T. Washington's Tuskegee Institute-based uplift "strategy of racial progress through self-reliance and entrepreneurship" adapted to the urban North.[10] Idlewild's black clientele largely followed this approach that, as one historian has noted, "deemphasized the fight for integration and dealt with discrimination by creating black institutions."[11] Du Bois wrote that black Chicago's Talented Tenth could enjoy a natural environment superior even to older East Coast African American resorts in part because it offered an unparalleled experience of "absolute freedom from the desperate cruelty of the color line."[12] Privately owned and fairly remote natural landscapes like Idlewild afforded many black Chicagoans access to environments they believed to be physically healthy, morally uplifting, and spiritually restorative, while also offering the promise of escaping the racial violence and discrimination that often plagued African American residential areas and Chicago's public green spaces such as Washington and Jackson Parks. Jesse Binga did not have to worry about bombings of his cottage in rural Michigan, and Idlewild flourished apparently free of racial violence at a time when the *Defender* lamented that white-on-black violence at Washington Park was its "permanent blister."[13]

Yet Idlewild's exclusively African American clientele meant that the color line simply moved outside the town limits, and any "absolute freedom" from it was an illusion: Idlewild's freedom from race violence was just as much a product of the color line as an escape from it because the resort was effectively an African American effort to establish a separate-but-equal institution. Race discrimination may have been less visible to resort goers who relaxed on Idlewild's beach or rowed on its lake, but it set the boundaries for the idyll Du Bois lauded— from the remote geographical location of the black resort to the discrimination resort goers sometimes faced when traveling to rural Michigan from urban centers across the Midwest. Outside the borders of the growing resort community, in the rural North that was almost exclusively populated by whites, race prejudice could rear its ugly head just as easily as it did in the South—or in the city's public green spaces such as Washington and Jackson Parks. Time and again in the Great Migration years, it seemed to many African Americans that the only way to fully realize the virtues of the natural environment was to establish communities and institutions entirely separate from whites, on privately owned land that was safer than public parks, beaches, or forest preserves where whites often resisted—sometimes violently—interracial use.

The members of the black cultural elite who retreated to Idlewild were well aware that the vast majority of black Chicagoans had neither the time nor the resources to escape the city, and they almost immediately set about making natural and landscaped environments more accessible to the working-class masses, acting on the same convictions that motivated their fight for the creation of Madden Park. Nearly a decade before it published Du Bois's ode to Idlewild, the NAACP's *Crisis* had already recognized that, even among its relatively affluent readership, few were "able to leave their work for any length of time. 'We're too busy trying to earn a living,' they write, 'to think about summer resorts.' To this large body of people the picnic, the evening car ride, the excursion to some neighboring park is the only escape from the city's toil and heat."[14] Urban green spaces such as Washington and Madden Parks were vital to black Chicagoans of all classes, but the black reformers who were fortunate enough to visit Idlewild and similar resorts worked throughout the Great Migration years to make sure that these landscapes of hope were not the *only* escape from the city's built environment.

As a result, thousands of working-class black Chicagoans—mainly children and young adults who represented a generation of African Americans with little direct experience of the South—retreated to rural landscapes that resembled Idlewild's, mainly through youth camps affiliated with segregated community organizations such as the YMCA, YWCA, and Boy Scouts. The same black Chicagoans who escaped to rural resorts like Idlewild in the summer also staffed and funded these organizations, adapting Booker T. Washington's ideas about self-help and nature's virtues to the perceived needs of urban dwellers, translating them from sites of Southern working-class labor onto sites of Northern middle- and upper-class leisure. These children of packinghouse workers and migrants growing up in collapsing tenements were most vulnerable to the "brute might of the Thing," after all—members of the working classes that reformers feared would struggle to adjust to the city and were in danger of lapsing into delinquency. The reformers' objective was to combat the negative impacts of industrial work on men and women—and street life on boys and girls—with religious instruction and physical activity, and so their programs perhaps naturally incorporated escapes to preindustrial, pastoral environments. Reformers hoped that, thanks to a few days or several weeks in more natural surroundings, these young men and women would become better workers and better citizens when they returned to Chicago's factories, streets, and neighborhoods. Reform the men, women, and children of the city by taking them to the country, the logic went, and when those reformed men, women, and children return to the city, it would become a better place for everyone to live.

Like white reformers, then, the black cultural elite took youngsters to the countryside in the hopes that they would gain the skills necessary for success in the city. In this, they followed the urban ecology logic of the Chicago School of Sociology that believed juvenile delinquency stemmed from social pathologies that developed in specific geographic locales. But at the same time, these rural youth camps that black Chicagoans established, staffed, and funded were also a powerful affront to racist ideologies, complicating primitivist images of working-class black youth falling prey to the supposedly vice-riddled leisure time of Chicago's Stroll. Although middle- and upper-class white reformers created nearly identical opportunities for white youth in this period, for African Americans the stakes were higher because escaping the city's artificiality also meant temporarily escaping the hazards of overt racism and its more covert manifestations that helped drive higher delinquency rates among African American youth. In the safe, privately owned space of rural camps, black leaders and their campers could try to forget, if only for a week or two, such distractions and focus on building character and building healthy bodies; instilling these values in the working classes would also ideally help reform the behavior in urban public green spaces that often frustrated the black cultural elite.[15] Just like Idlewilders, these working-class African Americans in unexpected places forged a hybrid relationship with nature that blended North and South, implicitly challenging primitivist ideologies even as they reluctantly accepted a certain amount of racial segregation.

To achieve these goals, black community institutions established seg-regated campsites in the rural Midwest during the Great Migration years: by the mid-1920s, building on its early success with camping programs for the South Side community, the segregated black Wabash YMCA had purchased its own camp in southwest Michigan and Chicago's African American Boy Scout troops operated a black division of Camp Owasippe in northern Michigan. Camps Wabash and Belnap, as they were respectively called, grew over the remaining years of the decade thanks both to sustained support from the black cultural elite and Chicago's ever-expanding African American population. By the time of the Depression, they had become integral parts of YMCA and Boy Scout programs for black Chicago's young men and boys. The city's black YWCA branch, meanwhile, established a short-lived campsite near Hammond, Indiana, mainly for young women who worked in the packinghouses, and scrambled to find a way to continue offering such opportunities when the site was deemed unsanitary and funding evap-orated. These community organizations also began utilizing the Cook County Forest Preserves, which were closer to the city, for hikes and weekend camping trips. Established in 1916, the same year Idlewild was founded, these forest preserves were more accessible and affordable to the working classes because they were just a short drive, streetcar ride, or even hike from Black Belt neighborhoods. But African Americans always needed to be prepared to face racial hostility in these public landscapes in ways that Idlewild residents or Camp Wabash campers did not; the vast majority of forest preserves were patronized by whites and were located very close to rural and suburban white neighborhoods.

As a 1924 *Defender* editorial titled "Vacation Time" hints, there was a vast and varied geography of exurban black recreation in natural and landscaped environments during the Great Migration years. Much like Du Bois did in the *Crisis,* the editorial set the stage by describing the crushing urban environment and quickly offered a refreshing alterna-tive: "When city pavements are sizzling in the torrid sun and scorching the feet of the weary pedestrian, . . . the back to the farm and the great outdoors movement is exceeding[ly] popular." In the Cook County Forest Preserves located on Chicago's outskirts, children could "romp at will out in the open, where there is an abundance of pure, fresh air, and far removed from the dangers confronted in their usual playground, the city streets." Even farther from the city than these rural green spaces, the editorial noted, were "hundreds of inviting resorts" in the rural Midwest that beckoned to black Chicagoans "blessed with a larger share of this world's goods." But regardless of one's wealth, the editorial concluded, "We . . . owe it to ourselves and to our children to get out if only for a week or two each summer in what we are pleased to call God's country." Such retreats were "better than all the medicine in the world when it comes to building up [children's] systems and restoring their youthful vigor."[16]

As the editorial indicates, private rural retreats merely represented an extension of public city parks for urban dwellers, providing an amplification of the supposed benefits offered by urban green spaces as small as Chicago's Madden Park and as large as the Olmsted and Vaux-designed Washington Park. Whereas Chicago's urban parks were bits of nature artificially landscaped into the city's grid and perilously close to what was believed to be moral and material filth, reformers of both races agreed with Daniel Burnham who, in his 1909 plan for the city, argued, "The existing public parks go far in this direction, but not far enough."[17] In other words, to achieve the most beneficial physical, mental, and spiritual influences on city dwellers (particularly children), reformers in the black cultural elite believed that "better than all the medicine in the world" was a retreat to landscapes of hope outside the city where relationships with nature could often be more easily cultivated and controlled.

Escaping to Beautiful Idlewild

In the fall of 1915, just as the first stirrings of the Great Migration were underway, four white land developers from Chicago and Michigan began to plat a portion of 2,700 acres in Lake County, Michigan, determined to create an African American resort just a few miles east of Baldwin, the county seat. More than 250 miles from Chicago's South Side, the landscape was undoubtedly more "natural" than the urban environment, but it was far from wild: much of the surrounding forests had been clear-cut at least a generation earlier, and the sandy soil had largely failed to support subsequent attempts at farming. Nevertheless, the marketing-savvy developers named their nascent town Idlewild, perhaps hoping to evoke images of spending idle, carefree leisure hours in a vacation spot where nature's wildness countered the city's ill effects on weary urban dwellers—or, as the *Chicago Whip*'s gossip columnist put it, someplace where there were "plenty of 'idle wild women' and 'wild idle men.'"[18] The development of Idlewild presumed a largely untapped market of well-off African Americans willing and able to spend significant amounts of money to escape the city for a rustic retreat hundreds of miles from the major Midwestern black populations in Chicago and Detroit and in an area surrounded by rural whites. Indeed, in 1910, the black population of Lake County was in the single digits—only five African Americans claimed the inland county as home.

There was more than a little justification for the white developers' gamble, because similar rural African American retreats were already popular on the East Coast, near older urban centers of black wealth and dating back to at least the 1890s. In the Midwest, one of the earliest such African American resorts was the West Michigan Resort, which opened in 1908 near Benton Harbor, Michigan, only a few hours' boat ride from Chicago. That resort's nearly decade-long run provided some evidence that there was a Midwestern market for such vacation spots, even before the Great Migration swelled the ranks of the urban black cultural elite seeking a temporary reprieve from the city. In its early years, this resort counted among its guests renowned Chicago surgeon and Provident Hospital's chief of staff George Cleveland Hall, lawyer and county commissioner Edward Herbert Wright, chef Rufus Estes (who would go on to publish a popular cookbook), and poet Fenton Johnson. Despite its notable clientele, the *Defender* alternated praise of the resort's natural beauty on the Lake Michigan shore and frustration at its poor management. Indeed, the West Michigan Resort failed to open its doors in 1915, perhaps not coincidentally the very same year Idlewild began courting vacationers and investors in a more remote inland area of Michigan.[19]

Idlewild initially drew hundreds—and quickly thousands—of vacationers annually from all over the Midwest and became the most famous of many rural African American resorts in the region, eventually growing into a town where many lived year-round. In characteristically hyperbolic fashion, the *Defender* billed Idlewild's 1916 dedication as "the biggest event of the year," touting "special trains" that brought those interested from Chicago, Detroit, and other Midwestern population centers to rural Michigan.[20] Perhaps after learning of Idlewild in the pages of the *Defender* or having gone to an informational meeting on Chicago's South Side—sometimes held in African Methodist Episcopal churches (which tended to have congregations consisting of the black cultural elite)—prospective lot owners would then go to see "Beautiful Idlewild" for themselves. In the late 1910s and early 1920s, when Idlewild was still building its reputation and working to attract buyers, it was common for those making the trek to organize an "excursion" with groups as large as three hundred. From Chicago, such groups would sometimes charter a Pullman sleeping car for the journey over the Pere Marquette railroad; once the train arrived in Baldwin, a bus service met groups and transported them the last few miles to the resort so they could inspect the lots for sale or, for those who already had purchased land or were just visiting, take a multiweek vacation from the city.[21]

Idlewild vacationers retreated to the resort from all over the Midwest and even beyond, but black Chicagoans constituted the majority of cottage owners, no doubt driven in large part by the city's thriving black cultural elite. By 1924, Idlewilders had built more than 400 cottages, and more than 4,000 lots had been sold; by the end of the decade, the resort boasted 700 cottages, a handful of small hotels, and an estimated summer contingent of more than five thousand that spilled over into adjoining summer communities, including Paradise Gardens, Idlewild Heights, and Idlewild Terrace. Although Idlewild was undoubtedly the most popular resort town in the Midwest where African Americans could actually purchase lots on which to construct modest vacation homes, it was far from alone in drawing visitors. Thanks to the relative prosperity of the Great Migration years, a host of similar leisure retreats increasingly dotted the rural Midwestern landscape, and more casual visitors could rent cabins or stay in rural hotels that catered to African Americans. By the late 1920s, many black Chicagoans regularly took weekend or weeks-long vacations at smaller rural Midwestern resorts in Illinois, Indiana, Michigan, and Wisconsin, many named for the natural features proprietors hoped would draw patrons. Among these landscapes of hope were the Homestead at Cedar Lake, Casa Loma, Waters Farm, Sunset Hills, Woodlawn, Paradise Lake, Chandlers, Ivanhoe, and Val-du-Lakes (short for "valleys, dunes, and lakes"), just to name a few.[22]

Among the proliferation of African American resorts in the rural Midwest, a large part of what made Idlewild such a uniquely smashing success in the Great Migration years was its ability to attract a veritable who's who of the South Side's black cultural elite. Along with Jesse

Binga, Oscar De Priest, and Robert Abbott, Idlewild counted among its most famous guests Dr. Daniel Hale Williams, surgeon and founder of Provident Hospital on Chicago's South Side (located on the northern boundary of Washington Park); Herbert Turner, medical doctor and Chicago NAACP president; Earl Dickerson, the lawyer who would go on to become president of the Chicago Urban League and argue the landmark *Hansberry* v. *Lee* case before the Supreme Court (a case that contested restrictive covenants in Chicago); Louis B. Anderson, Chicago's second African American alderman (who followed the city's first black alderman, Oscar De Priest, in representing the Black Belt's Second Ward and fought for park space on the South Side); George Arthur, Wabash Avenue YMCA executive secretary; and Dan Jackson, Chicago vice lord. Many if not most of these men retreated to Idlewild with their wives and families. In fact, reports of comings and goings at the resort town indicate that many wives spent considerably more time there than their husbands, whose business schedules allowed less vacation time. Several of the South Side's most prominent women also spent part of their summers at the most famous African American resort in the Midwest. Among them were Violette Anderson, who was married at Idlewild in 1920 overlooking "the limpid and placid waters of a perfectly mirrored lake, with the blue sky for a canopy and oak and Norway pines forming a background for the altar" and later became the first black woman admitted to practice law before the Supreme Court; Vivian Harsh, who would go on to serve as director of a Chicago Public Library branch; Irene McCoy Gaines, who worked for the Chicago Urban League and would eventually serve as president of the Chicago and Northern District Association of Colored Women's Clubs; and several officers of the South Side's African American YWCA branch.[23]

Although Idlewild was not reserved exclusively for those who were— or would become—notable black Chicagoans, the resort did primarily cater to "the leading colored people of Chicago and Evanston, physicians, college professors, real estate men, contractors, and professional people of wealth and acknowledged standding [*sic*],"[24] as the local Lake County newspaper put it even before the inaugural summer season. A decade later, the same newspaper elaborated that Idlewild's "rank and file are workers, professional people who labor under pressure ten months of the year or more and who have learned that they must rest at least once a year," but who were wealthy enough to travel from Chicago and other major Midwestern metropolises "in their town cars—many of them expensive and luxurious."[25] Idlewilders were workers, yes, but their white-collar labor occurred mostly in office buildings rather than the factories, mills, stockyards, and homes where most working-class black migrants manually labored. As a *Defender* editorial put it in 1924, Idlewild and other black resorts called to these office workers in the summer when "the electric fan in the office only churns hot air and makes collars and stiff shirts take on the appearance of dish rags"; they offered escape from an urban environment where one "daily breathe[d] air surcharged with the smoke of factory and workshop, with the odor from the stock yards for good measure."[26] For many working-class black migrants, in contrast, the stockyard stench described by the *Defender* would not have been merely "for good measure" added to factory smoke; jobs in the stockyards or steel mills were among the best-paying ones they could hope to find. Yet African Americans who worked in the stockyards invariably got the dirtiest, smelliest, least desirable jobs there, and the stench of dead animals on the killing floor or smoke from industrial furnaces would have been so deeply enmeshed in their clothes, even in their skin, that it overpowered everything else. Indeed, the urban sights and smells that signaled mostly ambient, environmental inconveniences and health threats to the Chicago's black cultural elite had far more intimate, bodily resonances for the working classes, the vast majority of whom could only retreat to urban public parks, unable to afford even a brief excursion to private resorts such as Idlewild.[27]

That critical class discrepancy reveals not only that African American resort culture in the early twentieth century developed in large part as a direct result of the Great Migration but also that those opportunities were distributed unequally: a geography of affluence effectively reserved what were perceived to be the healthiest, most beautiful, most pastoral landscapes for the black cultural elite, far from the environmental conditions created by the modern, urban industries that drew hundreds of thousands black migrants to Chicago from the South. Although the black professional classes that summered at Idlewild both predated the Great Migration and existed in select urban areas in the South, the Great Migration made these sorts of careers possible in the North on an unprecedented scale. Idlewilders like Jesse Binga, Robert Abbott, and Oscar De Priest could not have built their wealth and status without the influx of tens of thousands of working-class black migrants to Chicago who deposited their savings, read the newspapers, paid the rents, gambled their wages, bought the goods, and cast the votes that created the South Side's black cultural elite.

Idlewild was simply out of reach—both geographically and financially—for the average black Chicagoan. Owning an automobile was still out of the question for much of the working class in this period, and the train ride alone would have been expensive for even middle-class African Americans, had they aspired to go; in 1924 a round-trip ticket from Chicago's downtown Loop good for a return within three weeks cost $15. Even in the unlikely event that working-class African Americans could take a week or two off work, purchasing a lot for even as low as $24.50 in 1918—before prices rose to as high as $200 in 1921—would have been unthinkable for most of the black community in which the median income was about $100 per month, roughly half of which went to cover rent and food. In reality, this exclusivity was part of what attracted Chicago's black cultural elite to Idlewild: in rural Michigan they could escape both the city's unhealthy environment and the people—not just racist whites but working-class African Americans as well—who they felt often frustrated their ambitions. Resort goers made up precisely the same class of black Chicagoans, after all, that condemned ukulele playing and other markers of working-class Southern culture on Washington Park's tennis courts as "open-air performances of minstrelsy."[28]

Although vacationing in Idlewild certainly required money, not everyone was nearly as wealthy as Jesse Binga; what united resort goers were these shared cultural values and codes of behavior, manners, and morals. As the local newspaper reflected on the formation of the National Idlewild Woman's Club in 1927, "As silent workers, the women have brought the comunity [sic] to its present high standard, promoting interest in the beautifying of homes, raising the standard of entertainments to the present high class features, and creating a more wholesome atmosphere generally."[29] These clubwomen and urban professionals made up Du Bois's Talented Tenth, the well-educated class of black Chicagoans who would have appreciated poet Fenton Johnson's reference to reading Cervantes while listening to "the soft music of the waves and the breeze as it [came] through the trees" at the West Michigan Resort in 1911, or later the *Defender*'s 1924 Tennyson reference when it "paraphrased the poet" in claiming that in the "spring and during the summer and fall months almost everybody's thoughts are centered on the time and the place for their vacation."[30] One early vacationer somewhat hyperbolically described the value of the resort this way: "Idlewild is the greatest step forward we have made. We have always needed a nice, clean playground where cares and worries might be laid aside; where we might meet and mingle with our very best and in the course of the wonderful social contact here and there, pick out a friend."[31] Such statements implicitly compared Idlewild's remote, privately owned lots favorably to urban public green spaces such as Washington Park, subject as they were to the city's polluted environment as well as both race and class discord. For Du Bois, it was African Americans' "duty to develop, beautify and govern [Idlewild]. It must be a center of Negro art, conference and recreation," and just a year or two after the first lots were sold, cosmetics entrepreneur and millionaire Madam C. J. Walker had already envisioned Idlewild as a national meeting place for African Americans, ideal for combining business and pleasure.[32] Resorts like Idlewild, in other words, helped socially fortify a coherent black cultural elite in the Great Migration years.

Idlewild's landscape of hope was symbolic of the black cultural elite's uplift ideology that hybridized W. E. B. Du Bois's ideas about the Talented Tenth and Booker T. Washington's accommodationism, embodying the maze of contradictions with which black Chicagoans were confronted during the Great Migration era. This ideology was at once inspirational and exclusionary, simultaneously a measure of the great strides African Americans had made in the North and the racial barriers that persistently blocked them. Characteristic of the optimistic outlook that many Idlewilders possessed, early boosters exhorted "every Race man and woman [to] stand by his own and make [themselves] better citizens to our government by building up a city of [their] own and owning our own homes at Idlewild."[33] The year the resort opened, the local newspaper similarly contended, "The colored people have long wanted a place where they could enjoy their summers, by themselves, far enough from the resorts of the whites to be free from interference or prejudice and still be near enough to their homes and markets to be easy of access and supply."[34] This appeal was complicated somewhat by the reality that white land developers, not African Americans, were the original developers, and they, at least at the outset, stood to gain the most financially through Idlewild's success—not to mention that two of the white founders were members of the local Ku Klux Klan chapter, which apparently focused its animosity much more on Catholics than on African Americans.[35] Although it is unclear whether or not Du Bois knew of the founder's Klan ties, he rationalized a black resort begun by whites by arguing that the developers had dealt with buyers in an "absolutely open, square and just" way and that the responsibility for the town's subsequent development was assumed by the Lot Owners Association, which was "composed exclusively of colored folk."[36] At its worst, this sort of uplift ideology could verge on naked boosterism underwritten by an unjustifiably meritocratic worldview that alienated and marginalized the working classes, refusing to challenge segregation or racial discrimination. Idlewild's postmaster, who had also held a position with the segregated YWCA branch on Chicago's South Side, echoed Booker T. Washington's accommodationist rhetoric in a 1927 column that lauded the Tuskegee Institute along with philanthropic institutions such as the Julius Rosenwald Fund and the Carnegie Corporation; the column concluded, "The world in the main is fair minded. No one can be blamed for asking another to stay in his own backyard. Groups of peoples must rise within themselves. Demand does not always follow capability, for virtue has its own reward."[37]

Despite these sorts of rosy assessments, there are clues that Idlewilders knew full well that the world just outside their idyllic summer retreat was not "fair minded" and that vacationing in—and traveling through—areas in the rural North settled almost exclusively by whites brought its own risks and indignities. From its earliest days, for instance, Idlewild boosters framed their fledgling resort town as an economic boon to a fairly depressed region that was just beginning to promote nature tourism. Exhibiting an awareness that their presence might not be welcome in a region with an overwhelmingly white population, boosters claimed in the local newspaper that "in a business way it is going to mean a great deal to Baldwin, as the patrons of the resort are without exception people of means, people of professional pursuits and many of them ranking at the top of their professions."[38] Given a readership that would have been predominantly white, boosters were also clearly attempting to alleviate concerns about black working-class behavior and violence that were rampant among whites during the Great Migration years—the very same sorts of ideas that were grounded in primitivist ideologies. Boosters, in other words, were in part trying to assure white locals that Idlewilders would not be the sort of ill-behaved Southerners whom the black cultural elite themselves chastised in places such as Washington Park. No matter how the resort was framed to nearby white populations, however, the black cultural elite had to be prepared for embarrassing, if not violent, racial prejudice as they traveled through areas populated almost exclusively by whites, few of whom regularly encountered African Americans. Returning to Chicago from Idlewild by car in 1929, for example, three women were forced to relieve themselves in the bushes along Highway 12 near Michigan City, Indiana, after being refused use of the facilities at a gas station. *The Negro Motorist Green Book*, which offered African American travelers lists of friendly establishments along the road, was published nearly a decade later, partly to prevent precisely these sorts of indignities and dangers in rural America's white "sundown towns." The potential for such racial discrimination and humiliation that lay just beyond the bounds of Idlewild's pastoral idyll revealed the limits of racial uplift ideology that posited economic success and cultural refinement as a path toward equality.[39]

These difficulties, however, did little to deter boosters who were determined to prove not only that vacationing amidst Idlewild's rustic splendor was a restorative venture that uplifted the race but also that consuming nature represented a wise real estate investment. W. E. B. Du Bois was just one of many investors, for instance, who bought land but never developed it: at a time when the resort boasted around 500 cottages, there had already been more than 16,000 lots sold of the approximately 19,000 parcels into which the development had been divided. When Du Bois wrote about the virtues of Idlewild in 1921, he reflected that although lots had been sold at prices as low as $10 or $20 apiece just a few years earlier, their current price of about $100 was still a bargain. Investors who had gotten in on the ground floor stood to make a handsome profit if and when they sold their property, whether or not they had actually built a home. It turned out to be a wise investment in part because Idlewild was developed in the midst of a broader cultural move toward consuming nature that coincided with expanded automobile access. More than two hundred miles from large black populations in Chicago and Detroit, the trek to Idlewild could sometimes prove an arduous journey, and although the drive could be made in thirteen hours, one early visitor from Detroit recalled that, thanks to many flat tires along the way in his family's Model T, it took a full twenty-four hours to reach Idlewild. But already by 1925, a newspaper article noted that Idlewild was "becoming a thoroughfare for motorists, many of whom look in for an hour, purchasing supplies and refreshments and gaining a desirable viewpoint of our activities."[40] Representative of the ways car culture fueled the consumption of nature as a leisure outlet was Robert Abbott who, on a short visit to Idlewild in 1926, took "a motor sight-seeing trip [in which] he frequently left the car and tramped through the woods, plucking a wild flower, examining the soil, [and] commenting on the wonderful highway system of Michigan."[41]

If automobiles increasingly supplanted trains as the primary way black Chicagoans retreated to Idlewild, of course, they also paradoxically represented the conditions that boosters knew urban professionals wanted to—and had the means to—escape. In one paragraph of copy, a 1923 advertisement for the Woodland Park development, founded by the same men who began Idlewild and located less than twenty miles south, seamlessly transitions from problem to solution, from cause to effect:

> Spring is here at last and has brought with it that ever-returning longing to get back to Nature—away from the city with its close, stuffy atmosphere, the clang, clang of street cars—rumbling of heavy traffic and never-ceasing flow of automobiles. The big outdoors is calling. You cannot escape it. It is in your blood—you feel it with every breath and in every step you take. Somewhere off there in the distance the air is clear and refreshing—the birds are singing as they build their nests, the squirrels are chattering and fish are darting to and fro in pure crystal clear lakes and streams and all are glad that winter is past and spring is here at last.[42]

Like Du Bois, Woodland Park developers promoted rural northern Michigan's marked contrast with Chicago life: "Tired minds and bodies are not fit to perform the duties imposed upon them by the hard, strenuous life of a big city," another advertisement declared. "There comes a time to everyone, no matter how strong, when complete rest is needed, a change of atmosphere and scenery, and if you wish to keep pace with the times, you should take it."[43] Yet another half-page *Defender* advertisement promoted Woodland Park as a place for strengthening mental and communal well-being, as well as providing the conditions for healthy bodies: it was a "Happyland for all the family" where one could also find "pure, untainted air, scented only with the fresh perfume of the big outdoors" and "pure spring drinking water free from contamination and disease."[44] Many increasingly felt that modern urban life—which required one to "keep pace"—wore out minds, bodies, and souls. If the advertisements were to be believed, only an escape from such conditions could repair the damage and prepare one to return to a successful life in the city. Idlewild and similar resorts were marketed as landscapes of hope where African Americans like W. E. B. Du Bois could seek out "the great silence which is Peace and deep Contentment," impossible to find in the city.[45] Sometimes these resorts lived up to the billing.

Boosters used a variety of modern media to repeatedly promote nature as Idlewild's prime attraction, selling the rural outdoor experience to black professionals through film, song, and print. As early as Idlewild's opening summer in 1916, promoters had plans to produce a promotional film that would help sell the new resort to black Chicagoans, and in 1927 footage was shot for a twenty-three-minute silent promotional film called *A Pictorial View of Idlewild* that was screened throughout the Midwest to arouse interest in the already popular black resort. Promoting bucolic rural retreats in the heart of Chicago's urban entertainment district, the film was screened in black theaters such as the Pekin or the Regal on the South Side Stroll. A year earlier, Major N. Clark Smith, whose career had included stints as bandleader at Booker T. Washington's Tuskegee Institute and bandmaster of the *Defender* newsboys, also contributed to the advertising blitz, visiting the resort to "get the Idlewild atmosphere and gather inspiration from the woods and the streams of this wonderful playground, that they may be perpetuated in song."[46] The result was a tune that expanded on a song written by one of the original (white) founders of the Idlewild Resort Company:

> In a big Lake County, not many miles away,
> The countless pilgrims gather, for rest and play;
> Its trees of oak and lovely folk,
> Its Tabernacle or a church,
> Where maples grow with stately birch,
> 'Tis nature's wonderchild,
> Dear "Idlewild Fern Garden,"
> A dream of life come true,
> And old Pere Marquette river, so clear and blue,
> God made its waters sing a strain,
> To bubbling brook and spring remain
> They chant and sing a sweet refrain
> With nature's music dream.
> Dear Idlewild my Idlewild

I hear the birds a-calling,
I feel the dew drops falling;
To Idlewild, Dear Idlewild,
The candle lights a-burning,
My thoughts of love are turning,
To Idlewild (oh boy) Dear wild.[47]

The song wove together a diverse set of reasons to visit the resort: it was accessible to the city because it was "not many miles away" (although it was actually quite far away, of course, from the nearest big city); it boasted good social company; and it was a place where one could "rest and play" and feel closer to God. Idlewild itself was sold as "nature's wonderchild," but boosters also often linked the leisure enjoyed at the resort town to a rediscovery of one's own carefree childhood. An early Idlewild advertisement focused on the mental benefits derived from an escape to nature, urging potential buyers to "cast aside for the time all the cares and worries of their strenuous, nerve-racking routine lives, and romp and play once more as children, enjoy to the full nature in all her wondrous glory," for instance, and the full page of photographs accompanying Du Bois's 1921 *Crisis* article was captioned "Playing at Idlewild."[48]

Although Idlewild was explicitly promoted as a place where one could shed modern urban discomforts and stresses, in reality resort goers never completely left the city—or its modern conveniences—behind. Du Bois's 1921 version of Idlewild—a rural town that was "not fashionable: men in khaki, women in knickers and overalls, no servants, food cheap, victrolas for orchestra, no high-heeled shoes," and where one could enjoy "hiking, fishing, tennis, rowing, dancing, spooning and sleeping. Especially sleeping. Long, quiet, glorious naps, night and day, to the sound of dancing waters"—was accurate to an extent, but perhaps oversold the contrast with modern life.[49] Indeed, developers attempted to construct the best of both worlds, combining the amenities of the city with the virtues of nature in rural spaces—without the racism, filth, and ill health of the former or the potential hardships of the latter. It is true that during Idlewild's first decade, the accommodations provided by developers were fairly rudimentary: nine-and-a-half-foot by twelve-foot wooden platforms on which tents were pitched. But there were servants if vacationers desired them, despite Du Bois's claims to the contrary. Even during its inaugural summer, resort goers were assured that this "tent city" was to "be cared for by attendants who will change the linen, fill the water pitchers, make the beds, and do all the necessary work, so the guests will have nothing to tax their time or their patience."[50] By 1922 electricity came to the island and illuminated Idlewild's clubhouse and various dwellings, and by 1925 many small permanent structures, affectionately called "doghouses" for their resemblance in size and structure to actual doghouses, were built on the original wooden foundations. It was around this time that Dr. Herbert Turner, who had two cars at the time, recalled Idlewild's Paradise Hotel, built the same year Du Bois lauded the resort town's rustic pleasures, as "a hotel matching the standards of those most luxurious hotels in Chicago. The waiters came from the Palmer House. Orchestra played during both lunch and dinner. Ladies came in full dress. No man in shirt sleeves was permitted there."[51] This was a place far removed—both geographically and culturally—from the Washington Park tennis courts where the *Defender* worried about members of the working classes playing in inappropriate clothing.

In many ways, then, Idlewild's landscape of hope was a hybrid space: its summer residents remained inextricably bound to the cities they left behind for weeks or months at a time, transplanting a version of the material comforts and culture of urban living into a rural environment largely devoid of the smoke and filth, racism, the ill-behaved working classes, and work associated with the urban environment. But that is not to say Idlewild's culture was completely refined: the *Broad Ax* coyly noted that the town's first mayor might not enforce the prohibition of alcohol sales on Sundays, and as early as 1922, the *Chicago Whip*'s gossip columnist reported on "the wild scenes in the early morning hours as the tired political leaders of the Windy City sought to be carefree as they gathered unto themselves girls of tender years and sought to show them Bacchanalian orgies in the latest and most approved Hollywood style."[52] Whether or not that account of Idlewild's seamier side was an exaggeration, it seems clear that the rural Michigan retreat was not *only* as rustic and peaceful as Du Bois made it out to be. As Idlewild's postmaster noted in 1926, when the resort was just a decade old, "For two months of the year it is the retreat of thousands who have surrounded themselves with the comforts and conveniences of the city at vast combined expense in order that they may completely relax and enjoy their vacation."[53]

There were also indications that, by the late 1920s, Idlewild's entertainment culture was slowly but surely growing into a scene closely resembling that of Chicago's Stroll in miniature. In 1928, the Purple

Palace nightclub opened, featuring Chicago-based performers and "Or-pheum Circuit Headliners," boasting "Select Entertainment and the Best Dance Floor This Side of Chicago."[54] The following year, a *Pittsburgh Courier* correspondent, who noted the charms of the natural environment at Idlewild and pointed to daytime leisure activities like "bathing, fishing, hiking, horseback riding" as primary reasons to vacation there, also wrote that in the "evening one may enjoy the almost 'continuous vaudeville' at the clubhouse, furnished by visiting artists and others who volunteer."[55] Just as they did in the city, Idlewilders enjoyed such enter-tainment in conjunction with more pious engagements: AME and Bap-tist congregations gathered for Sunday services and Sunday school in the clubhouse, which functioned as a makeshift church when it was not hosting dances, games, and the like. Despite the idyllic setting, Idlewil-ders were similarly not divorced from the political and racial realities of the city. In August 1919, for instance, *Defender* editor Cary B. Lewis spoke to an audience of more than 150 "on the Chicago riot and the outlook for [African Americans] as a people, . . . stirring them up to greater Race activity," but he did so "on the spacious veranda overlooking the beau-tiful lake," not in a South Side lecture hall.[56]

Although Idlewild and other resort towns were inextricably bound up in the consumer culture of the Great Migration years, there was more than a grain of truth to advertisements' exaggerated claims of their natural beauty, no matter how many urban creature comforts they of-fered. Baseball games and the bridle paths Jesse Binga enjoyed may have resembled those in Washington Park—though they were presumably free of both the racial violence and the raw behavior that the black cul-tural elite felt too often plagued Chicago's Sunday School League—but resort goers' reminiscences largely focus on the same natural beauty that promotional materials touted. It is admittedly difficult to disentangle the promotional ideal from reality when, in 1925, Idlewild's postmaster noted that since the resort town opened a decade earlier, "there have been many resorts springing up in close proximity with big cities that have taken the sensation out of Idlewild, leaving a sentiment that links up with the out door life. . . . The climate is wonderful. It washes away the weariness of body and wakens the mind to a new view point on the beauties of na-ture."[57] But author Charles Chesnutt echoed Du Bois's promotional ver-sion of Idlewild when he wrote to his daughter in 1922 that he "danced every night . . . [and] spent a lot of time fishing and rowing; caught so

Figure 2.1. Bathing beach at Idlewild, circa 1930. Courtesy Archives of Michigan, Stanley Kufta Collection (MS 89–157), C-3713.

many black bass and blue-gills that your mother got tired of cooking them."[58] It was a haul more substantial than one could hope for in Washington Park's lagoon; like many others who visited Idlewild, Chesnutt took part in what was, according to the *Defender*, an "exquisite season of bathing, fishing and hiking" at the resort (see Figure 2.1).[59] By the same token, Chicago vice lord and undertaker Dan Jackson often visited Idlewild on winter hunting trips, and Woodland Park advertisements boasted the possibility of hunting partridge, duck, and rabbit. These were the sorts of excursions that translated the sport of hunting so common across the South into a northern context that was impossible in the city. Indeed, all these activities were evidence that, as Charles Chesnutt's daughter recalled, "nature was lavish at Idlewild" in ways that far outstripped public urban parks' ability to bring nature to the city.[60]

As Du Bois and many others recognized, because rural resorts like Idlewild marked such a contrast with city life, it made little difference to the black cultural elite that nature in most if not all of these places was actually not the wild, "undisturbed" nature that "wilderness cult" advocates like John Muir sought to protect. To the casual observer from the city, Idlewild's landscape no doubt would have appeared perfectly natural, even wild. Like much of the upper Midwest, however, Idlewild's environment was actually the product of decades of intensive human use—in this case industrial logging—rather than the pristine, untouched wilderness that promoters sold. In the late nineteenth century, like many counties along Michigan's western coast, Idlewild's Lake County provided much of the Midwest with lumber. One historian even traces the demand for lumber back to the Chicago fire of 1871, which would ironically mean that some of the South Side's rundown tenements that black working-class migrants occupied after moving to Chicago were constructed with wood that came from an area that would one day host the city's black professionals. At the height of the surrounding river valley's lumber production, more than two dozen sawmills employed around 1,200 people in the county. The small lakes that dotted the region and later played host to resort goers' rowing, swimming, and fishing were, decades previous, ideal holding tanks for floating lumber initially gleaned from vast stands of softwoods, most commonly white pine. Once it was ready to transport to market, the lumber floated down the rivers and lakes of Michigan on its way to Chicago to be distributed by rail to points farther south and west.

Railroads like the Pere Marquette had further opened up the region to logging near the turn of the twentieth century, making the wood from Lake County's hardwood forests more accessible and transportable. Unlike the softwood pines that by then had been largely clear-cut, hardwoods such as maple and elm did not float on the rivers and lakes—but they did stack on railroad cars. All of this intensive logging meant that, by the end of the nineteenth century, most of Lake County's virgin forests had been cut. Left behind were denuded landscapes particularly susceptible to erosion and wildfires; indeed, they were so treeless that some were convinced that northern Michigan would become "like Southern Illinois, a great rolling prairie of grass and grain, whose horizon is unbroken as the horizon of the ocean."[61] Yet those who attempted to farm the region like it was southern Illinois largely failed, mostly due to extremely sandy soils that held little moisture and eroded when plowed. Thus began northern Michigan's transition from a landscape of labor to a landscape of leisure. Soon, foresters instead began planting second-growth forests that would before long become key to northern Michigan's emerging recreation and tourist economy.

When they retreated to Idlewild—some on the very same rail lines (like the Pere Marquette) that brought timber from northern Michigan

Figure 2.2. Rowing on the lake at Idlewild, with cottages in the background, circa 1930. Courtesy Archives of Michigan, Stanley Kufta Collection (MS 89–157), C-3684.

south to Chicago in the late nineteenth century—black Chicagoans arrived in a region dominated by second-growth scrub oak forests, precisely the sorts of natural-growth trees that Chicago's South Park Commissioners had cut down in Washington Park decades earlier because they failed to fit Olmsted and Vaux's aesthetic vision. But although those scrub oaks fit the rough pastoral landscape of Idlewild just fine, the resort town's developers did undertake a variety of projects to make the landscape even more attractive to resort goers. To make the lake more conducive to swimming and rowing, Idlewild developers dredged the bottom, cleaning up underwater snags (see Figure 2.2). Early on, the lake was also stocked with fish, and by 1929 one of the resort town's developers boasted that "Idlewild Lake is one of the best lakes in the country for bass fishing."[62] Charles Chesnutt would have probably agreed. Although the surroundings were undoubtedly more rustic and less landscaped than the city's green spaces such as Washington Park, this reshaping of the lake effectively made it nearly as (un)natural as Olmsted and Vaux-designed lagoons, which were regularly stripped of unwanted aquatic plant growth and stocked with fish.

Although the region's vegetation and landscape had changed drastically over the half-century leading up to Idlewild's founding, its climate had remained more or less the same since glaciers had carved out Lake Michigan—the vast body of water that largely dictates surrounding climatic conditions. Idlewild was part of Michigan's fruit belt that extends along the full length of Lake Michigan's coast, and its climate proved as conducive to growing fruit as attracting resort goers (some Idlewilders did pick cherries while vacationing). Moderated by the westerly winds blowing across Lake Michigan (which takes longer to warm up and cool down than surrounding land masses), western Michigan stays cooler longer in the early summer and warmer longer in the early autumn. Although Chicago also benefits somewhat from this lake effect, prevailing weather patterns moving west to east make this effect more pronounced in western Michigan. Add to that Chicago's urban heat island effect, and those traveling to Idlewild from Chicago were leaving behind a city much warmer in summer than geographically similar rural areas.[63]

Rural Leisure Landscapes for the Masses

Chicago's black cultural elite who retreated to resorts like Idlewild knew that the working classes, living in unsanitary, rundown tenements and working in the city's dirtiest, most dangerous jobs, faced an even grimmer urban environment than they did. Yet those most in need of nature's ostensible curative powers were those whose dire financial straits meant they were least able to attain them. As the Chicago Council of Social Agencies observed in a study of camping opportunities near Chicago in the wake of the 1919 race riot, "The entire lack of provision for a vacation time for certain groups of people was a definite challenge: for instance, only 534 colored people were provided for."[64] In response, Chicago's black cultural elite set about the task of bringing Idlewild-like landscapes of hope to the black working classes, setting up camps in rural Michigan, Illinois, and Wisconsin for the children and young adults they believed to be most vulnerable to the city's hazardous environmental and social conditions—an effort that picked up on broader cultural ideas about the virtues of camping that had been in circulation since at least the 1880s.

But for the Great Migration generation that was newly adjusting to urban life, camping took on additional significance. The black cultural elite were ministering to an age group that, on the whole, would have had little direct experience with rural landscapes; many had migrated to Chicago with their parents when they were very young, and many more still had been born and raised in the city. In many ways, then, camping opportunities developed by black Chicagoans in this period—the vast majority of whom were migrants from the South—were guided by the conviction that the next generation would benefit from exposure to the sorts of raw nature from which all urban dwellers were increasingly isolated in the early twentieth century. These reformers believed that Washington and Madden Parks could work in conjunction with rural youth camps—a 1927 *Defender* photo collage, for instance, was titled "Enjoying the Out-of-Doors" and pictured children ice skating in Washington Park in the winter and swimming in the "ole swimmin' hole" at the Wabash Avenue YMCA's summer camp—but they shared the conviction that the closer one got to nature, the more beneficial the experience.[65] They were, in essence, attempting to replicate for the working classes the experience of one twelve-year-old urban dweller visiting Idlewild in the late 1920s, who would later recall that he "saw for the first time in [his] life snakes, porcupine, deer, bear, rabbit and many variety of birds in their natural habitat."[66]

Staffed and, to a lesser extent, funded by men and women in black Chicago's professional classes, well-known segregated community institutions like the YWCA, YMCA, and Boy Scouts—all of which were growing by leaps and bounds thanks to the influx of migrants—were logical pathways for bringing the working classes in closer contact with rural and wild landscapes of hope outside the city. In many cases, the members of the black cultural elite who themselves retreated to nature resorts such as Idlewild also tirelessly fought for working-class access to green space in both the city and country. Idlewild regulars Jesse Binga and Robert Abbott, for instance, were among the largest African American contributors to the segregated Indiana Avenue YWCA, and Abbott served on the Wabash Avenue YMCA's Committee of Management with several other prominent South Side businessmen throughout the 1920s. Irene McCoy Gaines, also an Idlewild regular, served as that YWCA's Industrial and General Secretary for many years and was a longtime advocate of the organization's camps, where officials and female volunteers were graduates from universities like Columbia, University of Chicago, Fisk, and Wilberforce. Foster Branch, another member of Chicago's black cultural elite who was deeply involved in promoting recreational opportunities for South Siders, served as assistant camp director at both the YMCA's Camp Wabash and the Boy Scouts' Camp Belnap before being appointed director of Jackson Playground (the predecessor to Madden Park) in February 1927.[67]

Although many of these institutions (the Urban League, for instance) were largely independent of white institutions, if not of wealthy white benefactors, the most notable institutions to become involved in rural camping had been established as segregated black branches of citywide and national organizations that were, like Idlewild, deeply informed by Booker T. Washington's uplift ideology recast for the North. The segregated Wabash Avenue YMCA, like many segregated black YMCAs across the country, was founded with significant financial backing from Chicago philanthropist (and part-owner of Chicago-based Sears, Roebuck & Company) Julius Rosenwald, who also sat on the Tuskegee Institute's Board of Directors; Washington himself delivered the Wabash Y's dedicatory address in 1913. Despite their segregation and heavy reliance on white philanthropists for funding, Chicago's black YWCA, YMCA, and Boy Scouts developed their own identities and became sources of intense race pride much like Idlewild, promoting uplift in the black community largely through the dissemination of middle-class values.[68]

Like their white counterparts, the African American black cultural elites who ran youth camps believed that these retreats to nature were perhaps the most important component of all the religious and character-building work undertaken in the city. The YWCA, YMCA, and Boy Scouts were all Christian organizations, and their work was intimately tied to churches across the South Side. Some Boy Scout troops were sponsored in part by Jesse Binga, for instance, but almost all of the troops that made up the segregated Douglas Division (which had its roots in the YMCA) were connected with a wide range of churches, including Catholic churches, St. Mark AME, Berean Baptist, and Olivet Baptist— Chicago's oldest and largest African American church that thousands of migrants joined.[69] The segregated Wabash YMCA worked in conjunction with the black Boy Scout troops organized through South Side churches to send boys to camp on land owned by Chicago's Moody Bible Institute at Cedar Lake in northwest Indiana.[70] Their earliest foray into summer camping featured "plenty of swimming, hiking, fishing, [and] games" and seemed so successful that by 1922 an extensive *Defender* article on the YMCA's work in Chicago's African American community already claimed that "by far the bulk of the religious work of the association is done in the gymnasium, on hikes, in camps, wherever the changing or directing of habits is possible."[71] These endeavors were no doubt guided in part by Henry Gibson's *Camping for Boys*, a 1911 book that quickly became a central text for the broader camping movement; it stated, "Whether the camp is conducted under church, settlement, Young Men's Christian Association, or private auspices, the prime purpose of its existence should be that of character building." Gibson went on to clarify the religious significance of character building, writing, "Camp life should help boys to grow not only physically and mentally, but morally. Religion is the basis of morality. The highest instinct in man is the religious. Man made the city with all its artificiality, but, as some one has said, 'God made the country.' "[72] Just three years later, a *Defender* editorial echoed Gibson (who was actually paraphrasing the eighteenth-century English poet William Cowper) that "man made the city and God made the country"; in 1927, the *Defender* similarly claimed, We "owe it to ourselves and to our children to get out if only for a week or two each summer in what we are pleased to call God's country."[73]

Even though most camping programs targeted young men and boys whom reformers feared were most vulnerable to delinquency, one of the earliest camping programs available to black Chicagoans was for young working-class women and was offered through the segregated Indiana Avenue YWCA, which had been founded in 1915. First opened in 1920 on the shores of Wolf Lake in the steel mill district along the Illinois-Indiana border about twenty miles southeast of Chicago, Camp Hammond was intended mainly to offer relief to "colored school girls and young women in business and industry . . . from packing houses [and] factories," some of whom were illiterate or mothers "caring for large families unassisted."[74] Well aware of the importance of camping for migrant women who worked in industries like meatpacking, YWCA officials spoke about "the miserable conditions under which many colored girls are obliged to work . . . the colored women are exploited, practically always given the poorest work and the least pay—often far below that paid other women for similar work. The negro woman offers the cheapest labor obtainable."[75] Reflecting on the Indiana Avenue YWCA's summer program in 1922, the committee in charge of Camp Hammond noted that the camp was "practically the only vacation spot in the vicinity of Chicago where the colored girl and woman may escape from the heat and toil of the city for a few days or weeks of life in the out-of-doors, with all that it implies of renewed strength and spirit."[76] Each year between 1920 and 1925, as many as 282 African American women were sent to Camp Hammond, and as many as an additional 200 annually took day trips there; sometimes high school aged girls and children retreated there with their mothers too. In 1924, it was the only one of the three Chicago YWCA camps filled to capacity; the two white camps remained under capacity that season. Although the number of black campers may seem small, African American women actually tended to be overrepresented in YWCA camps, accounting for roughly 10 percent of the full-period YWCA camping population at a time when African Americans accounted for only about 5 percent of Chicago's population.[77]

Like the annual Fourth of July "industrial picnic" that featured outdoor activities for thousands of stockyards employees and their families at Camp Hammond, the YWCA camp was the epitome of welfare capitalism in action, owned and subsidized by the very industries that exploited African American labor—and hence vulnerable to corporate support that could wax and wane. Although any girl or woman over the age of twelve was encouraged to attend camp whether or not she was affiliated with the YWCA—and assured that a round-trip train ride from the South Side would only cost 32 cents—it seems that industrial employees dominated the camping cohort each year. Swift & Company owned the camp's land and the extant buildings on Wolf Lake, loaning it to the YWCA rent-free and subsidizing or paying in full its employees' camping fees of $6.75 per week; as one camper was reported to have said, "Mighty funny that your boss pays you to take a rest, and pays your bills to boot!"[78]

Camp Hammond was mainly intended to give industrial workers a much-needed break that would return them to the city as stronger, better, and more loyal workers, but there is little question that the Indiana Avenue YWCA in the early to mid-1920s offered African American women and young girls an inferior camping experience to that enjoyed by whites. Whereas Chicago's permanent white YWCA camp on the Lake Michigan shore was romanticized by officials as "forty-three acres of hilly, wooded land, where flowers and wild berries grow," annual YWCA reports made no mention of Camp Hammond's natural virtues.[79] Already hamstrung by its tight budget, the Indiana Avenue YWCA was unable to change much about the campground only "dotted here and there with a clump of trees."[80] Making the best of it, YWCA staffers were able to host "volley ball and field games . . . and after much testing a place was found in the lake deep enough and safe enough for the girls to use for swimming."[81] Indeed, as with most camps (regardless of the campers' race), lake swimming was integral to the program; photographs of Camp Hammond in the YWCA's annual reports generally show women posed in or around the lake, dressed in swimsuits and caps. But YWCA officials soberly described even such basic outdoor recreational activities as swimming, baseball, and tennis as "exceedingly hard because of the unimproved condition of the grounds."[82]

The problems with Camp Hammond came to a head in 1925, when Indiana Avenue officials reported to the YWCA, "We regret exceedingly to have to recommend to you for consideration, the discontinuance of Camp Hammond, in as much as it has been condemnded [sic] as unsanitary and unhygienic and we feel should not be used further by our organization for camp purposes."[83] The YWCA, in other words, had unwittingly thrust young women into an environment uncomfortably similar to the ones that landscapes of hope were intended to counter: the Black Belt's decaying tenements and dirty industrial spaces that each presented health hazards. So YWCA officials determined that even though "camp was a vital part of their general program, Indiana Avenue Branch was in need of so many other and essential things . . . their committee felt it would have to eliminate camp in 1926."[84] This was in part because the Y had turned its attention to fundraising for a new building in the city, and it simply could not afford to tackle both projects at once. Reaching its fundraising goal was an uphill climb: as one somewhat naïve white YWCA official reported on the fundraising campaign for the new building in 1927, "I have found raising money for the colored people, by all odds, the most difficult thing I have ever undertaken. The amount of prejudice, and violent prejudice, which I have unearthed, is surprising in this enlightened age, and finding that small fraction of the community, whose hearts and minds are big enough to include an interest in their fellow beings, white and black, has taken time and strength."[85] Not until 1929 did the Indiana Avenue YWCA attempt to revive its camping program by purchasing a farmhouse in the Cook County Forest Preserves and spending $2,000 on improvements and maintenance. By that time, they were serving more than 13,000 girls and women total in a given calendar year and could claim 675 teenaged girls in various clubs.[86]

In contrast to the Indiana Avenue YWCA's short-lived segregated camping program that targeted young women employed in the stockyards, the Wabash Avenue YMCA's initial camping ventures took advantage of a handful of interracial camps designed for young boys. A few boys, for instance, attended camps for weeks at a time in Michigan and Wisconsin several hours' drive away from Chicago—picking cherries at the latter—through the Wabash Y as early as 1918 and continuing at least through the summer of 1922. The cost of a ten-day camping period was five dollars, which would have been affordable for many middle-class South Siders, and generous benefactors paid for a handful of "underprivileged boys who otherwise could not enjoy this outing" in 1922.[87] The interracial camping gambit was put to the test that year, however, when a troop of fifty-two Boy Scouts from Berean Baptist church was "driven from" the camp, garnering a front-page headline above the masthead in the *Defender*. The boys were exposed to race hatred from the manager of the camp, a "son of a Confederate state [who] object[ed] to their physical association with boys of the white race."[88] Plenty of white Northerners would have objected as well, of course— fear of this sort of "physical association" was what often drove racial violence at parks and especially beaches—but it was an unwelcome reminder of how easily the racial discrimination and violence that migrants sought to escape could follow them wherever they went. Yet rather than prompting Wabash Y officials to abandon camping as part of their program for young boys, however, it seems that they became more determined than ever to create a nature retreat more fully under their control. As migration continued and the population of African Americans served by the Wabash Y swelled, the institution committed itself to outdoor education and began looking for land on which it could establish and run its own privately owned camp as early as 1924.[89]

In 1925, the same year that was Camp Hammond's last, the Wabash Avenue YMCA's summer camping program for boys took a dramatic leap forward with the purchase of forty acres of campground on Rowe Lake near Dowagiac, Michigan. With the Great Migration in full swing and thousands more children coming to the city each year, Camp Wabash— named after the South Side branch—was an unprecedented and unique commitment to youth camping for Chicago's African American community. Although there were other church-affiliated black-owned camps on the East Coast, the Wabash Y proudly claimed to be "the only [African

American YMCA] branch in the country that owns and maintains its own summer camp."[90] Although the particulars of why the camp site was selected remain unclear, it was likely chosen not only for its lake access—integral to virtually every camping program in this period—but also for its proximity to Chicago (about 100 miles east of the city, much closer than Idlewild) and the area's small extant African American population. Camp Wabash's purchase and initial improvements—which at $14,000 accounted for about 15 percent of the Wabash Y's annual budget at the time—engaged the close attention of top Wabash Y officials from the very beginning: Physical Director Henry Crawford and Executive Secretary George Arthur (the latter of whom had taken note of the dangerous racial climate in Washington Park in the early 1920s and also vacationed at Idlewild in this period) joined a group that inspected the camp and identified improvements that needed to be made before it opened. In its first summer in operation, Camp Wabash served 277 boys who paid five dollars for a two-week period, the same fee charged by the Wabash Y a few years earlier. That number of campers more than doubled the previous total of boys that the Wabash Y sent to summer camp; clearly the new African American-owned campsite in its first year of operation had already greatly expanded camping opportunities for boys in the community. Camp Wabash quickly became an integral part of the South Side YMCA's program for boys, addressing the perceived needs of the working classes. As one Wabash Y official put it, nothing got "closer to the real needs of boy life than the Summer Camp"; it was also, as The Negro in Chicago put it, "for all boys whose parents must economize and yet are anxious to give their sons a good, clean, wholesome camp experience under Christian leadership."[91] Although the camp accounted for a fraction of the Wabash Y's yearly budget—about 5 percent in 1929, for instance—and was only active for a few months each year, YMCA officials repeatedly talked about how vital it was to the entire program and mission of the Y. Without a camp of its own, the Indiana Avenue YWCA held conferences hosting dozens of girls at Camp Wabash throughout the late 1920s as well. Now in full control of their own camp, Chicago's black cultural elite would not have to worry about forced closure or race discrimination tainting the camping experience.[92]

Wabash Y officials were clearly proud of their new black-owned camp, and promotional efforts that included hikes from Chicago to the Indiana Dunes soon paid off. Perhaps most importantly, Wabash Y camp committee officials "sent letters to the ministers of all the churches" asking for at least part of a church service be given over to promote the camp. They found at least some success, with entrepreneur and *Chicago Bee* publisher Anthony Overton supporting their efforts at Bethesda Baptist Church and some ministers holding meetings after their Sunday evening service to lecture and show "a health and camp picture" not unlike the film that promoted Idlewild.[93] The *Defender*'s regular "Boy Scout News" column even featured a few stanzas of promotional doggerel that bore some resemblance to the lyrics of Major N. Clark Smith's Idlewild song:

> Oh, boy, this summer you ought to go
> With the Boy Scouts to Camp Wabash,
> We'll hike, we'll fish, we'll swim and row,
> Two weeks for five bucks cash.
>
> That sum's nothing for the fun out there,
> For the benefit you are sure to get—
> Good food, good sleep and Michigan air,
> An outing you'll never regret.
>
> So gather the togs you'll need to wear;
> Your food will be better than hash.
> Five dollars will get you there,
> So pack up for Camp Wabash.[94]

The same column echoed W. E. B. Du Bois's praise of Idlewild, heralding Camp Wabash as "far away from the heat, bad air and 'humdrum' in Chicago city life," going on to promise that at "camp the Scout can relax, inhale the stimulating atoms from the purifying woods of Michigan for two weeks and return home a better boy and Scout, with a better, stronger determination to be a better man"[95] (see Figure 2.3).

The *Defender*'s promise that a retreat into nature would help one become "a better man" hints at the ways in which camping was tied to evolving conceptions of masculinity and sexuality in the early twentieth century, a period rife with anxieties that cities were feminizing young men. Boy Scout hikes in pastoral landscapes, no matter how constructed, became a way for young male scoutmasters to exhibit their own manhood and cultivate that manhood in the younger generation of scouts whom they led. These fears were perhaps all the more resonant for migrants, who had in many cases consciously given up close connections to rural landscapes in the South in favor of opportunity for advance-

Figure 2.3. Fishing and perhaps looking for mussels on Rowe Lake at Camp Wabash, circa 1930. Chicago History Museum, ICHi-79115. Photographer unknown.

ment in cities. Their children—unless they camped with the YWCA, YMCA, or Scouts—might never have the valuable experience of rural landscapes. Certainly many South Side parents determined that camp would be a beneficial experience for their children, but how many of them actually enjoyed camp life is substantially more difficult to discern. One late 1920s survey of Camp Wabash contended that "the natural beauty of the surrounding country is particularly enticing to a boy, especially one who is interested in the great out doors," but left unexamined just how enticing such a place would be to boys less enthused by "the great out doors."[96] By the same token, many black Chicagoans experienced their "first time in the woods" through the Boy Scouts, and troop leaders reported that boys came back from camp "happy and full of pep," having participated in "outdoor life with a purpose" that gave them "health, strength, happiness and practical education"—but the voices of the campers themselves are mostly lost to history.[97]

Regardless of any possible divergence between camp leaders' glowing accounts and campers' actual experiences, Camp Wabash was such an overwhelming success in its first few years that extensive improvements were underway by 1928, including the planting of about two hundred trees and, at the cost of $1,000, the construction of a bathing beach. Camp organizers expected a good yield of fruit from the new orchard and were so optimistic about the camp's prospects that they were already looking to expand on the original forty acres by purchasing adjacent wooded acreage. As those modifications of the environment suggest, the "natural beauty" of these youth camps—like Idlewild—was more akin to landscaped urban green spaces such as Washington Park than to true wilderness or backcountry. Most often these landscapes of hope were located on land that had been heavily farmed, logged, or otherwise intensively used only decades earlier; they were managed environments reclaimed for leisure activities that generally used and modified the land less intensively. Nonetheless, camp land was undoubtedly more rural and rustic than anything campers would have experienced in the city: there were more trees, more animals, and more natural bodies of water, not to mention far fewer buildings, streets, and people.[98] Ben Gaines, a counselor at Camp Wabash many years later, remembered the camp situated "in the wide-open country" that revealed the site as likely to be former farmland (indeed, in later years camp excursions were led to surrounding cornfields), with cabins looking out on the lake at a distance of about a hundred yards and a forested area beyond. A 1925 *Defender* article promoted the site as "40 acres of hills, valleys, plains and woods, exclusive of the beautiful lake" that gave campers the opportunity to swim and row, activities around which so much of camp life revolved[99] (see Figure 2.4).

While Chicago's African American Boy Scout troops took advantage of Camp Wabash in its early years, soon they began retreating to Camp Belnap—a segregated portion of the larger Camp Owasippe in Twin Lake, Michigan. In 1926, Camp Belnap hosted at least 150 boys from more than five different troops. Located in southwestern Michigan where farming was more tenable, Camp Wabash's land was mostly flat and open, begging improvements such as trees and beaches. By contrast, the Boy Scouts' Camp Belnap—nearly twice as far from Chicago as Camp Wabash and much nearer Idlewild—boasted an abundance of wooded area more characteristic of northern Michigan. As at Idlewild,

Figure 2.4. Swimming lessons on Rowe Lake at Camp Wabash, circa 1930. Chicago History Museum, ICHi-79113. Photographer unknown.

the natural environment at Camp Belnap was more lush than at Camp Wabash; it was situated on the edge of what would become the 844-square-mile Manistee National Forest, squarely in Michigan's fruit belt. Belnap could boast its location "on a hill between . . . two big lakes surrounded with an oak forest . . . where innumerable paths are almost endless," and as a 1929 promotional manual described it, "Miles of woodland surround the camp; innumerable lakes and creeks are within strolling distance and beckon explorers."[100] A swimming hole in the summer and a place for ice skating and ice boating in the winter, Lake O-Jib-way was the center of Camp Belnap's activities—just as life at Camp Wabash revolved around Rowe Lake.[101]

For African American Boy Scouts without the money or desire for longer camping trips to Michigan, there were ample opportunities to take advantage of the Cook County Forest Preserves encircling Chicago. Scouts generally retreated to Camp Kiwanis, located near Willow Springs, Illinois, little more than ten miles southwest of the heart of the Black Belt. Short overnight or weekend stays at the camp's tents and cabins included the usual Scout activities, such as nature study hikes, swimming, and campfires. If they encountered the "ground carpeted with flowers" that urban planner and architect Daniel Burnham had observed in what became the Forest Preserves, a 1925 *Defender* "Boy Scout News" column urged boys to "Save the Wild Flowers," reminding them, "When you are out in the open do not destroy the flowers. Millions of flowers are destroyed yearly by carelessness. Do all in your power to preserve the wildflowers."[102] In the spring of 1926, four troops combined to take nearly one hundred boys to Camp Kiwanis, who even gained the experience of helping fight a forest fire while they were there; later that year, another troop spent the Fourth of July holiday at Camp Kiwanis. Similar hikes occurred throughout the 1920s, and the Forest Preserves became a place for scouts to earn merit badges for activities such as conservation and bird watching; among other species, scout troops could expect to see phoebes, kingfishers, and ospreys.[103]

The Cook County Forest Preserves were evidence that Chicago government officials had joined the chorus of Americans who increasingly believed in the value of pastoral green spaces as retreats for urban citizens. Acting in part on recommendations in Daniel Burnham's 1909 *Plan of Chicago* (itself representative of the City Beautiful Movement), they picked up where Olmsted and Vaux's design of Washington and Jackson Parks had left off in the late nineteenth century. To counter the "disorder, vice, and disease [that] becomes the greatest menace" to densely populated cities like Chicago, Burnham's plan asserted that

> near-by woodlands should be brought within easy reach of all the people, and especially of the wage-earners. Natural scenery furnishes the contrasting element to the artificiality of the city. All of us should often run away from the works of men's hands and back into the wilds, where mind and body are restored to a normal condition, and we are enabled to take up the burden of life in our crowded streets and endless stretches of buildings with renewed vigor and hopefulness.[104]

Using the sort of language that *Defender* columnists would echo in the years to come, Burnham argued, "Those who have the means and are so placed in their daily employments that they can do so constantly seek the refreshment of the country," but the working classes still found these rural spaces largely inaccessible.[105] Purely coincidentally, land acquisition for the Cook County Forest Preserves began in 1916, the same year Idlewild was dedicated and just as thousands of black migrants had begun pouring into the city. Already by 1924, the Forest Preserves drew an estimated 7.65 million visitors annually, and expanding streetcar lines made them more and more accessible to those without automobiles. The same year, a *Defender* editorial encouraged South Siders to visit "a section of forest preserves north, west and south, that can be reached by the surface lines. Here a tent can be pitched and real camp life indulged in."[106] There was already evidence that many black Chicagoans were taking advantage of the new tracts of nature just outside the city. Just a few years after the preserves were formed, a group of prominent South Side African Americans (including Julius Avendorph of the Pullman Company) endorsed a Cook County commissioner candidate in part because he had "made members of our group especially welcome upon the vast and beautiful grounds of the forest preserve."[107] Notes in the *Defender*'s society pages about groups "motoring" to the preserves, holding social club picnics, professional outings, and interdenominational church picnics there, suggest that these rural, forested lands quickly became common day-trip retreats for Chicago's black cultural elite.[108] The preserves also served as a final resting place for those in the black community who could afford it. Accessible by train, Mount Glenwood cemetery was a prominent burial ground for black Chicagoans and the site of Decoration Day (later Memorial Day) observances. Promoted in part as an interracial burial ground, advertisements for the cemetery in 1922 also reminded potential investors that the cemetery was "surrounded by a County Forest Preserve, and thereby receives the benefits of the natural beauty of those tracts."[109] By 1928, the general superintendent of the Forest Preserves was expressing his appreciation for the *Defender*'s "co-operating whole heartedly with the forest preserve district campaign on preservation."[110]

White Chicagoans retreated in droves to such rural landscapes in this period, but for the black Chicagoans who picnicked in the Cook County Forest Preserves, summered at Idlewild, or spent a week at Camp Wabash, these sorts of spaces were doubly important. Writing on Idlewild in 1929, a *Pittsburgh Courier* correspondent perhaps best summed up the ways in which the black cultural elite viewed the importance of rural retreats in the Great Migration years: she contended that "freedom from criticism, of our own and other people," "independence," and "pride of ownership" could be found at Idlewild.[111] In other words, Idlewild and other private black-owned rural spaces like Camp Wabash were landscapes of hope that served as potent racial idylls: their remote locations, separate from whites, laid the foundations for race pride and dignity in ways that were difficult if not impossible in the city. If anything, the environmental inequalities, segregation, and racist treatment that African Americans suffered in cities such as Chicago only heightened the importance of these rural institutions as escapes in the Great Migration years. Indeed, the *Courier* columnist went on to make sense of Idlewild in the context of the migration and urbanization trends that had defined the previous decade and a half, claiming the resort town showed "that Negroes have worked through that mad cityward rush—when everything that savored of the primitive was taboo; and in a contemplative mood, which requires complete change to help crystallize their thoughts into plans and projects for the future, find solitude and undisturbed nature here."[112] In other words, the impulse to retreat to Idlewild or to camp in rural Michigan was not primitive; it was modern—a temporary, restorative escape from the cities in which tens of thousands of migrants now lived. Neither Idlewild resort goers nor youth campers ever actually needed to know how to camp, hunt, or fish to survive, after all; these leisure activities and skills were generally imparted to children with an eye toward the results they would deliver back in the city.

Whether the black Chicagoans who picnicked, camped, or summered in the rural North consciously realized it or not, then, their very presence in these environments wrestled with and often contested primitivist thought that inextricably and uniquely linked African Americans with nature during the Great Migration years and that the *Courier* columnist had identified as "taboo." The white art collector and patron Albert Barnes voiced one of the most positive spins on this primitivist worldview in his contribution to Alain Locke's landmark collection *The New Negro*. He contended that because African Americans had ostensibly "kept nearer to the ideal of man's harmony with nature," black artistic culture had "made [white Americans] feel the majesty of Nature, the ineffable peace of the woods and the great open spaces." But Barnes complicated this essentialist view by claiming that African American artistic production actually broke down these racial barriers, revealing "the essential oneness of all human beings."[113] In the end, then, when African Americans sought out nature, they were not expressing a unique impulse. Instead, they were expressing something many felt was universally human. For the *Courier* columnist, nature's power to bridge social and racial divides was precisely the value of Idlewild: it showed "that in spite of all that is said to the contrary—we sort of like each other, and like to be together, and just naturally drift toward the things that are human and American."[114] The black cultural elite retreated to rural Northern resorts in the summer months to fish in remote lakes and hike in the woods, just like the white middle and upper classes did. Black children swam and hiked at rural camps organized by the YMCA, YWCA, and Boy Scouts, just like white children. Taken together, these segregated enterprises all raised an uncomfortable question for whites steeped in the racial logic of primitivism: how different could African Americans be from whites if their landscapes of hope were virtually identical?

Rather than establishing unique racial attachments to nature, black Chicagoans laid claim to what many felt were universal affinities for nature in a modernizing, urbanizing culture—even as they were forced to forge those bonds with nature in a segregated context. When a *Defender* editorial published in the earliest days of the Great Migration noted, "From the daily routine of commercial life man becomes a very automaton, performing his duties in a methodical, perfunctory manner amid the smoke, grime and roar of city life," and that springtime in particular brought on the "uncontrollable feeling to get out in the open where nature is at its best," it described a modern condition that countless urban dwellers faced, regardless of race.[115] Black Chicagoans, like white Chicagoans, were modern Americans who retreated to resorts and youth camps, driven there by the same urban conditions that drove white Americans to the country. As the 1920s drew to a close, however, those urban conditions were about to take a dramatic turn for the worse: just two months after the *Courier* column lauded nature's virtues, Black Tuesday's stock market crash would throw the nation headlong into the Great Depression. The social and economic chaos that ensued would threaten to upend virtually all the institutions black Chicagoans had built during the Great Migration years, and no landscape of hope would be safe from its profound effects: not Idlewild, not Camp Wabash, and certainly not Washington Park.

PART II

THE DEPRESSION YEARS, 1930–1940

3

Playgrounds and Protest Grounds

"C HICAGO'S SOUTH SIDE went wild Saturday over Bud Billiken and his 'gang,'" the *Chicago Defender* triumphantly declared after its first annual Bud Billiken Day on August 16, 1930. "Gray skies and a chill northeasterly wind, which carried notice of fall, was not enough to dampen the spirit of the affair" that culminated in a picnic for approximately 12,000 in Washington Park that the newspaper none too modestly described as "the greatest picnic Chicago has seen to date." The heavily promoted day-long program had begun with a parade of "eight thousand or more children" two miles down South Parkway from 35th Street to the northwest corner of the park, and it featured free ice cream, baseball, tennis, track and field, and a "bathing beauty" contest for young girls in the park's duck pond.[1] From those relatively modest beginnings, the annual parade and picnic only grew in popularity during the Great Depression, and the festivities soon became a defining event not only for the *Defender*'s Bud Billiken youth club that had been founded several years earlier but also for Washington Park and black Chicago as a whole.[2] Even by its second year, the *Defender* claimed that the picnic had nearly trebled its attendance to 35,000, no doubt boosted by the popularity of featured guests such as Duke Ellington and the radio stars who portrayed Amos 'n' Andy. Much of that day's festivities were filmed and shown later at the newly built Regal Theater on the Stroll, with the

Defender declaring that the picnic in Washington Park featured enough "attractions to fill a Fourth of July, Labor day and Christmas eve."[3] By Bud Billiken Day's tenth anniversary in 1939, the picnic drew an estimated 150,000 from around the Chicagoland area (at a time when the city's black population was still less than 300,000) and featured stars such as heavyweight boxing champion Joe Louis at the height of his fame.[4] By World War II, the event had become so huge that one resident recalled, "We used to joke as kids during the war, that if Hitler wanted to win the war he'd have to knock out all the blacks in Chicago. All he'd have to do is drop a bomb on Washington Park during Bud Billiken Day."[5] Indeed, scarcely any place on the South Side other than the massive Olmsted and Vaux-designed public park could have entertained so much of black Chicago at one time, and Bud Billiken Day came to symbolize just how integral Washington Park had become to Chicago's diverse African American community year-round, the two symbiotically shaping one another in the 1930s.

The *Defender*'s annual community picnic in Washington Park enjoyed such wild success in part because it built on migrants' hybrid park use patterns established during the Great Migration years, which adapted Southern cultural practices to an urban landscape in an attempt to forge a unified black Chicago during the Great Depression. As two Great Migration historians have noted, at a time when more than three-quarters of black Chicagoans had been born in the South, Bud Billiken Day revelers included "thousands of recently arrived migrants, whose parents and grandparents had marched in southern Decoration and Emancipation Day celebrations" that dated back to the nineteenth century.[6] In addition to their familiarity with a deep tradition of church and community picnics, Southerners had also "long celebrated mid-August as lay-by time, a moment of tranquility between the second chopping, or weeding, and the laborious cotton harvest of the fall."[7] In Chicago, the *Defender* translated these late summer celebrations into an event that South Sider Jimmy Ellis recalled as a fun "back-to-school activity for the children" who "used to put a lot of streamers and fix their bikes up" to ride in the parade.[8]

Ellis was born in Chicago the same year the first Bud Billiken Day was held, but his parents had migrated from Alabama in the 1920s, and in many ways his family was fairly representative of migrants' aspirations of social equality and economic advancement when they uprooted

Figure 3.1. Bud Billiken Day picnic crowd, August 13, 1938. By permission and courtesy of the Chicago Park District Special Collections.

their families and moved northward to the "Land of Hope." His father had attained steady middle-class employment as a postal worker, and Ellis was indeed getting ready to head back to school when he participated in the *Defender*'s Bud Billiken Day in mid-August, rather than preparing to help his family with the fall harvest as so many African American children across the South did well into the 1930s and beyond. When tens of thousands of African Americans came together every summer in Washington Park for a celebration of black Chicago and its children, then, it represented a transformation and modernization of long-practiced African American celebrations in public space as well as a reminder of the sorts of communities, opportunities, and possibilities that the migrants who populated this city-within-a-city had come to the North to find (see Figure 3.1).

As the *Defender* was busy planning and promoting its first Bud Billiken Day picnic in Washington Park, however, the Great Depression seriously threatened those communities, opportunities, and possibilities. Indeed, it was hardly a coincidence that the inaugural festivities took place just a few short months after the catastrophic stock market crash that profoundly deepened an economic slowdown already in progress: the *Defender* likely created Bud Billiken Day in large part because the Black Metropolis it had helped build up during the Great Migration years found itself in danger of being torn apart at the seams by widespread social and economic turmoil. Although the worst was still yet to come, businesses everywhere were failing in the summer of 1930, and Chicago's Black Belt was especially hard hit. Even Idlewild regular Jesse Binga—a potent symbol of the Black Metropolis's possibilities for entrepreneurial success in the Great Migration years—was forced to shutter his bank in July 1930, just weeks before the *Defender*'s Washington Park picnic took place right across the street from his home. By the end of August, every bank in the Black Belt was closed, and "mobs cried in the streets for their savings"—mobs no doubt made up of many of the same black Chicagoans who had attended that first Bud Billiken Day earlier that month.[9] Along with migrants' meager savings, thousands of jobs that the *Defender* had encouraged Southern readers to come north to find during the relatively prosperous Great Migration years were also disappearing. If the Bud Billiken Day festivities in Washington Park in part represented the promise of migration to the urban North, then its genesis was also rooted in a response to the social and economic crisis that confronted the South Side in 1930.

More than merely an escapist celebration in trying times, however, the *Defender*'s Bud Billiken Day picnic used the South Side's most notable public green space to reinforce the idea that community institutions built up during the Great Migration years were now more important than ever; they were absolutely vital to stabilizing families and an entire social order shaken by the Great Depression. Even though the annual Washington Park celebrations centered mostly on black Chicago's youth, they promoted middle-class values and ideas—represented by institutions such as the Boy and Girl Scouts, the YMCA and YWCA, and church groups—among the entire community: young and old, women and men, working class and middle class. During the inaugural parade itself, "Boy Scouts from every South Side troop" led the march and were specially commended for helping handle the large crowds at the picnic, directing traffic and keeping other children in line while free ice cream was distributed.[10] South Side Boy Scout troops—and eventually the girls and boys of the Wabash YMCA, Girl Scouts, Camp Fire Girls, and the

National Association of Colored Girls as well—played a prominent role in the parade and picnic throughout the 1930s, continuing to promote these community institutions as productive outlets for children whose families grappled with ongoing economic distress.

Of course, these organizations' participation in Bud Billiken Day was merely representative of community-building work that went on all year. In the months leading up to the first parade and picnic in 1930, for instance, the *Defender*'s youth club launched a broader campaign spearheaded by "a large group of outstanding boy leaders, representing such organizations as the Boy Scouts, the Y.M.C.A., boys' clubs, church, Rotary, Kiwanis and Optimists clubs and the public and parochial schools" who would join "thousands of Billikens . . . along with their parents, teachers, pastors, social workers and policemen, in a city-wide campaign to reduce Chicago's juvenile delinquency rate."[11] Each year, then, Bud Billiken Day used Washington Park's urban green space to reinforce and build on the same middle-class ideas that valued rural and wild green spaces enough to establish Camps Wabash and Belnap in the Great Migration era. In fact, many of those who marched and picnicked on the South Side in early August had no doubt spent part of their summers camping in the rural and wild areas outside Chicago.[12]

Not everyone in black Chicago so readily adhered to the *Defender*'s middle-class vision for the Black Metropolis during the Great Depression, however. Indeed, Washington Park and other public green spaces in the Black Belt remained intraracial cultural and ideological battlegrounds in the 1930s, much as they had been during the Great Migration years. In particular, the turmoil of the early 1930s elicited politically radical responses from the working classes, and Bud Billiken Day was arguably as much a conservative attempt to quell these more subversive protests that threatened to upset the black cultural elite as it was a reaction to the challenges facing all of black Chicago. By early 1931, well over half of employable African American women and more than two-fifths of employable African American men in Chicago were out of work. Left with little to no income to feed their families or pay rent, black Chicagoans accounted for 25 percent of the city's relief cases and as much as 40 percent of eviction cases at a time when they made up only about 7 percent of the city's population. Many black Chicagoans—entire families, the homeless, and on some nights hundreds of "unescorted women of good character" according to the Welfare Committee—took to sleeping in Washington Park, and it was most commonly there that "stormy crowds met to listen to leaders of the unemployed."[13]

Newly influenced by the rampant unemployment and widespread evictions that so devastated the South Side, intraracial class-based conflicts over behavior and values that had coalesced in the parks during the Great Migration years transformed into pitched battles over the very structure of society itself in the early years of the Great Depression. As the *Defender* planned its first Bud Billiken Day in 1930, many black Chicagoans were joining communist-organized Unemployed Councils that held their first meetings in Washington Park and protested labor conditions citywide, and some founded their own versions of longstanding politically radical groups in the park. Indeed, one activist recalled that Washington Park was "the center of protest by Blacks against all forms of oppression" during the Great Depression, and a New Deal study noted that, on a walk through the park, "one might see a little knot of Communists, pamphlets in hand, disputing under the trees with ardent Negro Nationalists who still dream of Marcus Garvey and his Royal African Legions."[14] The black middle class worried that communists were gaining influence among the black working classes by organizing in public green spaces such as Washington Park. The creation of Bud Billiken Day was evidence that the *Defender*—along with other black-led middle-class community organizations allied with white city leaders—was scrambling to design counterprogramming that might undermine radical alternatives.

Especially during the early 1930s, then, thousands of black Chicagoans saw Washington Park and other public green spaces like it as contested places: either as conduits for radical protest or as bulwarks against it. Indeed, this was one of the most potent ways in which Washington Park was a reflection of black Chicago's diversity in the 1930s. It was a landscape of hope that helped forge a unified community in the face of adversity, as well as a battleground that helped define the conflict between middle-class reform and working-class protest.[15]

Of course, perhaps few of the tens and even hundreds of thousands of black Chicagoans who gathered for the Bud Billiken picnic every August in Washington Park thought of the South Side's public green spaces in precisely or explicitly those politically charged terms. For them, parks and beaches simply remained critical gathering places in a time of crisis, welcoming virtually everyone in the community whether they used it for leisure or protest, baseball and tennis, or soapbox oratory and political organizing. In a period when precious few black Chicagoans had much disposable income to spend on commercial entertainment, places like Washington Park were especially important because they were not only easily accessible to all ages but also free. Fewer and fewer could afford the attractions of the Stroll, but anyone could spend an afternoon in the park without spending a dime; indeed, this is partly what made Washington Park such a potent landscape for various groups trying to reach black Chicago's masses.

In *Black Metropolis,* the definitive sociological study of the South Side, St. Clair Drake and Horace Cayton took note of Washington Park's status as an ideological battleground, writing that it was "Bronzeville's equivalent of [London's] Hyde Park where 'jack-leg' preachers joust with curbstone atheists, and Black Zionists break a lance with sundry varieties of 'Reds.'"[16] But they also called Washington Park the "playground of the South Side"; the Olmsted and Vaux-designed acreage was where "Bronzeville's teeming thousands swarm[ed], lounging on the grass, frolicking in the Black Belt's one large swimming pool, fishing and rowing in the lagoon, playing softball, tennis, or baseball."[17] Simultaneously political and apolitical, Washington Park and other public landscapes of hope across the South Side were uniquely capable of meeting diverse black Chicagoans' needs during the Great Depression.

Citing trends already well underway in the late 1920s, Drake and Cayton deemed Washington Park a "major community institution" during the Great Depression, joining Olivet Baptist Church (which then boasted the "largest Protestant congregation in America"), Provident Hospital (founded and staffed by African Americans), the African American YWCA branch, and "the imposing Michigan Boulevard Garden Apartments for middle-income families."[18] In fact, Washington Park and other South Side public green spaces became such universally recognized community institutions that they were imaginatively memorialized in black Chicago Renaissance artists' poetry and painting; the winding thoroughfares designed by Olmsted and Vaux even make a brief appearance in Richard Wright's sensational 1940 novel *Native Son,* for example. So although Bud Billiken Day may have become Washington Park's signature event, those 371 acres of green space were important to Jimmy Ellis and countless other black Chicagoans all year. Ellis recalled that it was "the kind of center for [his] family" during the Great Depression in large part because it seemed like "everything was right there."[19] Timuel Black similarly remembered Washington Park as a "gathering place" that was "used by everyone," old and young, women and men, the wealthy and working classes alike—a place where the world-famous jazz musician Cab Calloway and his band, along with members of the Negro Leagues' American Giants, would play baseball in the park with neighborhood boys in the 1930s.[20] A new state-of-the-art swimming pool attracted hundreds if not thousands on hot summer days, tennis became so popular that one resident recalled needing to arrive at daybreak to have any hope of getting a court, and another remembered finding the quieter retreat of rowing on the lagoon with a date to be "quite romantic."[21] Thousands attended mass baptisms held in the same lagoon, and dozens of South Side churches held picnics in Washington Park throughout the decade. Summer remained the most active season in the park, but fishing in the lagoon during the month-long fall season remained popular in the 1930s, as did ice skating during the winter months (see Figure 3.2).[22]

Yet Washington Park became a "major community institution" for black Chicago in large part because it—along with many other public green spaces, institutions, and neighborhoods that made up the Black Belt—was also becoming increasingly segregated and isolated from the city's white population, trends that revealed the limits of urban landscapes of hope. As two Great Migration historians put it, the Bud Billiken Day festivities that culminated each year in Washington Park "rested on a shared sense of apartness that Chicago African Americans experienced daily."[23] Indeed, just a year after the inaugural Bud Billiken Day, sociologist Horace Cayton recalled that in Washington Park, "*only* Negroes played ball, strolled in pairs, or sat on the grass," and by the end of the decade the Chicago Park District confirmed that African Americans constituted virtually all of the park's visitors.[24] Communist organizing that promoted interracial collaboration or team sports that pitted black teams against white teams were the exception to the more general rule of diminished interracial contact—not only in public green spaces but also in many walks of city life. Timuel Black recalled that when it came to recreation in Washington Park, "whites just wouldn't come to the park unless they were invited by a team. They didn't venture into the park as they had done before blacks moved into the neighborhood."[25] By the same token, Drake and Cayton noted that because black Chicagoans did "not wish to risk drowning at the hands of an un-

Figure 3.2a. Two small children fishing in the Washington Park lagoon, circa 1934. By permission and courtesy of the Chicago Park District Special Collections.

Figure 3.2b. Fishing in the Washington Park lagoon, circa 1940. By permission and courtesy of the Chicago Park District Special Collections.

friendly gang . . . they swim at all-Negro beaches, or in the Jim-Crow sections of mixed beaches, or in one of the Black Belt parks."[26] Washington Park's new swimming pool was used nearly exclusively by black Chicagoans in the late 1930s, and Jackson Park beach remained as strictly segregated as it had been in the Great Migration era; African Americans were restricted to the north end while whites used the south end, and some residents recalled, "You could get into a fight if you crossed that line."[27] Ultimately, then, the fears that many black Chicagoans voiced during the racial tensions that broke out along the lakefront in 1929 were realized during the Great Depression: in its landscapes of hope and beyond, Chicago was increasingly becoming a city that resembled the Jim Crow South that migrants had escaped, accelerating and hardening segregation trends established during the Great Migration years even as some other racial barriers were coming down.

A whole host of infrastructural improvements and new recreational activities in public green spaces financed largely with New Deal funds in the mid- to late 1930s only reinforced this trend toward increasingly rigid racial separation that was also driven by residential segregation. Such investments were unquestionably long overdue boons to communities in desperate need, and they gained the wholehearted support of Black Belt leaders, who believed they reinforced the goals of the Bud Billiken Club and other middle-class institutions: mitigating juvenile delinquency and occupying the unemployed while undermining radical working-class protest. But each of these improvements, whether intentionally or inadvertently, further disincentivized venturing outside of one's own neighborhood and shored up the residential segregation that plagued black Chicagoans, effectively helping keep them geographically contained in public green spaces that whites had "conceded" to them. By 1937, the Chicago Park District had opened the city's largest swimming pool in Washington Park; Madden Park had been transformed from a small playground to a full-fledged park replete with recreational facilities and a swimming pool of its own after more than a decade of community protest; and 31st Street beach finally benefited from the city's transformation of the South Side's industrial lakefront into Burnham Park, a recreational destination that connected the Loop's Grant Park to Olmsted and Vaux's Jackson Park. All were made possible in large part by New Deal funding and labor, primarily through the Works Progress Administration (WPA), and all were almost entirely segregated. Washington Park's newest amenity was a realization of Jimmie Farrell's 1929 suggestion to "install a swimming pool" in a space that had already "been conceded to the Negroes by the whites"; the Chicago Park District saw Madden Park's improvements and the New Deal-funded public housing that surrounded it as "a recreational safety valve for one of the most badly decayed and poverty stricken areas in the black belt," and the Chicago Recreation Commission advertised 31st Street beach to tourists as a "Negroes only" beach in the late 1930s. The New Deal's ambitious foray into public housing, which in Chicago attempted to capitalize on Madden Park's public green space to uplift residents, only further reinforced these trends toward segregation in nearly all facets of urban life.[28]

Yet although segregation in landscapes of hope across the city undoubtedly restricted, limited, and discriminated against black Chicagoans, events like Bud Billiken Day were also evidence that de facto segregation could often paradoxically help turn places such as Washington Park into the culturally productive community institutions they became during the Great Depression. De facto segregation, in other words, simultaneously held back black Chicago and propelled it forward, allowing South Siders to attempt to build a diverse but unified community largely outside the bounds of white interference.[29] Once thought to be Washington Park's "permanent blister," interracial violence there became an exceedingly rare occurrence; what had been violently contested racial space during the Great Migration had become virtually uncontested African American space during the Great Depression. When Bud Billiken and his "gang" marched down South Parkway and joined tens of thousands of other black Chicagoans for the picnic in Washington Park each August, they could do so without fear of judgment or violence from white residents because virtually none lived immediately west of South Parkway in the 1930s. And when the marchers finally spilled into the park, they were just a few blocks north of Jesse Binga's South Parkway home; a decade earlier, he had had to staunchly defend it against multiple bombings, and now the entire area was solidly in the Black Belt.

With whites almost completely absent from Washington Park during the 1930s, middle-class African Americans' acute concerns about behavior and park use in the Great Migration years also seem to have dissipated. Critiques of tennis-playing attire vanished from the *Defender*, for example, and the outdoor baptisms that were fairly common among working-class migrants similarly failed to elicit the same middle-class criticism of Southern folkways they had just a decade earlier.[30] Perhaps even more telling was that, at the third annual Bud Billiken picnic in 1932, the *Defender* proudly promoted a three-man band of teenagers who played "the 'red hot,' 'low down' jazz" with a "jungle rhythm," with instruments including a "ukulele, a washboard and a box with 15 or more tin cans on it" that served as a drum—a performance clearly inspired by southern folk culture.[31] Now largely free from white observation and judgment in the park, the *Defender* wholeheartedly endorsed precisely the sort of musical performance it had chastised just a few years earlier when migrants played ukuleles on Washington Park's tennis courts. The fact that black Chicagoans could claim public green spaces such as Washington Park as their own places did have value for the community then, even within the context of evolving but strictly defined racial boundaries that precluded them from a variety of other city spaces.

For many in the Black Metropolis, these changes marked a sort of racial progress: black Chicagoans now had more—and objectively better—public landscapes of hope to call their own during the Great Depression. But it was without question a mixed blessing: these changes merely highlighted the fact that if one ventured outside certain ever-evolving geographical boundaries, one risked the same discrimination and violence that black Chicagoans had suffered in Washington Park, 31st Street beach, and other public green spaces during the Great Migration era. For most black Chicagoans, perhaps, both these perspectives held true at the same time. Jimmy Ellis, for instance, fondly recalled feeling like he "had everything that you would need in your community" in and around the park where African Americans "created our own society and entertainment." But Ellis, who joined Bud Billiken's benevolent "gang" in their annual parade down South Parkway, also very clearly remembered his parents telling him to not go more than a block east of Washington Park (toward Jackson Park, the white Hyde Park neighborhood, and the University of Chicago) at night. They were worried he would get accosted by violent white gangs, many of which continued to target African Americans in an effort to keep virtually all South Side spaces segregated—both public green spaces and private residential ones.[32]

"Reds" on the Black Belt's Green Grass

The Great Depression hit Chicago's Black Belt swiftly and sharply, and the deepening economic crisis in 1930 incited a range of radical grassroots activism, much of it catalyzed by the availability of public green spaces such as Washington Park across the South Side. One of the most notable protests occurred after community institutions ranging from the *Defender* to the Chicago Urban League failed to win any African American jobs on the extension of a streetcar line along the northern boundary of Washington Park (along 51st Street between South Parkway and Cottage Grove Avenue) despite its location in the heart of the Black Belt. During the Great Migration years, the Urban League had built its credibility within the African American community in part through negotiations with employers and city leaders that yielded jobs for the migrant working classes. Now it seemed to some working-class black Chicagoans that the League's effectiveness might have dissipated in an economic climate that practically worsened by the day, and a small group of protestors decided to take matters into their own hands. Little more than a month after the *Defender*'s inaugural Bud Billiken Day, hundreds of people gathered at the northwest corner of Washington Park and marched to the intersection of 51st Street and South Parkway where they "forced the white immigrant workers to lay down their work tools."[33] Faced with the prospect of a work stoppage, the streetcar company soon capitulated and hired a handful of African Americans on the construction project. It was a small victory that did gain the support of many in the black cultural elite, but that streetcar protest in 1930 also helped initiate a brand of more radical, grassroots working-class activism centered in Washington Park that would come to define the early years of the Great Depression on the South Side.[34]

When widespread economic hardship created the ideological space for more radical political thought among the hardest-hit working classes in the early 1930s, Washington Park's landscape of hope provided the physical space for those black Chicagoans to mobilize political action from the grassroots. Radical working-class protest took various forms in Chicago's public green spaces as the Great Depression deepened, but many who gathered in Washington Park increasingly believed that the Communist Party offered the best chance of combating rising unemployment and mounting evictions across the South Side. It was a situation that one prominent communist intellectual, with the dire consequences of the Mississippi River's catastrophic 1927 flood still fresh in his mind, called "a famine, a Mississippi flood, a major disaster to the human race."[35] For their part, communists believed that Chicago's African American population held a great deal of potential for the party not only because they were victims of capitalism's worst failings during the Great Depression but also because the jobs they had found during the Great Migration years made them "true proletarians, associated with essential heavy industry" in "the stock yards, the steel mills, the McCormick Harvester plants."[36]

Although the number of black Chicagoans who held official membership in the Communist Party was quite low—one historian found that the Chicago Communist Party could claim only 412 African American members at the height of its popularity in 1931—the thousands whom communists had the potential to reach every day in Washington Park posed a palpable threat to middle-class community institutions struggling to respond to the economic catastrophe. Chicago Urban League records, for instance, expressed anxiety that radical "communistic elements [were] taking advantage of the situation" to gain a following, and the sociologist St. Clair Drake noted that communists in Chicago "had more success in manipulating masses of the Negro people than any of the Negro organizations with the exception of the Universal Negro Improvement Association"—a group that had lost much of its potency by the early 1930s.[37] Observing a communist eviction protest led by an African American woman in 1931, Drake's future research partner Horace Cayton wrote,

> I have heard lots of radicals talk. I have attended the meetings of Anarchists, Socialists, I.W.W.s and Communists. I understand, more or less, the rituals of Karl Marx, Lenin, and the rest. I am familiar with the usual harangue of the "soap boxer"—but this was different. This woman was not talking about economic principles; she was not talking about empty theories, nor was she concerned with some abstract Utopia to be gained from the movement of the "lower classes." She was talking about bread, and jobs, and places to sleep in.[38]

Bread, jobs, and places to sleep: these were all things that the Urban League and the black cultural elite had helped provide for black Chicago in the Great Migration years. Now, despite the best efforts of many of these organizations and individuals to respond to the Great Depression's challenges (the Urban League almost immediately transformed itself into a relief organization, for instance), the economic catastrophe had opened up a golden opportunity for communists to win over the working classes. Indeed, the fact that black Chicagoans "were hungry, frustrated, angry people looking for a program of action" during the Great Depression was more than enough for the Communist Party to wield "considerable influence in the Negro community," most of it from their home base in Washington Park.[39]

Just as in other cities across the country, the Great Depression had a profound and disproportionate effect on African Americans in Chicago, who were often the last hired and the first fired. The communists' bold program of direct action addressed one of the most critical problems facing the Black Belt during the early 1930s: landlords were evicting thousands of families unable to pay their rent. In response to the growing crisis, communists formed hundreds of Unemployed Councils in cities nationwide to protest conditions and organize resistance to evictions. In Chicago, some unemployment protests were organized in Ellis Park, a tiny three-acre green space in the heart of the Black Belt practically adjacent to Madden Park and about a mile south of 31st Street beach. Washington Park hosted what was perhaps the largest Unemployed Council in Chicago, however, just a stone's throw away from the baseball games that continued on the park's massive meadow. When an Unemployed Council learned of an eviction in process, the speakers would lead the crowd from Washington Park through the streets of the Black Belt to the eviction and, defying landlords and often police, put the evicted family's furniture back in their home. A full year before the Communist Party's role in defending the Scottsboro Boys lent it a measure of legitimacy with African Americans nationwide, these effective eviction protests almost instantly gained credibility for the party among black Chicago's working classes. Throughout the fall of 1930 and into 1931, communist Unemployed Councils gained in popularity as evictions mounted, and citywide the Communist Party averaged more than one public protest per day between 1930 and 1934.[40] One African American participant recalled that these meetings that began in Washington Park cumulatively "put hundreds of families back into their homes," and another account noted that the daily meetings and orations had "nearly always" drawn about 1,000 listeners from as early as eight in the morning to as late as ten at night.[41]

Washington Park was a natural "center of protest," as one black communist organizer put it, for the same geographic and demographic reasons that made it a logical choice for the *Defender*'s Bud Billiken Day
picnic.[42] Not only was the massive public green space the site where
thousands of black Chicagoans already spent their leisure time but it was
also adjacent to African American neighborhoods suffering high eviction rates to the north and west. Even many of the stately homes that
attracted Jesse Binga to the area a decade earlier were being broken up
into multifamily kitchenettes, inhabited by black Chicagoans struggling
and often failing to pay their rent. Indeed, Richard Wright recalled that
many left unemployed and homeless by the Great Depression "filled all
the empty benches in the parks of Chicago's South Side" in the early
1930s when he would regularly drop by in the afternoons to "sample
the dialectic or indignation of Communist speakers" that "rang out over
the park."[43] Similarly, when one prominent communist intellectual visited Washington Park in the early 1930s, he saw hundreds of unemployed African American workers "lounging on the benches around the
speakers' stand, or arguing in groups under the trees of the massive
meadow," waiting for a soapbox speech later in the day.[44] One study of
the tactics and methods of communist organizing in Chicago noted that
these outdoor gatherings proved particularly popular and effective
because they were both more democratic than a lecture hall (which
tended to discourage high levels of crowd participation) and more spon-
taneous than organized meetings (which were vulnerable to police intervention). In open green spaces such as Washington Park, the audience
"felt free to discuss the subject among themselves [and] shout questions
or comments at the speaker or to move about and greet their friends as
the speech continued. All together, the lack of four walls gave this type
of gathering a spontaneity which added fire and color to the usual
speaking performances."[45] A typical gathering took place one summer
night in 1932, as men, women, and children from the Black Belt gathered around a platform in Washington Park and listened to speaker
after speaker. When an elderly African American man took the stage
and gave an impassioned speech, shouting, "We gotta start things goin'
ourselves. . . . A revolution is what we need. A revolution against white
bosses and black bosses!" the crowd murmured its approval. When the
next speaker, a young white man, took the platform to suggest reform
rather than revolution, a young black girl in the crowd shouted back,

"Hell, NO!" and the rest of the audience booed and catcalled the man off the stage.[46] Such radicalism must have sent a chill through the black cultural elite, which had built their status and credibility—among both African Americans and whites—on reform.

The very nature of Washington Park's wide-open green space—the "large meadow ground, of an open, free, tranquil character" that Olmsted and Vaux designed more than a half-century earlier, so very different from a lecture hall or street corner constrained by walls or traffic—ironically facilitated the anything but tranquil gathering of large protest groups during the early days of the Great Depression.[47] In addition to its open acreage that could host thousands and its geographical proximity to the Black Belt, Washington Park's political and racial history also made it an ideal place to stoke the fires of communist protest. At least since the turn of the century, well before African Americans lived nearby, Washington Park had hosted an "Open Forum" of radical political thought more colloquially known as the "Bug Club." Now, even as the long-running and overwhelmingly white Bug Club continued to meet in the park's southeast corner near neighborhoods that remained white, "Black Bugs" and "Black Reds" (as many called African American communists) continued that protest tradition in the northwest corner of the park nearest the African American neighborhoods hit hardest by the economic downturn.[48]

But while certain elements of radical political protest in Washington Park remained segregated, the Communist Party aspired to build an interracial working-class movement. Since Washington Park had only recently transitioned from the interracial battleground it had been during the Great Migration years and remained a border space between white and black neighborhoods, it was a logical place for communists to attempt interracial organization. Richard Wright witnessed firsthand that interracial collaboration in Washington Park in the early 1930s, and his short story "Fire and Cloud" is a transparent fictionalization of those efforts, transplanted into a small Southern town. In the story's climax, the town's African Americans are led by a farmer-turned-preacher who has been won over by the communist message, singing and marching to "the park that separated the white district from the black" where they join white protestors.[49] Wright's fictional vision of communists' interracial collaboration was an optimistic and even utopian vision of the South that migrants had left behind. Indeed, although communists were making modest inroads among African Americans in the South, much of their organizing was forced underground for fear of violent repression. Wright's short story fairly closely tracked reality in Chicago, however, where black migrants discovered and enjoyed considerably more political freedom. The racial composition of an estimated 60,000 marchers in a major 1931 communist parade through the Black Belt was approximately 60 percent African American and 40 percent white (although spectators were 90 percent African American, much more reflective of the surrounding neighborhood), and marchers regularly chanted phrases like "Black and white unite and fight."[50] Such interracial collaboration prompted one black Chicagoan who was more accustomed to the South's strict racial codes to recall that he had "never really even talked to a white man before, and I certainly hadn't said more than two words to a white lady" prior to his involvement with the Communist Party; the respect he was shown there "changed the way [he] thought about things."[51] These seemingly sincere efforts at interracial collaboration may be one reason that, as early as 1931, a Communist Party report noted that the "only mass organization where the Negro workers have been organized and feel at home is the Unemployed Councils."[52] Many black Chicagoans may have felt even more at home at communists' Washington Park gatherings when, despite continued interracial organizing, a grassroots movement for all-black leadership in the Black Belt district was upheld by the Communist Party in 1932.[53]

Regardless of interracial collaboration, working-class black Chicagoans left practically destitute by the Great Depression likely gravitated to the Unemployed Council in Washington Park's landscape of hope because it gave virtually the entire African American community a voice at a time when many felt powerless. Indeed, much like the annual Bud Billiken Day festivities, the Unemployed Council welcomed black Chicago in all its diversity: Southern born and Northern born, women and men, old and young. Dempsey Travis and Timuel Black—both born in Chicago to Southern migrants and both in grade school during the Great Depression—attended the anti-eviction protests in Washington Park with older family members and got early lessons in social justice. Travis regularly attended the protests with his older cousin, and although he recalled the Unemployed Councils' anti-eviction efforts as "free excitement for kids," his cousin told his father and uncles—all Southern migrants—"that they could get a liberal education in Washington Park by simply moving from one bench speaker to another."[54] Black similarly remembers attending some of the anti-eviction protests in Washington Park with his father, who believed the protestors "exemplified how you were supposed to behave when people mistreat you"; even at that young age, Black came away from the experience with "an example of learning very early to participate in things that brought about justice."[55] Indeed, one observer was struck by the multigenerational nature of the crowd that almost inevitably reflected black Chicago's Southern roots. She noted that on one representative evening, some spoke "with the blurring voice of Alabama, others with the clipped tones of Northern colleges," and listening to them were "hundreds of men and women [sitting] on coats and newspapers," as well as men standing ten deep behind "plump matrons and strangely quiet children" sitting on benches. Some wore work overalls while the Great Depression had left others "actually in rags," but all were "plainly dressed, serious, hard working people."[56] Another communist intellectual who visited the Washington Park protests confirmed that "fathers, mothers, grandmothers from the deep south, and scores of children—all the generations were at the forum"; in his mind, for working-class black Chicagoans communism had "become a folk thing. They have taken Communism and translated it into their own idiom."[57]

The communists' organizational successes in Washington Park were due in part to the same reason that helped make the *Defender*'s Bud Billiken Day picnic so accessible and popular, then: black Chicagoans could readily translate communism "into their own idiom" because the hybridity of Washington Park's public green space already invited them to translate their Southern roots to a Northern context, fostering new but still familiar ways of doing everything from playing baseball to practicing religion. Perhaps that was why one observer of the communist meetings in Washington Park felt as though she was "at an open air revival."[58] Horace Cayton similarly recalled that, at one anti-eviction protest in 1931, "the emotional responses of the Communists themselves reminded me more of a camp fire meeting than a mob of angry 'reds.' Evidently not all Communists, at least not all black Communists, are atheists."[59] Indeed, despite the generally antireligious party line, South Side communists organized through a range of religious community institutions from churches to the YWCA and welcomed religious expression at their meetings; given the religious affiliations of most black Chicagoans, they would have been hard-pressed to gain much of a

following otherwise. Parades sometimes featured marchers singing spiri-
tuals as well as decidedly secular communist songs or even blending the
two: the white communist intellectual who believed that communism
had become a "folk thing" on the South Side observed that black Chicagoans changed the lyrics of "Gimme That Old Time Religion" to "Gimme
That New Communist Spirit."[60] He further observed, "At mass meetings
their religious past becomes transmuted into a Communist present. They
follow every word of the speaker with real emotion; they encourage
him, as at a prayer meeting with the cries, of 'Yes, yes, comrade' and
often there is an involuntary and heartfelt 'Amen!'"[61] Rather than fully
abandon their "religious past," then, black Chicagoans clearly merged it
with communist organizing to create a hybrid form of community
building and working-class protest in Washington Park and beyond.

Despite allowing ample room for religiously inflected protest across
the South Side, however, communists often vilified the community's religious leaders—along with the politicians, landlords, bankers, lawyers,
and others who made up the black cultural elite—in their attempt to
forge an interracial working-class coalition in Washington Park. The
very same race leaders who saw green spaces such as Washington Park,
Camps Wabash and Belnap, and Idlewild as ways to disseminate middle-
class values and uplift the race in the Great Migration years now saw
many of these spaces leveraged against them to incite unrest among the
working classes and further destabilize a social order already disrupted
by widespread economic strife. One communist newspaper mirrored the
messages that those gathered in Washington Park received on a daily
basis, accusing Oscar De Priest and Mayor "Big Bill" Thompson of
"working hand in glove with [Jesse] Binga, the banker, [Robert] Abbott,
the editor of the Chicago Defender, and the Baptist and Methodist ministers" to mislead the Black Belt's working classes and undermine radical
protest that might yield jobs.[62] Communists singled out De Priest in particular, not only for his largely fruitless political efforts to ameliorate
suffering on the South Side, but especially for his alleged role in exacerbating it: as a landlord, they charged, he was "one of the leaders in
evicting unemployed Negro workers."[63] It was a bold but fairly representative indictment of a group that had become community pillars during
the Great Migration years and that now found themselves struggling to
adequately respond to the economic crisis. Anxious about the inroads
that communists were making among the working classes hardest hit

by unemployment and evictions, the charismatic Junius C. Austin—who for decades led Pilgrim Baptist Church, then one of the largest African American congregations in Chicago—unsuccessfully tried his hand at soapbox orating in Washington Park in 1931, later lamenting to the *Tribune* that, "you can't talk religion to a man with an empty stomach."[64]

The tumultuous summer of 1931 revealed just how much of an ideological battleground Washington Park had become during the early days of the Great Depression; it was key to a potentially dangerous rift between the working classes and the black cultural elite that had built up its power and influence during the Great Migration years. With roughly half of employable black Chicagoans out of work and no relief in sight, the tone of crowds gathered in the park grew increasingly militant after police began intervening to prevent evicted tenants' belongings from being put back in their homes. In late July, a race riot was narrowly averted as eviction protestors stood off against police, but on August 3, 1931, just days before the *Defender*'s second annual Bud Billiken Day, tensions finally came to a head. Word had come to the Unemployed Council leaders in Washington Park that a seventy-two-year-old widow was being evicted from her home nearby, and they quickly led a crowd of several thousand protestors just a short walk west to help put her furniture back into her home. When they arrived, however, police attempted to block their efforts, and although it remains unclear exactly what triggered the violence that ensued, police officers ultimately killed three African American protestors, who quickly "became the symbol of the city's unemployed masses."[65] The body of one of those killed was only recovered later that night back in Washington Park; communists who found him "shot through the head and badly mutilated" suspected that he had been "taken for a ride by the police" and dropped in the park, perhaps as a warning to those who protested there.[66]

In the days that followed what communists quickly dubbed the "Chicago massacre," the rift between the Black Belt's working classes and the Great Migration-era leadership threatened to rupture into a gaping chasm as enormous crowds as large as ten thousand flocked to Washington Park. Communists added fuel to the fire, declaring that Oscar De Priest had blood on his hands for conspiring with other city landlords and politicians "to demand that Chicago's chief of police take more severe measures to stop the anti-eviction activity" in the days leading up to the killings.[67] Attempting to quell the unrest, *Defender* publisher

Robert Abbott addressed the crowds assembled in the park that would soon host his newspaper's second annual Bud Billiken Day celebration. Counseling patience and denouncing communists as violent trouble-makers, he was booed off the platform. Herbert Turner, president of the Chicago NAACP (and, like Abbott, a regular Idlewild visitor), also blamed communist agitators for the escalating tension, but he could only look on with trepidation at the tenuous situation in Washington Park. City officials watched and worried too: the mayor's office sent a stenographer to the gatherings to "take down all orations delivered to the large Negro audiences," and the South Park Commission pledged to "not prohibit peaceful meetings in Washington Park" while rather idly threatening that "the south parks police would tolerate no Red speeches nor any appeal to the passions or prejudices of the colored people which might incite them to violence."[68] Realizing they needed to do something to address the root of the communist-driven working-class unrest that had coalesced in Washington Park, Black Belt leaders persuaded city officials to temporarily suspend evictions, an act that finally prompted "the city and the state [to begin] to make comprehensive plans for furnishing relief." Indeed, St. Clair Drake and Horace Cayton credited the eviction protests that Washington Park helped catalyze for inspiring city officials' "first serious attempts to face the economic crisis" and for "set[ting] in motion a chain of actions that was to benefit the entire city."[69]

Ultimately, however, the communists' victories that emerged out of organizing in and around Washington Park ironically sowed the seeds of their decline. Unemployment in the Black Belt peaked in 1931, and the city and state relief funds that their protests had helped secure began to make a small difference by 1932. As elected officials finally began to get a handle on the unemployment situation and conditions for the working classes marginally improved, communist protests in and around Washington Park gradually lost their potency, and the existential threat to the black cultural elite receded. Franklin Delano Roosevelt's federal New Deal programs began benefiting working-class South Siders in 1933, helping further shore up the black cultural elite against more radical challenges; increasingly black Chicagoans once again looked to their elected officials rather than communist protestors for solutions to economic problems. By the mid- to late 1930s, New Deal agencies like the Works Progress Administration (WPA) even significantly remade a variety of landscapes in the Black Belt. In a roundabout way at the very least, then, the "chain of actions" set off by the communist protests in Washington Park eventually had lasting impacts on both black Chicagoans and the South Side public green spaces on which they relied.[70]

The New Deal Builds New Landscapes on the South Side

While the Great Depression drove many to protest in the Black Belt's public green spaces across the South Side, widespread financial instability simultaneously forced officials to cut maintenance, improvement projects, and recreational programming to the bone citywide. Before federal New Deal programs took effect, the relatively meager city and state relief funds that the Washington Park protests helped spur barely helped put a dent in unemployment on the South Side, let alone fill gaping holes in the Park Commission's budget. Cuts were especially evident in the most impoverished sections of the Black Belt where, after years of community protest, there was still no appreciable progress in the transition from Jackson Playground toward the establishment of Madden Park for working-class African Americans. Evidence suggests that not only did park officials continue to deem the project a relatively low priority but also their diminished resources were simply stretched too thin to improve the space anyway. A South Park Commission study on the Madden Park neighborhood in February 1930, before cresting unemployment and evictions drove the formation of the Unemployed Council in Washington Park later that year, did set out to determine "what special [recreational] needs, if any, there are of negroes in Chicago as individuals or as a group," but the fact that "no funds were appropriated" made it difficult for the researchers to accurately assess what the community itself wanted. In addition, the lack of funding forced "the committee to carry out the study largely in their leisure" time, and the rushed timeline led to heavily qualified recommendations on which officials did not have the funds to act in any event.[71] In fact, budget cuts forced park officials to eliminate, not expand, recreational programming in the Black Belt despite claims from the community that the playground had "added 100 per cent to the social and civic uplift of this section and it would be disastrous now to turn the children out," and "social workers and interested civic leaders reported that delinquency in the Madden Park neighborhood doubled, following the indefinite closing of the supervised [Jackson] playground."[72]

Shabby facilities and reduced recreational programming for an already underserved community helped ignite a renewed community-driven movement to improve Madden Park and other public green spaces in the early years of the Great Depression, but to little effect. In September 1930, community leaders including Alderman Jackson and Congressman Oscar De Priest (whose home had been bombed on this very block in 1921) presented "a petition signed by numerous property owners and residents in the territory surrounding Madden Park" that urged a swimming pool and lagoon be constructed at the park.[73] A year later—just months after the "Chicago massacre" and more than four and a half years after the *Defender* had declared victory in its fight for a South Side park—the Urban League's A. L. Foster and Claude Barnett, the Wabash YMCA's Henry Crawford, and other community leaders were still protesting what they called "undue delay" in the park's construction and charging that the South Park "commissioners have shown too little interest."[74] In the coming months and years, hundreds of community members signed several more petitions requesting improved facilities and more adult supervision at Madden Park—so many, in fact, that the South Park's general superintendent felt "he was being importuned constantly" by residents.[75] The black cultural elite's continued fight for racial equality and improved services in public green spaces and beyond clearly challenged communists' claims that they were callously ignoring the working classes' rights and needs. Yet they struggled to produce substantial results, mostly failing to spur significant action on the much bigger problem of unemployment that devastated the South Side in the early years of the Depression.

It would take city, state, and especially the large-scale federal relief programs of Franklin Delano Roosevelt's New Deal to finally make a tangible impact on black Chicago and its South Side landscapes of hope. With the "Century of Progress" World's Fair approaching and communist protests perhaps having an impact, Madden Park and other South Side green spaces began to benefit from relief funding as early as 1932. That year, Madden Park was officially dedicated, finally making the transition from playground to park with the landscaping and infrastructural improvements that had been long sought by the community. The new facilities eventually allowed South Siders to enjoy annual field days, ice skate on a makeshift rink, take advantage of the park's open space to observe a solar eclipse, and play baseball and softball games on the park's three diamonds (as many as sixty teams of all ages, girls and boys, men and women, competed in one annual tournament sponsored by the *Defender* and the Wabash YMCA, among other community organizations).[76] Edgar Brown, Madden Park's director who would go on to serve as the Advisor on Negro Affairs for FDR's Civilian Conservation Corps (CCC), stoked Black Belt churches' interest in a "Ten Year Progress Plan for Colored Citizens of Chicago," which utilized emergency relief funds in part to put hundreds of men to work beautifying the Black Belt. The fruits of Madden Park's long overdue opening became apparent when the newly dedicated park served as ground zero for these efforts: the *Tribune* noted, "Not only were the weeds removed, grass planted, and old bricks used as a sidewalk and curb border [in the park], but the dressing up has spread to several individuals and community groups" across the South Side, who were "being urged to clean up their yards and plant grass, flowers, and shrubbery."[77]

An even bigger impact was made with the funding provided by FDR's New Deal programs, which began alleviating economic strife and social unrest as early as 1933. By far the most tangible improvements to public green spaces citywide came in 1936, when the WPA funded more than $25 million worth of parks projects in Chicago compared to less than $8 million that came from the newly consolidated Chicago Park District (CPD). It was enough to prompt the CPD's annual report to note that the city had "unquestionably . . . accomplish[ed] . . . more rehabilitation, repair and replacement work in the parks and on the boulevards of Chicago than has ever occurred in any previous year in their history."[78]

Perhaps the most important way the CPD and the WPA worked to make the South Side's public green spaces more attractive social centers in the mid-1930s was through multiplying black Chicagoans' swimming options. One of the largest projects that benefited from WPA funding was the long-planned Burnham Park (named after Daniel Burnham, one of Chicago's most famed city planners), which turned six miles of Chicago's industrial lakefront into grassy, tree-lined recreational grounds and sandy beaches that connected the Loop's Grant Park to the South Side's Jackson Park, and which at long last remade the justly maligned 31st Street beach. The beach had closed in the summers of 1933 and 1934 for use by the "Century of Progress" World's Fair, even further limiting black Chicagoans' already constricted swimming options and touching off protests within the community that eventually won assurances of equal treatment at 12th Street beach farther north. Soon after the fair ended, WPA workers began construction on 31st Street beach, and when it reopened for the 1936 summer season, it attracted an astounding one million visitors—no doubt nearly entirely African American—to its modest 300 feet of sandy lake frontage. Land that tens of thousands of African American migrants had traversed by train when they first arrived in Chicago had now been remade into a recreational space that overflowed with those very same migrants in the hot summer months. Working-class black Chicagoans finally had a respectable lakefront bathing option leagues better than the one that had been denounced in the Great Migration years as "fit only for dogs—or, rather, seals."[79]

New Deal funding also helped the Chicago Park District build new open-air swimming pools in Madden and Washington Parks, both of which opened the year after 31st Street beach overflowed with a million visitors. Madden Park's $100,000 pool was completed by WPA workers seven years after Oscar De Priest joined the community in petitioning for long overdue improvements, while hundreds more WPA workers finished a much larger pool in Washington Park just two miles farther south. Built just west of the lagoon designed by Olmsted and Vaux, Washington Park's pool could reportedly host at least one thousand black Chicagoans simultaneously and was in many ways the crown jewel of WPA improvements to the city's public green space. When it opened in 1937, it was the largest pool in all of Chicago and important enough to draw Mayor Edward Kelly to speak at its dedication. In fact, both parks' new swimming facilities were such a welcome addition to the South Side that black Chicagoans dedicated them on the same day and celebrated with a Bud Billiken Day-style parade in miniature, complete with "floats, children of the two parks in costume, softball and baseball teams, Boy and Girl Scouts, and delegations from business and civic organizations."[80] Much of the Black Belt knew they had the federal government to thank for these and other long overdue infrastructure projects as well. As the *Defender* noted of the many recreational amenities that Madden Park finally enjoyed in the mid- to late 1930s, "Social service workers sought for years to have a park built in this congested section of Chicago, but their efforts were futile until the Chicago Park District submitted the project to the Works Progress Administration."[81]

The South Side's new swimming pools were part of a federally funded wave of pool building nationwide, and they helped mark a new approach to urban park use that one historian has called the "recreation facility" era. Vying for citizens' recreation time, park officials attempted to compete with movie theaters and other popular commercial entertainment venues in the 1930s, which sometimes meant that parks' natural elements were either marginalized or ignored completely. That marked a significant departure from the approach reformers had taken up to and during the migration years.[82] Washington Park's massive new concrete swimming pool, for instance, eliminated a substantial portion of green space designed by Olmsted and Vaux; it was the type of project that the South Park superintendent had dismissed out of hand a quarter-century earlier on the grounds that "Washington park is one of the larger parks that is relied upon to furnish the lawn surfaces for the accommodation of those who wish to enjoy outdoor sports and games during the summer season. The demand for such areas is increasing greatly every year and the area to be devoted to this use is about exhausted."[83] Now, despite demand for park space that had only increased in the interim, park officials reversed themselves and decided that a new concrete pool would actually be more beneficial to the community. Although one community group had initially favored a new field house over an uncovered swimming pool in Washington Park because of the multiseasonal functionality it offered, there is little evidence that many black Chicagoans ultimately regretted construction of the South Side's new swimming pools.

In fact, the pools at both Washington and Madden Parks quickly became wildly popular in the summer months, drawing thousands from across the South Side. Photographs taken in their inaugural summers show them swarming with swimmers, and Madden Park's pool hosted an annual water carnival that featured a variety of swimming and diving activities for boys and girls alike (see Figure 3.3). Representative of the community's enthusiasm for these new amenities, Jimmy Ellis remembered that even black Chicagoans from distant neighborhoods flocked to Washington Park's pool because "it was a great facility [that] had about three pools, high diving board, a regular-sized pool, a pool where the children could play in. . . . Everybody went to the swimming pool, you know, even the so-called affluent, whoever they were. It was a class act. . . . Everybody was welcome."[84] Ellis, who grew up just a couple blocks north of Washington Park and often attended Bud Billiken Day in August, recalled visiting the pool with his siblings nearly every day in the summers when he was in grade school in the late 1930s. A

Figure 3.3a. Washington Park's new swimming pool in its inaugural summer, August 3, 1937, looking north toward the refectory. By permission and courtesy of the Chicago Park District Special Collections.

Figure 3.3b. Madden Park's new swimming pool in its inaugural summer, August 13, 1937. Note its small size and the lack of nearby trees compared to Washington Park's pool, then the city's largest. By permission and courtesy of the Chicago Park District Special Collections.

year after the pool opened, Jimmy Gentry (the man who dubbed black Chicago "Bronzeville" and created the popular "Mayor of Bronzeville" contest) even asserted that it blended right into the park's landscape:

> Spring officially is here and all Bronzeville is basking in the bright sunlight . . . the meadow in Washington Park is green with grass and clover . . . the wooded section of the Bronzeville side of the park has frisky little streams running through it. There are plenty of willows, some are "weeping." But the clump of trees that you see as you enter the park from Garfield boulevard hides a beautiful swimming pool that can accommodate a thousand or more swimmers at one time. But just lift your eyes and there beyond is the broad, shiny boating pond winding completely around twelve acres of yet dream-dispelling bits of ice and snow . . . melting away and sliding down into the lagoon.[85]

Although the pool represented a fairly significant departure from Washington Park's original design, for Gentry—and perhaps for many others—it was almost as if it had been seamlessly absorbed into Olmsted and Vaux's meadows and lagoons, part of a coherent whole that helped define Bronzeville during the Great Depression.

Published the same year the South Side's two new pools opened to great fanfare, Frank Marshall Davis's 1937 poem "Washington Park, Chicago" imaginatively captures the many reasons why that landscape of hope in particular—unparalleled in sheer size and accessible to all—had quickly become one of Bronzeville's key "community institutions" where "everybody was welcome" during the New Deal era. Davis, who worked as a journalist for the Associated Negro Press and was invited by Richard Wright to join the South Side Writers Group, portrays the park as black Chicago's mental and physical refuge from the jungle-like city, which he calls "Chicago's Congo."[86] The poem begins,

> The heat roars
> Like a tidal wave
> Over Chicago's Congo
> . . .
> High breakers of heat
> Split into dry mist—
> A harmless spray—
> As the tidal wave
> Dashes against strong rocks
> Of tall trees
> In Washington Park.
> . . .

> In Washington Park
> The people go—
> When the heat
> Is an African python
> Crushing amid its coils
> The black carcass
> Of Chicago's Congo. . . .

Washington Park's shady trees and its new pool literally cooled off visitors, but Davis suggests that its cultural power runs deeper. Within the park, black Chicago is strong and unified like the "strong rocks of tall trees," just as the *Defender*'s Bud Billiken Day picnic willed it to be each August, and the urban environment's myriad forms of oppressiveness and destructiveness—powerful as a tidal wave and malevolent as a python—dissolve into mere "harmless spray" at the park's borders. Yet although Davis clearly favors Washington Park's "humble waving grass / That crawls on its belly" to the city's skyscrapers and other human inventions that "boast of Progress," the South Side's most important public green space does not exist in complete isolation from the surrounding urban environment. Indeed, the poem suggests that much of Washington Park's virtue stems from its hybridity and capaciousness, capable of mediating conflicts between nature and culture:

> Along pretzel crooked roads
> Race horse autos gallop
> In great herds
> Or stand in insolent silence
> Rubber feet among green blades of grass
> Sniffing in mechanical disdain
> At those who walk
> And barely dodge
> A mile a minute hoof.
>
> The park shoulders
> Its people and cars
> On a verdant back
> And marches on
> To the steady boom
> Of the taut heat drum.

Washington Park was made up of the urban environment's roads, cars, buildings, and concrete swimming pools just as much as it was made up of pastoral meadows and lagoons. Here, just as in Jimmy Gentry's ode to early spring, everything blends together into a coherent—if precariously balanced—whole that lends the Black Belt strength (see Figure 3.4).

Washington Park not only acts as a mediator between nature and culture in Davis's poem but its strength also lies in its unique ability to bring together disparate elements of Bronzeville to shoulder the lingering burdens of the Great Depression. Joining a homeless man sleeping under newspapers on a park bench and a destitute woman gathering kindling for a fire in her "fallen-in house" is a "lanky Communist" who

> Tosses baited words
> To faces beneath him,
> Faces fish-mouthed
> In a sitting sea
> Of human forms.
> "Proletariat" . . . "Bourbon"
> "Workers" . . . "Starvation"
> "Equality" . . . "Comrades"
> Are flung at 'em
> By the glib fisherman
> On the angler's stand.

With an ingenious metaphor that grafts the fishing so popular in Washington Park's lagoon onto communists' continued, if less successful, efforts to build support among the black working classes in the mid-1930s, Davis manages to capture the vital nature of public green space to both leisure and protest during the Great Depression. In addition to the communist soapbox orator exhorting his audience and those laid low by the Depression, however, one also sees the "Queen of the Burlesque Houses," a young couple in love, a lagoon fisherman, and a reverend who join

> Faces of infants and con men
> Of turnip breasted virgins
> And worn out prostitutes
> Their bodies piled along the grass
> Or poured into wooden benches.

Taken together, those in Washington Park are a collection of "kaleidoscopic faces / Twirling slowly against the light." Much more than merely a passive setting for Bronzeville's diverse multitudes, however, Washington Park becomes an active, nurturing mother to all black Chicagoans. In

Figure 3.4a. Aerial view of the northern half of Washington Park, November 2, 1938. Note the baseball diamonds and faint outlines for football and soccer fields on the meadow, the armory along Cottage Grove avenue at the park's eastern edge, as well as the duck pond encircled by a pathway along South Parkway at the park's western edge; communist protests coalesced in the northwest corner. Chicago Aerial Survey 1938 #283, Michigan to Drexel, 51st to 57th, CAPS_1938_18617_283, Chicago Aerial Photo Services Collection, University of Illinois at Chicago Library, Special Collections.

the second verse, willows and oaks watch park goers like "anxious mothers," and the poem's concluding image is that the park is

> Inarticulate, strong;
> Holding Chicago's Congo
> To its soothing breast
> While the heat roars
> Like a tidal wave
> Dashed to harmless spray
> Against strong rocks
> Of tall trees. . . .

Like a good mother, Davis's Washington Park welcomes and shelters all her children, whatever their needs; somehow the park manages to balance Bronzeville's diversity and contradictions, both fostering community and nurturing solitude. Stimulus is all around as "Voices swing like

Figure 3.4b. Aerial view of the southern half of Washington Park, November 2, 1938. The newly constructed pool, drained for the winter, is the bright white structure; adjacent to the pool, tennis courts bordering South Parkway line the entire western edge of the park from Garfield Boulevard to 60th Street. Note the contrast with the surrounding urban grid and built environment. Chicago Aerial Survey 1938 #284, Michigan to Ingleside, 55th to 61st, CAPS_1938_18617_284, Chicago Aerial Photo Services Collection, University of Illinois at Chicago Library, Special Collections.

monkeys / Through a thick forest / Of continuous sound," but nevertheless, "Here one may be / Surrounded and alone" (see Figure 3.5).[87]

Two contemporaneous paintings by Archibald Motley, "The Picnic" (1936) and "Lawn Party" (1937), similarly suggest the potential power that public landscapes of hope like Washington Park held for Bronzeville in the New Deal era. Although its composition is indebted to Renoir's "Luncheon of the Boating Party," the African Americans of varying skin tones who crowd under a large tree in Motley's "The Picnic" are also reminiscent of the "kaleidoscopic faces" in Davis's "Washington Park, Chicago." The African American community's intraracial diversity was a consistent feature of Motley's corpus, but of particular note in "The Picnic" are a singing guitar player and a large, dark-skinned man with rolled-up sleeves seated in the foreground, both of whom also appear in Motley's "Jazz Singers" (1934)—and the latter of whom also appears in

Figure 3.5. A couple strolling in Washington Park, April 1941. Farm Security Administration / Office of War Information Black-and-White Negatives, Prints and Photographs Division, Library of Congress, LC-USF33–005166-M3, Edwin Rosskam, photographer.

Motley's "Black Belt" (1934). Their appearance here suggests a night-club's patrons gathered in an urban park: Motley combines the vibrant reds that dominate many of his nightlife scenes with cooler greens and blues for a color palette indicating the Stroll's vibrant urban culture blending seamlessly into the Black Belt's pastoral landscapes. As one critic has pointed out, the characters in "The Picnic" are "familiar inhabitants of Motley's Bronzeville. Indeed, they seem to have strolled directly from its streets to the South Side's parks or Lake Michigan shore, for their attire, from the men's suits and hats to the stylishly exaggerated high heels of the woman in the foreground, all indicate an urban milieu."[88] Motley's "Lawn Party" (1937) depicts a similar scene—the same fashionable dress and an abundance of fruit and wine appear in both paintings—but here the canvas is much less crowded, and the color palette tends even more toward cooler greens and blues, influenced by the scene's trees, grass, and a body of water in the distance. "Lawn Party" reminds the viewer of Davis's "Washington Park, Chicago," in which one can be both "Surrounded and alone," but both paintings suggest the extent to which public landscapes of hope had become African American "community institutions" during the Great Depression, as vital to Bronzeville's cultural landscape as the Stroll.

Although the South Side's new federally funded swimming pools helped attract thousands of black Chicagoans who turned Washington and Madden Parks into the sorts of culturally vibrant places one sees in Davis's poem and Motley's paintings, New Deal-era reformers firmly believed that they also needed to guide the masses' experience of those public green spaces. As one city official warned when WPA labor cleared thirty-three vacant lots (an area that amounted to more than three acres) in the heart of the Black Belt, "simply to turn over a vacant lot to a bunch of youngsters might easily develop a jungle instead of an aid in checking delinquency."[89] So the massive infusion of WPA funds not only spurred a flurry of building projects but also expanded recreational programming on the South Side, thereby reasserting the middle-class values that reformers in the black cultural elite had promoted throughout the Great Migration years. But now the Great Depression had raised the stakes: widespread unemployment fueled fears about how young and old alike—such as the destitute in Davis's poem—might spend unwanted leisure time in public green spaces such as Washington Park. As Mayor Kelly explained the rationale behind New Deal relief initiatives, "Recreation . . . IS a problem in Chicago" that had increased "as a result of a period of economic adversity" because "we have hundreds of thousands of people who need to have their leisure time filled with constructive activity . . . that not only educates and builds character . . . but which diverts minds from negative influences."[90] Another assessment similarly contended, "The depression has given a pointed, almost dramatic emphasis to the problems of recreation and leisure time. The enforced leisure of unemployment . . . constitute[s] a social need which has been given attentive consideration by the Federal government."[91]

These New Deal reformers were, of course, concerned about the potential for increased delinquency and social ills that often followed economic downturns, but the "negative influences" from which Mayor Kelly wanted to divert citizens' minds clearly also included the radical politics that had threatened the established social order earlier in the decade. After communist protests had coalesced to dramatic effect in Washington Park and beyond during the worst days of the Great Depression, New Deal reformers and Black Belt leaders alike knew that public green spaces without adequate recreational programming could just as easily foment social unrest as they could help defuse it. In other words, they hoped to reclaim public green spaces from influences like the "lanky Communist" who appears in Davis's poem, luring the masses away from radical protest with the bait of recreational activities. As the *Defender* bluntly put it in 1934 when widespread communist protests were still quite fresh in South Siders' minds, it advocated federally funded concerts and other activities in city parks in part because "making the parks a desirable place for citizens means diverting their attention from communistic ideas and associations."[92] The Chicago Park District, working mostly with WPA funds, was on the same page: one report contended that although the parks were "originally intended to conserve health," officials had since decided that "in times of general irritation and unrest, the parks have been a steadying influence. No radical or revolutionary movements have gained foothold among those busy in parks schedules of recreation."[93] Indeed, many if not most of these recreational programs—which included activities ranging from traditional athletic competitions like baseball and softball tournaments to new ventures such as lessons on birdhouse building and sandcastle building competitions—appear to have been rooted in the same impulses behind Bud Billiken Day: both mitigating delinquency and countering the inroads that communists and other political radicals had made among the working classes in the early years of the Great Depression (see Figure 3.6). Although the control and use of these public landscapes of hope had been thrown into disarray in the early 1930s, New Deal funds allowed city officials and Black Belt institutions to redouble their efforts with the black working classes by the mid-1930s.[94]

Yet no matter how many infrastructural improvements and recreational programs the New Deal helped fund in public green spaces, city and community leaders still had good reason to fear they were still far from sufficient to combat myriad social ills exacerbated by the Great Depression. After all, even though many black Chicagoans took part in recreational programs sponsored by the Chicago Park District and belonged to community institutions like the Girl and Boy Scouts, these programs could not occupy citizens twenty-four hours a day. More importantly, they tended to focus their activities on young children and fell far short of reaching the entirety of the Black Belt; as St. Clair Drake observed, "On the whole, recreational activity of the lower middleclass

Figure 3.6. Girls affiliated with Washington Park building sand castles at Jackson Park beach as part of a Park District competition, circa 1938. Looking north toward the Loop, skyline in distance. By permission and courtesy of the Chicago Park District Special Collections.

and lowerclass is unorganized."[95] Even when public green spaces across the South Side were flush with federal money in the late 1930s and the new pools in Washington and Madden Parks hosted publicly funded community swimming lessons as well as weekly summer concerts, they themselves were vulnerable to the sorts of social ills they were intended to counter. A *Defender* editorial published two years after the dedication of Washington Park's pool claimed, "In Washington Park, where Race families must seek recreation, bandits roam almost unmolested with citizens often afraid to enter this public place after five P.M."[96]

Segregation in the Black Belt's Public Green Spaces

For observers like Richard Wright, New Deal reformers' recreational programs were doomed to fail because they turned a blind eye to the elephant in the room: race discrimination, most strongly rooted in residential segregation, that spilled over into virtually every urban landscape, public and private. Wright, who worked for the South Side Boys' Club during the Great Depression, came to view its activities in public green spaces (swimming, baseball, and the like) merely as "stopgap" measures, "utterly inadequate" to counter the "centuries-long chasm of emptiness which American civilization had created" and perpetuated in African American neighborhoods.[97] He even went so far as to suggest that New Deal-era reformers promoted recreational activities in public green spaces such as Washington Park (directly adjacent to the University of Chicago and the white Hyde Park neighborhood) to prevent young African Americans from "roam[ing] the streets and harm[ing] the valuable white property which adjoined the Black Belt."[98] His cynicism was understandable. When a Chicago Park District report described Madden Park as "a recreational safety valve for one of the most badly decayed and poverty stricken areas in the black belt," the implication would have been unmistakable for Wright: places like Madden and Washington Parks, complete with their swimming pools funded by the New Deal, were simply tools to help the city avoid another 1919 race riot, a way to contain and pacify black Chicagoans with crumbs of recreational retreats while denying them the whole loaf of full equality.[99]

Even Park District policies that appear to have been well-intentioned efforts to empower communities inevitably reinscribed race segregation. Well aware that virtually every park and beach were segregated, officials did attempt to structure investments "around local community needs," and a CPD newsletter noted that when there was "a large predominance of colored people, practically the entire program [was] turned over to them and the park is manned by a colored staff."[100] Even though that situation was certainly preferable to an African American park run by white officials, it also represented a capitulation to the broader trend of segregation. Although it is difficult to fault officials for strategies that actually met the sorts of demands made in the "Don't Buy Where You Can't Work" campaign earlier in the Great Depression, black Chicagoans undoubtedly recognized other markers of segregation that bore more than a passing resemblance to the Jim Crow South. When 31st Street beach reopened after closing for the "Century of Progress" World's Fair that took over the lakefront in 1933 and 1934, for instance, a tourist pamphlet published by the Chicago Recreation Commission designated it as "Negroes only."[101]

In addition, even though Frank Marshall Davis's "Washington Park, Chicago" and Archibald Motley's "The Picnic" and "Lawn Party" depict diverse African American park goers coming together to build community in public green spaces, the subtext of all three works confirms Richard Wright's critique: there is not a white park goer to be seen in any of the segregated parks. But perhaps Motley's most provocative and visually stunning critique of segregation in public green spaces is "Sunday in the Park" (1941), one of the first paintings in the South Side Community Art Center's permanent collection. The canvas is dominated by a muted green that colors nearly everything: trees, shrubbery, and grass are all green as one might expect, but so too are the tree trunks, park benches, men's suits, a woman's dress, a police officer's uniform, a nanny's apron, a horse, and a newspaper. The dominant aqua green suggests a natural landscape that swallows its visitors into a dreamlike, leisurely, even romantic escape from the urban Bronzeville scenes for which Motley is best known. Much as Frank Marshall Davis depicts the tall trees of Washington Park warding off the heat from the surrounding city, the cool colors of "Sunday in the Park" reflect a contrast with city life—perhaps even evoking the "combination of the fresh and healthy nature of the North with the restful, dreamy nature of the South" that Olmsted and Vaux sought.[102] Like the well-manicured trees in Motley's "Lawn Party" or the "pretzel crooked roads" in Davis's poem, tree trunks enclosed by wrought iron and the hedgerows' straight lines betray the constructedness of Olmsted and Vaux's landscaping of urban green environments, a reminder that the planned city grid is just beyond the park's borders.[103] And just as in Davis's poem, that environment still promotes community, even romance: couples lounge on a bench, lie in the grass, stand amid the shrubs, and, in the background, ride horseback.

But when one looks more closely at Archibald Motley's "Sunday in the Park," the viewer realizes that this pastoral scene appears to differ in one key way from "Lawn Party" and "The Picnic": instead of featuring park patrons that are entirely African American (though diverse in skin tone), "Sunday in the Park" undoubtedly depicts an interracial scene in which, as one critic has put it, "black figures are quietly marginalized in a world of whites."[104] Partially cropped by the frame, two figures stand out: the only African Americans in the park. At the far left of the canvas is the same burly African American bartender who appeared in "The Picnic"; there he was in the middle of the action, engrossed in conversation, but here he is alone and reading a newspaper. To the far right, meanwhile, is his bookend, so to speak: an African American nanny caring for a light-skinned blond child. Even when black Chicagoans temporarily escaped the urban jungle, Motley seems to suggest, they were still unable to break free from the alienating and isolating segregation that dictated the city's recreational and residential geography.[105]

Motley may hint at the pernicious effects of segregation in the South Side's public green spaces, but Wright practically bludgeoned his readers with them in his 1940 novel *Native Son*. Indeed, the book depicts a nightmare scenario in which New Deal-era recreational programs fail to reach the Black Belt's youth; referencing the book's main character, he called the South Side Boys' Club "an institution which tried to reclaim the thousands of Negro Bigger Thomases from the dives and the alleys of the Black Belt."[106] Bigger Thomas only briefly interacts with Washington Park in *Native Son*, but the pivotal scene suggests why Wright believed that New Deal-era reformers' efforts to salvage the Black Belt's Bigger Thomases with the help of public green spaces were pitifully insufficient and doomed to fail. When Bigger drives Mary Dalton and her boyfriend, Jan Erlone, (both white) "round and round the long gradual curves" of the park's winding thoroughfares for two hours, Bigger's "sense of the city and park fell away; he was floating in the car."[107] Much like Motley's "Sunday in the Park," the dreamlike interlude initially hints at the park's potential as a refuge for black Chicago, but its effect is fleeting at best. Bigger continues to drive the car—one of the "Race horse autos" that represent the overwhelming and potentially destructive urban environment in Davis's poem—and never experiences the park on foot despite spending hours there; he never fully escapes Chicago's urban environment, and just pages later he murders Mary.

Native Son's brief, dreamlike Washington Park scene is an outlier, and most of the novel reveals Wright's indebtedness to the Chicago School of Sociology's ideas about urban ecology, stuffed with references to the "jungle" of the urban environment that has inexorably led to Bigger committing murder.[108] When Bigger goes on the lam, he muses that hiding out in one of the many old, abandoned tenements on the South Side would "be like hiding in a jungle," and when he is captured, the fictional *Tribune* article describes Bigger as a threatening "jungle beast." Later, when Bigger stands trial for murder, his communist defense lawyer blames the "rank and choking vegetation of slums" in the "wild forest of our great cities" for Bigger's violence, likening him to a jungle animal.[109] So although Davis's poem and Motley's paintings suggest that places like Washington Park can be a refuge from the heat of "Chicago's Congo," Wright's novel unmistakably contends that the urban jungle is inescapable, defining Bigger's existence and determining his fate. There is no community, no common ground in *Native Son* as there is among the jazz singers in "The Picnic" or the down and out in "Washington Park, Chicago"—for Wright there is only alienation. Davis and Motley tend to see public green spaces as potential conduits for community building and solidarity, but according to Wright, Bigger Thomas is too "estranged from the religion and the folk culture of his race" to fully realize the potential of public green spaces like Washington Park for fostering that folk culture. Instead, because Bigger is "trying to react to and answer the call of the dominant [white] civilization whose glitter came to him through the newspapers, magazines, radios, movies, and the mere sight and sound of daily American life," Washington Park's pastoral offers only a brief reprieve at best.[110] That view helps explain why another of Chicago's most famous fictional juvenile delinquents, James T. Farrell's Studs Lonigan, is able to find repeated refuge in Washington Park's green spaces—just as reformers hoped children like him would—while Bigger Thomas remains unreformed by that same landscape: Studs is white and Bigger is black.[111]

The New Deal Builds Residential Green Space in the Black Belt

Not only did New Deal reformers' policies fail to challenge race segregation in public green spaces citywide, their most ambitious effort to reshape the South Side's urban landscape ultimately perpetuated rather than countered the environmental and social conditions that they—and Wright—believed produced working-class Bigger Thomases. When the Ida B. Wells Homes public housing project surrounding Madden Park opened in 1941, it represented an audacious attempt to combine residential and public green spaces into a synergistic whole. In the initial plan, less than one-third of the site's thirty-five acres was slated to be built on, leaving the rest for park space, lawns, trees, flower beds, sidewalks, and the like. It was a vision that reaffirmed and expanded reformers' long-held convictions about nature's potential for shaping working-class communities negatively affected by the densely built urban environment; the neighborhood had come a long way since Jackson Playground was dedicated fifteen years earlier. Named in honor of the civil rights activist who had helped fight for the creation of Madden Park more than a decade earlier, the Wells Homes had been proposed as a federal housing project as early as 1935, two years before Madden Park's pool was dedicated. Financing and bureaucratic delays slowed construction, however, and although the $9 million project did not open until much of the economy had rebounded from the worst days of the Great Depression, many black Chicagoans were still struggling to make ends meet. According to St. Clair Drake and Horace Cayton, half of all African American families "were dependent on some type of government aid for their subsistence" as the 1940s began, and African Americans made up approximately 40 percent of those on relief—about five times their proportion of Chicago's population.[112] Those factors alone make it clear why the Wells Homes' nearly 1,700 apartment units were in such high demand among working-class black Chicagoans; only a small fraction of the 18,000 applicants could be accepted. Although affordability alone made the Wells Homes attractive to prospective residents, many who lived there saw public housing as a way to achieve a more middle-class lifestyle. As one historian put it, "By quantitative income standards, the first residents of Wells were decidedly poor, but by social standing among African Americans, their tenancy in public housing marked a step up and planted many on a path out of poverty."[113] The early successes of public housing in Chicago should not be underestimated, but the roots of its ultimate failure would not have escaped Richard Wright: the Wells Homes, along with other Chicago Housing Authority (CHA) developments, were entirely segregated.

It should have come as no surprise that the Wells Homes were entirely segregated in part because Madden Park—itself entirely segregated like the extant surrounding neighborhoods—was central to the CHA's middle-class vision for residential and recreational landscapes of hope working in tandem to uplift the poorest sections of the Black Belt. A Chicago Park District report proudly claimed that Madden Park—as it had when Edgar Brown directed cleanup campaigns a decade earlier, in the depths of the Depression—fueled changes in the Wells Homes and beyond, saying that it was "the pride of its neighborhood . . . inspir[ing] people for a full square mile around it to bend to the job of maintaining green lawns, well preserved shrubbery and flower boxes in their own yards and parkways."[114] By the same token, a CHA pamphlet published soon after the Wells Homes opened rather optimistically contended,

> When you come upon one of Chicago's public housing developments, it is like stepping into a different world. Everywhere you see green—green of lawns, green of shrubbery, green of trees. Pleasant, vine-covered buildings stand in harmonious groups, with plenty of space left for sun and air and children's play. Everywhere you see gardens, and overhead stretches a sky that somehow looks bluer and sunnier than it did in the slums. For many of the people who live in these homes, this is the first time in their lives that they have known anything but dusty pavements and crowded rooms. They have learned, for the first time, what it is to handle damp earth, to see tiny green shoots poking up through the ground, to smell growing things. They buy seeds; they plant vines around their doorways, flowers in their window-boxes, shrubs and grass in their front yards. They are immensely proud of their lawns and flowers and of the whole community of homes.[115]

Of course, for many black Chicagoans, this close connection to nature was something that they had known in the South.

Whether they realized it or not, CHA officials fostered African Americans' ability to reconnect with and adapt their more rural, Southern folkways that could be difficult, though not impossible, to maintain in the Black Metropolis. Indeed, the Chicago-born playwright Lorraine Hansberry fictionalized just such a working-class migrant in the character of Lena Younger, the family matriarch in her play *A Raisin in the Sun*. Having moved to Chicago from the South years earlier, Younger wistfully says that the one thing she "always wanted" in the city was "a garden like I used to see sometimes at the back of the houses down home." It was a dream that was all but impossible to realize in the crowded tenements of Chicago's South Side, so impossible that a "little old plant that ain't never had enough sunshine or nothing" is as "close as [she] ever got to having" the garden she dreamed of.[116] Like her little plant, Lena perseveres, resisting her children's entreaties to spend her recently deceased husband's life insurance money elsewhere and instead opts to purchase a home in a predominantly white middle-class neighborhood where she hopes to have a chance to plant the garden she has deferred for so long. For most black Chicagoans, however, restrictive covenants, racial hostility, and financial barriers made her suburban dream a near impossibility. Instead, in the late 1930s and early 1940s, the Wells Homes were the CHA's attempt to bring a version of that middle-class, green suburban landscape to the urban Black Belt's working classes, connecting many migrants like Lena Younger back to their Southern roots and countering urban landscapes' ostensibly negative physical and moral impacts.[117]

Although Richard Wright would have no doubt dismissed the CHA's vision as fundamentally flawed and the promotional pamphlet as na-ively utopian, many early residents appear to have embraced the middle-class aesthetics that informed the Wells Homes and Madden Park. One man whose family moved into the Wells Homes in 1941 when he was only seven years old, for instance, recalled that life there was "a won-derful experience for us. . . . We had a little yard, it was a pretty good size yard. . . . We played softball in our backyard, and we played baseball in Madden Park [which] also had a swimming pool. So we could swim in the summer, and in the winter they would freeze a smaller playground— that's where I learned to ice-skate. We were poor kids in the community, but we didn't know we were poor, really. We had everything kids could ever want."[118] Similarly, the housing project's first manager echoed Edgar Brown's sentiments a decade earlier when he recalled,

> We made [residents] think that flowers were something fine. So all of them wanted to plant flowers. The place had flowers everywhere. Wher-ever there was a vacant space. . . . They had flowers in the windows, flowers everyplace. So much so that the people outside Wells who had thought it was going to deteriorate their neighborhood said after two or three years, "You've improved the neighborhood."[119]

His recollection that management encouraged those aesthetic values among residents has an undeniable air of paternalism about it, par-ticularly when many Wells Homes residents—like the fictional Lena Younger—surely thought "flowers were something fine" well before they moved into the public housing project. Nevertheless, the CHA helped give working-class migrants the space and the pride of place to realize those aesthetic ideals—both of which were in short supply in much of the Black Belt that was plagued with dilapidated housing.

Just as they did in multiple public green spaces across the city during the Great Depression, everyone from city and community leaders to resi-dents echoed reformers from the Great Migration years who believed it was critical to fund organized play to guide residents' experience in the Wells Homes. The CHA attempted to cultivate middle-class recreational opportunities for Wells Homes residents at Madden Park, actively building relationships with the Chicago Park District, the YMCA and YWCA, and Boy and Girl Scout troops—many of the same community institutions that had promoted youth camping since the Great Migration years and with which the *Defender*'s Bud Billiken Day had been allied since 1930 (see Figure 3.7). At least for some children who grew up in the Wells Homes, these strategies seemed to work. One man who moved to the Wells Homes in 1941 when he was ten years old recalled that Madden Park's many activities were like "a magnet to enhancing socialization among the children."[120] Indeed, Madden Park had finally matured into a fully functional community center by the time the Wells Homes opened, boasting "outdoor facilities available for swimming, softball, football, soccer, croquet, horseshoes, ice skating, track and field activity, games and nature lore," in addition to playing host to "open air movies, musical programs and water carnivals" in the summer months.[121] It was a far cry from the poorly funded and equipped space of a decade earlier.

In many ways, New Deal reformers intended Madden Park's and the Wells Homes' landscapes of hope to emulate and democratize the environmental aesthetics of the Michigan Boulevard Garden Apartments, a large-scale housing development just a few blocks northwest of Washington Park that Drake and Cayton had reported was already fast developing into a "major community institution" by the late 1930s.[122] It, too, was entirely segregated, but affordable only to the black middle classes. The Michigan Boulevard Garden Apartments complex was completed in 1929 and financed entirely by Julius Rosenwald (who also helped underwrite the Wabash YMCA and its camping program, among many other philanthropic ventures in black Chicago and well beyond). The company that managed the complex had "always considered it a semi-public undertaking" that "was conceived of as a demonstration to determine the possibilities and limitations of private capital in providing large-scale housing and community facilities for a moderate income group" that included railroad and postal workers.[123] The Great Depression's effects on the Black Belt had made it exceedingly difficult for the Michigan Boulevard Garden Apartments to turn a profit with even moderate rents, however, and by 1937—the same year the Madden and Washington Park pools opened—those managing the apartments had

Figure 3.7a. Cub Scouts meet in the Ida B. Wells Homes community center, March 1942. Farm Security Administration / Office of War Information Black-and-White Negatives, Prints and Photographs Division, Library of Congress, LC-USW3-000286-D, Jack Delano, photographer.

determined that financing and building costs made "an attempt to pro-vide desirable accommodations for the low-income group . . . beyond the scope of private enterprise."[124] All of which meant that, if commu-nity and city leaders wanted to provide similar housing to the working classes, the government would have to finance it. Robert Rochon Taylor, an African American migrant from Alabama who helped de-sign and manage the Michigan Boulevard Garden Apartments, surely took notice—he also helped oversee the construction of the Wells Homes after he became the first black board member for the CHA in 1938.

Both in terms of landscaping and recreational programming, Taylor and the CHA apparently modeled many aspects of the working-class Ida B. Wells Homes on the middle-class Michigan Boulevard Garden Apartments. But what exactly did these reformers believe was worth at-tempting to replicate? Much like Idlewild and other segregated resorts

Figure 3.7b. In Madden Park adjacent to the Ida B. Wells Homes, kindergarteners head to class, April 1942. Farm Security Administration / Office of War Information Black-and-White Negatives, Prints and Photographs Division, Library of Congress, LC-USW3–000649-D, Jack Delano, photographer.

outside the city, neither housing development challenged the South Side's segregation, instead attempting to uplift black Chicagoans in part with middle-class aesthetics that privileged green space. The "boulevard" and "garden" in the apartment complex's name connoted not only Chicago's tree-lined boulevards (despite the fact Michigan Avenue was not itself one of these boulevards) but also the pastoral ideal transplanted into the city. The corporation touted the complex's ample green space, noting that the buildings that housed approximately 1,600 residents in 421 units swallowed up

> an entire city block, comprising approximately six acres, three of which are laid out in a garden and courts. The building incloses [*sic*] an inner garden, landscaped with grass, trees, flowers, and shrubbery, which is visible from practically every apartment. Toward the north end of the garden, partially hidden by trees and shrubbery, is a well-equipped playground for the younger children who live in the apartments.[125]

This ample green space, enjoyed in a directed and orderly way, was integral to the Michigan Boulevard Garden Apartments' vision—hardly surprising given that the Wabash YMCA's George Arthur, the man after whom Camp Wabash would be named, served on the corporation's board of directors. Much like in the Wells Homes' adjacent green spaces, the complex even took on a camp-like atmosphere, as "recreational activities [were] provided by the building for children between the ages of 6 and 15" at the on-site playground.[126]

But the complex's design perhaps inadvertently turned the buildings into a virtual fortress, walling off the grassy interior courtyards from the surrounding neighborhood and reinforcing intraracial class divisions. Waters Turpin describes a lightly fictionalized version of the apartments in his 1935 novel O Canaan!: "With spacious outer and inner courts artistically landscaped and abundantly scattered with trees, shrubbery and play spaces for children, it was a complete community within itself—an oasis in the desert of the surrounding areas, which, like the rest of the South Side invaded by the horde, were fast deteriorating into slums."[127] Even by the late 1930s, it was evident that the accessibility of the Michigan Boulevard Garden Apartments' "oasis" was mostly limited to the black middle classes. By contrast, as the CHA's promotional pamphlet makes clear, reformers saw the publicly funded Wells Homes and Madden Park as a green "oasis" for the working classes. But no matter how much influence the Wells Homes and the Michigan Boulevard Garden Apartments may have had on surrounding neighborhoods, they themselves could only house a few thousand black Chicagoans, a mere fraction of the more than 275,000 African Americans who crowded into the city's segregated Black Belt by 1940.

Perhaps no South Sider's personal experience—and the art it produced—illustrates the impacts of residential race segregation spilling over into the South Side's public green spaces quite so well as that of the playwright Lorraine Hansberry. Born in Chicago in 1930, just three months before the first Bud Billiken Day and in the midst of increasing unemployment protests in and around Washington Park, Lorraine was the daughter of Carl and Nannie Hansberry, both migrants from the South.[128] Although Hansberry herself was not a Southerner, she fondly recalled Southern culture's influence on her experience of the South Side's public green space as a child growing up during the Great Depression:

Sometimes, when Chicago nights got too steamy, the whole family got into the car and went to the park and slept out in the open on blankets. Those were, of course, the best times of all because the grownups were invariably reminded of having been children in the South and told the best stories then. And it was also cool and sweet to be on the grass and there was usually the scent of freshly cut lemons or melons in the air. Daddy would lie on his back, as fathers must, and explain about how men thought the stars above us came to be and how far away they were.[129]

Family excursions like these, even amidst the turmoil of the Depression when the homeless also slept in Washington Park, enabled the park's green landscapes to help "the grownups" reconnect to their Southern folk culture and keep those memories alive in a new Chicago-born generation. Indeed, it is not difficult to see in Hansberry's own life story the inspiration for these themes and especially Lena Younger's character in *A Raisin in the Sun.* But that childhood idyll was broken in 1937, when Hansberry turned seven years old. The same year that Washington Park's pool opened and Frank Marshall Davis published his ode to the South Side's "community institution," the Hansberrys bought a home just a few blocks south of the park at 6140 South Rhodes Avenue, in a neighborhood bound by racially restrictive covenants. As a Chicago Park District study noted, their new home was in an area that, as the Black Belt had expanded, "had become a virtual island of whites [and] the white residents of this area were fearful that they would soon be isolated in an all-Negro district."[130]

White residents' resistance to the Hansberrys' move to the neighborhood directly south of Washington Park was swift and fierce. While Carl Hansberry was busy fighting a legal battle against the restrictive covenants that had barred African Americans from the neighborhood, Lorraine recalled that the house was surrounded by "howling mobs" that forced her mother into "patrolling our house all night with a loaded German luger, doggedly guarding her four children"; during the days, Hansberry herself was "spat at, cursed and pummeled in the daily trek to and from school." The Hansberrys eventually won their legal battle in 1940, the same year Wright published *Native Son,* when the Supreme Court invalidated the restrictive covenant on a technicality in *Hansberry v. Lee.* But Lorraine Hansberry recalled mostly "the cost, in emotional turmoil, time and money," visited on her family as the case took years to wind its way through the courts. The toll was particularly harsh on her father, and Hansberry was convinced the battle over their home near Washington Park led to her "father's early death as a permanently embittered exile in a foreign country when he saw that after such sacrificial efforts the Negroes of Chicago were as ghetto-locked as ever."[131] And yet the Hansberrys could have perhaps predicted that segregation would be the ultimate result of their blockbusting efforts: they and their fellow petitioners had submitted as evidence that Washington Park at the time was "used predominantly by colored people."[132] Already by 1941, when the Ida B. Wells Homes next to Madden Park opened to working-class African American families, the neighborhood just south of Washington Park that Carl Hansberry and his family had fought to integrate just four years earlier had once again become segregated: now nearly entirely African American instead of white. Neither the black working classes nor the professional classes were able to stem the tide of segregation that continued to wash over the South Side and its landscapes of hope in the Great Depression years.

The embitterment Hansberry expressed after racial segregation persisted despite a Supreme Court victory echoed both Richard Wright's dim outlook and the frustrations that W. E. B. Du Bois had expressed years earlier. In the early 1930s, Du Bois observed that segregation nationwide was "steadily growing worse" since the Great Migration. He contended that, in the depths of Depression, "faced by starvation and economic upheaval, and by the question of being able to survive at all . . . it is ridiculous not to see, and criminal not to tell, the colored people that they can not base their salvation upon the empty reiteration of a slogan" of integration.[133] The only viable solution to such widespread privation, Du Bois controversially argued, was to "voluntarily and insistently . . . organize our economic and social power, no matter how much segregation it involves."[134] Du Bois thundered, "We have got to renounce a program that always involves humiliating self-stultifying scrambling to crawl somewhere where we are not wanted; where we crouch panting like a whipped dog. We have got to stop this and learn that on such a program they cannot build manhood. No, by God, stand erect in a mud-puddle and tell the white world to go to hell, rather than lick boots in a parlor."[135]

In a sense, Washington Park became the Black Belt's most diverse, largest, and greenest unbroken stretch of Du Bois's metaphorical mud puddle during the 1930s. And for many black Chicagoans, public green spaces such as Washington Park became precisely the sorts of places where they could "stand erect" not only on days like Bud Billiken Day but also in the wake of the 1931 "Chicago massacre" that claimed the lives of three black communist protestors. They were at once segregated places that held back black Chicagoans and productive places where African Americans strengthened communal bonds while contesting community norms, retreating for recreation while mobilizing political action. At base, then, the Great Depression's economic and social challenges along with increasing racial segregation in many cases led many in the wider African American community to, as one historian has put it, seek to "build a self-sufficient, independent black community."[136] As W. E. B. Du Bois had concluded when he urged African Americans nationwide to "stand erect in a mud-puddle," it was perhaps the least worst option available to a community violently rebuffed virtually every time it fought for integration and one that many black Chicagoans had already explored in myriad landscapes of hope outside the city during the Great Migration years. From Idlewild to Camp Wabash, these places, too, were shaped by the devastating impacts of the Great Depression.

Back to Nature in Hard Times

S ETTING OUT JUST days after the *Defender*'s inaugural Bud Billiken Day parade in August 1930 at which Boy Scouts led the way, a teenaged South Side Boy Scout named William Van Arsdale hiked the roughly 250 miles from Chicago to Idlewild, a journey that took three full days. His knapsack full of sleeping blankets and other provisions, Van Arsdale reportedly arrived in the nation's premier African American resort town "well and hearty and of splendid deportment," a testament to the supposed virtues of rugged, healthful outdoor living and the values that South Side Boy Scout leaders had striven to instill in their members since the first African American troop had formed in Chicago a decade earlier.[1] But if Van Arsdale himself was "well and hearty," the same could not be said for the South Side as a whole, which was reeling from the closing of Jesse Binga's bank the month before and the rapid disappearance of the jobs that migrants had ventured north to find.

The financial shocks of the deepening depression had reverberated well beyond the South Side, and Van Arsdale arrived at an Idlewild that was somewhat less tranquil, remote, and insulated from the city's troubles than it had been in the Great Migration years. As Idlewild's postmaster put it that summer, "The panic following the failure of four banks in Chicago turned Idlewild upside down for a few days, as many Chicago depositors and a scattering of shareholders have summer homes here." Putting a positive spin on the growing crisis that was then only dimly apparent, she continued, "It seemed for a time that Idlewild would be a deserted village. But the call of the woods and the lakes won, and, with a few exceptions, all are here."[2] No doubt one of those few exceptions was Binga, who would be absolutely ruined by the Great Depression. Not only was he forced to close his bank and driven bankrupt that year but he was also indicted for embezzlement in 1931. Despite maintaining his innocence, he was convicted in 1933, began a three-year prison stint at the age of seventy, and eventually died a virtual pauper in the Black Metropolis he had helped build. Binga's story is more tragic than most: on top of his dramatic financial fall, his wife with whom he often retreated to Idlewild sued him for mismanaging their money and then died just months before his embezzlement conviction. But despite its larger-than-life proportions, Binga's story suggests the profound nature of the social and cultural upheaval the Great Depression produced and, by extension, the challenges facing the rural landscapes of hope that those of Binga's class had founded and expanded in the Great Migration years— from Idlewild to Camp Wabash and beyond.

The social and cultural disorder spurred by the Great Depression both motivated cross-class unity in the face of near-universal poverty and exposed class tensions in the rural Midwestern outposts that black Chicagoans had established in the Great Migration years, reflecting the same trends that played out in the Black Metropolis's public green spaces. Indeed, if Chicago's black cultural elite were eager to give many migrants and their children the same sort of edifying rural experiences they themselves enjoyed at resorts such as Idlewild, they were equally protective of their private rural retreats' class exclusivity. They struggled, in other words, to insulate places like Idlewild from the sort of class strife that roiled urban green spaces such as Washington Park in the early years of the Great Depression, fighting to keep the resort a nature-based leisure space for the well-off even as poverty rates in nearby communities skyrocketed. For the most part, they succeeded, and Idlewilders were no doubt eager to welcome the middle-class Boy Scout William Van Arsdale in 1930. But as jobs in the city's stockyards, steel mills, and kitchens disappeared, some migrants decided to head "back to the land" and attempt to make a living by subsistence farming or picking up odd jobs in the country. That move marked a return to a lifestyle similar to the one they had left behind in the South, turning the northern Michigan landscape into one of working-class labor rather than one of leisure for the black cultural elite. Despite Idlewilders' resistance, then, these macroeconomic factors in combination with longer term trends in transportation and leisure culture brought the resort town ever nearer to Chicago's spatial and social orbit in the Great Depression years—and to many of its attendant tensions and troubles. Indeed, the culture and politics of the city increasingly penetrated into rural green spaces such as Idlewild and Camps Wabash and Belnap, sometimes highlighting class tensions even as black Chicagoans worked to strengthen these places of community solidarity in the country, separate from whites.

City and country were bound as tightly together as ever, then, even as black Chicagoans' hybrid experience of the country that blended elements of North and South increasingly left behind any semblance of "primitive" landscapes. Idlewild had promoted a rustic luxury from its origins in the Great Migration years, but during the Great Depression—and particularly when the economy began to recover in the latter portion of the decade—its entertainment opportunities came to increasingly resemble those available in Chicago and Detroit. The same *Defender* society page article that noted William Van Arsdale's arrival in Idlewild gave some indication of the transition. Among the entertainment options for those who could spare the money and the time were beach parties, luncheons, and fashion shows with orchestral accompaniment that featured "bathing beauties, dancing dolls, hot dogs and lemonade booths, dancing, songs and a train of beautifully gowned women and girls moving about in a maze of colorful ensembles"—all attractions not so different than those offered at the *Defender*'s annual Bud Billiken Day parade and picnic in Washington Park.[3] Conspicuously absent in that account and many others was any mention of activities that more directly engaged with the surrounding natural environment, such as hiking, fishing, or boating; references to beauty were reserved for society women and not rural Michigan's "sheer physical beauty" about which W. E. B. Du Bois had rhapsodized in 1921.[4] By the same token, youth camps like Camp Wabash expanded their programming to encompass activities and content that had little or nothing to do with the surrounding natural environment, just as programming in Washington Park sought to address youth delinquency by any means necessary.

Nevertheless, Chicago's black cultural elite remained convinced that the natural environments themselves still mattered, despite the con-

tinued encroachment of city leisure practices into country places. Progressive-era beliefs that leisure activity in the rural outdoors made for
citizens healthier in mind, body, and character—assumptions that led
to the founding of various African American resorts and youth camps
during the Great Migration years—persisted into the 1930s, even taking
on a more urgent tone as reformers tried to head off youth delinquency
that they believed the Depression's widespread poverty only exacerbated. The very same beliefs undergirded the anti-delinquency efforts
undertaken in Madden and Washington Parks, but reformers remained
convinced that environments far from city vices were more effective in
guiding youth. The black cultural elite hoped that, on their return from
rural green spaces to the city's offices, factory floors, schools, and streets,
black Chicagoans would become better employers, employees, and students in the modern urban environment that very few were seriously
trying to escape permanently.

William Van Arsdale's hike to Idlewild from the South Side certainly
embodied the nature-based values Chicago's black cultural elite continued
to inculcate in young men and women during the Great Depression, but
his own biography also indicates the ways in which the hybrid meanings
of these environments began to change for a new generation of black
Chicagoans. Born in Chicago at the onset of the Great Migration to a
mother from Illinois and a migrant father from Mississippi, Van Arsdale
was an exception on his South Side block in living with his Northern-
born, middle-class grandparents (on his death, his grandfather was hailed
by the *Defender* as a "pioneer newspaperman among the Race"). They
lived on the edge of the Black Belt about a mile west of Washington Park,
where the 1930 census revealed that his neighbors were mostly working-
class African American families originally from Mississippi, Louisiana,
Texas, and Alabama, along with a smattering of working-class whites.[5]
But regardless of his family's class status, Van Arsdale was also characteristic of a young generation of black Chicagoans—many the children of
migrants from the South—that reached adulthood during the Depression
when migration had slowed to a trickle. Like Lorraine Hansberry, who
fondly recalled how Chicago's green space inspired grownups to tell stories about their youth in the South, Van Arsdale was part of a generation
connected to the South's more rural landscapes mostly through occasional trips back down South to visit extended family and through
the memories of parents and grandparents.[6]

Convinced that the Great Depression's impact on urban-dwelling youth only stood to increase juvenile delinquency rates, Chicago's black cultural elite doubled down on their efforts to maintain and even expand camping opportunities that exposed Chicago-born children like William Van Arsdale to rural landscapes. Without the federal New Deal funding that flowed to government entities such as the Chicago Park District and underwrote improvements to and programming in urban green spaces, reformers sought out charitable and philanthropic support when funds within the community fell short. Evidence abounds that young women and the working classes left nearly destitute by the economic catastrophe actually had greater access to these natural and landscaped environments than they had during the Great Migration years, thanks both to community institutions and ad hoc individual efforts that only grew into the 1940s. Although he never went to YMCA or Boy Scout camps like many of his adolescent friends, for instance, South Side resident Jimmy Ellis—who regularly spent summer days at Washington Park's pool and marched in the annual Bud Billiken parade— recalled spending a handful of summers in Bangor, Michigan, a small town about twenty-five miles due north of Camp Wabash. Thanks to a neighborhood man who took an interest in children, Ellis and about a half-dozen other boys traveled to Bangor, not to participate in any official program or activities, but "just to get out of the city [which was] nothing like the country, you know, which is more open air and everything."[7] For Chicago-born children like Ellis, a retreat to rural landscapes offered an experience wholly different from the urban environment that reformers worried would breed a generation of Bigger Thomases.

Although the majority of these camping opportunities available to black Chicagoans during the Great Depression remained segregated just as they had been in the Great Migration years, a handful of integrated camping options (both charitable and not) emerged late in the 1930s, revealing the promises and pitfalls of pursuing social equality in these landscapes of hope across the rural North. Indeed, black Chicagoans continued to work toward establishing and strengthening segregated institutions like Camp Wabash during the Depression, effectively following W. E. B. Du Bois's exhortation to "stand erect in a mud-puddle and tell the white world to go to hell, rather than lick boots in a parlor," in part because African Americans could control every aspect of the program.[8] This strategy proved doubly important because interracial charitable camps run by whites in the Cook County Forest Preserves had, at best, achieved mixed results in terms of providing an experience free from urban ills. At worst, they were plagued by racial discrimination and hatred. The YWCA's integration efforts in a Forest Preserves camp in the late 1930s were much more successful thanks to socially engineering a small group of campers amenable to interracial experiences, but even they had to contend with nearby rural Cook County residents' racial prejudices that sometimes boiled over into violence just as they did at Jackson Park beach. The Cook County Forest Preserves came within reach of a broader swath of black Chicagoans mainly because of improved transportation options (better and cheaper automobiles as well as extended streetcar and bus lines) and Chicago's growing geographical footprint that effectively brought the Black Belt ever closer to the ring of green space that encircled the city. But officials posted signs that read "For Colored People Only" on these public lands, ostensibly to ensure African Americans' safety in places where whites would not tolerate interracial contact. For many black Chicagoans, the racial climate in these rural green spaces would have not only closely resembled what they confronted at the city's parks and beaches but it would have also been an all-too-familiar reminder of the Jim Crow South they had left behind in search of landscapes of hope.

Nature and Class at Idlewild during the Depression

Although many resort goers tried to put on a brave face, an escape to Idlewild did not mean an escape from the effects of the Great Depression. Leisure retreats required wealth that was vanishing with startling rapidity in the early 1930s, and as Jesse Binga's case so vividly illustrated, the black cultural elite fell on hard times along with members of the working classes. Signs of a sluggish economy had been evident to Idlewilders as early as 1927, when the local newspaper noted that, although the vast majority of the premier resort town's cottages were occupied, "surounding [sic] resorts report a falling off in attendance due to money depression."[9] By 1930, just months after the stock market crash, the *Defender* article that celebrated William Van Arsdale's arrival attempted to frame declining summer attendance in a positive light by emphasizing the presence of stalwart Idlewilders: "Notwithstanding all expectations to the contrary," the resort town's postmaster wrote, "this has been one of the best seasons that Idlewild has ever had, for, with the transients falling off, the summer cottages, the bone and sinew of Idlewild, became active along all lines of entertainment with splendid results."[10] By January 1931, however, it had become difficult to maintain such optimism as the Great Depression's profound effects on Idlewild were becoming ever clearer: the local newspaper noted, "Idlewild reports little sickness, except that of the purse," and with "taxes due and payable," one could only "hope they will be paid."[11] At the conclusion of that year's summer season, despite boosterist assertions (once again) that it was "perhaps the best we have ever had," Idlewild's postmaster admitted that "sales were almost at a standstill" and went on to say that for those who were able to visit, Idlewild was a refuge from the chaos in the city: "Surely the vacationists were in sore need of [rest and recreation]," she wrote, "for it had been a terribly hard year outside as well as here, and to bring Idlewild up to an approximation of its standard was the problem."[12] It was during that same "terribly hard year," after all, that rising unemployment led to intensifying communist protests in Washington Park and the so-called Chicago massacre roiled the South Side—all of which had undermined the legitimacy of Chicago's black cultural elite, many of whom vacationed at Idlewild.

Indeed, for those in the black cultural elite who could still afford a leisure retreat to Idlewild and other similar landscapes of hope, surely one of the added attractions of such escapes in the early years of the Great Depression was that, despite the vulnerability to hard economic times, such retreats enabled them to remain largely insulated from the sorts of political unrest the working classes fomented in Washington Park. For men like J. C. Austin and Louis B. Anderson, that attraction would have been especially important. When Austin (who led Pilgrim Baptist Church, then one of the largest African American congregations in Chicago and the birthplace of gospel music) escaped to Idlewild, he was also leaving behind his futile attempts to win over the working classes from a soapbox in Washington Park; there were no working-class communists to challenge his authority in rural Michigan.[13] By the same token, Louis B. Anderson (Chicago's second African American alderman, following Oscar De Priest in the Black Belt's Second Ward) was escaping the black communists who protested outside his Chicago home in 1931; he did not have to listen to their demands while he relaxed by the lake.[14]

In part simply because many in the first generation of Idlewilders were growing old and dying and in part because the Great Depression upset black Chicago's established class structure, it was also at about this time that a new generation began frequenting the resort town. Prominent, long-time residents like Dr. Daniel Hale Williams and author Charles Chesnutt died in 1931 and 1932, respectively, for instance, and Jesse Binga was convicted of embezzlement the following year. Despite these challenges, Idlewild survived and even prospered in part because it attracted prominent newcomers: among the most notable regular resort goers during the 1930s were Arthur Mitchell, the first black Democrat elected as a congressman anywhere in the nation, who served from 1935–1943 (succeeding Oscar De Priest); Dave Kellum, who ran the *Defender*'s Bud Billiken program and organized the annual parade and picnic; John Sengstacke, *Defender* general manager and nephew of founder Robert Abbott; Ed Wright, who served as county commissioner and Chicago's first black ward committeeman; and the "Jones Boys" (Mac, Ed, and George), who were perhaps Chicago's wealthiest and most renowned gambling kingpins. Idlewild also began attracting national celebrities during the Great Depression, both to vacation and to perform: trumpeter Louis Armstrong vacationed there well into the 1930s, and heavyweight champion Joe Louis, at the height of his fame, spent some of his summer days at Idlewild before appearing at the Bud Billiken Day parade and picnic in Washington Park.[15]

Idlewild's ability to attract national celebrities in the 1930s offers some small indication of how the resort town's character continued to change in the Depression decade, bringing ever more city attractions to the growing rural outpost. Despite the evaporation of wealth on the South Side, the continued rise of automobility had made Idlewild more accessible to a much broader cross-section of African Americans, particularly as the economy slowly recovered in the late 1930s. No longer were resort goers as bound to train travel as they had been when Idlewild was founded. Indeed, consistent with broader national trends, rural tourism to northern Michigan grew across the board in this period, and the automobile's increased prevalence enabled even more city dwellers to enjoy its natural pleasures: road conditions improved and automobiles became faster and more reliable, drastically reducing the amount of time needed to reach formerly remote destinations. The relative ease and speed of travel also meant that it was easier than ever for visitors to spend only weekends at Idlewild, rather than several weeks or the entire summer. Although economic hardship appears to have curtailed the visits of these "weekenders" or "transients," who were perhaps less well insulated from financial ruin than the uppermost classes, particularly in the early years of the Depression, a 1930 *Defender* article still noted that it was "remarkable how much recreation one can get out of a weekend trip up here, away from everything that sours city life, with its hustle and bustle. To get the tang of the air, the odors of the wild flowers and a vision of a lake dancing in ripples is a treat indeed."[16]

Despite the flowery rhetoric lauding the natural environment that matched Du Bois's words nearly a decade earlier, Idlewild's increasing accessibility and size meant that in many ways it was coming to resemble a miniature version of the cities that resort goers sought to escape. There had always been elements of the city's social refinement at Idlewild, but gradually Idlewild contrasted less and less with the city's "hustle and bustle." Even the town's built environment—while not approaching the "brute might of the thing" that Du Bois had been so relieved to escape a decade earlier—came to more closely approximate the city's.[17] A *Defender* society page article from 1931, for instance, noted, "The sultry days are responsible for the great exodus of prominent personages who are numbered among the elite. The summer resorts, governed by the three S's—sun, sand and sea—are being filled with the fashionable set. They are like magnets, drawing the society groups in throngs." It went on to describe one consequence of such popularity: "Every highway is jammed with cars loaded with baggage and filled with families. Some are trying to get away from the crowds, and others are trying to get with them."[18] In contrast to Du Bois's exhortations, increasingly it seemed that those who retreated to Idlewild were trying to get with the crowds. Five years later, when Idlewild had added Baptist and Seventh Day Adventist churches to complement the lone church that had served resort goers through the 1920s, a *Defender* article noted, "The atmosphere of the city blend[ed] harmoniously with the beauties of nature, giving a perfect background and tone to any affair."[19] No longer casting Idlewild as a retreat isolated from modern city life, the writer instead figured the resort town as an ideal hybrid, offering a perspective similar to Jimmy Gentry's treatment of Washington Park's new swimming pool. Seen this way, Idlewild became a blend of natural and landscaped environments that emphasized the social, relegating nature to a backdrop rather than the main attraction. During the post–World War II migration years, this trend became even more glaringly apparent. One visitor went so far as to liken Idlewild's social scene in the 1950s to that of the Stroll, claiming, "While we might have been in the country, there was clearly as much gaiety—loud, raucous, and sometimes dangerous gaiety—as there was along any strip of bars and clubs in urban Negro America."[20]

Despite these undeniable changes, many resort goers and the promotional materials that brought them to Idlewild still mimicked the tone of Great Migration-era accounts like those of W. E. B. Du Bois that emphasized the resort town's beautiful and healthy natural environment, which ostensibly resulted in soundness of body, mind, and spirit. Given the economic and social turmoil associated with the urban landscapes they were escaping in the Depression decade, nature's tranquility perhaps seemed particularly attractive to resort goers. Just before the 1929 market crash, for instance, a *Pittsburgh Courier* correspondent marveled that "nature has been so lavish in her gifts to the entire section, that a few minutes from anywhere, there are beautiful lakes, beautiful walks and the peace and calm which no man-made resort can duplicate." Echoing Du Bois, she wrote that at Idlewild there were thousands of African Americans who preferred "knickers and linen, Indian trails and dirt roads, cabin cottage and tent to places more sophisticated" and were willing to travel great distances to the "Michigan woods instead of resorts nearer their home."[21] Even with Idlewild's expansion and increased popularity, it was not difficult for residents to peacefully enjoy the eight miles of lake shoreline; according to a 1930 *Courier* article, "Forests of hemlock, pine and spruce [which] add to the attractiveness of the spot and despite the hundreds of cottages, unless one is on the lake, it is difficult to see more than a dozen at once, so tucked away are they in the recesses of the woods."[22] Born in northern Alabama before migrating to Chicago in the 1890s, the widow of county commissioner Ed Wright seems to have agreed. As she told an interviewer in 1938, "I love the country. I usually spend at least three months up [at Idlewild]. I have friends go up and spend a week or ten days at a time with me. They always seem to enjoy it about as much as I do."[23]

Even as late as 1940, an advertising campaign undertaken by the Chamber of Commerce and the Idlewild Lot Owners Association echoed the resort town's earliest promotional efforts and followed broader national trends in emphasizing the natural environment as the primary selling point for prospective visitors and landowners. One advertisement featured a lake scene with evergreen trees and summed up the attraction of the leisure escape: "It's scenery like this that makes people leave home and spend the Summer in Idlewild, and it's the perfect fishing, boating and swimming that brings the many thousand vacationers back to Idlewild every year."[24] Another advertisement mentioned the recently established Manistee National Forest that abutted the resort town, telling prospective vacationers, "If you like hiking or are a lover of nature, early morning saunters into the surrounding woods will reveal to you deer and other wild life which thrive and multiply under the strict protection of the State."[25] Indeed, one young visitor recalled that his grandparents approached the wildlife surrounding Idlewild as "naturalists: they wanted to record species, observe does with their young, count the points on antlers."[26] There was plenty of wildlife that had naturally returned to the region since its intensive logging decades earlier, but other human interventions were more obvious: by 1940 the lakes and streams near Idlewild had been stocked with fish for years, and more recent New Deal-era wildlife management and conservation efforts had consciously worked to make such rural retreats even more attractive to recreational tourists. Across Lake County, millions of pike perch, brook trout, brown trout, rainbow trout, black bass, perch, bluegills, and grayling were stocked, which no doubt influenced an ad in the 1940 advertising campaign promoting Idlewild as a "Fisherman's Paradise . . . situated in a county where there are 156 lakes and 46 trout streams"; it was much more than an angler could ever hope to find in the stocked Washington Park lagoons.[27] But even if a vacationer was uninterested in those myriad recreational activities, yet another 1940 advertisement reminded prospective visitors that at Idlewild you could "Keep Cool As a Penguin," and that compared to the city, the resort town offered a "refreshing change of climate . . . cool, fresh air, just the right temperature for perfect comfort."[28]

The 1940 advertising campaign was apparently a rousing success, effectively promoting the resort town to a new generation of African Americans, many of whom had either left the South long ago or been born in the North. In just a few months, the Chamber of Commerce was pleased to have already received "more than 1500 letters of inquiry" from prospective landowners, and Irene McCoy Gaines—prominent Chicago clubwoman and president of the Lot Owners Association—proudly asserted that "Brown America was made aware, as never before, of Idlewild, 'The Fisherman's Paradise,' 'Nature's Perfect Health Resort.' " Gaines went on to echo the sort of glowing praise Du Bois had lavished on Idlewild's natural splendor in the pages of the *Crisis* nearly two decades earlier, saying that even "those who had never heard of Idlewild were enticed to come and enjoy our crystal nights and sparkling stars, our lakes and streams, our great pine forests, and last but not least the great fellowship which is found here." She concluded her report to the Lot Owners Association by writing, "We are heartily glad at this season for all the hundreds of resorters who have not had the opportunity of sunshine and the out-of-doors for long, long months, and now the beauty of it all is available to them."[29] But there remained some question as to just for whom Gaines and the Lot Owners Association wanted Idlewild's "great fellowship" and "the beauty of it all" to be available as the resort emerged from the depths of the Great Depression.

It seems likely that the 1940 advertising campaign was in part a response to the fact that nearby residential developments began attracting a more working-class—and poverty-stricken—element from Midwestern cities as the 1930s wore on, heightening the very class tensions Idlewilders hoped to escape during the Great Depression. In 1930, a *Pittsburgh Courier* reporter laid bare this simmering class antagonism, baldly stating, "If hard times and unemployment are prevalent throughout Negro America, there were few evidences of their ravages" at Idlewild, which possessed an "unmistakable class and gentility" in part because it was "too far from the cities to attract undesirables and the character of the permanent investors who own their cottages and are determined to maintain the standards of the place keep it on a high plane."[30] As early as the mid-1920s, Idlewilders had subtly discouraged working-class African Americans from attempting to settle there. The postmaster, for instance, accurately noted that "Idlewild is an ideal summer resort and a beautiful place in Indian Summer. Surrounded by lakes and woods it has never failed to please the vacationist. But its best friends would scarcely recommend it for a poor man's winter residence. The winters are long and cold, resort activities are at a standstill and there are no nearby factories to provide employment. Living expenses are high—at least they are not cheap. It costs as much to live here as elsewhere and there are few 'jobs' to be had, at least at present."[31] This is not to say that more well-off Idlewilders callously ignored less fortunate Lake County residents as the Depression deepened and there were even fewer jobs to be had, however. Just a few months later, for instance, as the holiday season approached, Idlewilders banded together to offer relief in the form of food, clothing, and even money for those most in need. As the local newspaper put it, "There are many in Idlewild who depend upon common labor and in these days of scarcity of work, it is refreshing to note the spirit of helpfulness manifested."[32]

Yet for many long-time Idlewilders, nearby working-class settlements remained a source of frustration, and even if they were not so bold as to call them "undesirable," many euphemistically referred to these new-comers as a "less progressive" element in their community.[33] When Gaines and the Lot Owners Association launched their publicity cam-paign in 1940, the choice to focus on Idlewild's natural environment as its primary attraction and downplay its burgeoning Stroll-like nightlife was perhaps an attempt to cement its status as a landscape of hope exclu-sively for the black cultural elite, not the members of the working classes whose behavior and protests in Washington Park could cause such con-sternation. Nearly a decade before the Depression hit, advertisements for the nearby Woodland Park residential development had told prospective working-class lot buyers that they could "be independent, have a home, raise and grow your own food, sell enough to do well, and bring up your children in the right way."[34] But it was not until the Depression that these sorts of developments proliferated, drawing significant interest from those in the working classes who had lost their jobs or wanted to opt out of punishing jobs in the city's stockyards, steel mills, and kitchens. Land developers catered to this working-class clientele in part by adver-tising on Chicago streetcars and raffling off lots as door prizes, selling five-acre plots where one could eke out a living subsistence farming with a few cows and chickens.[35] Perhaps most attractive to Southern migrants who had been hit hardest by catastrophic unemployment in Chicago and other Midwestern urban centers, the broader "back to the land" movement in the Great Depression offered an opportunity to return to a more agricultural, rural lifestyle with which many were familiar. For these new working-class Lake County residents, northern Michigan became a year-round landscape of labor, not a summer leisure escape; it was a shift that not only threatened to undermine the exclusivity that was part of Idlewild's attraction to Chicago's black cultural elite but also left the region much more vulnerable to poverty. Subsistence living off the land in Lake County had turned out to be less than Edenic: by 1935, nearly half the year-round residents of Idlewild's Lake County were on some sort of government relief, more than in any surrounding county. One longtime resident of the area recalled that, during the Great Depression, "The people out in the townships couldn't even afford to go to the nightclubs; they were out in the fields picking beans, cherries, and peaches so they could eat through the winter."[36]

While the working classes drawn to rural Michigan in the hopes of subsisting on the land found themselves hungry and poverty stricken in the Depression—forced to pick the produce of Michigan's fruit belt to eke out a living, not unlike John Steinbeck's Joad family in *The Grapes of Wrath*—Idlewild resort goers forged a very different relationship with food and the land. In 1935, the very same year during which nearly half of Lake County residents were on relief, the resort seemed to have turned the corner: "Idlewild has just closed the best season since 1929," the local newspaper declared, "Thousands visited us and the general returns from all sources were very encouraging. Many sales of valuable properties were made and new homes are already in the course of erection."[37] Symbolic of the resort town's recovery as a vacation destination that summer, Mamie Ellis Kelly's garden was flourishing. Kelly, Irene McCoy Gaines's mother, was typical of the long-time Idlewild residents of the black cultural elite who must have been relieved to see the resort town weather the storm of the Depression: she had joined the Chicago Urban League and YWCA after migrating to Chicago in 1898. She wrote to her daughter in Chicago that she had two dozen eggs fresh "from the barn yard" and that although she was dead tired "from spading and putting in my garden" at Idlewild, she was "really getting a kick out of it"—she had planted seeds from Gaines and neighbors, ranging from "snap beans squash onions cucks [cucumbers] sweet corn sweet potatoes mustard green pop corn watermelons pumpkins beets carrots down to peanuts."[38] In a letter a few days later, she wrote, "Everyone [was] going wild over their gardens. I have planted one hundred and one things. I hope you will not have to buy many vegetables this summer from watermelons on down to red and green pepper."[39] Although she expressed hope that vegetables would not have to be purchased, there is little doubt that the family could have afforded them.

In many ways, Gaines's gardening—and that of other Idlewilders—represented both the realization of Booker T. Washington's ideal relationship with nature transplanted to the rural North and the real-life fulfillment of Lena Younger's middle-class dream of having a backyard garden in Lorraine Hansberry's *A Raisin in the Sun*. In 1901, more than a decade before the Great Migration was underway in earnest, Washington had written in *Up from Slavery*, "Somehow I like, as often as possible, to touch nature, not something that is artificial or an imitation, but the real thing," and went on to describe a temporary escape from the modern world not that different from the escape Idlewild offered. In the garden he cultivated outside his office at the Tuskegee Institute, Washington would "spend thirty or forty minutes in spading the ground, in planting seeds, in digging about the plants," activities that gave him "rest and enjoyment" and the feeling that he was "coming into contact with something that [was] giving [him] strength for the many duties and hard places that await[ed him] out in the big world."[40] Indeed, Washington valued gardening so much that he pitied "the man or woman who has never learned to enjoy nature and to get strength and inspiration out of it."[41] Now, in the midst of the Great Depression that forced myriad "duties and hard places" onto Idlewilders, it was little wonder that its residents—steeped as they were in Washington's logic of racial uplift grafted onto a Northern landscape—took such solace in their gardens. Those gardens, were, after all, the realization of Lena Younger's lofty aspirations in a landscape of hope: a sign they had made it. But as the poverty of surrounding rural Lake County suggested, for many in black Chicago's working classes left hungry by the Great Depression, vegetable gardens could take on a much different, more urgent resonance.

Camps Wabash and Belnap Weather the Great Depression

Planted and harvested with the help of campers themselves, Camp Wabash's two-acre truck garden began in 1929 as the economic slowdown was already evident; while planning for that summer season, a YMCA official noted that "the unemployment situation in Chicago is becoming acute and is being felt at this time by the colored population" and gave control of a Camp Subsidy Fund to Alderman Louis B. Anderson, an Idlewild regular.[42] Indeed, as the Great Depression deepened in the early 1930s, the Wabash Y turned its attention to providing services to "the so-called 'underprivileged boy' . . . , the poorest and most neglected boy in the community," many of whom had families so destitute that they found it difficult to feed them properly.[43] The large truck garden that by 1931 had expanded to three acres served a dual purpose then. On the one hand, it fed undernourished young boys who—according to Washingtonian logic—would benefit physically, mentally, and even spiritually from the food they cultivated: a 1937 promotional pamphlet touted the fact that "fresh vegetables are served daily from the camp and nearby farms." On the other hand, YMCA officials noted that the on-site farm helped enable "the camp fees to be the smallest of any of the many camps in Chicagoland."[44]

In many ways, then, Camp Wabash's garden was a hybrid landscape that incorporated both labor and leisure, transforming Booker T. Washington's Southern-inflected philosophy to address the privation wrought by the Great Depression among the products of the Great Migration. Providing food for campers summer after summer for two decades, the truck garden even produced enough vegetables to ship back to Chicago for use in the Wabash YMCA's cafeteria, where it fed both lodgers and working-class men who stopped in for a meal. By the 1940s, when campers were also enjoying fresh milk from local farms, camp organizers had planted fruit trees, and the campers themselves planted and harvested so many fresh vegetables that hundreds of quarts of food were canned each year. Young boys and girls enjoyed plenty of leisure activities during their stays at Camp Wabash, of course, but their gardening more closely resembled labor born of economic necessity—like the subsistence farming of working-class year-round Lake County, Michigan, residents or even of Southern sharecroppers—than it did the leisure activity Mamie Ellis Kelly had taken up at Idlewild and got such a "kick out of." Indeed, photographs of campers cultivating Camp Wabash's truck garden are eerily reminiscent of images of laborers in Tuskegee's demonstration gardens and of sharecroppers working in the fields (see Figure 4.1). For campers who had been born and raised in Chicago, this would have been a new experience, working in the fields as did many of their parents and grandparents, who fled the South in part to escape this sort of labor. The difference was that these campers were not only working on land in the North that was owned by African Americans but that their labors were also supplemented by a host of leisure activities. By the same token, campers' parents had actively chosen this temporary escape to the country for them, but like many choices made in the South, it was a choice that for many was born of economic necessity.[45]

Figure 4.1. Working in the truck garden at Camp Wabash, circa 1930. Chicago History Museum, ICHi-79114. Photographer unknown.

As Camp Wabash's truck garden indicated, the Wabash YMCA essentially turned into a relief organization during the depths of the Great Depression, expanding and tailoring the camp's operations to minister to the needs of working-class boys *and* girls whose families had been devastated by the South Side's dire unemployment situation. Enlisting the support of aldermen and other community leaders to identify and recruit more than 300 boys to camp in both 1929 and 1930, the Wabash Y more than doubled the previous record total of summer campers. But camp operations expanded even more dramatically when officials effectively doubled the pool of prospective campers by adding camping periods for South Side girls and young women. Camp Hammond had been closed for years, and it was painfully apparent to reformers in the black cultural elite that "Negro women and girls on the south side fare much worse than the boys, for the Y.W.C.A. branch on S. Pkwy. has almost no recreational equipment, and no camp"; it was little surprise that a

1930 poll of social workers repeatedly cited "camp opportunities for girls" as one of the greatest needs for the South Side African American community.[46] Camp Wabash had hosted girls affiliated with various South Side Sunday schools since at least 1929, but it was not until the summer of 1933 that girls began regularly attending Camp Wabash following the creation of a women's division in the Wabash Y. That year, nearly three dozen girls paid their fees by raising money through social events like teas, and by 1935, over half of the more than five hundred campers who spent part of their summers at Camp Wabash were women and girls—a trend that held throughout the late 1930s and early 1940s.[47]

Few of these campers paid their fees in full. Reformers in the black cultural elite, who themselves often financially struggled to afford their retreats to resorts such as Idlewild, were increasingly forced to turn to funding sources outside the black community to keep camps afloat during the Great Depression. Wabash YMCA officials did still enlist the aid of local businesses in funding the camp, planning a fundraiser at the popular Regal Theater on the South Side's Stroll (25 cents of every ticket sold to the show on "Camp Wabash Nite" was to be contributed to the camp subsidy fund) and helping organize a newsboys contest with the *Defender* in which the winners were sent on an all-expenses-paid trip to camp. But with money tight across the whole South Side and the Wabash YMCA deluged with requests from both parents and community organizations to offer camping opportunities to children whose families were much too poor to pay the fees themselves, officials relied most heavily on charitable and philanthropic funding to maintain and even expand camp programming. More than half the children who retreated to Camp Wabash in the mid- to late 1930s had their fees (which ranged from $8–$13 per camping period) subsidized or paid in full by charitable or philanthropic organizations. Sometimes, virtually all the campers were subsidized: in 1936, for instance, when an estimated 10,000 South Siders were on relief and more than 70 percent of boys served by either the camp or in-city summer programming were on relief, only 36 of 218 boys paid their fees in full.[48]

In Chicago, a robust assortment of charitable and philanthropic organizations—the Provident Hospital Child Welfare fund, the Illinois Children's Home and Aid Society, the Elizabeth McCormick Memorial Fund, and the Golden Gloves boxing tournament fund (a *Chicago Tribune* charity) among others—prioritized camping opportunities for black

South Siders, but none helped more than the charitable organization founded by Julius Rosenwald. Rosenwald, the Sears, Roebuck & Company magnate and Tuskegee Institute board member whose financial support and public backing had been so integral to the founding of the Wabash YMCA and many other African American YMCAs across the country, died in 1932, but charitable donations from the Rosenwald Fund were integral to the camp's survival in the mid-1930s. In 1934, for instance, a $1,500 contribution kept the camp afloat and accounted for nearly half its income; the following year, a $725 donation allowed the camp to stay open an additional two weeks and serve dozens if not hundreds more boys. Having weathered the worst of the Great Depression, Camp Wabash even undertook a series of capital improvement projects—planting trees, improving the lake beach, reroofing camp cottages, and adding electric lights—with the aid of charitable and philanthropic support in the late 1930s. By 1940, officials had planned an ambitious five-year $25,000 expansion that would more than double Camp Wabash's capacity to accommodate two hundred children at a time.[49]

Camp Wabash undeniably stepped up to serve a community devastated by the Great Depression, but in training their sights so directly on helping those unable to pay camping fees, officials perhaps unintentionally highlighted the intraracial class tensions rooted in the Great Migration years that—as the simmering discord in Washington Park and even rural Lake County, Michigan, revealed—persisted during the 1930s. The fresh produce from the camp's truck garden contributed to the "healthful summer environment" that inspired the director of Provident Hospital's children's clinic to rave that twenty-two boys sent to Camp Wabash came back to Chicago "in splendid condition and [were] all aglow from their experiences as well as much improved physically."[50] No doubt it also helped feed the "undernourished" boy dubbed "Little Chief Oatmeal" because he consumed so much of the breakfast food.[51] But in 1935, when Mamie Ellis Kelly and other Idlewilders were "going wild over their gardens," Camp Wabash had become almost exclusively a camp for these "undernourished" and "problem children"—more than 75 percent of the campers fit that description that year. It was a development motivated by the widespread poverty that had devastated the South Side and forced camp leaders to eliminate the lone period of fully paid campers when, in a stark reminder of intraracial class strife that continued and in some cases even worsened during the Great Depression, many parents began sending their boys to the more expensive Boy Scout Camp Belnap "because of the feeling that they did not want them to go with the underprivileged group."[52]

While Camp Wabash's truck garden pointed to an evolution toward a landscape of leisure *and* labor for underprivileged campers who planted and harvested fresh vegetables during the Great Depression, Camp Belnap largely remained a recreational landscape that followed the scouting tradition established decades earlier. Camp Wabash officials used the truck garden in part as a way to help keep camp fees as low as possible, but there is little evidence that the Boy Scouts made similar changes to the camping program or significantly altered their fee structure to accommodate Chicago's widespread poverty. Likely financially insulated by its more middle-class clientele and its direct association with the Boy Scouts' adjoining white Camp Owasippe, Camp Belnap appears to have relied much less on charitable and philanthropic subsidies during the Depression than did Camp Wabash, and camp fees point to a small but tangible class difference from Camp Wabash that was already evident by the late 1920s. An eleven-day outing to Camp Wabash, transportation included, cost only $10 to $12 in 1929, whereas a full two-week escape to Camp Belnap cost $16.50 including transportation. By 1936, the year after Camp Wabash eliminated the full-fee camping period, the difference was even more stark. Camp Belnap's fee had risen to $17.50 for a two-week period including transportation costs, while Camp Wabash's fees had fallen (even disregarding charitable subsidies) to $11 for a twelve-day period for boys and $8 for a one-week period for girls, both including transportation costs. The cost was hardly a deterrent, however, to camp participation: in the early to mid-1930s, approximately one hundred African American Boy Scouts annually retreated to Camp Belnap—nearly 20 percent of the 500 to 600 African American Boy Scouts in about thirty-three Chicago troops—and made up around 8 percent of the boys at Camp Owasippe in a given summer, slightly outpacing African Americans' share of Chicago's population.[53]

The fairly clear class divide between Camps Wabash and Belnap did not mean, however, that Boy Scouts were drawn exclusively from black Chicago's wealthiest black families: the fact that troops were formed from residents of the Ida B. Wells Homes public housing development when it opened in 1941 is evidence enough of that. Indeed, Chicago's African American Scout leaders were well aware that camp fees were prohibitively expensive for a large part of the population they ultimately wanted to reach, and for those children unable to pay, they promoted shorter, more affordable excursions to Cook County's Forest Preserves, often to Camp Kiwanis on the South Side. In 1931, for instance, a five-day summer camp in the Forest Preserves was conducted for the first time "in order to make it possible for youngsters who could not afford to go to the summer camp in Michigan to get a brief stay at camp at a very inexpensive rate. The charge to each boy was $3.50, the balance of the cost being subsidized by the Chicago Tribune," and several black Scouts from the segregated Douglas Division took day hikes in the Forest Preserves.[54] These shorter excursions were popular as well: in 1935 and 1936, black Boy Scouts accounted for between 5 and 8 percent of participants in day trips and overnight hikes to the Forest Preserves, not far off from African Americans' percentage of Chicago's population. Similar to the fundraising teas that girls organized to help pay for a trip to Camp Wabash, there were also opportunities for black Boy Scouts to work to raise their own camp fees. In 1935, the same year some parents began sending their children to Camp Belnap rather than Camp Wabash, Colgate Palmolive cooperated with the Douglas Division scouts, allowing boys to collect coupons for soap products and redeem them for an all-expenses paid trip to either Camp Kiwanis in the Forest Preserves (a five-day stay) or, for more coupons, Camp Belnap (a two-week stay). Charles Davis recalls raising money for his camp experience with a similar fundraising scheme that no doubt capitalized on Scouts' high visibility in community events such as the annual Bud Billiken parade, "by going door-to-door and selling tickets to . . . a talent show that the troop put on" at Good Shepherd church.[55]

The Camping Experience in the 1930s

The black cultural elite built on rationales for leisure retreats in nature developed during the Great Migration years, but the stakes were higher with poverty rates so high, particularly in the early to mid-1930s before Franklin Roosevelt's New Deal programs began to have a tangible impact on the South Side. Although place remained important, sometimes nature was pushed to the margins as it was in Washington and Madden Parks. For some reformers, the objective was simply to get children away from the city's negative influences, whether or not nature factored prominently into the camping program. As one Wabash Y official stressed during the summer of 1933, when the World's Fair drew thousands of visitors to Chicago's lakefront and South Side, one of summer camps' primary goals was simply to keep children from "getting into trouble" in the city.

To achieve these goals, activities at Camp Wabash—similar to antidelinquency efforts in South Side parks or even a weekend at Idlewild— were wide ranging, featuring nature only as a part of much broader offerings. Boys and girls could expect to take part in "classes in citizenship, nature study, boating, canoeing, swimming, life saving, art, archery, Indian lore, dramatics, singing, Negro History, belt weaving, and corrective gymnastics" (see Figure 4.2).[56] South Side reformers maintained this approach into the 1940s as the second wave of the Great Migration began: one pamphlet from this era depicted an African American girl looking off camera and pleaded with the reader, "Won't you send her to camp? One week at Camp may change a whole life." Camping, the inside of the pamphlet argued in no uncertain terms, would "decrease delinquency among our boys and girls."[57] One reformer similarly reflected, "Our camping program has helped more boys and girls than any other project sponsored" and that girl campers in particular "express[ed] the joy of getting away from their crowded homes and dirty streets. Camping [gave] them a desire to work for something much better than what they have been accustomed to all of their life."[58]

Although nature-oriented activities were just one part of a more comprehensive program, just as at Idlewild, the marked contrast of rural landscapes of hope with cramped city environments remained a central virtue of youth camps. Indeed, reformers and parents alike may have felt they were countering the city's hazards by providing children—many of whom had been born and raised in the city—with an idealized version of the more rural South that many had left behind. In a sense, these camps owned and operated by African Americans were landscapes of hope amid countless public and private green spaces which could all too often prove dangerous, South and North. At the Detroit Urban League's summer camp not very far from Camp Wabash, for instance, reformers promised that campers would experience rural landscapes that were a "counter-irritant for . . . social evils" for children "menaced by the vices of Detroit, by the destitution of Detroit, the selfishness of Detroit, the

Figure 4.2. Original print captioned "A boxing bout at Camp Wabash, August 1930. Left, Arthur Garner, age 7, vs. Frank (Little Giant) Garner, age 9. Referee, TL Hickman, Senior Program Secretary for Wabash Department. This was the second year in camp for the Garner brothers, who were the youngest at camp." Note both the cabins and the large camping tents in the background. Chicago History Museum, ICHi-79116. Photographer unknown.

race prejudices of Detroit." Perhaps influenced by its close connections to Chicago's Wabash YMCA, the Detroit Urban League had created an environment where campers "found pine needles in place of city pavements, clear water instead of muddy alleys and bird songs rather than roaring trolley cars."[59] When Irene McCoy Gaines advocated for more youth camps in 1937, she used similar language that also echoed her praise of Idlewild's virtues: she wanted places where children could "find clean streams—where they can be inspired by the majesty of trees and the songs of birds . . . and listen to the quiet music of the stars."[60]

Gaines and other reformers wanted as many South Side children as possible to experience natural environments like those at Idlewild and Camp Wabash so that they could benefit physically, mentally, and spiritually, just like one camper who was "inspired by a sermon heard at Camp Wabash" to write a poem titled "Sonnet for Lake Rowe" that was published in the *Defender* in 1938. Echoing Du Bois's purple prose that praised Idlewild's aesthetic beauty in 1921, the poet rhapsodized about how the lake, trees, clear sunny skies, and, indeed, "all nature shows [God's] love." For the writer, going "back to nature and the dust from whence we came" helped to "purge our souls of arrogant pride and lust" and break "the chains of sin and woe" that led to a path of delinquency and vice in the city.[61] Rather than leaving nature behind at camp, these lessons were supposed to carry over to the city. In 1930, for instance, attendees at the Illinois State Federation of Colored Women's Clubs meeting noted that in the Cook County Forest Preserves, "we must teach our children not to destroy the beauties of these Forest Preserves by picking the wild flowers, pulling up the shrubbery and killing the birds," linking this lesson to beautification efforts in the city: "We should beautify our homes by keeping the grass and weeds out, planting flowers and shrubs and protecting the trees."[62]

Not only did these landscapes remain an integral part of the camping experience but also evidence abounds that many campers engaged with nature well beyond merely swimming or canoeing in a lake. At Camp Wabash, for instance, parents were told that nature study was particularly rewarding for children unaccustomed to the country: "Boys and girls at camp become acquainted with new beauties through lessons on insects, flowers, birds, wood, lore, fields and streams." Camp leaders claimed, "City children becoming acquainted with these new beauties, first inquire, then appreciate, and finally respond to them. Nature is always an excellent teacher."[63] By the same token, a 1937 promotional pamphlet for Camp Wabash noted that the program was intended to promote "Recreation, Relaxation, Education" that would "give to youth a healthful summer environment, an appreciation of Nature, development of attitudes and habits which will make for successful and harmonious living, training for rugged physique, and fun under proper supervision"—precisely the types of virtues that William Van Arsdale had ostensibly exhibited on his three-day hike to Idlewild.[64]

Some South Siders apparently displayed a real eagerness to embrace these environmental lessons. In the summer of 1932, one "undernourished" but enthusiastic boy attending Camp Wabash thanks to a charitable donation was learning "how to tell the difference between the many birds and wild animals that live in and about camp," and the "camp director [felt] certain that the delinquency problems that [had] been confronting this boy in the past will be corrected during this two months stay at Camp Wabash."[65] That same summer, a group of ten boys "successfully passed Indian tests" and lived "in true Indian fashion in teepees that they . . . built themselves in the 10-acre stretch of woods just south of Camp Wabash."[66] These boys, apparently more than the rest of the campers, learned "how to live out next to nature, secure their food, make friends with the animals, and learn about the many varieties of wild flowers and trees that [grew] in and about camp," as well as making bows and arrows and identifying bird species "by their size, color of their feathers, the types of nests they build, the places they build them, and the size, shape and color of the eggs that the mother bird lays."[67]

Although accounts from reformers in the black cultural elite who operated and staffed camps unsurprisingly tended to emphasize the beneficial experiences and outcomes of youth camping, how did African American children actually respond to these programs in the rural Midwest? Many children would have no doubt preferred to spend their summers with their friends and taking advantage of urban amusements rather than being surrounded by woods and wildlife, far from home. Even the Forest Preserves could seem far away, especially for children who still rarely ventured beyond the Black Belt: growing up on the South Side, Charles Davis recalled that even going to the relatively nearby Dan Ryan Woods required traveling a "considerable distance" from where his family lived at the time.[68] Add to this the fact that the quality of the camping experience could vary widely. At one small camp just two miles outside Idlewild where about a dozen Chicago children stayed in the summer of 1938, for instance, conditions were quite different than they were at the nearby resort. Reflective of the poverty that devastated Lake County's black residents outside Idlewild's bounds, the children had "little milk and meat seldom. . . . There seemed to be nothing provided for any kind of activity—not a book or even a ball. . . . The children seemed to spend their time on the road trying to beg rides to the lake where they could play in the water."[69]

Yet although the evidence is sparse and largely anecdotal, it appears as though young black Chicagoans' reactions to their camping experiences were little different from those of their white city-dwelling counterparts: some loved going to camp, some hated it, and plenty fell somewhere in between. For some children accustomed to certain urban conveniences, even if they lived in relative poverty in the city, the adjustment to camping life could be negatively affected by homesickness and generate a resistance to camp programming. Others did not like the rustic conditions: for instance, although Carl Davis eventually grew to appreciate his summer at Camp Wabash because it allowed for unique experiences such as rowing a boat, he remembers that at the time he hated camp primarily because of its primitive accommodations—rudimentary sleeping quarters, outhouses, and the like. One report on African American campers' experience similarly noted that it was "slightly unclear as to how they reacted to the camp. For many of them this constituted their first experience outside of the city. . . . The only severe physical inconvenience with which they had to contend was a pestilence of mosquitos. The presence of these pests put a severe strain on camp morale from time to time." The report concluded, however, that despite these challenges, "many of the boys expressed a keen interest in returning the following year for another camp period."[70]

Clarice Durham was one South Sider who recalled enjoying her camping experience as a child in the 1930s, the purpose of which she recalled was "to just be in the open spaces, to learn something about nature, to learn how to live together away from home." At the relatively new Good Shepherd Church camp near Idlewild, Clarice cooked out, tried to learn to swim in a lake, and bathed in a nearby trout stream—all the sorts of activities that W. E. B. Du Bois had cherished at the elite resort more than a decade earlier.[71] Ben Gaines, who served as a Camp Wabash counselor for several years, recalled that children who had been born and raised in Chicago and scarcely ventured outside the city often found camp entirely new, exciting, and sometimes frightening. Accustomed to city lights illuminating the night sky, many of the children had never seen a darkness quite as pitch black as in the country; other children had never seen fireflies' blinking glow or heard the chirping of crickets at night before traveling to Camp Wabash. Gaines also remembered taking a group of campers to a nearby farm to milk cows, gather eggs in a henhouse, and pick corn in the field; some of them "found it very fascinating that the stuff that they eat out of cans actually grew in the ground."[72]

Brothers Timuel and Walter Black are a good example of how two children with nearly identical backgrounds and experiences could respond quite differently to camping. Both children spent several summers at Camp Wabash in the late 1920s and early 1930s because their parents, migrants from Alabama, wanted them to "get a sense of the rural, country community" and have a "break away from the hectic life of the city." Walter took to the camp activities immediately; Timuel remembers that Walter loved the camp experience in part because he could bring some of those camping skills back to the city. Along with his father, Walter would regularly fish in Lake Michigan and in park lagoons, and even took hunting and fishing trips to downstate Illinois. Timuel, in contrast, remembered camping primarily for its discipline— it was "kind of a militaristic thing," he recalled—rather than for any rural, outdoor experiences impossible in the city. Camp counselors tried to teach him how to fish, but he never really got the hang of it. The best part of the camping experience, he recalls, was meeting other children he would not have met otherwise: making new friends from different areas of the city and different economic backgrounds gave him a stronger sense of community. Perhaps it was for those reasons that, despite his own relative lack of enthusiasm for Camp Wabash, Timuel later sent his own children to camp too—a choice that speaks to the African American community's transgenerational valuation of such experiences in natural environments.[73]

Whether or not individual campers enjoyed their summers at camp, the community's shared convictions about nature's importance— particularly given fears over how the Great Depression's widespread poverty only stood to exacerbate juvenile delinquency in the city—led reformers in the black cultural elite to push for ever-expanding camping opportunities. Like Washington and Madden Parks, Camps Wabash and Belnap were important, but they were far from sufficient to handle the large numbers of African American children. In 1935, for example, the Chicago Urban League secretary noted in the *Defender* that "one of the great needs of the negro population is camp and outing service," and three years later the Chicago and Northern District Association of Colored Women (for which Irene McCoy Gaines served as president) elaborated, "All of our institutions, settlements and children's homes have many children in their groups who need more nourishing food and fresh air. A trip to a summer camp is one of the things that can be done every year, and will prove most valuable for underprivileged children."[74] Instituting a fund for these purposes, the report went on to state, "would make one of the outstanding and most significant of the district's social services."[75] Black reformers had to continue to push for expanded opportunities because segregation and race discrimination still limited black Chicagoans' options. Some community institutions like the Newberry Avenue Center on the near South Side, for instance, struggled to find "camps for [their] large number of registered colored boys and girls," finding it "disconcerting . . . to have to explain to the colored boys why they could not be selected" for camp.[76]

Despite these limitations, reformers' efforts were paying off. By the end of the 1930s, Chicago's African American parents could send their children—members of a generation who were increasingly born and raised in the city—to any one of more than a dozen camping programs, more than twice the number that existed a decade earlier. In 1935, for instance, the wife of a Baptist minister began a summer camp hosting African American boys and girls in a thirteen-room house in the Forest Preserves west of the city; by the end of the decade, the Church of the Good Shepherd's youth group organized both summer and winter excursions to a different camp in the Forest Preserves. Community organizations like the Abraham Lincoln Center and the Good Shepherd Community Center (for which Irene McCoy Gaines served on the board) began their own camps, and smaller black-owned and operated camps were established. Longstanding social service organizations were beginning to expand service to African Americans as well. In 1938, Jane Addams's Hull House finally admitted twenty-one African Americans to Bowen Country Club, its camp in the Forest Preserves forty miles north of Chicago; up until that point, one official noted that the camp "had just absolutely ignored the Negro."[77]

·By 1940, more than 2,000 African Americans annually—as compared to more than 25,000 whites—were taking advantage of these sorts of "Free and Low Fee Camping Services" in the Chicago area. Thus African Americans made up roughly 7 percent of this camping group, a figure roughly in line with their share of the city's population. Only thirteen free and low-fee camps served black Chicagoans, and African Americans—both campers and staffers—made up roughly 18 percent of those camps. On the one hand, 2,000 African American campers in 1940 seems a small number, accounting for less than 1 percent of the total African American population of Chicago and only slightly more than 4 percent of the population aged 8 to 18 (the age range of the vast majority of campers). On the other hand, that number of African American campers excludes those who participated in full-fee, unsubsidized camping (like many who attended Camp Belnap), not to mention the more ad hoc rural experiences of South Siders like Jimmy Ellis. It also suggests that camping was roughly as common for black Chicagoans as it was for whites, particularly by the end of the Depression decade. Factoring in a conservative ratio of first-time to repeat campers, it does not seem unrealistic to suggest that a good deal more than just 4 percent of black Chicagoans attended a summer camp before they graduated from high school. And although direct adult participation does not seem to have extended much beyond the black cultural elite who oversaw the camps' daily operations, the commitment of hundreds of mothers and fathers to send their children there—year after year, summer after summer—speaks to the value that many black Chicagoans, the vast majority of whom were migrants, placed on rural green spaces.[78]

These rural youth camps were unique to the major Great Migration destinations across the North for at least two main reasons. First, since youth camping developed in large part as a remedy for juvenile delinquency and a range of more general concerns about modern urban living, it follows that these opportunities would be far more plentiful among the products of the Great Migration and not those still living a more rural lifestyle in the South. The 1930 census revealed that more than 70 percent of African Americans in Southern states such as Mississippi and Alabama lived in rural areas. In states like Illinois and Michigan, those numbers were practically reversed: more than 90 percent of African Americans lived in urban settings. Second, and perhaps more importantly, Jim Crow all but guaranteed that limited social services were unequally distributed in the South during the 1930s. These inequalities often characterized the North as well, but several studies have shown that the situation was particularly dire for a variety of New Deal agencies in the South, a trend that also held for organizations not affiliated with the government.[79]

Although such statistics reveal that youth camping was almost exclusively a privilege of urban-dwelling children of the Great Migration, those opportunities were limited. Branches of the Brooklyn and St. Louis YMCAs were the only others beside Chicago to own their own camps, and only the St. Louis branch approached the Wabash YMCA in the number of campers it accommodated each summer. A 1934 report, for instance, found that only fourteen of twenty-five African American

YMCAs nationwide ran summer camps, and only two—Atlanta and Washington, DC—were outside the North. The contrast between North and South remained stark, however; a similar survey found that across the South, "no provisions at all are made for Negroes and if such provisions were made they would be separate." As a Family Service Organization representative from Louisville stated, "At no time could there be any question of the colored and white groups visiting the camp at the same period."[80] This was not the case in the North, where many "tax supported free camps for under-privileged mothers and children or for children only" in New York, Cleveland, Philadelphia, and Pittsburgh made "no distinction as to race or camping periods for different racial groups," and several other private camps across the North accepted "mixed racial groups without discrimination."[81] Chicago's charity camps that, unlike Camps Wabash and Belnap, were operated by white counselors and administrators, were only beginning to pursue such interracial policies by the end of the 1930s. But as the experiences of many African Americans in these interracial nature camps illustrate, integration could be a mixed blessing: race discrimination they encountered there all too often resembled that which they sought to escape.

Integration and Discrimination in the Forest Preserves

Segregated camps such as Camp Wabash were important to black Chicagoans in part because they were owned and operated by African Americans, and like many other segregated community institutions, they became sources of race pride. But they fell far short of meeting the entire community's needs, and as early as 1925 social service organizations such as the Chicago Urban League also sent working-class African American mothers and children to charity camps owned, operated, and staffed by whites. Foremost among these were Camp Algonquin (operated by United Charities of Chicago in association with the *Chicago Tribune*) and Camp Reinberg (operated by Cook County), both located in the Cook County Forest Preserves near Palatine, Illinois, about thirty-five miles northwest of the Black Belt. Much like the other rural green spaces that Chicago's black cultural elite considered restorative, Camp Algonquin was described as an historic twenty-acre "Indian campground" consisting of "virgin forests and living springs" where the "natural resources" were "practically endless, [including] oaks, maples, blackwalnut, butternut, hickorynut, wild cherry" trees, a place that was supposedly "better than city parks" because it was more wild.[82] Explicitly intended to help families recover from the exhausting and unhealthy urban environment, these camp outings were thought to be, as one United Charities superintendent described them, valuable for mothers who were "on the verge of breakdown as a result of overwork and worry [and] needed a complete change, a chance to get away from their tenement homes and rest and relax."[83] Campers could expect not only a similar environment to Camps Belnap and Wabash but also similar programming. Camp Reinberg's program, for instance, was "based on the Scout program, since it has been found by experience to be the best so far developed," and included mornings "devoted to hikes, swims, instruction in nature study, or miscellaneous activities" and afternoons "devoted to tournament games, special events, swimming, or hiking."[84]

Hundreds of black Chicagoans were sent to these charity camps each summer, where their proportion of the campers often far outpaced their share of the city's population. At Camp Algonquin, a racial quota limited African Americans to roughly 10 percent of all campers (in line with the proportion of the city that was black, it amounted to roughly one hundred campers annually), but at Camp Reinberg the proportion of African American campers ranged as high as 19 percent throughout the early to mid-1930s. In 1932, when unemployment in the Black Belt reached an all-time high, Camp Reinberg's segregated camping group was made up of 530 African American campers (246 boys, 214 girls, and 70 mothers) out of fewer than 2,800 campers that summer. When Camp Reinberg eliminated the segregated camping period and "accept[ed] guests without discrimination as to race or color" for the first time in 1938, 637 African American campers made up nearly 30 percent of camp guests, a rate that was more than triple black Chicagoans' share of the city's population.[85]

That striking disproportionality likely stemmed from African Americans' high levels of poverty in the 1930s, because these campers were drawn from the same demographics from which Camp Wabash pulled: the undernourished and nearly destitute, laid low by the Great Depression. When Camp Reinberg closed after the summer of 1942, it dramatically reduced the number of black Chicagoans able to retreat to nature: one report noted that a 30 percent decrease in the number of

African American children served by free and low-fee camps between 1938 and 1944 was "due entirely to the closing of Camp Reinberg."[86] Clearly, Camps Algonquin and Reinberg were important resources for working-class black Chicagoans, but what were campers' actual experiences at these charity camps that, unlike Camp Wabash, were owned and operated nearly exclusively by whites?

All too often, African American mothers and their children were greeted at these camps with the sort of Jim Crow segregation and race discrimination redolent of the South—and of Chicago's racially contested parks and beaches. At Camp Algonquin, even though African Americans and whites attended in the same camping periods, residential quarters were segregated—an arrangement that apparently did not change until 1939. Even following desegregation, one building was reserved for white mothers who complained about having to live in close proximity to African Americans. To make matters worse, African Americans' living quarters were cramped and the only ones lacking indoor plumbing. As one observer noted, "They are placed in quarters, expressly the reverse for which they came to camp. They came to camp to get away from these same conditions under which they live in Chicago. It brings about a nervous restlessness of body and spirit which is to be regretted."[87] Clearly the *Defender*'s rosy 1932 caption of a photograph depicting mothers and children heading to camp was misleading at best when it proclaimed, "No color line is shown in the selections of mothers and kiddies for the outing. Such a scene as is here depicted could never happen below the Mason and Dixon line."[88]

If the facilities were worthy of regret, treatment from white campers and staffers could be even worse. African American girls complained of racial harassment from white girls; in 1931, one girl "was able to adjust to the group very well considering the fact that she was colored," but another continued to be "very sensitive to teasing about being colored."[89] Such racial conflict was evidently fairly normal, as one particular summer was described as merely "comparatively happy" for black campers, who often withdrew from camp activities.[90] Noting this tendency not to take part in activities at Camp Algonquin, for instance, one caseworker eventually found that African American campers were particularly excited by the opportunity to fish, a fact that white camp staff had apparently made little effort to discover (one need only have looked elsewhere in the Forest Preserves or to the Washington Park lagoons to realize many black Chicagoans were eager to fish).[91] At Camp Reinberg, meanwhile, racial tension could easily boil over between African American campers and white staffers. After a stay there in August 1934, a group of African American mothers claimed that they and their children had been the victims of discriminatory treatment, including being served poor food and being inappropriately disciplined—they were slapped and hit with a stick after misbehaving on a hike. A thorough investigation by a special committee that included the Urban League's A. L. Foster "found no evidence of discriminatory procedure against the colored group nor of racial prejudice upon the part of the staff," but it did find that the camp superintendent's unwarranted decision to call police after campers expressed anger at the corporal punishment only exacerbated racial tensions rather than quelling them.[92] Yet in spite of the racial unrest at Camp Reinberg, it received generally positive reviews from African American social service agencies and was even credited with promoting positive interracial contact (see Figure 4.3). One report claimed to have observed "a change of attitude in [one of the] White clients towards mothers of the Negro race, whom she had met at camp." The white camper reflected that her experience had prompted her to realize that "they are just like us, and I am glad that I had the opportunity to meet them before forming any further opinion from outside reports."[93]

So although interracial camps could reinscribe the very social and environmental inequalities they were meant to counter, these rural landscapes of hope also had transformative potential beyond that which the segregated Camps Wabash and Belnap could boast. As the assessment of interracial contact at Camp Reinberg indicated, these and other integrated camps had the potential to break down racial barriers that were growing ever more rigid in the city: they were relatively isolated and controlled environments in which camp organizers and campers themselves could forge a new society in miniature. Easily the most notable of these carefully conceived attempts at integration occurred at the YWCA's Camp Sagawau, which opened in the Forest Preserves south of the city in 1936 and supplemented the segregated camping opportunities available to YWCA girls at Camp Wabash. Even though YWCA and YMCA branches in the city remained segregated, the YWCA's rationale for attempting integration at camps was clear: as early as 1923, a YWCA official had told its board, "Much of the prejudice existing today on the part of white people is due to lack of any real understanding of the mind

Figure 4.3. Interracial group of boys apple-bobbing at Camp Reinberg in Deer Grove Forest Preserve, 1938. FPDCC_00_01_0006_038, Forest Preserve District of Cook County records, University of Illinois at Chicago Library, Special Collections.

and soul of the best colored people and it is contact alone which can bring understanding."[94] The YWCA knew that if its camps were going to integrate with better success than either Camps Algonquin or Reinberg, it would have to go out of its way to painstakingly manage interracial contact in a manner that was virtually unprecedented in the city. As one YWCA official reflected, "Making our camps interracial was a step in advance of the community. The Y.W.C.A. of Chicago is certainly far ahead of many community organizations in its interracial policy."[95] With Camp Sagawau, then, the Chicago YWCA was effectively asking, "How far can an institution deviate from the community pattern in attempting to carry out its own philosophy"?[96]

Almost immediately after Camp Hammond closed in the mid-1920s, the YWCA tentatively began to pursue these interracial objectives in camp by inviting two African American girls from Wendell Phillips High School for the last period at Camp Millhurst, near Plano, Illinois, about fifty miles west of Chicago. YWCA officials were extremely wary of pushback from both white campers and their parents, however, and went through great pains to make it clear that these last two weeks of camp would be interracial because "it was definitely felt that there would be a considerable misunderstanding and criticism if girls went to a camp which their parents assumed was a white camp and found colored girls there."[97] Camp Millhurst closed just a few years later, however, not only because of sanitation problems similar to those that closed Camp Hammond but also in large part due to the deepening economic turmoil that led to "the decreased income of the families from which these girls come"; even before it closed, officials had noted, "Negroes were feeling the early effects of the depression and no Negro girls could be found who could afford to go to camp."[98] This predicament was quite familiar to the YMCA. Indeed, like the YMCA, the YWCA noted that, in the 1930s, "Our club membership in the Negro community had been catering to the girls who, to a large extent, were from poorer homes with unemployed parents of families on relief. As a result the club membership was not a cross-section of the Negro community and most of the club girls could not afford to go to camp."[99]

In 1934, at about the same time that girls made up the majority of campers at the YMCA's Camp Wabash, the YWCA gained control of two hundred acres south of the city that would become Camp Sagawau. Adjoining Forest Preserves land along the Des Plaines River, the area "had been intended by its owner as a country estate including a bird and wild flower sanctuary," and YWCA officials valued its new acquisition for its "nearness to Chicago, its accessibility, its canyon and fossil areas; its flowers & birds; its wide feeling of expanse; its small lake and fishing area [and] the way it is seemingly hidden from the highways, which encircle it."[100] But the camp also had drawbacks similar to those of Camp Hammond: its grounds were largely unimproved by camping structures, it had a critical "lack of trees and top soil," and mosquitoes were abundant in "low areas and swamps" that could be particularly miserable in the summer when there was "little breeze on very hot days." Those handicaps meant that, in contrast to the Boy Scouts' Camp Belnap, there was the "lack of opportunity for a real woodsy outdoor camp—either a large lake or a big woods," but YWCA officials were undeterred.[101] They optimistically concluded that despite the acreage having "only a small farmhouse and a few scattered buildings, . . . its many natural advantages of woods, orchards, meadows, and lake were a challenge to the far-seeing eyes and imagination of the Girl Reserve Department." It took until 1936 to get Camp Sagawau ready for its first camping group composed of "high school girls of whatever creed or color," for which officials established a racial quota proportional to the percent of African American girls in the YWCA's Girl Reserve Department citywide.[102] Given that African Americans made up around 20 percent of Girl Reserves at the time (roughly twice their proportion of Chicago's population), that translated to four African American girls for each two-week camping period.[103]

The YWCA carefully vetted prospective campers of both races to all but guarantee success in what amounted to a bold but admittedly small-scale social experiment at a time when interracial conflict was still the norm in contested urban recreational spaces such as Jackson Park beach. Officials thoroughly screened white girls and their parents for racial prejudice, and examined black girls and their families to make sure they would represent the middle-class values that the YWCA believed would cast African Americans in the best possible light. Indeed, the YWCA staff personally recruited African American girls they decided came from a "comparable background" and met with them prior to camp in part to "help them realize that they were standing for more at camp than their own good time, in other words, they were contributing their share in working out the interracial policy of the Y.W.C.A. through education by contact."[104] Exactly how those backgrounds were determined remains unclear, but what does seem clear is that the YWCA wanted their African American campers to resemble much more closely the campers at Camp Belnap rather than at Camp Wabash; there would be no "undernourished" or "problem children" here. Camping fees alone may have been enough to guarantee the sort of African American camper they sought: in its inaugural year, a two-week camping period cost $17 at Camp Sagawau—significantly more expensive than Camp Wabash, but just fifty cents cheaper than Camp Belnap and "the same fee charged by the Girl Scouts and the Camp Fire Girls."[105]

Early on in the process, parents of both races received letters "indicating the inter-racial aspect of the camps, so that all parents and campers themselves were prepared to make this inter-racial experiment a success"; if parents called to inquire about sending their child to camp, they were explicitly informed that it was an interracial camp.[106] As a result, some white parents chose not to register their girls for camp, and others "wrote in ahead of time to find out how many Negro girls would be there when their daughters were there," ultimately deciding to go ahead and send their daughters to camp when YWCA officials explained that Camp Sagawau promised an opportunity "to meet Negroes of comparable background and culture, an opportunity equivalent to that offered by travel."[107] At least according to YWCA officials themselves, all that preparation paid off. As one internal report stated, "A special study was made of the reactions of campers at the close of camp, and it was discovered that the camp experience had been in almost every way a complete success."[108] Camp Sagawau was such an apparent triumph, in fact, that reflections from white campers are almost too glowing to believe. One girl said that her two weeks at camp had taught her "not to feel superior to others or treat them indifferently as when I first came here. But I find it is lots and lots of fun to mingle with different race [sic]." Another admitted that she had "always dreaded going to . . . High School because of the colored people. I thought they were all cruel and selfish. But since coming to camp I have learned that they are a people, can laugh and play, have opinions of their own and are very real and full of fun. I think that mixing the different races and religious people is fine—it gives us a chance to know other types of peoples' opinions." Yet another claimed, "I never did have much racial prejudice and I am now completely cured."[109] Perhaps inspired by these early successes, the YWCA finally lifted the "ban on Negro girls at Forest Beach Camp" in Michigan by the end of the decade, and applicants for positions as counselors were rejected if they expressed any aversion to interracial camps. By 1941, when the YWCA counted more than 2,200 black Chicagoans as constituents and more than 40 percent of teenaged Girl Reserves were black, nearly three hundred African American girls attended camp.[110]

Although the YWCA's interracial camping experiment seems to have been a success, internal documents reveal that officials struggled to promote Camp Sagawau among both black and white girls. Through the end of the Depression decade, YWCA officials noted that Camp Sagawau's racial quota was "not designed to limit the attendance but to secure an adequate proportion of attendance" from black Chicagoans.[111] Indeed, the YWCA found it difficult to recruit the handful of African American girls to camp each summer, despite its own "special promotion . . . on camp" and the Defender's enthusiastic endorsement of Camp Sagawau as a positive "interracial experience."[112] One official lamented, "I wish I knew the reasons why the Negro girls do not participate in the activities open to them," before going on to speculate: "Lack of participation may be due to the fact that (1) only in recent years have they been made welcome; (2) many volunteers carry a heavy responsibility in the local center; (3) because of housing segregation in Chicago, the area in which Negroes live is almost self-sustaining, with all community organization duplicated within the area."[113] In a decade when even the most prosperous black Chicagoans were struggling to make ends meet, the YWCA seemed curiously blind to the possibility that the camp's cost could be a significant deterrent for many prospective campers in an already relatively small black cultural elite.

The suggestion that the South Side's social services and community institutions were "self sustaining" rationalizes the YWCA's recruitment failures, but it does perhaps inadvertently hit on developments that followed Du Bois's exhortation to "stand erect in a mud-puddle and tell the white world to go to hell, rather than lick boots in a parlor."[114] Shut out of too many public and private natural landscapes to count, African Americans had forged their own community institutions such as Camp Wabash. Even when given the opportunity to integrate white institutions, then, it appears many black Chicagoans simply chose to support their own privately owned segregated ones. Given the way African Americans were often treated at places like Camps Algonquin and Reinberg, this would hardly be surprising. The YWCA knew it was swimming upstream by attempting to counter divisions and animosities virtually embedded in Chicago's landscape. To integrate in the 1930s was to fight the same uphill battle Carl Hansberry and his family fought just south of Washington Park.

Indeed, it was clear to the YWCA that any interracial understanding it was able to foster at Camp Sagawau was not the rule, but the hopeful exception to broader social trends. But the goal was to inculcate values in a younger generation whose racial views were perhaps more malleable than those of their parents' generation. YWCA officials knew that they were reaching campers at formative ages, stating that Camp Sagawau "has helped the youth of Chicago to have an understanding of the likenesses and differences in people and to have a tolerance which is hard for adults to obtain after attitudes and minds have been set."[115] Racially prejudiced adults proved a significant barrier to recruiting open-minded young campers, however. Many whites' racial prejudices meant that they continued to believe that the "intimate nature of camp activity"—just like swimming at Jackson Park beach along the lakefront—made it unsuitable for interracial contact. When one community organization conducted a survey of its white constituents on the possibility of interracial camping, "all but one parent [had] check[ed]: 'I would prefer that my children would not be with Negroes.'"[116] Indeed, despite the YWCA's efforts to inform both campers and their parents about the nature of interracial camping, some white parents "missed the point in the letter of the interracial camp. We knew this by comments they made when they brought their daughters to camp."[117] Even after several years of promoting interracial camping, the YWCA felt that "in spite of our attempts at cooperation in Girl Reserve groups we still feel that many Girl Reserves do not participate in our camp program due to the fact that it is an interracial camp. This is something of which staff are very conscious and on which they work continually. On the other side of the picture is the fact that those girls who do attend camp are very enthusiastic about it and seem honestly concerned that anyone should take exception to the interracial plan."[118]

Signs of the outside world's racial prejudices were not difficult to find, even in Camp Sagawau's meticulously controlled social environment. In one case, a photographer refused to photograph black and white campers together, leading a YWCA official to express frustration, saying, "We can have our own inter-racial policies, but we can't force their acceptance by commercial concerns who feel differently about the whole thing."[119] Nor could they force acceptance among the local whites who lived near the camp. This was something that the YWCA had known about from the very beginning; when they took control of the land and started planning for an interracial camp, they euphemistically noted in one report that nearby "neighbors are little interested in 'our' type of camp" before going on to more explicitly state that "Lemont people not interested in an inter-racial camp at 'the sag.'"[120] More than just "not interested," many small towns near Chicago displayed the same virulent racism black Chicagoans often encountered in the city's green spaces, opposing any African American use of the nearby Forest Preserves.

This racial prejudice, at times violent, led county officials to institute a Jim Crow segregation policy in the Forest Preserves, ostensibly for African Americans' own safety. The policy was news to many black Chicagoans who had been doggedly fighting for the integration of the city's parks and beaches, however. In 1930, the *Chicago Whip*'s A. C. MacNeal demanded a response to an "incident that happened not long ago where officials of the Forest Preserves refused to allow a group of colored clerks of Neisner Brothers to hold a picnic in the Forest Preserves" in Palos Park Woods, just a few miles east of Lemont and the site where Camp Sagawau would be established.[121] The general superintendent responded that he "sincerely regret[ted] the incident in the Palos area of which you speak" and assured MacNeal that "proper disciplinary measures have been taken with the one who was really responsible," even expressing a desire to "meet a group of you and discuss the matter of the colored people and the Forest Preserve District."[122] Yet despite the conciliatory response, little changed. When the Chicago Urban League's A. L. Foster inquired about the de facto segregation policy three years later, he specifically asked about rumors "that some of the leaders of the colored race are acquainted with these plans and approve them. Please let us know with whom you have consulted regarding this policy."[123] Even as late as 1937, the year after Camp Sagawau opened, a Jim Crow policy that mimicked the one at 31st Street Beach was in place: MacNeal (who by this time had succeeded Idlewild regular Herbert Turner as Chicago NAACP president) wrote to officials to complain about a sign posted in the Forest Preserves near Chicago Heights that read, "For Colored People Only."[124]

Yet it seems that African Americans living in nearby Chicago Heights, approximately twenty-five miles due south of the Black Belt, *had* accepted officials' de facto segregation policy unbeknownst to Chicago race leaders, a move that suggested the limits of racial politics in public natural and landscaped environments outside the bounds of the Black Metropolis. Confronted with the same sort of potential for racial violence that black Chicagoans faced at Jackson Park beach but without the safety of numbers that the city's burgeoning black population offered, these locals had decided that Jim Crow was their best option to continue to enjoy Cook County's natural landscapes. The policy dated back to 1931, when a Forest Preserves lake near Chicago Heights "opened for swimming" and "due to no part of the colored people of the area [Forest Preserves officials] were shortly confronted with near riots and serious injury to the law abiding colored visitors."[125] As many officials did when similar trouble broke out on Chicago's beaches, the general superintendent contended, "The trouble was perpetrated by a rough foreign white element who frequently visited the section and started trouble before our police could act."[126] Such race violence was not unique to that particular lake: that same year, when a group of black Chicagoans made the hour-and-a-half journey from the city to fish in the Des Plaines River that ran through a Forest Preserves area, one of the members of the party was shot and killed in an apparently racially motivated conflict.[127]

Indeed, race violence in the Forest Preserves appears to have been a widespread, longstanding problem; one official confessed to the Chicago Urban League's A. L. Foster that the Forest Preserves' "policy to refuse to permit the use of swimming pools and beaches to white and colored people at the same time and [refusal] to permit colored people to use some of the pools entirely" was because "we have in some eight or ten instances narrowly averted tragedies where we attempted to permit mixed bathing."[128] Internal Forest Preserves correspondence suggested that officials would "be glad to remove the sign but . . . in the event it is removed there may be a reoccurrence of the uncontrolable [sic] trouble with which the Chicago Heights negroes were so concerned."[129] Years earlier, another Forest Preserves official suggested to the Chicago Urban League's A. L. Foster, "To be sure I am a thorough believer in equal rights and liberties and perhaps lives in the abstract are not important in the consideration of such matters, until that time when the life affected is your family or my family, and then the civil liberties idea becomes unimportant."[130] Race violence thus had propped up Jim Crow and trumped equal rights in the Cook County Forest Preserves, just as it did all across the South that tens of thousands of black Chicagoans had fled.

Race violence and Jim Crow segregation may have plagued the Cook County Forest Preserves during the Great Depression, but that did not stop African Americans from retreating to these public green spaces—just like they would not be deterred from retreating to contested landscapes in the city such as Jackson Park beach. In all these spaces, African Americans forged connections with nature despite the racial barriers and violence that confronted them. With the Forest Preserves serving as a sort of middle ground between urban parks and more distant rural landscapes like Idlewild, a 1937 assessment estimated that "the entire population of the city is within a thirty-minute ride of some forest preserve" and deemed them "easily accessible" by automobile as well as rail, streetcar, and bus lines.[131] Arguably the area in the Cook County Forest Preserves most frequented by black Chicagoans was along the Des Plaines River north of Chicago, where Mr. and Mrs. Robert L. Taylor (the former of whom was a prominent black attorney in the city) also ran a segregated youth camp. Perhaps having decided not to make the long trek to Idlewild so late in the season—or constrained by the economic collapse that seemed to worsen by the day—the *Whip's* A. C. MacNeal and *Defender* publisher Robert Abbott, along with whom the latter described as "many of the leading business and professional men and women in this community" picnicked there one September Sunday in 1930.[132] That particular retreat was characteristic of the way black Chicago's cultural elite used the Forest Preserves, as high society and clubwoman picnics were exceedingly common during the Depression.[133]

But it was not just the well-heeled Idlewild set or children affiliated with the YWCA or the Boy Scouts who retreated to the Forest Preserves; there are ample indications that these natural landscapes became more accessible to the average black Chicagoan during the Great Depression. In coordination with the Wabash YMCA, the working-class employees of Chicago's meatpacking plants (still among the largest employers of African Americans) assembled in ever-larger crowds at the annual Fourth of July picnic, which had relocated from Hammond, Indiana, to Dan Ryan Woods on the far South Side—the same Forest Preserve where Charles Davis was initiated into Boy Scout Troop 547, Mohawk Patrol, a camping excursion that he recalled as the "highlight" of the scouting program. And just as Washington Park fostered black Chicagoans' political and religious culture, so too did the Forest Preserves. In the late summer of 1932, when communist organizers and soapbox orators were still lecturing daily in Washington Park, Congressman Oscar De Priest reportedly drew more than 100,000 supporters to the Preserves for a Republican Party rally and Labor Day picnic in the midst of his reelection campaign. South Side churches also regularly used the Forest Preserves for large gatherings; in 1935, for instance, an interdenominational picnic drew more than one thousand African Americans from Chicago AME, Baptist, Presbyterian, and other churches. The same year, a *Defender*-sponsored petition-signing campaign for the addition of bicycle paths in the parks and Forest Preserves hinted at the broad African American support for such green recreational spaces. *Defender* newsboys helped collect 35,000 signatures for the campaign, and the top-performing newsboy won a new bicycle for his effort in collecting more than 4,200 signatures. It comes as little surprise, then, that South

Sider Jimmy Ellis, who lived near Washington Park and regularly visited its pool on hot summer days, also remembers retreating to the Forest Preserves for picnics with his family in the late 1930s. Sometimes they would go on special occasions like birthdays or to entertain an out-of-town visitor to enjoy the "relaxing" forests and lakes that were "a good place for people to go."[134]

Whether they realized it or not, the Forest Preserves to which Jimmy Ellis and countless black Chicagoans retreated during the Great Depression were constructed landscapes undergoing dramatic changes in the 1930s, much like Washington and Madden Parks that benefited from New Deal funding through the WPA. Along with hundreds and even thousands of other rural landscapes, the Forest Preserves' green spaces were reshaped thanks to another of Franklin Delano Roosevelt's New Deal agencies, the Civilian Conservation Corps (CCC). Following the same sort of segregation policy instituted at Camps Belnap and Algonquin, the CCC established segregated work camps north, south, and west of the city, housing hundreds of young black Chicagoans who planted trees and dug ditches on thousands of acres. Nearly identical camps sprang up on rural landscapes nationwide, including near Idlewild, where young men reshaped the landscape to rehabilitate cut-over forests and depleted farmlands, making it more productive as well as more attractive to resort goers and tourists. Taken as a whole, the CCC was perhaps the most notable and substantial pathway for black Chicagoans to come into contact with these rural landscapes of hope during the 1930s; in many ways, the agency was meant to inculcate the very same nature-based values embodied by William Van Arsdale's hike from Chicago to Idlewild. But for these young men, the Cook County Forest Preserves, downstate Illinois, and rural Michigan were landscapes of hope that demanded labor more than they invited leisure.

5

Building Men and Building Trees

D AVID L. COHN, a white native of the Mississippi Delta and celebrated chronicler of the region, wrote in 1935 that "the Negro's identification with the life of the Delta is fundamental and complete. He came here as a slave with the earliest settlers. He has remained to live and multiply as freedman. The land is first and last his handiwork. It was he who brought order out of a primeval wilderness, felling the trees, digging the ditches, and draining the swamp. . . . Wherever one looks in this land, whatever one sees that is the work of man, was erected by the toiling, straining, bodies of blacks."[1] Cohn was right: the South's landscape and wealth were built largely with the labor of black slaves and, later, of freedmen and freedwomen. But Cohn was also wrong: although African Americans' identification with the Delta and its landscape may have been strong, it was never so "fundamental and complete" as to prevent them from attempting to leave their own handiwork (and that of their ancestors) far, far behind.

Individuals and families made their own choices and calculations, but remaining in the Delta's oppressively racist and impoverished society was never the first choice for African Americans as a people, no matter how fertile and beautiful the land may have been: those were landscapes of despair, not hope. As Richard Wright so poignantly conveyed in *12 Million Black Voices*, his 1941 assessment of African American history and the Great Migration, remaining on that land was something to strain and strive against, because remaining usually meant suffering. By the time Cohn ruminated on African American environmental labor in the midst of the Great Depression, for a full generation the Mississippi Delta had already been the land from which thousands and thousands of African Americans had escaped to find better, freer lives for themselves and their families in cities across the North. And more often than not, African Americans who had grown up in the Mississippi Delta migrated to Chicago, riding the Illinois Central railroad northward. They sought a society and a job market in the North that—despite its own racial discrimination and the indignities thrust on African Americans at nearly every turn—allowed them to vote, respected them more, paid them better, and, if they were lucky, allowed them advancement beyond the sort of manual environmental labor that had cleared and cultivated the South.

Yet at the very moment in 1935 when Cohn was reflecting on generations of African Americans digging the Delta's ditches and draining its swamps with hard manual labor, thousands of young African American men between the ages of 17 and 28 were toiling for the Civilian Conservation Corps (CCC) in the rural Midwestern landscape: digging ditches, draining swamps, clearing land, and planting and felling trees. Both migrants themselves and the sons of migrants, a great many of them Chicago residents, they were undertaking the same sorts of labor African Americans had done for centuries throughout the South. For African American CCC enrollees in the South, their labor on the land was akin to the predominantly rural environmental work African Americans continued to perform in the region's fields and forests. But in the North, it was something new. By an overwhelming majority, African American migrants and their families had settled in cities in the 1910s and 1920s, living and laboring in the heart of America's thriving urban industrial economy—not in the North's rural spaces.

When the Great Depression struck, that urban industrial economy was thrown into disarray: millions nationwide were left unemployed, and thousands protested evictions in Chicago's Washington Park. At the same time as the WPA was remaking the South Side's landscapes of hope, President Franklin Delano Roosevelt created the CCC as a way "to build men and to build trees" nationwide.[2] Sending the working-class unemployed to the countryside to labor on the land for six-month periods, he thought, would rehabilitate and strengthen both the hungry young men at risk of delinquency and the landscape denuded by generations of intensive resource extraction that had fueled the nation's industrial expansion. For black Chicagoans, this meant mostly manual environmental labor in landscapes of hope: the Cook County Forest Preserves, downstate Illinois farms, and northern Michigan's forests near Idlewild.[3]

Hit hardest by the Depression, African Americans in the North—most of them working-class migrants living in urban places such as Chicago, Detroit, Pittsburgh, and New York City—joined CCC companies at a rate that was often far higher than their percentage of the population. The CCC enrolled an astonishing 250,000 African Americans nationwide—roughly 10 percent of all eligible young black men—over the course of its existence from 1933 to 1942; at its peak in 1935, it enrolled 50,000. The enrollment rate was even higher in northern states such as Illinois, where the CCC's adherence to a racial quota of roughly 10 percent of total enrollment actually meant that African Americans were overrepresented in states that still had relatively small African American populations, even after a generation of intense in-migration. Nearly 390,000 African Americans in Illinois in 1940 accounted for only 4.9 percent of the population, for example; almost 278,000 of those African Americans lived in Chicago, accounting for 8.2 percent of the city's population. Census figures reveal that in Illinois there were between roughly 49,000 and 61,000 CCC-eligible African American men, approximately 70 percent of whom lived in Cook County, which encompasses Chicago. CCC statistics suggest that total African American enrollment statewide appears to have been at least 16,000. In other words, between one-quarter and one-third of all eligible African Americans living in Illinois—young men born between 1907 and 1925, more than three-quarters of whom had been born in the South (and were hence migrants, even if they came to Chicago as young children)—were at some point enrolled in the CCC.[4]

It is safe to say, then, that if a young African American CCC enrollee was from Illinois, he was much more likely than not to be a southern-born man now living in the Chicago metro area. The impact of African American participation in Midwestern CCC companies is truly staggering, particularly when one realizes that, given the CCC's rules about the vast majority of the dollar-a-day wages being sent back to enrollees' families—mothers and fathers, sisters and brothers—the CCC seems to have directly benefited between one-quarter and one-third of African American enrollees' families statewide, most of whom were working-class migrants living in Chicago. Although rural leisure spots in the North such as Camp Belnap and especially Idlewild tended to draw more well-to-do African Americans, environmental labor in the CCC represented the most notable connection to nature for working-class black Chicagoans during the Great Depression, far outstripping the opportunities that Camp Wabash and other free or low-fee camps were able to provide boys and girls.[5]

So what is to be made of this widespread—albeit somewhat fleeting—return to manual environmental labor in rural landscapes for working-class migrants now living in cities in the North? Regardless of race, all enrollees performed similar environmental labor, but it was their shared cultural history of the Great Migration and environmental labor in the South that made African Americans' CCC experience in the North unique. In 1904, before the first stirrings of the Great Migration, Booker T. Washington exhorted African Americans across the South, "Our pathway must be up through the soil, up through swamps, up through forests, up through the streams and rocks."[6] Underway just a decade later, the Great Migration had in part been a repudiation of this sort of environmental labor and gradualist thinking; hundreds of thousands of African Americans were beginning to trade hopeless toil in Southern soil for the prospect of advancement in Northern cities' factories and businesses. And the African Americans who retreated to the North's rural spaces in the Great Migration era—from Idlewild to Camp Wabash and beyond—had explicitly recast nature as a place primarily for leisure, not labor. Yet during the depths of the Great Depression, thousands of young working-class black Chicagoans found themselves undertaking precisely the sort of labor that so many migrants—and now their children—had consciously rejected. As one woman who worked in a Chicago laundry said, "I think that the object of the white man is to force all the colored people to go on the farm but I will never go there. I was born in the city and there is where I belong."[7]

For black Chicagoans themselves—as well as Detroiters, Pittsburghers, and New Yorkers—CCC labor represented a hybrid experience with the natural environment, blending the cultural memory of

Southern labor practices with rural Northern landscapes that were mostly new to working-class migrants and their children. To be sure, there were many differences between environmental labor in the Delta and in the rural Midwest, not the least of which was the fact that these young men earned decent wages from one of the federal government's many Great Depression-era New Deal relief programs rather than scraping together a living on what white landowners saw fit to pay them. But there were many similarities too. African American workers largely performed this environmental labor for white overseers in segregated CCC companies across the North, and they often did so in the midst of racist white communities that were quite hostile to their presence. Perhaps even more important, the most direct environmental fruits of black Chicagoans' labor in these landscapes—rehabilitating farmland, building recreational areas, planting state and national forests—would mostly accrue to whites, just as it had accrued to whites in David L. Cohn's Mississippi Delta. Now the Midwestern landscape, too, would owe an environmental debt to African Americans, a debt that has largely been effaced by time and nature itself.[8]

Black Labor on the Land in the Great Depression

Soon after the CCC's creation, an April 1933 "Questions and Answers" bulletin from the Department of Labor—which was distributed for recruitment purposes to community and relief organizations around the country, such as the Urban League—made the CCC's objective plain: "In a word, the purpose of this work is both to build men and to build trees."[9] The CCC was one of the first relief agencies Franklin Delano Roosevelt proposed on taking office, and the dual goals of building men and building trees seem to have come directly from the new president. Indeed, in his initial proposal to Congress, FDR noted that the CCC would "make improvements in national and state domains which have been largely forgotten in the past few years of industrial development": these would be the rural counterpart to WPA-funded infrastructural improvements to city spaces such as Washington and Madden Parks. In the very next breath, however, FDR argued that "more important" were the "moral and spiritual gains" of putting young people to work, further elaborating, "We can take a vast army of these unemployed out into healthful surroundings. We can eliminate to some extent at least the threat that enforced idleness brings to spiritual and moral stability."[10] Three years later, FDR declared the CCC a success on both counts. Addressing all enrollees, white and black, he stated, "Although many of you entered the camps undernourished and discouraged through inability to obtain employment as you came of working age, the hard work, regular hours, the plain, wholesome food, and the outdoor life of the C.C.C. camps brought a quick response in improved morale. As muscles hardened and you became accustomed to outdoor work you grasped the opportunity to learn by practical training on the job and through camp educational facilities." He continued, "Our records show that the results achieved in the protection and improvement of our timbered domain, in the arrest of soil wastage, in the development of needed recreational areas, in wildlife conservation, and in flood control have been as impressive as the results achieved in the rehabilitation of youth."[11]

FDR's account of the benefits of CCC work for both the land and those who labored on it reveals that the agency's ideological roots were a synthesis of two longstanding ideas about nature that culminated in an immense reshaping of America's rural landscapes that helped both rural *and* urban Americans of all races. The first idea derived from early twentieth-century Progressivism and conservationism in the mold of Gifford Pinchot, the first chief of the United States Forest Service, and its impact was reflected in the scientific approach to environmental management in the CCC. From forestry to soil conservation and beyond, CCC labor was intended to turn the natural environment itself into something of a productive factory space, maximizing the material returns of labor on the land to produce goods for human consumption (whether recreational space across the Midwest, agricultural commodities on the Illinois prairie, timber in northern Michigan, or otherwise). The second idea was one that Chicago's urban parks and its youth camps and resorts in the hinterlands had been addressing for generations: that exposure to the natural environment, whether through leisure or labor, could have beneficial physical, mental, and spiritual effects, especially for urban dwellers. Chicago's black cultural elite in particular was already deeply conversant with this second idea, which can be traced back through the Boy Scouts, Teddy Roosevelt, and Frederick Law Olmsted, as they advocated rural escapes as tonics for city life that corrupted and wore on everyone regardless of class. In other words, although the CCC prescribed both labor *and* leisure in nature (and primarily targeted young men rather than boys still in grade school), its goals and methods dovetailed seamlessly with those of the YWCA, YMCA, and Boy Scouts, organizations through which Chicago's black cultural elite hoped to build the character necessary for success in a modern, urban environment through outdoor education and camping in rural environments. The key difference from places like Camps Wabash or Belnap, however, was that African Americans had little if any control over how segregated CCC camps were run by white officials.[12]

The CCC was never conceived as an antimodern or permanent back-to-the-land enterprise; just like a retreat to Camp Wabash or Idlewild, it depended on nature as a temporary rural antidote to persistent—and growing—urban problems. Although the CCC did seek to rehabilitate or "improve" rural land that had been abused—or neglected, as FDR put it—by the consequences of a growing population and industrial development, it also somewhat paradoxically intended to train men to enter those very industries once the Depression-ravaged economy recovered. In other words, the CCC was both intended as a corrective response to modern industrializing trends that devastated natural environments and as a way to spur and support those very industries by preparing young workers to one day return to work in urban metropolises such as Chicago. In a column addressed to CCC enrollees in the organization's earliest days, for instance, FDR wrote, "You should emerge from this experience strong and rugged and ready for a reentrance into the ranks of industry, better equipped than before."[13] The CCC intended to both physically and mentally strengthen young men by transplanting them into nature, where they would exercise bodies ostensibly weakened by the Depression while also educating their minds by attaining marketable skills and following a regimented, moral lifestyle. Officials hoped that improvements in both areas, achieved largely through manual environmental labor, would address concerns about urban youth delinquency and produce a motivated industrial workforce once jobs became available. A full-page drawing in the January 1940 issue of an Illinois African American camp newspaper visually portrayed the transformation that the CCC was intended to produce: from carousing delinquent to respectable quasi-soldier. A CCC veteran in uniform greets a new enrollee who, with suitcase in hand and dressed to the nines in a zoot suit, black shirt with tie, and black hat, looks as if he had arrived in camp straight from a night on Chicago's Stroll; the latter, the drawing insinuates, will soon transform into the former. From an enrollee's perspective, though, the drawing may have also illustrated the kind of lifestyle many CCC enrollees regretfully left behind in cities while simultaneously subtly poking fun at the lack of preparedness of many new urban enrollees for environmental labor in the rural Midwest.[14]

So what did the CCC labor mean for the young black Chicagoans who enrolled, and how did it further develop working-class migrants' hybrid ways of understanding nature that blended the environmental cultures of North and South? In the peak years of the Great Migration when African Americans migrated north to find jobs that were relatively plentiful, these young working-class men would have gone to work in industries like meatpacking or steel in cities like Chicago. By 1920, Chicago's African American population had swelled to nearly 110,000, and an estimated 70,000 held some sort of urban industrial job. Although many migrants lived in the urban South before making their way northward, most migrants left rural agricultural economies for urban industrial economies, further removing themselves from the land in the process.[15] A sociological study of Mississippi Delta culture in the depths of the Great Depression backed up this disjuncture between the rural agricultural South and urban industrial North when it noted, "Even among the town Negroes there is a feeling of closeness to the soil" in the South that could not be maintained in an urban metropolis like Chicago; when the authors asked a woman who had visited her son in Chicago "how she would like to live there, she replied that it was all right for a visit, but she wanted to live some place where she could 'put a stick in the ground.'"[16]

But where the Mississippi Delta study emphasized a rupture in migrants' connections to the land, St. Clair Drake and Horace Cayton emphasized continuity in 1945's *Black Metropolis*. They wrote,

> The Chicago adult world is predominantly a working-class world. Over 65 per cent of the Negro adults earn their bread by manual labor in stockyard and steel mill, in factory and kitchen, where they do the essential digging, sweeping, and serving which make metropolitan life tolerable. During the Depression, whether on public projects or in private industry, the bulk of the employed adult Negroes, with a minimum of education and still betraying their southern origin, were toilers, working close to the soil, the animals, and the machinery that undergird Chicago's economy.[17]

Migrants no longer held the same jobs in Chicago as they had in the South, in other words, but the manual labor most migrants undertook meant they still worked "close to the soil." Hands that once picked cotton bolls in rolling fields now skinned hogs' heads in sprawling slaughterhouses or washed clothes in cramped laundries. Hands that once felled trees in the turpentine forests now poured molten iron in immense steel mills. For Drake and Cayton, then, urban manual labor was simply another version of rural manual labor. Working-class migrants may have wanted to reject Booker T. Washington's logic of uplift through manual labor when they left the South, but discriminatory practices and other factors meant that in some ways the vast majority of African Americans "betray[ed] their southern origin" when they labored in Chicago's factories, stockyards, steel mills, and homes.

Viewed another way, urban African American laborers were simply one more level removed from the land than they had been in the South. In Chicago, the hogs and cattle they slaughtered still depended on the land, and the iron ore they forged into steel was still mined from it. But African American migrants were no longer generally involved in raising those hogs and cattle on the land or extracting iron ore from Midwestern mines: those were rural jobs. In the urban metropolis, the jobs that processed these raw materials into consumer goods and the stuff of civilization were as "close to the soil" as it got. But as Drake and Cayton pointed out, even though migrants more often worked in the North's heavy industries that were largely indoors and insulated from the seasonal rhythms that affected sharecropping and other extractive industries in the South, "metropolitan life" in the North did not mean a complete detachment from soil or animals. Living in Chicago, migrants had simply relocated to the hub of major industrial networks they were already at least somewhat familiar with in the South. But when the Great Depression eliminated many of the urban industrial jobs for African Americans, who were so often the "last hired, first fired," the CCC turned the rural Midwestern marshes, farmlands, and forests into the sites of that manual labor for thousands of black Chicagoans during the New Deal era. It returned these migrants to the land.[18]

By inducing thousands of young working-class black Chicagoans to reshape the landscapes of the rural Midwest, the CCC effectively blended a long history of rural manual labor in the South with the modern logic of industrial progress in the North, creating a hybrid culture of labor in nature for African Americans. Although enrollees of all races performed manual environmental labor, the context of the Great Migration made the African American experience unique: the CCC intended to train black enrollees for the sorts of jobs they and their families migrated North to find while employing them in the sorts of jobs they or their parents had left behind in the South. It should perhaps come as no surprise, then, that the CCC itself and some of its African American enrollees reached back to that longer cultural history in the South to make sense of their new endeavors. Just as Booker T. Washington's ideas loomed large at Idlewild and Camps Wabash and Belnap, so too did they in the CCC. A 1939 *Defender* article, for instance, noted that, throughout the country, 143 African American companies celebrated the CCC's sixth anniversary by "dedicating their programs to Dr. Booker T. Washington and National Negro Health Week."[19] Similarly, one enrollee in an Illinois company addressed seemingly disgruntled fellow enrollees in his company's newspaper, writing, "CCC life is strenuous in all its departments. The out-door work is sometimes a little hard but invigorating, this makes us hungry which insures us better physical health." He then went on to counsel, "There is no use to 'crab' about work if you wish to earn an honest living, the late Booker T. Washington once said, quote, 'If we work hard we can do things. Anything that is good is worth working for. It is no disgrace to do manual labor.' "[20] At the same time, however, the ways in which the rural natural environment turned into a sort of Northern factory itself were not lost on enrollees. One forestry news article in an African American CCC newspaper, for instance, echoed the urban factory's language of efficiency when it noted, "The planting season is short and all the component activities of getting the trees into the ground must move with clock-like precision."[21] More generally, as another article put it, "every one should learn to work efficiently at a real job, in order to become a useful and productive citizen."[22] At least one Chicago enrollee seemed to have internalized these lessons in the CCC. Described as "the hardest and steadiest worker" his CCC camp "had ever known," on returning to the city he landed a job in the steel mills, "the kind of work a hard-work loving man . . . would pick."[23]

Although some African American enrollees in Illinois may have reached back to Booker T. Washington to make sense of their environmental labor, it was clear that CCC work—especially in the North—was a hybrid labor culture that offered far more training and opportunity for advancement than had sharecropping, timbering, or mining in the South. Add to that African Americans' overrepresentation in Illinois CCC companies, and the CCC underscored one of the key pull factors that led migrants to leave the South in the first place: cities in the North almost invariably offered better jobs, better wages, and more hope of advancement. While African Americans in the South were struggling just to get into CCC companies, blocked by racial quotas and low turnover, black Chicagoans could use their tenure in the CCC to gain skills that would make them more employable when they returned to the urban industrial workforce. In a camp focused mainly on rehabilitating Illinois farmland, for example, there was the "unusual opportunity for enrollees to learn to become dragline operators, oilers, machine operator and skilled mechanics" and perhaps even "become experts."[24]

But not all working-class African American CCC enrollees gained marketable skills that would help them advance in the workforce when they returned home to the city. Although the CCC estimated that 90 percent of African American enrollees attended vocational classes teaching trades and skills such as "carpentry, shorthand, typing, forestry, auto mechanics, [and] landscaping" and 11,000 enrollees were taught to read and write, there was little education beyond the trades and little opportunity for advancement within the CCC.[25] In other words, despite the *Defender*'s proclamation that the CCC was "like a big university" whose "main campus extend[ed] from the Atlantic to the Pacific oceans and from the Gulf of Mexico to the Canadian border," the vast majority of African Americans who served in the CCC undertook hard physical labor in rural environments that may have better prepared them for work on the slaughterhouse floor, but not a middle-class office.[26] Most entered the CCC as members of the working class, and they left it working class. As the superintendent for a CCC project in the Skokie Lagoons north of Chicago remarked, although education and training benefited many enrollees, first and foremost enrollees would learn "what manual labor really is. They will acquire the ability to create and build. The visible results of their perseverance and efforts will mold in them the determination to stay with a job, undertaken, until their part of that job is completed."[27] This was Booker T. Washington's uplift agenda translated to the Great Depression-era North.

So although many African American enrollees took advantage of the voluntary education and training available after long workdays in the field, the bottom line for black Chicagoans in the CCC was that the vast majority of their time was spent reshaping rural Midwestern landscapes, many of them far from a city of any appreciable size. Had widespread unemployment not forced millions of young men to support themselves and their families by looking for work in government programs outside the city, it is doubtful that many of them—regardless of their race— would have voluntarily chosen to spend six or more months of their lives in rural spaces often far from their families, friends, and city life. Like campers away for a week at Camp Wabash, enrollees away from family for weeks at a time could get homesick too.

For African American migrants, a CCC stint meant giving up some of the very attractions that pulled them to cities in the first place; for those born and raised in Chicago, they were leaving the only environment they had ever known. Even one new enrollee who reflected that "it is wonderful here in camp" and "there is nothing like it in the world" went on to say that he would "give [his] last dime to remain here if it weren't for what I left behind in the city."[28] Highlighting the hardship of CCC life compared to what he left behind in the city, one African American enrollee in Illinois penned "The CCC Blues":

> Of all the sad words of tongue or pen,
> The saddest are these, I'm in the 3 C's again.
> It seems so hard to part with my girl,
> To travel to camp for another whirl.
>
> I can't sleep till noon, can't dance till morn,
> Have to don those dennims [sic] so tattered and worn.
> There goes the whistle, it's six o'clock
> Time to work, else my pay they'll dock.
>
> It seems that the world is very unfair,
> It has me down, holding me by the hair.
> I've worked so hard all these summers and Falls,
> And I'm spending my winter in overalls.
>
> They tell me of a home way off somewhere
> We'll all get an equal chance up there
> I'll bet I can gold brick up there all day
> With no officer saying, "You get fined today."[29]

Although the location of the author's home away from camp remains unclear, the poem evokes wistfulness for the sort of leisure African Americans enjoyed on Chicago's Stroll, and its title ironically plays on the sort of music the author wishes he was enjoying there. "The CCC Blues" idealizes the city life the author was forced to leave behind, as well as the influences from which reformers explicitly sought to remove young men. But the last stanza reveals his awareness that the city's promise may be illusory. He is told "of a home way off somewhere" where the work would not be as difficult as that in the CCC and where "we'll all get an equal chance." But had he returned to the city and found employment, it seems unlikely that his life would have been as carefree as he imagines. Indeed, plenty of African Americans were finding that the "world [was] very unfair" in cities devastated by the Depression, particularly because they were so often the victims of racial discrimination there.

Exacerbating the sense of isolation and relative privation of rural Midwestern environments compared to the city life that African American enrollees temporarily sacrificed while in the CCC, enrollees were sometimes forced to build their camp from scratch before they could even begin their environmental labors. Particularly because many black Chicagoans were initially trained on the job at the relatively well-established and well-provisioned African American camps in the Skokie Valley's Cook County Forest Preserves just north of Chicago, transferring to a more distant and remote location—sometimes nothing more than an unused parcel of Illinois prairie—could come as something of a shock. At a newly established downstate campsite, for example, one African American enrollee recalled that the enrollees arrived "on a very hot and sultry August afternoon" only to find "no barracks or other conveniences which we had expected." In the first weeks of camp, they "struggled against all kinds of obstacles, mainly lack of materials to work with, rainy weather which made [their] camp a pool of mud, windy weather which blew [their] tents down, and a shortage of water."[30] At another western Illinois camp, enrollees recalled that when they first arrived from their Skokie Valley camp, they "pitched tents and built a cook shack, hauled water, went without baths, [and] sweated and worked to make this camp what it is today."[31] Another enrollee who arrived once the camp was established put the struggle of those pioneering enrollees in verse:

> Do I remember way back when?
> Of course not, I was absent then
> But from the news I have at hand
> This place was not a fairyland.

According to the news I got
This place was quite a dismal spot.
And one glance at this area
Would give a guy hysteria![32]

Whether they induced hysteria in young men more accustomed to the hustle of city life or not, new campsites around rural Illinois and Michigan were often described by African American enrollees as exceedingly bleak places: one was "just a field of clover"; another was "a most deserted spot"; and yet another was "an 'eye sore' to a casual observer," composed of "grass, corn stalks, weeds, shrubbery and deposits of decayed vegetation" that "provided a comfortable habitat for grasshoppers, crickets, rabbits and other pests."[33] Implied, of course, was that these desolate environments did *not* provide a "comfortable habitat" for enrollees who were facing on-the-job environmental and climatic challenges much more similar to those faced by Southern sharecroppers than even the poorest industrial workers in the North. It was a far cry from Chicago's bright lights and broad streets and an extreme version of the sort of hardship William Van Arsdale had faced during his hike from Chicago to Idlewild.

Perhaps most important for African American enrollees, however, the remote locations of Midwestern camps meant that they spent their six-month enrollment periods not just in rural landscapes some saw as "desolate" but also in segregated companies amid almost exclusively white villages and "sundown towns" often hostile to their presence. Usually far from the nearest African American population of any appreciable size, the remote, isolated locations of many African American CCC camps were almost certainly a trickle-down effect from the racism of rural white communities in the North. For the first two years of its existence, the CCC organized racially integrated companies (with segregated barracks and work units); Chicago's own Oscar De Priest—the South Side congressional representative who was at the time the only African American serving in Congress—had authored an amendment to the original CCC bill barring discrimination on the basis of race, color, or creed. Prefiguring the government's approach to African American servicemen in World War II, however, CCC officials repeatedly bowed to nearby towns' racist pressures, seeking to avoid or mitigate race conflict at all costs, rather than taking a stand in favor of African American enrollees' rights. In 1935, the year before Chicago's YWCA embarked on its interracial camping experiment in the midst of a hostile local population, the CCC director yielded to complaints from several rural American communities that voiced racist objections to nearby mixed-race camps by mandating completely segregated companies. Rather than attempting to break down racial boundaries in green space, the federal government opted instead to take the path of least resistance and conform to the segregation patterns evident in countless landscapes during the Great Depression, both rural and urban—from Camp Belnap to the Forest Preserves, from Washington Park to the Ida B. Wells Homes.[34]

Segregated companies, however, invited their own problems for CCC officials, because these same rural white communities—many if not most of them in the North—also vocally resisted exclusively African American camps being located nearby. Clearly if a racially mixed company that included a few dozen African American enrollees incited racist anger and anxieties, a company of two hundred or more young African American men would not suit these towns any better. The CCC director capitulated, stating, "Whether we like it or not, we cannot close our eyes to the fact that there are communities and States that do not want and will not accept a Negro Civilian Conservation Corps Camp" and therefore he was unwilling "to compel any community to accept a Negro company . . . against its will."[35] In 1937, for example, plans for an African American camp in Illinois were dropped after "objections [were] voiced by churches, civic organizations and public officials" in a nearby white town.[36] The CCC's solution to this conundrum was to place as many African American camps as possible on remote state and federally owned lands while also minimizing the total number of African American camps by moving, reshuffling, or merging existing companies. In Lake County, Michigan, this meant that the initial site for an African American company was rejected when "local people suggested that the location closer to Idlewild would be more acceptable and the transfer was made by the federal officers."[37] On the whole, it was a policy that further discriminated against African American enrollees, isolating many of them in places far from the families they were supporting.

Although many small towns in the North welcomed the environmental labor of CCC enrollees regardless of their race, companies located near potentially hostile white communities could experience situations fraught with racial tension. In a decade when the Scottsboro Boys trials dominated racially charged headlines and fueled prejudices about the relationships between black men and white women, the tacit context of the CCC handbook's guidelines concerning interactions with local women would have been unmistakable for African American enrollees. Reprinted in a rural Illinois company's newspaper, the handbook echoed behavioral concerns voiced by the black cultural elite in the migration years, reminding the young men that "proper dress and behavior will help to make these people [in nearby towns] friends and neighbors," and that "making remarks to or about women . . . while riding in trucks, on trains, or on foot is strictly forbidden." The code of conduct was not only part of the broad agenda of character education that the CCC undertook but also an explicit component of the CCC's own public relations campaign. As the same handbook put it, "The public sees only the uniform, and it is difficult to distinguish between one man and another in uniform"; poor behavior of an individual, officials worried, would reflect poorly not only on the individual company but also on the CCC—and the race—as a whole.[38] For African American enrollees in rural Northern camps, however, nearby towns clearly saw both the CCC uniform and the color of their skin.

African American CCC camps almost inevitably ran the risk of causing friction with nearby communities just by virtue of the enrollees' race. In 1938, for instance, the *Defender* reported that white citizens in one small northern Michigan town insulted, abused, and wrongfully imprisoned African American enrollees from the nearby CCC camp for having done nothing but walk along the highway in town; many of those citizens wanted the CCC camp moved apparently because "most of the citizens were 'afraid of colored people.' "[39] African American enrollees working in the Deer Grove Forest Preserves just north of Chicago were suspected by a business owner of repeatedly breaking into his building near the CCC camp, even though, as the Forest Preserves' general superintendent rather drily pointed out, "some of the breaking occurred prior to the establishment of the CCC camp." Given the racial climate throughout the Forest Preserves, officials could not have been surprised by this sort of complaint.[40]

The racist resistance to African American CCC camps could be even more virulent far outside the Chicago metropolitan area. In 1940, after visiting a western Illinois African American company a camp inspector wrote to the CCC director, "The town of Mt. Carroll is a town of approximately 1400 population with no negro population. It is evident that the town has an intense desire and movement on to have the camp moved." He went on to write, "It is further evident that the town feels that there is a great deal of possibility of one of the town white girls being attacked by one or more of the boys."[41] At a different western Illinois camp, CCC officials similarly noted that a nearby town had "an intense hatred for negroes and will not rest until the camp is moved."[42]

Often moving the camp simply was not practical given the work that needed to be done, and the CCC sometimes attempted to promote interracial understanding between white locals and African American companies by hosting sporting events—boxing, baseball, and the like—that drew mixed-race crowds.[43] Rather than consistently fostering interracial understanding, however, CCC officials more commonly adhered to the institution's segregation policy in designing leisure activities for enrollees. Boxing matches, baseball games, musical performances, lectures, and tours and celebrations of CCC work were promoted in African American newspapers such as the *Defender*. Occasionally "cards of admission" to the camps were available from South Side African American institutions such as the Wabash YMCA, the South Parkway YWCA, or various community churches.[44] CCC officials brought city dwellers to remote camps, but they also took enrollees to the city for their leisure time. Instead of allowing enrollees to seek out recreation in nearby white towns on their days off, the CCC regularly transported them to the nearest African American community. Whereas enrollees stationed at the Skokie Valley camp in the Cook County Forest Preserves could travel within the county to nearby Evanston (less than ten miles away) or even Chicago (roughly twenty-five miles away) for recreation, those stationed in more rural places had to travel to more far-flung cities with smaller African American populations, such as Rockford, Peoria, Rock Island, or Galesburg, Illinois.[45]

African American CCC camps often attempted to maintain close ties to black communities in nearby cities like Chicago and in Idlewild such that enrollees never entirely left behind urban life; the result was a hybrid experience that blended long periods of rural environmental labor with shorter spurts of more urban-inflected leisure. Enrollees working in the Skokie Lagoons took a company trip to the second summer season of Chicago's World's Fair in 1934, for instance, and in 1941 enrollees participated in the annual Bud Billiken Day parade and picnic.[46] In 1936, the staff poet at one western Illinois camp composed a poem poking fun at a fellow enrollee's boasting about his weekend exploits, beginning a five-stanza poem with these lines: "He's been a playboy in Chicago / Is a great lady-killer he say."[47] Idlewild, which by the 1930s was developing into a center of black entertainment and was not nearly as rustic as it had been a generation earlier, drew enrollees who piled into a truck for the hours-long drive to the "glamorous and beautiful resort of lower Michigan," as one CCC newspaper put it; there they could take a break from labor in the forests and join summer resort goers for a weekend of leisure activities as diverse as horseback riding, baseball, hiking, boating, and swimming.[48] Even in the off-peak autumn, winter, and early spring months when Idlewild's tourist population dwindled, CCC enrollees traveled there for masquerade balls, Easter services, or simply a night of entertainment and socializing at the resort town's Paradise Club.[49] For the CCC's working classes, it was a taste of how the black cultural elite spent their leisure time in rural locales.

More generally, the CCC promoted sports and other leisure-time activities as a way to make the CCC's program of manual environmental labor in remote rural locations more palatable to young men, creating a hybrid experience by bringing elements of the city to the country. Just as in Chicago's Washington Park and other green spaces, sports were exceedingly popular among young men, and virtually every issue of African American CCC company newspapers was suffused with breathless reporting on each company's athletic achievements. For reformers and CCC officials, participating in sports was also a way to symbiotically supplement the supposed moral and physical development afforded by manual labor in the rural environment. As one African American company newspaper put it, a championship basketball team "proved the value of the physical development and stamina derived from the various projects and healthful living in camp."[50] Sports were, in other words, akin to the leisure activities increasingly organized by the black cultural elite in city green spaces such as Chicago's Washington Park or rural youth camps like Camp Wabash: reformers attempted to promote physical activity in nature as an antidote to idleness and the threat of urban delinquency, particularly among the working classes. Indeed, the official publication of Chicago's American Negro Exposition in 1940 explained that the CCC exhibits there were in part "designed to show what the federal government is doing to improve the leisure activities of unemployed Negro youth," reflecting the black reformer mentality that had for a generation led to the development of African American youth camps and resorts in the rural Midwest.[51]

The education and training programs offered by the CCC, the leisure excursions that necessitated trucking African American enrollees to nearby cities with black populations, and its sporting culture all highlighted the fact that enrollees were only visitors in the rural Midwest, destined—and usually eager—to return to their homes in Chicago and other urban areas. As one African American enrollee stationed at a western Illinois camp mused in 1937, "All the boys who left camp in March to go to the 'windy city' seem to be doing fine. I think that I will go on a leave pretty soon, for I long to see the bright lights again."[52] Another former CCC enrollee noted how, once back in the city, enrollees seemed to revel in the urban entertainments they had had to leave behind for the past several months: "If you ever want to find some of your old CCC friends on Sunday night here in Chicago" he wrote, an excellent place to check would be one "of the three leading theatres on the South Side" known for hosting gambling. At the Regal Theater on Chicago's Stroll, he met a handful of other former enrollees who had returned to the city for work.[53] One enrollee in a rural Michigan company stationed near Idlewild used the onset of autumn weather to reflect on the impending discharges of all enrollees when they completed their term of service: "Just as Mother Nature has spent her idle hours the summer long, so have we. We have been content only in ferreting out pleasure. Just as she becomes the cool, calculating, level-headed planner of tomorrow, so should we. Now is the time for us to consider that there is no career, no future for us in the CCC." He went on to encourage his fellow enrollees to take advantage of the training and education offered in the CCC because "we must fit ourselves for our return to civil life."[54] Even though no individual enrollee had a long-term future in the CCC, serving as little as six months before returning to civilian life in the city, the collective labor of thousands of African American enrollees over the agency's decade-long existence transformed the landscape for generations to come.

Black Chicagoans Reshape the Rural Midwestern Landscape

No matter the specific type of environmental labor, African American CCC companies in Illinois and Michigan, like their white counterparts, employed efficient division of labor techniques that had long since shaped urban factories. They effectively turned the countryside into a factory that produced new leisure opportunities in nature, farm fields with higher yields, and timber for Midwesterners'—and Americans'—consumption. On projects in the Cook County Forest Preserves, African American enrollees shaped the land and built the infrastructure enjoyed by Chicago-area leisure seekers for generations to come. In countless rural Illinois fields, enrollees rehabilitated farmland depleted by neglect born of Depression hardship and worn down by generations of intensive grain and livestock production necessary to feed a growing nation—virtually all of which was filtered through Chicago's commodities markets for distribution nationwide. In northern Michigan's sandy soil that was largely unsuitable for farming, enrollees attempted to reverse the effects of timber extraction that had clear-cut the area with factory-like precision in the nineteenth century; they planted millions of trees in vast new forests intended to both produce timber and draw even more recreation seekers and resort goers like those who vacationed at Idlewild.[55] One poetic interpretation of the meaning behind the quarter-million African Americans' service in the CCC framed that labor as a contribution to what the American people as a whole owed to nature. Titled "Back to Nature," the 1936 poem published in an African American Illinois company's newspaper figured nature as both needy and generous, requiring humankind's attention for rehabilitation but holding great potential for recovering from the Depression's poverty. The poem reads,

> Now, the depression has run its course
> And the debris cleared away.
> We've returned to old nature, dear,
> To help her gain her sway.
>
> We owe it to old nature, dear
> Because she was so loyal and true,
> She fought with us, our battle great
> Upon her beautiful meadows of dew.
>
> She fought with us with tireless fear,
> To help us drive the enemy away.
> She fought with us on every side,
> To help us stem depression tide.
>
> Now nature welcomes us into her fold,
> To share her wealth that's never been told,
> So that's why we're in the C.C.C.
> To receive her blessings and forever be free.[56]

A "return" to nature could refer not only to an enrollee's personal journey from the city to the country but also to a broader understanding of African Americans' historical cultivation of American soil. Cleared debris seems to metaphorically reference the human, financial, and other wreckage that the Depression ("the enemy") wrought, but it also more literally doubles as a reference to the some of the work CCC companies were doing in the natural environment: clearing brush and weeds that stalled drainage from cornfields and attempting to right the wreckage left behind by the logging industry. In the end, nature is a resource that offers possibility; once the debt is paid, nature offers the ability to "forever be free"—a sentiment that carried special resonance for African Americans still grappling with the toxic legacy of slavery.

Although enrollees were welcomed into nature's fold and paid relatively well for their time there, "her blessings"—with the help of countless hours of African American labor—would be primarily bestowed on rural white communities for decades to come. Indeed, the most direct and lasting environmental benefits of African American CCC enrollees' manual labor accrued primarily to whites—just as it did in the Mississippi Delta and the South more broadly. In the Midwest, African American enrollees had few if any permanent ties to these rural communities that saw recreational opportunities develop on public lands and crop yields increase on private lands. Indeed, they were the very same rural white communities that were so often hostile to African Americans' mere presence.

Although there is no question that otherwise unemployed African American enrollees and their families benefited from the dollar-a-day wages and job training they received in the short term, they largely were not able to enjoy the longer term environmental impacts of their work when they returned to their homes in Chicago and other Midwestern cities. When African American enrollees helped construct a massive network of lagoons and channels to control floods and draw recreation seekers to the Skokie Valley north of Chicago, they did so on public land near white communities. A report by the Cook County Forest Preserves on the completion of the project noted, "The ultimate development of this area will offer many opportunities for outdoor recreation"—including hiking, horseback riding, picnicking, canoeing, and fishing—but failed to note that Cook County's residential segregation meant that most African Americans were unlikely to benefit from these opportunities.[57] When African Americans cleared ditches, laid drainage tile, and terraced Illinois croplands intended to boost agricultural production, they did so almost entirely on or near white farmers' private land; the "unlimited value" that an African American Illinois company's agronomist saw in the "knowledge that can be gained by individuals of [the] community as to how they may attack their own problems" accrued to white communities, not African American ones.[58] And when African Americans planted trees in what became Michigan's state and national forests, they did so on land that few African Americans outside of those who retreated to resorts such as Idlewild could easily access; the "hundreds of thousands of tourists, campers, and picnicers [sic]" who would visit a northern Michigan state park and benefit from the seedlings planted by African Americans that replaced "species of less beauty and value" were almost exclusively white.[59]

Just twenty-five miles north of Chicago's South Side, the Skokie Lagoons were perhaps the most notable CCC work project in Illinois with which African Americans were significantly involved. The Skokie area was home to the "largest concentration of CCC camps in the nation," both black and white, hosting approximately twenty camps over the course of the CCC; in January 1935, there were over 800 African American enrollees stationed in three Skokie Lagoons companies, and when the CCC expanded later that year, more than 700 African American enrollees were trained in ten separate companies at Skokie before many of them moved to other, more remote sites around Illinois.[60] However, as with other projects around the state, the lasting environmental benefits in Skokie largely have been enjoyed by nearby white communities with more direct cultural and geographical ties to the landscape than the African American enrollees who worked there.

Undertaken on land owned by the Forest Preserve District of Cook County, construction of the Skokie Lagoons was a massive engineering project that had two main goals: "flood control and the creation of a marsh and water landscape with facilities for outdoor recreation."[61] The plan called for the creation of "190 acres of lagoons and channels with a normal water depth of five to six feet, a flood plain of four hundred and thirty-four acres, and restraining dikes at both sides of the flood plain," which were to be reconstructed such that "receding waters will drain rapidly toward the central lagoons and leave no stagnant mosquito breeding pools."[62] Aesthetic advantages followed from these more practical considerations, playing into the nation's burgeoning culture of recreation in nature that also helped drive Idlewild's success. A Forest Preserve District report noted that the "Skokie Marsh had long constituted a unique form of landscape scenery of striking beauty at certain seasons" that "could not be fully appreciated from available vantage points"; CCC work created "flood control dikes of varying widths and heights, and the gently rolling topography with sodded slopes and forested areas planted with native trees and undergrowth now produce[s] a series of marsh and water landscapes at such a scale that they may be taken in by the human eye"[63] (see Figure 5.1).

The network of lagoons and channels marked a massive reshaping of nature, but just like virtually every other Midwestern landscape, the environment was far from untouched by human hands when the CCC began its work in the 1930s. As an initial report on the area noted, "Many changes in physical character of the swamp [had already] taken place during the past one-hundred years," brought about by municipalities' construction of storm drains and runoff ditches, as well as roads built across the marsh that essentially created dams that impounded upstream waters and exacerbated flooding problems. Additionally, previous attempts to drain the marsh had already lowered the water table in the region and caused "swamp grasses and wild rice that afforded cover and forrage [sic] for wild bird life [to disappear and] be replaced by a weed infested bottom land. The drying out of the marsh exposed hundreds of acres overburdened with peat which together with annual accumulations of rank weed growth was always susceptible to fire."[64] When one CCC company gave visitors tours of the worksite, a CCC officer contended, "The greatest and most lasting impression seems to be the fact that it is possible to make so much out of what has always been considered a worthless tract of land," and the Secretary of War was particularly impressed with the "progress being made in transforming the Skokie marsh into a healthful park and playground."[65] In other words, rather than simply replacing a pristine wild marshland with an engineered recreation space, CCC work in Skokie was intended to resolve flooding problems and create recreational opportunities on land that had already been deeply shaped by decades of human intervention.

The great majority of African American enrollees' manual environmental labor in the Skokie Lagoons could be summed up in one word: digging. Measured in cubic yards, the vast quantities of earth excavated from what would become the network of lagoons and connecting

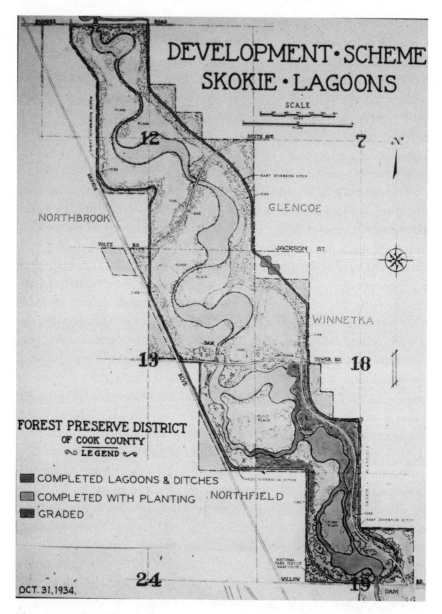

Figure 5.1a. The "development scheme" of the Skokie Lagoons. The southern-most shaded-in portions were in various stages of completion by October 31, 1934. FPDCC_00_01_0017_008, Development Scheme Skokie Lagoons, Forest Preserve District of Cook County records, University of Illinois at Chicago Library, Special Collections.

Figure 5.1b. Aerial view of the Skokie Lagoons on April 13, 1935, looking north (Lake Michigan at upper right). Compare to the state of completion map approximately six months earlier, above. Skokie Lagoons #15164, CAPS_1935_15164, Chicago Aerial Photo Services Collection, University of Illinois at Chicago Library, Special Collections.

channels easily tallied into the hundreds of thousands over the course of the project. Much of that dirt, excavated with pick and shovel, was then hauled by wheelbarrow—load after load, day after day, month after month, year after year—to adjacent areas to be transformed into the dikes that would retain the lagoons' and channels' water. Working in the Skokie Lagoons from 1933 to 1941, just one of three African American companies that spent more than a year working on the project excavated 90,000 cubic yards of soil in just the first two years and nine months on the job. At that rate, African Americans working in those three companies cumulatively excavated the equivalent of approximately ninety-three acres—or the area of seventy football fields—to a depth of one yard over the course of the CCC's work in Skokie. Across the rural Midwest, environmental work in the CCC—as it was for enrollees regardless of race—was much the same: labor with hand tools that moved dirt, cleared land, and planted trees[66] (see Figure 5.2).

Black Chicagoans' work on the Skokie Lagoons may have been the most notable and permanent contribution to the Illinois landscape, but it was merely a small fraction of the total work done to create, rehabilitate, and shape both publicly and privately owned environments across the Midwest—virtually all of which had already been extensively engineered since the nineteenth century. On other projects throughout the Cook County Forest Preserves and similar publicly owned conservation areas, enrollees dug ditches, planted trees and shrubs, laid sod, and built recreational infrastructure such as bridges, trails, picnic shelters, bathing beaches, and dams. Some black Chicagoans also served in Michigan, where tree planting was enrollees' main task: there the objective was not only to build up the nation's timber supply but also to create a vast recreational resource on public land unable to support agriculture.[67]

Black Chicagoans also worked extensively on privately owned Illinois farms (or on publicly owned parcels and infrastructure that abutted and directly affected privately held land), where they typically focused either on drainage or soil conservation projects. Both types of projects attempted to manage rainfall and water flow so that the land produced corn (and, to a lesser extent, oats, soybeans, and wheat) at optimal levels. Both were also part of a unified approach to modifying the land shaped by Progressive-era ideals of efficiency termed "wise land use practices" and "include[d] not only land drainage but also good rotations, and soil improvement to maintain soil fertility on level lands, and contour tillage, strip-cropping, terracing, and tree planting to control erosion on sloping lands."[68] Drainage projects were intended to dry out low-lying land by expediting the removal of water via streams, ditches, and tiling systems. To this end, African American companies improved existing tile and ditch drainage systems—at least some of which dated to the 1860s, and many of which had fallen into critical disrepair when the Great Depression financially devastated farmers—and constructed new ones to augment "sluggish" and "meander[ing]" streams, thereby boosting crop production.[69] Blocked by trees, weeds, and debris, ditches carried only a small fraction of the water they had been designed to drain, which led to excess soil moisture, prolonged floods, and, eventually, suppressed crop yields. As one CCC report pointed out, cleaning

Figure 5.2a. CCC enrollees from Company 610 excavating a channel south of Tower Road in the Skokie Lagoons, March 18, 1935. Series 0: Photographs and Illustrations, Sub-series 3: Skokie Lagoons Project #1, ca. 1930–ca. 1940, Box 0-3-9, Group 154 Item 1, FPDCC_00_03_0003_077, Forest Preserve District of Cook County records, University of Illinois at Chicago Library, Special Collections.

Figure 5.2b. CCC enrollees from Company 610 posing for a photograph with their main tools—shovels and wheelbarrows—on March 18, 1935. Series 0: Photographs and Illustrations, Sub-series 3: Skokie Lagoons Project #1, ca. 1930–ca. 1940, Box 0-3-9, Group 154 Item 6, FPDCC_00_03_0003_082, Forest Preserve District of Cook County records, University of Illinois at Chicago Library, Special Collections.

and clearing work in drainage ditches was especially important because it was a relatively simple, if labor intensive, solution that could "often double or treble [the] capacity" of a ditch to remove water from pasture-land and farmland.[70] Soil conservation projects, by contrast, were intended to make hilly land wetter and more nutrient rich by stemming the flow of water and soil into watersheds. African American companies mainly undertook projects such as constructing terraces and contour furrows in fields and pastures to reduce runoff from sloped lands, crushing limestone into dust to be used as fertilizer on "erosion resisting legumes and grasses [to] be grown on land retired from cultivation," and "tree planting on badly eroded areas."[71]

In much the same way agricultural land had been worked in the South for centuries—and was still worked by laborers in the 1930s despite decades of creeping mechanization—African American CCC enrollees across the rural Midwest mostly used hand tools such as shovels, spades, scythes, saws, mattocks, and axes to do the digging, hauling, clearing, and planting on private and public lands. Men cleared ditches of brush, weeds, and other debris largely by hand, and the same was true for deepening and widening ditches; one report estimated that 85 percent of ditch clearing was done with axes and saws, and 95 percent of excavation was done with spades and shovels.[72] According to another official report, one ditch-clearing job undertaken by an African American company in Illinois was "practically a logging operation" because the growth of large trees—likely willows—"had apparently never been cleared before."[73] Two units of an African American soil conservation company in rural Illinois, meanwhile, spent the winter months of 1937 thinning trees from "a dense forest of oak and elm trees" to produce cordwood and fence posts from the resulting lumber before planting around one million black locust and walnut trees later that spring. As the other unit working in the forests put it, "Trees, Trees, Trees! And still more trees! Trees in an indefinite number, and all to be planted! Not by machines but by labor of some CCC boys. . . . Some day, we hope, [these trees] will be useful in holding the soil."[74] In Michigan, where tree planting was the primary focus, a single company could expect to plant around 2.5 million trees over approximately 2,000 acres (or roughly three square miles) in a year's two planting seasons in spring and fall, given decent weather. Setting out in units of twenty-five men, enrollees who were especially adept could plant up to 1,200 trees over an acre and a half in a single day, but had to take more care planting small saplings only a few inches long than ones that had already grown to a few feet. With a workday of approximately seven hours, enrollees could plant between two and three trees every single work minute.[75]

Regardless of whether a given assignment's ultimate objective was rehabilitating private farmland to increase yields or creating public recreation space, the value of African American environmental labor that shaped hundreds of thousands of acres across rural Illinois and Michigan easily ranged into the millions of dollars and most directly benefited whites; the Idlewilders who hunted or fished amid millions of newly planted trees were more the exception than the rule. Environmental benefits that accrued to predominantly white communities were perhaps most pronounced in downstate Illinois farmland. On the completion of one Illinois drainage project that lowered the water table by as much as two and a half feet in some places, for example, a report noted that CCC work "meant just the difference between good crops and poor or no crops," and in wetter years, "practically the entire crop is saved, to say nothing of the peace of mind of the farm operators."[76] Although CCC work clearly had an immediate impact on local, overwhelmingly white communities, it also had more lasting impacts: the effect of ditch clearing was expected to last about three years before weeds and willows encroached again, but repaired tile systems could last a decade or more before needing additional work.[77]

More generally, though, such efforts were the first steps in a longer term project to boost farmlands' productivity. If productivity indeed increased, agronomists and foresters hoped that more marginally productive acreage could be "gradually removed from production and returned to grass, parks, woodland, game, and Forest Preserves," hence creating the types of leisure spaces already under development in the Forest Preserves of Cook County.[78] For example, one African American company that primarily focused on soil conservation and drainage on Illinois farmland planted 10,000 trees on a 256-acre farm's ten-acre woodlot intended for "game bird protection" and cleared a nearby area in preparation for the construction of a Boy Scout camp.[79] In Michigan, meanwhile, the forests planted in part by African Americans were on a much larger scale and meant to draw recreation seekers in the much nearer term; they still stand today, protected as state and national forests. Like the Skokie Lagoons and other areas of the Cook County Forest Preserves that benefited from the CCC's environmental labor, they too continue to draw leisure seekers and buoy property values long after African American enrollees returned to their Chicago homes. Sometimes these recreational inequalities were even more immediate and readily apparent to enrollees: a bathing beach used by Camp Reinberg in the Deer Grove Forest Preserves north of Chicago was off-limits to the young black men who constructed it.[80]

The African American Experience of Environmental Labor in the Rural Midwest

The scale and duration of African Americans' environmental labor in Illinois and Michigan are staggering, but ultimately fail to convey CCC enrollees' actual experience in far-flung Midwestern landscapes. What did their work mean to them? Reflecting on just how closely many African American laborers were tied to nature in the agricultural South, Richard Wright said, "When the time comes to break the sod, the sod must be broken; when the time comes to plant the seeds, the seeds must be planted; . . . The seasons of the year form the mold that shapes our lives, and who can change the seasons?"[81] Although the crops cultivated in the South varied from the Mississippi Delta to the rolling hills of Kentucky to the coastal plains of the Carolinas, the common thread was that environmental labor ebbed and flowed in cycles with the growing seasons: if one worked in agriculture, there was no breaking free from the tyranny of spring planting and fall harvest. But by and large, migration to the urban industrial North *did* break working-class African Americans free from the tethers of the seasons. In cities like Chicago, workers' lives were governed by the clock and the workweek, not the weather and the climate. Working-class migrants held jobs that, although they were "close to the soil, the animals, and the machinery that undergird Chicago's economy," were largely insulated from the changing seasons (though some industries such as meatpacking retained some seasonal variability, workers still labored indoors).[82] By contrast, the CCC thrust African American enrollees back onto the mercy of the seasons, and in some ways to an even greater extent than Southern agriculture demanded of its laborers. Indeed, the CCC's year-round adherence to the industrial factory model's full workday exposed enrollees to wildly variable extreme conditions—particularly, winter cold—for which no amount of environmental labor in the South could have adequately prepared them.

Working in remote camps under white commanding officers and foremen in conditions that could range from punishing heat to numbing cold, not to mention rain and snow, African Americans developed their own unique environmental labor culture that blended familiar elements of environmental labor in the rural South with modern industrial labor practices in unfamiliar Northern climates and landscapes: it was the factory system grafted onto the land. Indeed, although the rhythms of CCC work in Midwestern fields, forests, and marshes were partially governed by the seasons (some types of work were simply impossible once the ground froze in the winter, for instance), the seasonal ebbs and flows that shaped environmental labor in the South were greatly attenuated. Like a factory in nature, CCC work continued virtually year-round at full speed, ceasing only for hours or a day or two in the most extreme conditions. Although a Department of Labor informational bulletin made it clear that recruits need not "have experience in camp life or work in the forests"—acknowledging that most men would "be 'green' at this sort of work" and assuring recruiters that "physical health and strength, willingness to work hard, and good conduct are enough to carry any man through successfully"—plenty of enrollees who arrived fresh from Chicago had trouble adjusting to life in remote rural camps, having had little to no experience with or interest in rugged outdoor work in such a climate.[83]

Even in the relatively moderate weather of spring and fall, the sheer drudgery and physically demanding nature of the work could easily wear on enrollees. In the Skokie Lagoons, a company commander noted that the enrollees welcomed any departure "from the routine of pushing one wheelbarrow of dirt from the channel up a long incline to the dike, only to dump it and return for another."[84] But there was little allowance for deviation from that routine; hour after hour, day after day, month after month, enrollees dug ditches and hauled dirt. Some officials tried to break the monotony by promoting "a friendly rivalry" between groups of men over "which one will move the most dirt or make the largest hole," but the dirt was moved and the holes dug regardless.[85] In Michigan, meanwhile, the moderate weather of spring and fall meant that enrollees planted millions of trees.[86] Having to plant between 1,000 and

1,200 trees every single workday while conditions allowed—one company newspaper noted that fall planting continued until the ground had frozen "absolutely too hard for a dibble to be driven into the ground or until the snow is so deep that it must be raked away"—predictably led many to bodily and mental exhaustion. When the same article jokingly noted that the resumption of the fall tree-planting season was "much to the distress of the boys," there was more than a grain of truth in it.[87] As one company official noted, with the spring and fall planting seasons in Michigan's forests also came "long line[s] of boys in front of the camp hospital [who] complained of sore muscles and backs, hoping the doctor would put them on the sick book so they wouldn't have to go to the woods."[88] Much like at the Skokie Lagoons, some company officers tried to boost morale, promote good-natured competitiveness, and increase efficiency by framing the work itself as a contest. During 1938's fall planting season, for instance, Michigan CCC camps statewide were pitted against one another in a tree-planting competition that was monitored with daily reports on each company's progress.[89]

Spring's mild weather inevitably gave way to summer's sweltering heat and humidity that could easily approach that of the South, and there was little relief for CCC enrollees laboring outdoors because work paused only briefly even during the most extreme heat waves. The CCC work program, a hybrid of the factory workweek and agricultural labor, often demanded labor regardless of high temperatures or the day of the week, forcing enrollees to make up for time lost to thunderstorms or other inclement weather. In 1934, as African American enrollees working in the Skokie Lagoons used picks and shovels to dig the hard black dirt and clay baked by summer sun, temperatures in the field approached 120 degrees one day and 110 on others. According to the company commander, it was "monotonous work" in punishing heat, enough to prompt him to remark, "July will be long remembered by the C.C.C. boys . . . on account of working every Saturday to make up time lost during the week, and on account of the excessive heat which drove the boys into camp early on two days and kept them from going out at all in the afternoon on two other days."[90] The next month, the company was moved to another area in the lagoons where it began preparing dikes for planting with grass and trees. Before holes could be dug and black dirt spread, the dikes needed to be cleared of weeds and brush that had sprung up in the preceding months. In temperatures that ranged as

Figure 5.3. CCC enrollees from Company 609 clearing the "luxuriant growth" of enormous weeds along the dikes bordering the north branch of the Chicago River near the Skokie Lagoons, August 8, 1934. Series 0: Photographs and Illustrations, Sub-series 3: Skokie Lagoons Project #1, ca. 1930–ca. 1940, Box 0-3-8, Group 61 Item 6, FPDCC_00_03_0005_076, Forest Preserve District of Cook County records, University of Illinois at Chicago Library, Special Collections.

high as 110 degrees, enrollees cleared this undergrowth, much of which "had attained a luxuriant growth and required no little effort on the part of the boys to pull. Considerable time was put on this work, for besides pulling the large weeds, all small ones were also pulled and the ground put in suitable condition for seeding." Given the photographs of enrollees standing alongside weeds that stood taller than they did, it is little surprise that "no little effort" was required (see Figure 5.3). Once the weeds were cleared, picks were once again needed to dig the holes for trees, not just because high temperatures had baked the soil into a hard crust but also "because in some cases the clay dike [had] been pounded and packed by the constant passing of trucks and heavy equipment."[91] Regardless of the conditions, the factory in the countryside chugged along, slowly building the Skokie Lagoons with African American labor.

Downstate, meanwhile, African American enrollees who were in drainage and soil conservation camps worked through the same summer heat waves. At one camp made up of World War I veterans, they complained that not even taking refuge "under the shade trees and by the streams" could provide relief from the "sweltering temperatures on the bleak, low prairie."[92] At another camp, drought made the ground too hard for enrollees in soil conservation companies to terrace rolling fields effectively; they simply had to wait until rain loosened the ground enough for them to resume work. But their labor did not cease: quarrying and crushing limestone that would fertilize depleted Illinois cornfields continued no matter how dry the soil may have been. In Michigan, the dry soil and heat were not ideal for planting trees, so the summer was spent creating and improving roads and truck trails by uprooting stumps, clearing brush, and grading the land; rebuilding and repairing bridges; and, perhaps most of all, scalping small patches of land to prepare a space for each tree to be planted in the fall.[93] Scalping involved "removing an eighteen inch square of sod at seven and a half foot spacings," one for each tree to be planted—a task that could be quite tedious.[94] One company newspaper article titled "Chicago Rookies Can't Take It" jokingly referred to the thirty-two new enrollees coming down with "scalpingitis," a term the men had no doubt invented to refer to the enrollees' difficulty "scalping" the land.[95]

Winter in the field brought its own challenges, as African American enrollees regularly faced temperatures and snowy conditions rarely seen in the South; compelled to work as long as temperatures were above 10 degrees, some enrollees effectively quit instead. Official CCC reports are littered with instances of dozens of African American enrollees refusing to work in such frigid temperatures and being dishonorably discharged as a result. Brutally cold temperatures in the Skokie Lagoons in January 1935 meant that "the progress of the work has been greatly retarded by the frost in the ground to a depth of 2 feet or more caused by the recent rains and severe cold weather. All the dirt moved must be broken out in large chunks by the use of frost wedges and sledges and then broken into pieces that can be loaded into wheelbarrows."[96] Reflecting on several days at or below zero degrees that caused another company in the Skokie Lagoons to call off work for half the month of January, one report noted, "These low temperatures, accompanied by strong winds, make for much discomfort and no little suffering among men who are not accustomed to working in cold weather."[97] Richard Wright described his similar winter experience digging in the Cook County Forest Preserves in two separate stints for non-CCC relief organizations as "cold, bitterly hard work. I rode in zero weather

Figure 5.4. CCC enrollees from Company 609 hauling a wheelbarrow through the mud in the Skokie Lagoons, February 15, 1935. Series 0: Photographs and Illustrations, Sub-series 3: Skokie Lagoons Project #1, ca. 1930–ca. 1940, Box 0-3-9, Group 144 Item 2, FPDCC_00_03_0005_235, Forest Preserve District of Cook County records, University of Illinois at Chicago Library, Special Collections.

for miles in open trucks, then spaded the frozen earth for eight hours, only to ride home again in the dark, in an open truck."[98]

For enrollees working in the Skokie Lagoons, even warmer winter days could prove miserable. When the marshland was not frozen, mud and standing water were everywhere. In the late winter of 1935, one company commander noted, "Often times the boys would be in water and mud up to their shoe tops," and the mud and wet clay made pushing a laden wheelbarrow along gangplanks especially precarious.[99] Another boss in the Skokie Lagoons noted that winter that "the use of hip boots is in order at all times, and the handling of the wet, sloppy clay from such a depth to a dike 200 feet away by wheelbarrows is a tedious task and the use of cinders on the plank runways was necessary to prevent slipping while pushing the wheelbarrows"[100] (see Figure 5.4). Downstate, limestone quarrying carried on virtually regardless of the temperature; as one official for an Illinois African American company noted in January 1936, "In spite of an unusual amount of very cold weather, we

have quarried 1120 tons and quarried and ground 580 tons of limestone" in just a bit more than two months.[101] Nor did work stop on even
the coldest winter days in Michigan's forests: when the ground was too
frozen to prepare for planting, companies worked to improve existing
forest stands by clearing out old and diseased trees.[102]

Despite the climatic conditions that at times could be undeniably
challenging, company newspapers indicate a diversity of enrollee reactions to the CCC experience, much like the campers' varying reactions
to a stay at Camp Wabash or Camp Belnap: for every enrollee who was
miserable, another found enjoyable aspects to his environmental labor
in the countryside. Rather than complain about the cold winter he had
just endured, for instance, one African American enrollee in Illinois
thoughtfully reflected on nature in late March 1937: "The cold, bitter and
icy winter is almost over. There are a few signs of spring. The winter
winds have calmed a little, the sun is shining beautifully, thawing out
ground. And the life that has been inactive all Winter has finally started
on its way again toward an unknown destination, some of our birds that
make their Winter home in the South are flying homeward again to the
North."[103] Similarly, men who endured the hardship of establishing a new
camp in Illinois idealized their previous camp in the Skokie Lagoons by
comparison, where "the woods were full of flowers, [and] beautiful and
glamorous butterflies flitted hither and yon."[104] Reminiscent of W. E. B.
Du Bois's flowery assessment of Idlewild, one could scarcely guess that
the environmental labor enrollees undertook there involved digging
ditches and hauling countless wheelbarrow loads of dirt.

There are also signs that working-class enrollees took pride in their
rustic surroundings, beautifying camp areas in ways not that different
from how Idlewild's black cultural elite cultivated gardens or community institutions encouraged South Siders to plant grass and flowers each
spring—a development that should not be surprising given that Edgar
Brown, Madden Park's director who initiated Black Belt cleanup efforts
in the early 1930s, also served as the CCC's Adviser on Negro Affairs. At
a camp in the Cook County Forest Preserves, the company newspaper
contended that the "considerable competition between members of each
barracks in beautifying the areas around their barracks with trees,
shrubbery, and flowers" was evidence of "an outward expression of the
appreciation of the camp by members of the company."[105] Months of
labor had transformed the rougher, wilder nature they encountered on

first arriving there into a more pastoral landscape. In more rural downstate camps, meanwhile, some African American enrollees hunted rabbits, squirrels, and even skunks on the Illinois prairie in their free time—opportunities that would have been in short supply for migrants in Chicago, but that were abundant across the South.[106]

Of course, the surrounding natural environment was not always hospitable, and sometimes enrollees used humor and imagination to deal with difficult circumstances. For those working in the marshy land north of Chicago, mosquitoes and other pests could prove especially uncomfortable until an autumnal frost thinned their numbers. The company newspaper of the same Cook County Forest Preserves camp that beautified its grounds attempted to make light of enrollees' plight with an article titled "Mosquitoes Attack Camp Deer Grove: Casualties Heavy." The article, written by an enrollee, began by contending that "the age old question as to whether insects will some day conquer man and overrun the earth has been answered at Deer Grove"; it continued by joking that "in addition to there being so many of them that it was impossible to see two feet ahead, these were unusually vicious, some of them had spears two feet long (believe it or not)." Although a fall frost had improved the situation, the enrollee continued, "We are all waiting for the arctic mosquitoes which are on their way. Yes there are such mosquitoes because we will believe anything we hear about those flying reptiles."[107] An ingenious way of both venting enrollees' frustrations and not running afoul of camp officials' likely desire to promote high morale by maintaining an optimistic outlook, the company newspaper's farce found humor in what must have been at times a truly miserable summer.[108]

Other enrollees attempted to make sense of their environmental labor on the prairie in the pages of their company newspapers, poetically connecting limestone quarrying to its larger ecological purpose or metaphorically linking it to a musical performance. In the short three-stanza poem titled "Limestone," one African American Illinois enrollee imagined the long-term ecological benefits outweighing the short-term hardship he and his fellow limestone crushers endured:

> Working in the sun all day
> Grinding limestone is no play
> Still we get a thrill to know
> Limestone makes the tall corn grow.

Tho' the dust blow in our eyes
Still we always realize
Limestone makes the clover sweet;
So the cows and sheep can eat.

So we know it's work we must!
Grinding limestone into dust
Cause it makes the soil so pure,
Makes the farmers' crops secure![109]

Whereas that poem took an expansive view of enrollees' limestone-crushing task that internalized the official goals of the company's soil conservation experts, an enrollee in a different downstate African American company imaginatively recast the labor itself as a musical endeavor that connoted Chicago's Stroll. Having just mentioned his desire to return to Chicago as soon as possible, that enrollee turned to anticipating the coming summer's work in the quarries, claiming that he "long[ed] to swing the hammer once more and hear the musical notes of the crusher."[110] It was as if his mind had returned to the jazz clubs of the Stroll while he was still destined to labor in the quarries for at least another few months. Earlier that year, that same enrollee had admitted, "All the [other] boys [in the company] seem to think that we have a hard way to go," but he went on to say, "Well, we boys don't think so. We think, working in a rock quarry is all in a day's run. On our project, all you can hear is the drumming of the sledges and the musical sound of the crusher. After all, some one had to work in the quarry, and we were chosen to do the job. All I can say is that we boys are trying to do a good job."[111] Exuding a sense of resignation to the difficulty of his environmental labor, the enrollee's musical metaphors also make plain the ways in which some enrollees longed for city life.

For good or ill, many enrollees remarked on just how different CCC camp life was from city life, echoing reformers' observations of the changes in boys and girls after spending a week or two at youth camps in similar environments. One white CCC officer in African American and mixed-race camps in Illinois and Michigan "observed the change that came over the city bred enrollees" when they began working in the woods. Although enrollees clearly missed the attractions of city life, the officer wrote, "The majority had lived in rat-infested alleyways and crowded streets, so getting out into the forest primeval and discovering its landlocked lakes, and fish-stocked streams wandering wildly through the lowlands, with game in every thicket, revealed a new side of life to them."[112] Although the officer's beliefs hint at an anti-urban bias as well as racism and delinquency fears, they were echoed by an African American CCC enrollee in Michigan, who reflected, "One of the greatest and most impressive things in the CCC is working in the fields. Traveling by truck for many miles into the far recesses of the forests is an opportunity that many people from large cities would not ordinarily have."[113] He believed that the CCC had improved his health, given him educational opportunities and practical training experiences he would not have had otherwise, and allowed him to travel across the state on the company's sports teams—all of which gave him "a new slant on life."[114]

At the same time, however, those truck trips to remote worksites could just as easily evoke misery in an enrollee. Another Michigan enrollee recalled his early CCC experiences in a poem published in his camp's newspaper, writing that he arrived "Deep in God's country with naught to see but a tree, / Where Nature is in the raw, and paved roads you never see." His invocation of "God's country" recalls the *Defender*'s exhortation decades earlier to enjoy leisure time in the natural environment. But the tone of the poem quickly changed when, on his first day on the job, the enrollee "boarded the truck at work call, to the woods I then did go, / It didn't strike me as funny, slaving out in that cold and snow." His closing assessment was that "life in the three C's, my man, as you can plainly see, / May be a snap for others, but was a pain in the neck to me."[115] Whether he meant to or not, the enrollee's allusion to slave labor highlighted the fact that, for African American enrollees working under white officers in the Midwest, the "pain in the neck" of environmental labor in the CCC sometimes carried with it the racial discrimination that migrants had been eager to escape when they had left the South.

CCC Labor: "Achievement by the Race" or "All the Earmarks of a Peonage Farm"?

The *Defender*'s CCC coverage underscored the New Deal agency's hybrid environmental resonance for African American migrants in the North, highlighting both the possibility of racial and individual advancement that CCC's environmental labor offered while also denouncing the ways in which it sometimes perpetuated a long history of racial discrimination and hard labor on the land. In some cases, the newspaper lauded both African American accomplishments in the CCC and the organization itself. Soon after the Skokie Lagoons project north of Chicago began, for instance, the newspaper had declared African American labor on the massive endeavor to "transform an erstwhile marsh into a beautiful forest and a series of seven lagoons" to be a "a tacit proclamation of achievement by the Race."[116] In other words, the *Defender* contended that the results of that environmental transformation—the network of lagoons, channels, and levees in the Cook County Forest Preserves from which Chicagoland residents would benefit for generations to come—constituted a landscape of hope: a silent but material testament to African American capability and progress. Even more specifically, it was the sort of racial progress that African American migrants found most possible in the North, in some cases underwritten by the federal government. The *Defender* reiterated similar ideas in 1940, when it reported that hundreds of CCC enrollees from ten African American companies in Illinois were set to converge on the American Negro Exposition in Chicago for "CCC Day," which opened with the singing of the Negro national anthem, "Lift Every Voice and Sing," and was followed by a program of prayer, song, and lectures. Conceived of as a black World's Fair marking the seventy-fifth anniversary of slavery's end, one historian has argued that the exposition "sought to inventory the progress made by African Americans since slavery, and therefore buttress claims to full civil status and belonging."[117]

In many ways, the *Defender* was simply assenting to ideas about the CCC's purpose in a nation fractured by the Great Depression, ideas that were foundational to the agency's administrative rationale and that were in much wider circulation than just in the African American community. Indeed, the CCC's presence at Chicago's American Negro Exposition demonstrated just how fully many African Americans had accepted FDR's notion that the agency succeeded in building men and building trees during the Great Depression, with benefits accruing to *all* Americans regardless of race. In fact, both the American Negro Exposition and the *Defender*—bastions of African American middle-class thought—largely agreed with the white superintendent of an African American company in the Skokie Lagoons who loftily predicted, "The C.C.C. will, eventually, become the one institution in the United States in which sectionalism cannot maintain and in which racial and nationality prejudice will be obliterated. The time is not far away when the Skokie Lagoons development, aside from becoming a Park of unexcelled beauty, will stand out as a silent testimonial of the foresight and ability of those men of this State who have made the development possible."[118] These were notions that echoed the *Pittsburgh Courier* columnist's assertion that Idlewilders' attraction to nature showed how African Americans "just naturally drift toward the things that are human and American."[119]

The question, though, was whether the "tacit proclamation" and "silent testimonial" would stand like the tacit proclamations and silent testimonials of black environmental labor in David L. Cohn's Mississippi Delta landscape, performed under white overseers and landowners who derived the most lasting value from it. Or did these landscapes in the rural Midwest represent something new? Were they truly landscapes of hope? Because while the CCC and the landscapes it shaped could hold hopeful, symbolic power for African Americans' integration into the narrative of American progress, the *Defender* was also quick to point out that they could also reflect the persistent racism and lack of opportunity that all too often dogged migrants long after they had left the South. After all, even though the dollar-a-day wage was the same for enrollees regardless of race, one could make a case that segregated labor under white foremen and overseers was a step back for working-class migrants who ordinarily would have found urban industrial jobs that, although they were almost invariably unskilled entry-level jobs under white bosses, were not so strictly segregated as in the CCC companies.

In December 1937, for instance, the *Defender's* front page demanded a federal inquiry into a downstate Illinois camp near the confluence of the Mississippi and Ohio Rivers that twenty-three African American enrollees claimed had "all the earmarks of a peonage farm in the southland." Earlier that fall, several young men who had been working at a Skokie Lagoons camp—the conditions at which were described as "ideal and within government regulations"—had been routinely transferred to the downstate camp where they claimed to have encountered poor food and sanitation, not unlike some black Chicagoans who stayed at Camps Algonquin and Reinberg in this period. More damningly, they said that the white commanding officer warned other enrollees not to join them in protesting camp conditions by saying, "These boys from the North think they are better than you boys from the South, and you must not get any silly notions of the northern Negro in your heads."[120] Although the *Defender* failed to follow up on its initial story and inform its readers of what happened to the accusers or the camp from which they were discharged, the scrutiny generated by the article did prompt an internal investigation that revealed both the opportunities and limitations for African Americans in the CCC—opportunities and limitations that were more broadly representative of those faced by working-class migrants in the North. Despite the absence of testimony by the discharged enrollees who registered the complaint, the resulting investigation offered a revealing glimpse at the ways in which the Great Migration forged a hybrid environmental culture among black Chicagoans serving in the CCC, showing how the long history of oppressive and discriminatory environmental labor in the South sometimes persisted in Northern landscapes.

A deeper analysis of the 1937 conflict over race and environmental labor in downstate Illinois reveals how the products of the Great Migration had come to expect equal treatment, demanding more respect from whites than many Southern African Americans dared to; indeed, they displayed the same self-confidence with which many black Chicagoans responded to race conflict at Jackson Park beach. In some cases, enrollees ran headlong into a culture of manual environmental labor and racism in the CCC that too closely resembled Booker T. Washington's accommodationist South for their liking; after all, this was the oppressive culture that their families had rejected when they migrated to the North. In part, the investigation simply revealed common complaints and difficulties among CCC enrollees nationwide, black or white: the work was difficult and often unpleasant, in remote locations far from home. All of the interviewees—both white commanding officers and African American enrollees—agreed that the trouble began almost immediately, when many of the new transfers did an exceptionally poor job planting trees in the field. The transfers complained that tree planting was hard work and that they "didn't want to get down on their knees"; as a result, they were reprimanded and sent back to camp.[121] But although the investigation concluded that the transferred enrollees did seem to be poor workers and that their allegations of inadequate food and sanitation were without merit, it corroborated the young men's claims of racist treatment and grafted that racial conflict over environmental labor onto the geography of the Great Migration.

White or black, virtually everyone who spoke to the investigator—and eventually the investigator himself—interpreted the incident as the product of marked differences between enrollees accustomed to urban Chicago and those accustomed to rural downstate Illinois. From the perspective of the company's white commanding officer, the new transfers "arrived at this camp with the idea of not staying, and their method of getting out was to refuse to work in order to get transportation back to Chicago."[122] Having ample incentive to corroborate the commanding officer's account, both the company's African American doctor and educational advisor largely agreed, discounting the transfers' claims about poor food and sanitation; they too believed the root of the problem was that the transfers "didn't want to come down here; it was too far from home."[123] The doctor agreed with the investigator not only that more generally "the boys from Chicago require more for entertainment than the boys from the country" but also that "the boys from the city are ready to strike quickly" as compared to country boys when met with poor labor conditions out in the field: these were lessons that many, like Dempsey Travis and Timuel Black, had perhaps learned at protests in Washington Park just a few years earlier.[124]

But the perceived differences between the enrollees fresh from the Chicago area and those who had worked longer at the rural downstate camp went even deeper. The white commanding officer went on to state, "It seems that the idea was to show up the enrollees of Camp Pomona, as being dumb and ignorant. Chicago boys could and would get things done their own way."[125] And one of the company's white foremen offered perhaps the most comprehensive assessment of the conflict between city and country: "These boys were city boys and had just come down from Chicago; they had probably never been out of the city before. They came from Skokie Valley, and after they got down here they were very much disappointed. So back here in the woods they grumbled and didn't want to stay. . . . They thought we were out in the sticks out here."[126] He elaborated, "Bringing those boys from the city and putting them in a place like this was like putting them in slavery to them. They felt like the conditions were awful. I don't mean it was, but suppose a man in your standing would suddenly become very poor and had to go to shoveling. You know how you would feel and that's just how these boys felt, and they didn't stay long enough to get lined up, to get accustomed to muddy, country life."[127] The foreman's reference to slavery was perhaps more telling than he meant it to be, as the investigator's findings revealed a racist geography of South and North grafted onto the perceived divide between expectations and lifestyles in urban and rural places.

Indeed, it was little wonder that the enrollees transferred from Chicago chafed under the camp's environmental and social conditions, because for the enrollees of this particular southern Illinois company, it was as if the culture of slavery and sharecropping had been transplanted from South to North. The investigator's interviews revealed the racist ways in which enrollees were treated, confirming the *Defender*'s reporting that the commanding officer and at least one white foreman believed that "Northern colored boys thought they were better than Southern boys" and finding that another white foreman in the camp "said he has no use for these niggers that strike for something to eat, if them niggers don't [*sic*] get them trees planted right, he . . . was going to take his fist and knock hell out of them."[128] The commander's and foremen's racism, reminiscent of slave masters' threats of physical violence, could not be more plain.

Yet the commander's distinction between "Northern colored boys" and "Southern boys" introduced a cultural idea that seemed to negate actual geographical origins, given that every enrollee in the company was from Illinois, even those who had recently migrated from the South. The commander's meaning became clear in the CCC investigator's conclusion, however, when he noted that many enrollees complained of being underfed and "any number of boys told me [the white commanding officers] were slave drivers," keeping them working in the fields too long; he concluded that the commander in question "would be a good commander with a white company, but owing to the fact he comes from Mississippi, I am afraid he cannot adapt himself to the colored people ways in the north."[129] For the Southern company commander, geography became shorthand for behavior. Hence his racist critique of the products of the Great Migration: the "Northern colored boys" were "the New Negroes" more likely to demand respect and fair treatment from white superiors and institutions, while the "Southern boys" knew their place. Mississippi and the "earmarks of a peonage farm in the southland" had followed these enrollees North, challenging their aspirations to reject white supremacy in search of a better life.[130]

A survey of records from African American CCC camps across Illinois and Michigan where black Chicagoans were stationed reveal similar, if less blatant, instances of enrollees subjected to the racist prejudices of white camp officials and a more general atmosphere of racial discrimination within the agency. Based on seemingly little evidence whatsoever, for instance, one CCC investigator said of an eastern Illinois African American company, "As in most of the colored companies thruout [sic] this northern section of the country, it is difficult to show the negro boy the value of property, and make him realize that he has a large responsibility in the camp. There seems to be little personal pride for the organization."[131] Another official at the same camp voiced similar criticisms a few months earlier when he wrote to the federal CCC director in 1941 to explain that the high attrition rate for the company over the past year was "not considered excessive due to the fact that colored enrollees in the Sixth Corps Area are not generally up to the standard of white enrollees and require more discipline. All camp supervisory personnel have made and are continuing to make every effort to reduce discharges and dismissals. However, discipline cannot be relaxed or chaos will prevail."[132] White CCC officials may have been responding to black enrollees who actually performed their work less satisfactorily than the average white enrollee, but they were largely—if not wholly—oblivious to a long African American tradition of intentional work slowdowns and sabotage when confronted with racially hostile work environments.[133] Regardless, when one combines reports like those with other reports from African American camps across the state, the balance of evidence tilts quite convincingly toward a climate of racism within the CCC that working-class migrants were unable to escape in the North. Even the photographic record speaks volumes; images of white foremen supervising African American enrollees' manual labor in rural environments connote the racially unequal labor conditions African Americans endured across the South (see Figure 5.5).

The CCC's racial climate in Illinois and Michigan, then, was conversant with the racist tropes of the indolent and incompetent African American worker, which subjected many African American enrollees to "more discipline" of the sort that those at the "peonage farm" downstate experienced. According to an investigator, for instance, another African American Illinois camp made up primarily of enrollees from Chicago was so remote that "recreation for the enrollees are weekly trips a distance of 45 miles where the nearest colored population is located," and their problems with high desertion rates over the preceding year "could be

Figure 5.5. CCC enrollees clearing a channel south of Willow Road, at the southernmost border of Skokie Lagoons with a white foreman looking on, August 8, 1933. Series 0: Photographs and Illustrations, Sub-series 3: Skokie Lagoons Project #1, ca. 1930–ca. 1940, Box 0–3–8, Group 5 Item 6, FPDCC_00_03_0001_048, Forest Preserve District of Cook County records, University of Illinois at Chicago Library, Special Collections.

directly attributed to poor messes, run-down condition of the camp and a commanding officer who did not make any effort to gain the respect of the members of this company, and was prejudiced against the colored race."[134] At yet another rural Illinois company composed primarily of enrollees from Chicago, the investigator found that "morale was very low in the company"; it was so low, in fact, that he "was led to believe that the camp was on the verge of an uprising" by enrollees who were entirely "justified in their complaints." He concluded, "This is a colored company and it is felt that neither of [the commanding officers] knows how to deal with the boys"—no doubt a euphemism for the officers' racial prejudice.[135] Indeed, just a few months later, enrollees from that very same camp wrote a letter to the investigator, pleading that "the boys of camp Carroll are again in need of your help" because the commander "goes through the barracks in the morning and turn[s] beds over with the boys in them, and hitting them accross [sic] the head with pillows to wake them up. It is said the reason he is so bold is that he carries his gun, then if you speak up for your self it is a dishonorable discharge."[136] Such accounts made the CCC sound more like Mississippi's infamous prison work camp at Parchman Farm than a federally administered relief program in the North.[137]

Brutally cold winter weather seemed to bring to the surface some white CCC officials' racial prejudice, as they voiced stereotypes that dated back to slavery and sometimes even echoed Southern whites who had attempted to deter African Americans from migrating North with warnings that they would freeze to death. In 1935, one company officer working in the Cook County Forest Preserves noted, "Considerable snow fell during the last two weeks of December and although the temperature was not extremely low it was not the kind of weather when colored enrollees do the best kind of work."[138] That same month, a company commander in the Skokie Lagoons reflected on the African American company's reaction to working in single-digit temperatures, saying that some "seem to have a greater dread of the cold weather than of the work" and that "many are totally ignorant of ways of keeping themselves warm other than getting as close as possible to artificial heat."[139] The following winter, company officials in the Skokie Lagoons blamed the cold weather for enrollee desertions, noting, "The morale of the company is somewhat below good weather average. Enrollees seem to resent being required to work when weather is such as to cause them discomfort."[140] Although desertions leading to dishonorable discharges from the CCC may have increased in particularly cold weather, there is little evidence that African American enrollees were discharged at a higher rate than white enrollees—despite the racist treatment many received—and contrary to the generalizations of CCC officials who explained high attrition rates in terms of racial capabilities or dispositions.[141]

Regardless of weather conditions, it seems clear that African American enrollees' environmental labor in Illinois and Michigan sometimes triggered white officials' racial prejudices, which then influenced the sort of work assigned and informed their perceptions of enrollees. In the Skokie Lagoons, for instance, a company commander determined that the more skilled labor of leveling and grading the soil "could be done to a better advantage by white boys," and so he assigned African American enrollees the more physically strenuous and less skilled job of excavating soil to be hauled to a nearby stockpile. The commander justified his decision by saying, "This work is more to the liking of the colored boys and they made a good showing in moving black dirt."[142]

The African American enrollees may have performed that more difficult job well, but it remains substantially less clear whether the work was actually more to their liking, given that other officers had described the very same job as painfully monotonous. Similar racial stereotypes were evident after a lightning strike killed a white enrollee in another Skokie Lagoons company. A commanding officer of that African American company claimed that the "accident caused uneasiness among the boys and especially the colored boys as they are naturally superstitious," going on to note that, although some work time that month was lost due to rain, "the morale of the enrollees is of the highest standard, as can be noted by their continual laughter and song while at work."[143] Similarly, another white officer in the Skokie Lagoons observed of his African American workers that "at all times the morale of the enrollees has been excellent. They are cheerful and willing workers, often moving a pick to the rythm [sic] of group singing or chanting," all despite conditions making progress "very slow and arduous."[144] Enrollees' work songs in the rural North, transported from the South, clearly marked a hybrid culture of African American environmental labor in the CCC. Here, too, singing and chanting may have enabled white bosses to overlook or misinterpret the actual experience of African Americans performing sometimes grueling environmental labor.[145]

The atmosphere of the CCC camp located near Idlewild was one of the more egregious examples of the ways racist views could permeate companies. The same white officer who had praised the CCC for exposing urban-dwelling African Americans to "the forest primeval" littered his memoir with African American stereotypes ranging from the violent Zip Coon to the indolent laborer to the innately talented musician—embodying the lingering prejudice of racial essentialism and primitivism that sometimes hung over the CCC. Employed at a camp near Idlewild, he was introduced to the area by the company's white doctor who told him, "It used to be a colored summer resort but now a lot of riff-raff got in and the place is full of blind pigs, cheap whore houses and whatnot. Anything to make money because there's no way to make a living there—most of them are on County Relief. Real estate highbinders pulled in a lot from the towns—got their last cent and dumped them." Going on, he hinted at the paranoia surrounding the communist influence on African Americans in the early years of the Depression, saying, "That kind of stuff makes people meat for radical ideas—and we've got a few of those in the camp, too."[146] Later, the doctor told the new white officer that "a lot of these men in camp right now were ex-convicts or had a criminal record of some kind—dumped on the CCC by the cities to get them out of their communities" and that the culture of the black enrollees was "so primitive. And if you stay here long enough alone at night you get that jungle feeling; you imagine you hear drums and tom-toms."[147] It was precisely such insultingly racist perceptions that Idlewild's black cultural elite had worked against for years; indeed, they would have been deeply infuriating and horrifying to Irene McCoy Gaines and the Idlewild Lot Owners Association.

So did African American CCC camps in the rural Midwest have "all the earmarks of a peonage farm in the southland," or were the results of countless hours of environmental labor performed by enrollees "a tacit proclamation of achievement by the Race"? Of course the answer is that, on balance, it was both: black Chicagoans digging ditches, clearing brush, and planting trees across Illinois and Michigan were constructing landscapes of hope of which they could not take full advantage. And in doing so, they forged a hybrid environmental culture that blended elements of African Americans' long history of rural agricultural labor in the South with elements of black migrants' newfound urban industrial labor patterns in the North, both of which largely revolved around manual environmental labor that primarily benefited white communities. In both the North and South, African Americans labored under some white overseers and bosses who would prove to be incredibly racist and unjust. Yet although African American enrollees could still be subject to the racial prejudices of white officials in the CCC, the dollar-a-day wage, available training, and, perhaps most importantly, the ability to challenge and freedom to escape such discrimination made CCC labor in the North quite different from environmental labor in the South. Much about the environmental labor itself was the same, but the context was vastly different from North to South. In sum, the Great Migration mattered a great deal to the working-class African American men who labored in the CCC—and their families back in the city who received a large portion of their monthly paycheck.

From the perspective of the Great Migration, perhaps the most remarkable impact of African American CCC camps in the North during the Great Depression was the temporary reintroduction of working-class migrant men to rural environmental labor that the vast majority had left behind when they left the South (and some even before that). It was a temporary reintroduction not only because enrollees generally served only six- or twelve- or eighteen-month stints in the CCC but also because the CCC itself lasted only from 1933–1942. By the time the much larger second wave of the Great Migration began during and after World War II—a surge of migration that nearly tripled Chicago's African American population to 813,000 by 1960—the shuttered CCC camps across Illinois and Michigan were already fading into memory, as was the immense reshaping of the landscape that enrollees made possible. The channels and lagoons African American enrollees dug in Skokie became as "natural" a part of the Cook County Forest Preserves as any other land that officials had reclaimed and shaped earlier in the century, the drainage ditches African American enrollees cleared on downstate farms would need to be cleared again while the drainage tile they laid and the limestone they crushed continued to boost crop production, and the trees African American enrollees planted in Michigan became a leisure resource for millions. And enrollees shaped all these landscapes in areas where virtually no African Americans lived, then or now. By the end of the Depression decade, urban life had already largely severed African Americans' close, everyday connection to the rural environment through labor. The CCC was merely a hiccup in broader historical trends of modernization and industrialization that only accelerated once the second wave of the Great Migration began in earnest. Along with the persistent and even intensified forces of race discrimination and segregation that confronted new migrants in the years after World War II, accelerating modernization and industrialization would also make it increasingly difficult for many black Chicagoans to connect to nature through leisure.

Epilogue

A CENTURY OF MIGRATION TO
THAT GREAT IRON CITY

A FTER MORE THAN a decade away, Richard Wright returned to Chicago in 1949 to film an adaptation of *Native Son*. What were his impressions of the Black Metropolis he had once called home? "Truthfully," he wrote in an article for *Ebony* magazine, "there is but one word for it: ugliness." Never one to mince words, Wright found that after living in New York and Paris, the "atmosphere of Chicago's turbulent and tumultuous industrial activity" was striking; the detritus of urban life littering the South Side "all but took my breath away," he reflected, and "above all, I missed the presence of trees to which I had grown so accustomed in Paris!"[1] It was a lament that recalled the moment when he "first glimpsed Chicago through the naïve eyes of a young Mississippi Negro to whom the South Side loomed as the Promised Land, the longed-for Mecca," and found that "there were no curves here, no trees; only angles, lines, squares, bricks and copper wires."[2] Although there was much more than a grain of truth to those two snapshots of Chicago nearly a quarter-century apart, both impressions similarly effaced the more complicated history of Chicago's landscapes of hope by emphasizing elements of the city's hostile environment that symbolized the racial hostility faced by African Americans there.

More accurate were the observations Wright offered about how dramatically the South Side's Black Belt had changed and grown since he

had left during the Great Depression's later years. Seeking the same freedoms and opportunities that drew migrants from the Jim Crow South
to the North in the first wave of the Great Migration, black Southerners
had flooded into Chicago in the 1940s. This time, the industrial demands
of World War II that helped pull the country out of the Great Depression spurred an even larger wave of migration: black Chicago grew by
more than 200,000 residents in the 1940s alone, nearly as much as it
had between 1910 and 1940. Recovering from the social and economic
turmoil of the 1930s, the Black Metropolis Wright found was thriving
as a city-within-a-city despite confronting continued and even intensified race prejudice and segregation. The massive influx of migrants,
returning World War II veterans, and the same sorts of discriminatory
housing practices and violent racism that had confronted Jesse Binga's
family in the early 1920s and Carl Hansberry's family in the late 1930s
had all conspired to create a critical housing shortage in the Black Belt.
As a result, Wright observed, "The South Side apartment buildings
were jammed to bursting with Negroes from Mississippi, Texas, Louisiana, Arkansas, Tennessee, and points South. The South Side was still
a Black Belt, but it had swollen and burst its banks!" Even after Hansberry's Supreme Court victory and, later, the 1948 *Shelley* v. *Kraemer* decision that outlawed restrictive covenants, the barriers of segregation
were as strong as ever due in part to racially discriminatory practices
adopted by the Federal Housing Administration and the Home Owners'
Loan Corporation. Indeed, despite its growth, Wright observed that the
South Side Black Belt "remained an undissolved lump in the city's
melting pot."[3] What did Wright make of these trends and of the pros-
pects for black Chicagoans? "The situation among the white citizens of
Chicago is *bad*, but it contains elements of hope," he wrote, while "the
situation among the Negroes of the South Side is not *too* bad, but it is
distinctly hopeless. Meaning this: Chicago whites still grudgingly with-
hold from the Negro the right to living space, full citizenship, job opportunities; but the Negro, within these hopeless limits, is making progress
in his material standards of living, in education, in business, in culture
and in health."[4]

Among those marks of progress bounded by hopelessness, Wright
could have counted black Chicago's landscapes of hope. In an admittedly
sanguine evaluation of the social potential in Chicago's natural and
landscaped environments, a special mayor's commission in 1946 con-

tended, "Where members of different racial and cultural groups participate in common activities of play, they come to understand that fundamentally the needs of all people are the same. . . . Chicago is rich in beaches, in city parks, in forest preserves. And here, where the city plays and learns to play better, we have an outstanding expression of a united people."[5] No doubt born of lessons learned from fighting fascist regimes in World War II, this assessment was more aspiration than reality: Chicago was no more united than it had been during the first wave of the Great Migration. The mayor's commission conspicuously ignored the persistent race segregation in myriad public green spaces, enforced by whites' fierce resistance to the mixed-race use of parks, beaches, and Forest Preserves that inched ever closer to the Black Metropolis as its frontiers expanded. Yet despite these persistent challenges, Washington Park and other segregated landscapes of hope on the South Side continued to thrive as community institutions, helping welcome the flood of new migrants from the South. Ultimately, they all continued to embody W. E. B. Du Bois's frustrated, defiant advice to "stand erect in a mud-puddle and tell the white world to go to hell, rather than lick boots in a parlor."[6]

Much the same held true in black Chicagoans' rural landscapes of hope outside the city. Idlewild remained segregated, but the resort town thrived in the 1940s and 1950s, spurred by a growing black cultural elite with disposable income.[7] By the same token, an entirely new generation of migrants and their children found ample opportunities to connect with nature through youth camping. A substantial bequest from George Arthur, the Wabash YMCA's longtime executive secretary who died in 1941, was devoted to doubling Camp Wabash's acreage and improving its facilities; then nearly two decades old, it was renamed Camp Arthur in his honor.[8] Beginning in 1942, the South Side Community Committee began sending children to Camp Arthur and other camps in Michigan, Indiana, and Wisconsin, with money raised from charitable organizations and small five- and ten-cent contributions from community members put in collection boxes in participating South Side businesses. By 1945, the Community Committee sent more than 500 children to camp each year, introducing an entirely new generation of South Siders to a program that had not changed appreciably since Camps Wabash and Hammond began operating in the 1920s. Children could expect to spend their time engaged in "campcraft, handicraft, games,

Negro history, archery, nature study and camp songs [and] hiking
through the vast expanse of wooded areas [that] brought forth a galaxy
of vari-colored flowers, bugs, small garter snakes, frogs and a number
of small birds."[9] Although some children took to these experiences more
than others, a boy who wrote to Myrtle Sengstacke at the *Defender* to
say "I love Camp Arthur and I love you for sending me to Camp Arthur"
in the summer of 1950 was indicative of the camp's continued influence.[10] Despite financial struggles not unlike those it faced during the
Great Depression, Camp Arthur continued to host hundreds of South
Siders well into the 1950s, drawing children affiliated with a new YMCA
branch established just three blocks west of Washington Park in 1951.[11]

The trends that motivated Wright to call black Chicagoans' situation
"distinctly hopeless" in 1949 only grew more pronounced as migrants
continued to flood into the city, however, and "Land of Hope" began to
seem more of a misnomer in the 1950s and 1960s than it ever had before. Hundreds of thousands more black Southerners migrated to strictly
segregated neighborhoods on Chicago's South Side and, increasingly, the
West Side. All told, the second wave of the Great Migration helped nearly
quadruple black Chicago's population to more than 1.1 million between
1940 and 1970; roughly half of that increase can be attributed to in-
migration from the South. Chicago's total population remained virtually unchanged in this period, however, which meant that African
Americans' share of the total population nearly quadrupled as well,
jumping from just over 8 percent to more than 32 percent in what had
become, by some measures, America's most segregated city.[12]

Chicago was perhaps the most extreme example, but one could tell
a virtually identical story about countless other cities nationwide: urban
areas were becoming dramatically blacker not just because of in-
migration but also because "white flight" grew middle-class suburbs
ringing the city by leaps and bounds. At the same time, racially discriminatory housing practices such as redlining, underwritten by government policies, precluded the vast majority of African Americans from
realizing the homeownership dreams of *A Raisin in the Sun*'s Lena
Younger. When black Chicagoans did attempt to integrate these suburban spaces—as one family did in Cicero in 1951—they were often
met with virulent race hatred and violence. At the same time, the prospect of decent and affordable public housing was evaporating; the
promise the Ida B. Wells Homes had represented when they opened in

1941 was fading into distant memory. In Chicago, the Robert Taylor Homes and the Dan Ryan Expressway, which opened adjacent to one another on Chicago's South Side in 1962, were emblematic of these growing urban problems. Named after the man who had been so integral to the Wells Homes and the Michigan Boulevard Garden Apartments, the former was a cluster of high-rise buildings that housed 27,000 and came to symbolize the way postwar public housing nationwide concentrated black poverty and exacerbated segregation; the latter was symbolic of the way that highways nationwide were constructed to connect suburban white commuters to downtown business districts, gutting Black Belts and literally dividing communities with concrete. All these trends and more contributed to a tragic feedback loop that plunged black Chicagoans—and products of the Great Migration across the country—into what became known as the "urban crisis."[13]

Black Chicagoans' landscapes of hope were no more immune to the urban crisis than the Black Belt as a whole. The Du Sable Museum of African American History would eventually move to an abandoned Park District building in Washington Park and fortify black Chicagoans' symbolic ownership of that public green space that St. Clair Drake and Horace Cayton had deemed a "community institution" decades earlier. But the poverty and crime that troubled the adjacent, nearly all-black neighborhoods inevitably spilled over into the park. Not even the *Defender*'s annual Bud Billiken parade and picnic were safe from the threat of violent crime, and the deteriorating condition of the Olmsted and Vaux-designed landscaping further reflected the community's struggles.[14] Idlewild, meanwhile, fell victim not only to the corrosive social and economic forces that were tearing apart the South Side but also to a post–civil rights era that favored integration and eroded segregated resorts' customer base.[15] The Wabash YMCA, in dire financial straits despite an Emergency Finance Campaign, suspended the operation of Camp Arthur in 1960 and considered closing it for good.[16]

Martin Luther King's ill-fated Chicago Freedom Movement, which began in earnest in 1966, was perhaps the best indication that black migrants' aspirations were on life support. After more than a decade of civil rights activism in the South, King brought his program of nonviolent direct action to the North to contest racial inequalities that coalesced around discriminatory housing practices. To King, those practices—and the wide array of forms of discrimination that African Americans faced in

Northern cities—had clearly undercut the aims of the Great Migration: "The Negro has come North, crowding into the confines of already teeming black ghettoes, seeking a Promised Land," he told a Chicago crowd in March 1966. "Lured by the promises of a better life," King continued, "he found not a land of plenty but a lot replete with poverty. He experienced not the buoyancy of hope but the fatigue of despair. He found not a Promised Land but rather another Egypt-land of denial, discrimination and dismay."[17]

A few months later, the Freedom Movement's nonviolent protests on the city's South and West Sides were met with white resistance as virulent and violent as anything black Chicagoans had faced in Washington and Jackson Parks during the first wave of the Great Migration. The frontier of the Black Belt having expanded south and west, the most dramatic confrontations took place at Marquette Park, six miles southwest of Olmsted and Vaux's Washington Park. On July 31, 1966, amidst 323 acres of meadow and lagoon designed by Olmsted's sons, a mob of angry whites threw rocks, bricks, and bottles at peaceful marchers and vandalized their cars. Dozens were injured, more than a dozen cars were set on fire, and two were even pushed into the park's lagoon. Five days later, King joined another peaceful protest in Marquette Park, where the nation's most famous civil rights leader was struck in the head with a rock.[18]

The violence the Chicago Freedom Movement encountered at Marquette Park and across the city's South and West Sides was enough to prompt King to reflect, "Swastikas bloomed in Chicago parks like misbegotten weeds." King—a man who had endured bombings, beatings, and death threats for years—continued, "I've been in many demonstrations all across the South, but I can say that I had never seen, even in Mississippi, mobs as hostile and as hate-filled as in Chicago."[19] It was a sobering assessment of Chicago's dismal race relations, especially for the hundreds of thousands of migrants who had fled Jim Crow in search of a better life. Ultimately the Chicago Freedom Movement's campaign to end slums fell far short of its lofty goals, and the city's dismal housing situation persisted—just as it did in Great Migration destinations across the North. On March 1, 1968, a presidential commission tasked with studying the causes of race riots that had roiled the nation famously concluded that America was "moving toward two societies, one black, one white—separate and unequal."[20] When King was assassinated a month later, riots once again erupted across the country. In Chicago, the impoverished West Side neighborhood where King had lived two years earlier suffered the worst destruction. Mobilized to quell the violence, troops occupied the Black Belt's landscapes of hope. Hundreds were stationed at Washington Park's armory, and hundreds more set up camp on Jackson Park's baseball fields of "soft, green grass" near where a *Tribune* reporter noticed that "three Negro boys fished in the muddy, brown water of a lagoon."[21]

One could scarcely dream up a more fitting representation of the ways persistent race discrimination and segregation after World War II made it harder and harder for black Chicagoans to forge and sustain the hybrid environmental relationships that had flourished since the Great Migration began. Maintaining and adapting their Southern kinship with the soil had been central to the way migrants sought out, fought for, built, and enjoyed the promise of the Great Migration in the North's Land of Hope. Experiencing nature mainly as a place for leisure rather than labor was one of the many ways migrants became modern in Chicago's urban environment. But with the circumstances of the urban crisis deepening poverty and disinvestment on the South Side, it was becoming increasingly difficult for many African Americans to access and enjoy the landscapes of hope that had mattered so much to earlier generations, let alone establish new ones.

This was the Chicago into which Michelle Obama (nee Robinson) was born in 1964. A product of the Great Migration, Michelle's grandparents had migrated to Chicago from the South. The last to arrive was her paternal grandfather Fraser Robinson, who came to Chicago from South Carolina in 1931, the same year Clarice Durham and Charles Davis migrated to the city. More than three decades later, Robinson felt the frustrations King experienced during the Chicago Freedom Movement, felt the weight of the Great Migration's fading promise. But even for him, a World War II veteran who was able to build a career as a postal worker, Chicago remained a Land of Hope. Growing up on the South Side, Michelle remembered that her grandfather "filled my brother and me with big dreams about the lives we could lead. He taught me my destiny had not been written before I was born—that my destiny was in my hands."[22] That sense of freedom, possibility, and hope would help lead Michelle to attain degrees from Princeton and Harvard, begin a successful law career back in Chicago, and eventually become the first African American First Lady of the United States. Although he was raised far from the Black Metropolis, Michelle's future husband had been instilled with a similar outlook on life, an outlook that helped drive his community organizing on the South Side and perhaps even brought them together.

Well before Barack and Michelle Obama ever crossed paths, Barack was conscious of his adopted city's history, of the hopes and dreams harbored by thousands of black migrants—migrants like Michelle's grandparents and like the aging poet whom Barack had met growing up in Hawaii, Frank Marshall Davis. Introducing himself to Davis's South Side in the early 1980s, Barack drove down Martin Luther King Jr. Drive (formerly South Parkway) and up Cottage Grove Avenue—streets that not only run past Michelle's first childhood home but also mark the east and west boundaries of Washington Park—and thought about "the thousands who had come up from the South so many years before; the black men and women and children, dirty from the soot of the railcars, clutching their makeshift luggage, all making their way to Canaan Land." Rather than the hopeless, treeless, ugly city that Richard Wright lamented, however, on that drive Barack Obama saw a South Side with more room for hope. He remembered that "the sun sparkled through the deep green trees" that summer, not unlike the "strong rocks of tall trees" that sheltered black Chicagoans in Frank Marshall Davis's 1937 poem "Washington Park, Chicago."[23]

The South Side's landscapes of hope run through the life stories of Michelle and Barack Obama, just as they do for countless black Chicagoans past and present. Grade school aged in the mid-1970s, Michelle would ride her bike out to Rainbow Beach Park, three miles south of Jackson Park beach. She attended a Park District-sponsored day camp there and remembers an area where she "could walk along the rocks way out into the lake and have a beautiful view of the city."[24] An idyllic spot that colors some of Michelle's earliest memories, it too had been racially contested space just a few years before she was born. Only a series of "freedom wade-ins" that provoked violent confrontations and drew hundreds and sometimes thousands had turned Rainbow Beach Park into another one of black Chicago's landscapes of hope—the newest and southernmost Lake Michigan beach in a story that included 31st Street and Jackson Park beaches.[25] Years later, after a courtship rooted in the Hyde Park neighborhood once bound by restrictive covenants,

Michelle and Barack Obama held their wedding reception along the lakefront between Jackson Park beach and Rainbow Beach Park, at a venue that itself had historically excluded African Americans.

Perhaps those connections to the South Side's natural and landscaped environments help explain why Barack Obama, a man who campaigned on a slogan of "Hope" in 2008, has announced that his Presidential Library will be built on the far west side of Jackson Park. Constructed in a green space with more than a century of African American history, a central piece of the legacy of the nation's first black president may help write the next chapter in the story of black Chicago's landscapes of hope. Still among the most segregated and impoverished areas in the nation, plagued with school closures, record levels of gun violence, and a police presence that many community members believe hurts more than it helps, Chicago's South Side is in need of hope now as much as ever.[26]

Abbreviations

ASF   Abbott-Sengstacke Family Papers, Vivian G. Harsh Research Collection of Afro-American History and Literature, Chicago Public Library

CAP   Chicago Area Project Records, Chicago History Museum

CBGC   Chicago Boys and Girls Clubs Records, Chicago History Museum

CPD   Chicago Park District Special Collections

CUL   Chicago Urban League Records, Special Collections and University Archives, University of Illinois at Chicago Library

DUL   Detroit Urban League Papers, Michigan Historical Collections, Bentley Historical Library, University of Michigan (microfilm edition, 1973)

EWB   Ernest Watson Burgess Papers, Special Collections Research Center, University of Chicago Library

FPDCC   Forest Preserve District of Cook County Records, Special Collections and University Archives, University of Illinois at Chicago Library

IMG   Irene McCoy Gaines Papers, Chicago History Museum

IWP   The Illinois Writers Project: "Negro in Illinois" Papers, Vivian G. Harsh Research Collection of Afro-American History and Literature, Chicago Public Library

JPA   Juvenile Protective Association Records, Special Collections and University Archives, University of Illinois at Chicago Library

JR   Julius Rosenwald Papers, Special Collections Research Center, University of Chicago Library

MB   Martin Bickham Papers, Special Collections and University Archives, University of Illinois at Chicago Library

MVF Master Vertical File, Chicago History Museum

RG 35, NACP Record Group 35: Records of the Civilian Conservation Corps, 1933–1953, National Archives at College Park, MD

RG 79, NACP Record Group 79: Records of the National Park Service, 1785–2006, National Archives at College Park, MD

RG 114, NACP Record Group 114: Records of the Natural Resources Conservation Service, 1875–2002, National Archives at College Park, MD

RW Richard Wright Papers. Yale Collection of American Literature, Beinecke Rare Book and Manuscript Library

SCD St. Clair Drake Papers, Sc MG 309, Manuscripts, Archives and Rare Books Division, Schomburg Center for Research in Black Culture, New York Public Library

TB Timuel D. Black Jr. Papers, Vivian Harsh Research Collection of Afro-American History and Literature, Chicago Public Library

UCC United Charities of Chicago Records, Chicago History Museum

VMP Vivien M. Palmer and University of Chicago Local Community Research Committee, Documents: History of the Communities, Chicago, Chicago History Museum

WC Welfare Council of Metropolitan Chicago Records, Chicago History Museum

WM William McBride Jr. Papers, Vivian Harsh Research Collection of Afro-American History and Literature, Chicago Public Library

YMCAM YMCA of Metropolitan Chicago Records, Chicago History Museum

YMCAW Young Men's Christian Association—Wabash Avenue Records, Special Collections and University Archives, University of Illinois at Chicago Library

YWCAM YWCA of Metropolitan Chicago Records, Special Collections and University Archives, University of Illinois at Chicago Library

Notes

Introduction

1. Richard Wright, *12 Million Black Voices* (1941; New York: Thunder's Mouth Press, 1988), 32, 43. Countless others, both black and white, have ruminated on the fertility and beauty of the American South; in this same era, see especially David L. Cohn, *God Shakes Creation* (New York: Harper & Brothers, 1935), 168–189.

2. Chicago's black population growth more than quadrupled African Americans' share of the city's total population, from 2.0 percent in 1910 to 8.2 percent in 1940. St. Clair Drake and Horace Cayton, *Black Metropolis: A Study of Negro Life in a Northern City* (1945; Chicago: University of Chicago Press, 1993), 8–9. On Chicago as symbolic of the Great Migration for African Americans in this period, see chapter 1 in Wallace D. Best, *Passionately Human, No Less Divine: Religion and Culture in Black Chicago, 1915–1952* (Princeton, NJ: Princeton University Press, 2005).

3. Richard Wright, "Introduction by Richard Wright," in Drake and Crayton, *Black Metropolis*, xvii.

4. This book does not become involved in debates about wilderness or which landscapes, if any, are really "natural" for two primary reasons. First, nearly every environment that black Chicagoans frequented in the first half of the twentieth century was in some way altered by human hands: "nature" was almost always what William Cronon calls "second nature." William Cronon, *Nature's Metropolis: Chicago and the Great West* (New York: W. W. Norton, 1992). The touchstone collection that considers debates over nature's social

construction remains William Cronon, ed., *Uncommon Ground: Toward Reinventing Nature* (New York: W. W. Norton & Co., 1995). The second and
perhaps more important reason that this book largely ignores these debates is because I am concerned mostly with the ways people used and
perceived their environments at the time. In other words, I care about how
black Chicagoans valued, thought about, and experienced what they
saw as nature, and I use the term "nature" much as they did. In this book,
therefore, "nature" (which I often refer to as "natural and landscaped environments") perhaps most closely approximates what environmental historian Neil Maher calls "landscape"—"nonhuman nature altered by human
labor"—places that represent "the nexus of interactions between society
and the natural environment, between culture and nature [and are] thus
neither solely the ecological nature of trees, soil, and water nor the socially
constructed nature of ideas about the natural world, but rather a fusion of
the two." Neil M. Maher, *Nature's New Deal: The Civilian Conservation Corps
and the Roots of the American Environmental Movement* (New York: Oxford University Press, 2008), 6.

5. Although this book is a case study focusing on one of the major Great Migration destinations for black Southerners, it reveals that nature was ma-
terially and imaginatively important to the everyday lives of urban-dwelling
African Americans in ways that have been largely lost to history. The stories
of other cities and other black communities are just waiting to be told. The
most significant example of scholarship on nature and black Chicagoans, on
which this book builds, is chapter 4 in Colin Fisher, *Urban Green: Nature, Recreation, and the Working Class in Industrial Chicago* (Chapel Hill: University of
North Carolina Press, 2015). On African Americans and nature, see in particular Kimberly K. Smith, *African American Environmental Thought: Foundations* (Lawrence: University Press of Kansas, 2007); Dianne D. Glave and
Mark Stoll, eds., *To Love the Wind and the Rain: African Americans and Environmental History* (Pittsburgh: University of Pittsburgh Press, 2006); Andrew Wiese, *Places of Their Own: African American Suburbanization in the
Twentieth Century* (Chicago: University of Chicago Press, 2004); Andrew
Kahrl, *The Land Was Ours: African American Beaches from Jim Crow to the Sunbelt South* (Cambridge, MA: Harvard University Press, 2012); Carolyn Finney,
*Black Faces, White Spaces: Reimagining the Relationship of African Americans to
the Great Outdoors* (Chapel Hill: The University of North Carolina Press,
2014); and Dianne D. Glave, *Rooted in the Earth: Reclaiming the African American Environmental Heritage* (Chicago: Lawrence Hill Books, 2010). Scholars
are only beginning to uncover the significance of nature for African Americans, but the importance of geography and place has long been recognized
in migration studies—primarily through the ways in which racially restrictive covenants, redlining, blockbusting, and white violence shaped
the contours of African Americans' urban lives in the North. Although
they do not examine nature or the environment specifically, outstanding

place-conscious studies of black Chicago and the Great Migration include Davarian L. Baldwin, *Chicago's New Negroes: Modernity, the Great Migration, & Black Urban Life* (Chapel Hill: University of North Carolina Press, 2007); Amanda I. Seligman, *Block by Block: Neighborhoods and Public Policy on Chicago's West Side* (Chicago: University of Chicago Press, 2005); Mary E. Pattillo, *Black on the Block: The Politics of Race and Class in the City* (Chicago: University of Chicago Press, 2007); and Ira Berlin, *The Making of African America: The Four Great Migrations* (New York: Viking, 2010).

6. Werner Sollors defines modernity as a "continuing processes of urbanization, industrialization, secularization, and migration," and he tends to emphasize the similarity between white ethnic and black modernities. Werner Sollors, *Ethnic Modernism* (Cambridge, MA: Harvard University Press, 2008), 10–12. On African American modernity and the Stroll, see chapter 1 in Baldwin, *Chicago's New Negroes.* On black Chicagoans and post–World War II modernity, see the introduction to Adam Green, *Selling the Race: Culture, Community, and Black Chicago, 1940–1955* (Chicago: University of Chicago Press, 2007). If, as one cultural critic has argued, the jazz and blues pouring out of the Stroll's dance halls were ways of reflecting and making sense of "the speeded-up tempo of life produced by industrialization in the American workplace and the mechanization of urban life," spending leisure time in natural and landscaped environments represented a conscious and complementary effort to deal with urban life by temporarily removing oneself from its speed and mechanization that could just as easily prove wearisome. Joel Dinerstein, *Swinging the Machine: Modernity, Technology, and African American Culture between the World Wars* (Amherst: University of Massachusetts Press, 2003), 5.

7. James N. Gregory, *The Southern Diaspora: How the Great Migrations of Black and White Southerners Transformed America* (Chapel Hill: University of North Carolina Press, 2005), 12–32.

8. Wright, "Introduction by Richard Wright," in Drake and Cayton, *Black Metropolis,* xxii. On these trends and their environmental consequences in Chicago, see Cronon, *Nature's Metropolis;* and Harold L. Platt, *Shock Cities: The Environmental Transformation and Reform of Manchester and Chicago* (Chicago: University of Chicago Press, 2005). On the longer, broader evolution of these historical changes, see especially Raymond Williams, *The Country and the City* (New York: Oxford University Press, 1973).

9. James R. Grossman, *Land of Hope: Chicago, Black Southerners, and the Great Migration* (Chicago: University of Chicago Press, 1989), 31. Racial discrimination and violence, natural disasters such as the growing boll weevil infestation and devastating floods, and a sharecropping system that left most farmers in debt peonage conditioned many Southern African Americans to a peripatetic lifestyle, always searching for better land or a way off the land completely. On African American sharecropper mobility within the South, see ibid., 26–28; Peter Gottlieb, *Making Their Own Way: Southern*

Blacks' Migration to Pittsburgh, 1916–30 (Urbana: University of Illinois Press, 1987), 17–28; and James C. Cobb, *The Most Southern Place on Earth: The Mississippi Delta and the Roots of Regional Identity* (New York: Oxford University Press, 1992), 106. On the boll weevil and other natural disasters, see James C. Giesen, *Boll Weevil Blues: Cotton, Myth, and Power in the American South* (Chicago: University of Chicago Press, 2011); Carole Marks, *Farewell, We're Good and Gone: The Great Black Migration* (Bloomington: Indiana University Press, 1989), 33; and R. H. Leavell and J. H. Dillard, *Negro Migration in 1916–17: Reports* (Washington, DC: Government Printing Office, 1919), 93.

10. After decades of study, Great Migration historians still disagree about just how much urban experience migrants attained before they arrived in northern industrial cities like Chicago. While it seems clear that many migrants undertook a step migration, due to small sample sizes and the snapshot nature of decennial censuses it is substantially less clear how much time migrants spent in those intermediate Southern cities and towns and what they may or may not have gained from those experiences. On these and other complex questions concerning migrants' urban or rural character before arriving in cities such as Chicago, see Grossman, *Land of Hope*, 28–33, 112, 181–183; Gregory, *The Southern Diaspora*, 22; Gottlieb, *Making Their Own Way*, 22–32; Marks, *Farewell, We're Good and Gone*, 37–42; Baldwin, *Chicago's New Negroes*, 38–39; Gavin Wright, *Old South, New South: Revolutions in the Southern Economy since the Civil War* (New York: Basic Books, 1986), 203–205; Berlin, *The Making of African America*, 161; Jacqueline Jones, *The Dispossessed: America's Underclasses from the Civil War to the Present* (New York: Basic Books, 1992), 209–210; J. Trent Alexander, "The Great Migration in Comparative Perspective: Interpreting the Urban Origins of Southern Black Migrants to Depression-Era Pittsburgh," *Social Science History* 22, no. 3 (Autumn 1998), 358–359; Chicago Commission on Race Relations, *The Negro in Chicago: A Study of Race Relations and a Race Riot* (Chicago: University of Chicago Press, 1922), 95; Leavell and Dillard, *Negro Migration in 1916–17*, 19; Florette Henri, *Black Migration: Movement North, 1900–1920* (Garden City, NY: Anchor Press, 1975), 69–70; Emmett J. Scott, *Negro Migration during the War* (1920; New York: Arno Press, 1969), 189; Abraham Epstein, *The Negro Migrant in Pittsburgh* (1918; New York: Arno Press, 1969), 74; and Carter Godwin Woodson, *The Rural Negro* (Washington, DC: Association for the Study of Negro Life and History, Inc., 1930), 91–106.

11. The other two northern cities with African American populations between 100,000 and 200,000—themselves Great Migration destinations—were Detroit and St. Louis.

12. On these environmental differences migrants encountered, see Grossman, *Land of Hope*, 112; Gottlieb, *Making Their Own Way: Southern Blacks' Migration to Pittsburgh, 1916–30*, 22–25; Hortense Powdermaker, *After Freedom: A Cultural Study in the Deep South* (New York: Viking Press, 1939), 7–8, 75; and Jeffrey Helgeson, *Crucibles of Black Empowerment: Chicago's Neighborhood Pol-*

itics from the New Deal to Harold Washington (Chicago: University of Chicago Press, 2014), 1–2. On Chicago and its hinterlands in the nineteenth century, see Cronon, *Nature's Metropolis.*

13. "History of Grand Boulevard: Document #8," VMP, Volume 5, Part 1, p. 2–3; Chicago Commission, *The Negro in Chicago,* 137. Although a few prospective migrants seemed intent on finding "some good farming country" either "near Chicago or some small town near Chicago," most who resisted the pull of city life simply made plain they would rather not live in a place so big: a man from Starkville, Mississippi (with a population hovering just above 2,500, qualifying it as urban by the Census Bureau's definition), bluntly declared that he did not "care for the large city life I rather live in a town of 15 or 20 thousand." Emmett J. Scott, "Letters of Negro Migrants of 1916–1918," *Journal of Negro History* 4, no. 3 (July 1919), 305; Emmett J. Scott, "More Letters of Negro Migrants of 1916–1918," *Journal of Negro History* 4, no. 4 (October 1919), 435–436. For other letters to this effect, see Scott, "Letters," 307, 309, 319, 331, 337, 339; and Scott, "More Letters," 415, 429, 430.

14. Most notably near Chicago, African American communities developed in places such as Morgan Park, Lilydale, and Robbins, all between ten and twenty miles farther south of the city's South Side Black Belt; Morgan Park and Lilydale claimed only about 1,000 and 2,200 residents, respectively, when Chicago's black population exceeded 200,000. Frederic H. H. Robb, *The Negro in Chicago: 1779–1929, Vols. 1–2* (Chicago: Washington Intercollegiate Club, 1929), 229. Thomas Philpott argues that these places turned into African American settlements in part because whites stayed away from these areas, which were "remote, uninhabited, and ill-suited for residential development"; he calls the site of Morgan Park a "swampy no-man's-land" near railroad tracks. Thomas Lee Philpott, *The Slum and the Ghetto: Immigrants, Blacks, and Reformers in Chicago, 1880–1930* (Belmont, CA: Wadsworth Publishing, 1991), 183–185. See also Ruth Evans Pardee, "A Study of the Functions of Associations in a Small Negro Community in Chicago" (master's thesis, University of Chicago, 1937); "History of Douglas: Document #5c," VMP, Volume 4, Part 2, p. 2; Earl Richard Moses, "Community Factors in Negro Delinquency" (master's thesis, University of Chicago, 1932), 46; St. Clair Drake and United States Work Projects Administration, *Churches and Voluntary Associations in the Chicago Negro Community* (Chicago, 1940), 171–172; Alfred O. Philipp, "Robbins, Ill.—A Folklore in the Making" (U.S. Work Projects Administration, Federal Writers' Project, Library of Congress: Folklore Project, Life Histories, 1936–39, 1939); "Morgan Park Growing," *Broad Ax,* June 14, 1919, p. 8; and "Morgan Park in Bloom," *Broad Ax,* July 15, 1922, p. 3. Although these places—along with Chicago's notable West Side black community—are important to consider when contemplating how black migrants forged hybrid environmental cultures, I focus on black Chicagoans on the city's South Side because this book strives for a representative rather than exhaustively comprehensive account of African

American migrants' ideas about and experiences with nature. The best account of these types of small African American migrant communities in the North remains Andrew Wiese's *Places of Their Own,* but even by his rather expansive definition of "suburbs" (which includes places like South Chicago), only one in six migrants lived in these more rural settings. Wiese, *Places of Their Own,* 5. On African American suburbs, see also Bruce D. Haynes, *Red Lines, Black Spaces: The Politics of Race and Space in a Black Middle-Class Suburb* (New Haven, CT: Yale University Press, 2001); Becky M. Nicolaides, *My Blue Heaven: Life and Politics in the Working-Class Suburbs of Los Angeles, 1920–1965* (Chicago: University of Chicago Press, 2002); Christopher Sellers, "Nature and Blackness in Suburban Passage," in *To Love the Wind and the Rain: African Americans and Environmental History,* ed. Dianne D. Glave and Mark Stoll (Pittsburgh: University of Pittsburgh Press, 2006), 93–119; and H. Paul Douglass, *The Suburban Trend* (New York: Century, 1925). The essential history of this broader, longer impulse toward suburbanization in part for its environmental benefits remains Kenneth T. Jackson, *Crabgrass Frontier: The Suburbanization of the United States* (New York: Oxford University Press, 1987). See also chapter 3 in Michael Rawson, *Eden on the Charles: The Making of Boston* (Cambridge, MA: Harvard University Press, 2010).

15. Wright, *12 Million Black Voices,* 100. As Lawrence Buell has pointed out, suggestive of this cross-cultural reaction to new, modern conditions were figures as diverse as John Muir and Jane Addams, the former a champion of wilderness and the latter a champion of the urban poor, who both "valued open space as therapeutic" for "a society sickened by industrialization's growing pains." Lawrence Buell, *Writing for an Endangered World: Literature, Culture, and Environment in the U.S. and Beyond* (Cambridge, MA: Belknap Press of Harvard University Press, 2001), 13. On nature's common connotation among urban dwellers as a leisure landscape rather than a work landscape in this period, see (among many others), Fisher, *Urban Green;* Robin Faith Bachin, *Building the South Side: Urban Space and Civic Culture in Chicago, 1890–1919* (Chicago: University of Chicago Press, 2004); Victoria W. Wolcott, *Race, Riots, and Roller Coasters: The Struggle over Segregated Recreation in America* (Philadelphia: University of Pennsylvania Press, 2012); Richard White, " 'Are You an Environmentalist or Do You Work for a Living?': Work and Nature," in *Uncommon Ground,* ed. William Cronon (New York: W. W. Norton & Co., 1995), 171–185; Paul Sutter, *Driven Wild: How the Fight against Automobiles Launched the Modern Wilderness Movement* (Seattle: University of Washington Press, 2002); Kevin C. Armitage, *The Nature Study Movement: The Forgotten Popularizer of America's Conservation Ethic* (Lawrence: University Press of Kansas, 2009); Matthew W. Klingle, *Emerald City: An Environmental History of Seattle* (New Haven, CT: Yale University Press, 2007); Lawrence M. Lipin, *Workers and the Wild: Conservation, Consumerism, and Labor in Oregon, 1910–30* (Urbana: University of Illinois Press, 2007); and Roderick Nash, *Wilderness and the American Mind* (New Haven, CT: Yale University Press, [1967] 2001).

Grossman counts leisure and church as "arenas in which blacks exercised the greatest autonomy." Grossman, *Land of Hope*, 264.

16. After more than a decade of rapid population growth, African American migration lessened during the Great Depression, and Chicago's African American population stabilized, increasing by less than 3,000 between 1930 and 1934 and only gaining another 30,000 people in the remaining years of the decade (indeed, during the 1930s, Chicago's population as a whole remained relatively stable, increasing only from 3.376 to 3.396 million). To contrast Depression-era migration levels with those of the World War II era, note that between 1940 and 1944, Chicago's African American population increased by nearly 60,000 to 337,000. Drake and Cayton, *Black Metropolis*, 8–9.

17. For representations of these South Side environments from the Chicago School of Sociology onward, see (among many others), Chicago Commission, *The Negro in Chicago;* Edward Franklin Frazier, *The Negro Family in Chicago* (Chicago: University of Chicago Press, 1932); Drake and Cayton, *Black Metropolis;* Allan H. Spear, *Black Chicago: The Making of a Negro Ghetto, 1890–1920* (Chicago: University of Chicago Press, 1967); Philpott, *The Slum and the Ghetto;* Grossman, *Land of Hope;* Nicholas Lemann, *The Promised Land: The Great Black Migration and How it Changed America* (New York: A. A. Knopf, 1991); and Rick Halpern, *Down on the Killing Floor: Black and White Workers in Chicago's Packinghouses, 1904–54* (Urbana: University of Illinois Press, 1997). These are also the urban environments that most commonly inform an environmental justice perspective on racial and ethnic minorities' relationships to nature: inequalities expressed through the denial of environmental goods or exposure to environmental hazards, and social movements to combat those inequalities. For representative environmental justice histories, some of which focus on Chicago and its environs, see David Pellow, *Garbage Wars: The Struggle for Environmental Justice in Chicago* (Cambridge, MA: MIT Press, 2002); chapters 10 and 14 in Platt, *Shock Cities;* Sylvia Hood Washington, *Packing Them In: An Archaeology of Environmental Racism in Chicago, 1865–1954* (Lanham, MD: Lexington Books, 2005); Andrew Hurley, *Environmental Inequalities: Class, Race, and Industrial Pollution in Gary, Indiana, 1945–1980* (Chapel Hill: University of North Carolina Press, 1995); Robert R. Gioielli, *Environmental Activism and the Urban Crisis* (Philadelphia: Temple University Press, 2014); Rob Nixon, *Slow Violence and the Environmentalism of the Poor* (Cambridge, MA: Harvard University Press, 2011); Dawn Biehler, *Pests in the City: Flies, Bedbugs, Cockroaches, and Rats* (Seattle: University of Washington Press, 2013); Julie Sze, *Noxious New York: The Racial Politics of Urban Health and Environmental Justice* (Cambridge, MA: MIT Press, 2007); Klingle, *Emerald City;* Carl Zimring, *Clean and White: A History of Environmental Racism in the United States* (New York: New York University Press, 2015); and Dorceta Taylor, *Toxic Communities: Environmental Racism, Industrial Pollution, and Residential Mobility* (New York: New York University Press, 2014). The Chicago

School of Sociology famously borrowed ecological ideas from the natural sciences to analyze the geographical distribution of migrant communities and describe how various migrant cultures interacted with one another and adapted to the city, but in this book the ecological metaphor becomes much more literal. The seminal works that borrow ecological thinking to describe human populations in cities and that explore ideas of hybridity and migration are Robert Ezra Park et al., *The City* (Chicago: University of Chicago Press, 1925); and Robert Ezra Park, "Human Migration and the Marginal Man," *American Journal of Sociology* 33, no. 6 (May 1928), 881–893. On the whole, this book seeks to complicate and often challenge Wright's fairly reductive visions of natural and landscaped environments—North and South, urban and rural—which were no doubt influenced by ideas generated by the Chicago School of Sociology and meant to emphasize the racial discrimination that African Americans suffered nationwide. For a more thorough treatment of the Chicago School of Sociology as well as its influence on Richard Wright, see both Chapters 2 and 3.

18. In its focus on the importance of public and private green space to black Chicagoans rather than on the more well-studied discriminatory forces that confronted them in every square foot of the city's built environment, this book offers an environmentally grounded complement to Jeffrey Helgeson's account of black Chicago's "community building and largely neighborhood-based politics that reinforced longstanding traditions of self-help, racial uplift, and race-conscious liberal pragmatism" after the first wave of the Great Migration. Helgeson, *Crucibles of Black Empowerment*, 12. See also Baldwin, *Chicago's New Negroes;* and Green, *Selling the Race*. In a sense, this book seeks to uncover black Chicagoans' unique "topophilia," which Yi-Fu Tuan defines as "the affective bond between people and place or setting." Yi-fu Tuan, *Topophilia: A Study of Environmental Perception, Attitudes, and Values* (New York: Columbia University Press, [1972] 1990), 4. Models for black Chicagoans' varied connections to nature could be drawn from Lawrence Buell's frameworks for mapping "place-connectedness"—in particular one that models "concentric areas of affiliation decreasing in intimacy as one fans out from a central point" and another that models "a scattergram or archipelago of locales, some perhaps quite remote from each other." See Buell, *Writing for an Endangered World*, 64–72.

19. Those complexities only multiply after 1940, when the arrival of hundreds of thousands of black migrants once again dramatically alters Chicago's social and cultural geography in the second wave of the Great Migration (see the Epilogue). That increased complexity, in addition to broader historical trends such as suburbanization and deindustrialization that have a marked impact on urban environments, is why this book effectively ends before the post–World War II era. In periodizing the book this way, I follow classic studies of Great Migration-era Chicago and scholars like James Gregory who mark two distinct phases of migration centering on economic and so-

cial opportunities surrounding the two world wars, separated by an interlude of attenuated migration during the Depression. See Grossman, *Land
of Hope;* Baldwin, *Chicago's New Negroes;* and Gregory, *The Southern Diaspora,*
23–38. For works that take the longer view, see, for example, Best, *Passionately Human, No Less Divine;* and Wiese, *Places of Their Own.*

20. Terminology concerning class status within the African American community can be confusing and controversial, in part because social and economic statuses did not always match and in part because of the way it
maps—or does not map—onto class status among whites. I use the term
"black cultural elite" to emphasize cultural capital and behavioral norms
(rather than monetary wealth) among the group of middle- and upper-class
black Chicagoans who tended to be well educated and employed in skilled
"white-collar" jobs (as opposed to the less well-educated working classes
who tended to work in unskilled "blue-collar" jobs)—this group is similar
to but somewhat more expansive than what W. E. B. Du Bois famously
termed the "Talented Tenth." My use of "black cultural elite" is also meant
to include what Michele Mitchell has termed "the black aspiring class" in
her study of turn-of-the-century African American culture. Mitchell
writes, "From seamstresses to small proprietors to teachers to skilled
tradesmen, the black aspiring class was comprised of workers able to save
a little money as well as those who worked multiple jobs to attain class mobility; significantly, it included self-educated women and men as well as
those who had attended normal school or college." In Chicago during the
Great Migration era, many of these women and men held respectable
working-class jobs at restaurants, the post office, or on the railroad. Mitchell
argues that, like the black cultural elite in this book, "The characteristic
common to the overwhelming majority of the black aspiring class during
the late nineteenth and early twentieth centuries was an abiding concern
with propriety—not to mention a belief that morality, thrift, and hard work
were essential to black progress." Michele Mitchell, *Righteous Propagation:
African Americans and the Politics of Racial Destiny after Reconstruction* (Chapel
Hill: University of North Carolina Press, 2004), 9–10. As Mitchell's attention to propriety indicates, this is also the class of African Americans in-
vested in "respectability politics" and "race uplift." See Victoria W. Wolcott,
Remaking Respectability: African American Women in Interwar Detroit (Chapel
Hill: University of North Carolina Press, 2001); Evelyn Brooks Higginbotham, *Righteous Discontent: The Women's Movement in the Black Baptist Church,
1880–1920* (Cambridge, MA: Harvard University Press, 1993), 204–211; and
especially chapter 3 in Kevin Kelly Gaines, *Uplifting the Race: Black Leadership, Politics, and Culture in the Twentieth Century* (Chapel Hill: University of
North Carolina Press, 1996). My understanding of the complex class structure among black Chicagoans is most deeply informed by chapters 18–23
in Drake and Cayton's *Black Metropolis,* which make it clear that, because
of systemic social and economic race discrimination, the "cultural elite" in

the black community actually maps very closely onto "middle class" in the white community. Contrasting black and white societies, they write, "The white upper class in [Chicago] is a wealthy leisure class[, whereas black Chicago's] upper class is a well-trained but only moderately well-to-do group who have more leisure than the rank and file, but who nevertheless must work for a living," and "whose standards of behavior approximate those of the white middle class." They point out that those members of what I call the black cultural elite tended to have "what the people call 'positions'— professionals, proprietors, managers and officials, clerical and kindred workers." Drake and Cayton, *Black Metropolis,* 529, 563, 507. James Gregory points out that this group consisted of "attorneys, social workers, writers, musicians, and other professionals along with merchants, preachers, and teachers." Gregory, *The Southern Diaspora,* 28. See also chapter 5 in Grossman, *Land of Hope;* Carter Godwin Woodson, *The Negro Professional Man and the Community* (Washington, DC: Association for the Study of Negro Life and History, 1934); and Lorenzo J. Greene and Carter G. Woodson, *The Negro Wage Earner* (Washington, DC: Association for the Study of Negro Life and History, 1930). Members of this group were famously criticized in E. Franklin Frazier, *Black Bourgeoisie* (Glencoe, IL: Free Press, 1957).

21. A more interesting question than whether or not we can call the environments to which black Chicagoans retreated "nature," then, is *to what degree* these myriad places were shaped by human labor and how the access to and experience of these places may have varied along lines of race and class. These issues are discussed in the chapters that follow.

22. Drake and Cayton, *Black Metropolis,* 99; Harold Foote Gosnell, *Negro Politicians: The Rise of Negro Politics in Chicago* (Chicago: University of Chicago Press, 1967), 18.

23. For the most part, historians agree that migrants sought ways to maintain or adapt cultural practices to the Northern context rather than abandoning them. Particularly in recent years, historians have richly explored the ways that migrants created new hybrid cultures of religion, labor, leisure, and the like rather than completely jettisoning their Southern culture or completely assimilating to a Northern one. This book adds to those stories. See, among many others, the conclusion in Grossman, *Land of Hope;* Gregory, *The Southern Diaspora;* Best, *Passionately Human, No Less Divine;* and Joe William Trotter, *The Great Migration in Historical Perspective: New Dimensions of Race, Class, and Gender* (Bloomington: Indiana University Press, 1991). Although the story of two migrants like Clarice and Charles could never be absolutely representative of the migration experience (and recollections of childhood at a distance of seventy years come with their own caveats), their story is fairly typical. Like thousands of other migrants they followed a step migration, having moved with their family from Mobile, Alabama, to Chattanooga in 1924 when their father took a promotion from the Atlanta Life Insurance Company. Like many other migrants, they

also had considerable urban experience before migrating to Chicago, where strong kinship networks aided their adjustment to the city. Easily the most notable book to use individual migration stories as a way of understanding the Great Migration is Isabel Wilkerson, *The Warmth of Other Suns: The Epic Story of America's Great Migration* (New York: Random House, 2010).

24. Charles Davis and Clarice Durham, interviews with the author, January 20 and July 28, 2010; "How Bigger Was Born," in Richard Wright, *Native Son* (New York: HarperCollins, [1940] 1998), 453.

25. Davis and Durham, interviews with the author. On nature, urban space, and the psychological impact of migration on migrants, see chapter 12 in bell hooks, *Sisters of the Yam: Black Women and Self-Recovery* (Boston: South End Press, 1993); and Toni Morrison, "City Limits, Village Values: Concepts of the Neighborhood in Black Fiction" in *Literature and the Urban Experience: Essays on the City and Literature,* ed. Michael C. Jaye and Ann Chalmers Watts (New Brunswick, NJ: Rutgers University Press, 1981), 35–43.

1. "Booker T." Washington Park and Chicago's Racial Landscapes

1. Richard Wright, *Black Boy (American Hunger): A Record of Childhood and Youth* (New York: HarperPerennial Modern Classics, [1946] 2006), 262.

2. Frederick Law Olmsted and Calvert Vaux, "Report Accompanying Plan for Laying out the South Park," in *The Papers of Frederick Law Olmsted. Supplementary Series,* ed. Frederick Law Olmsted, Charles E. Beveridge, and Carolyn F. Hoffman (Baltimore: Johns Hopkins University Press, 1997), 216.

3. Ibid., 217. Olmsted and Vaux's design simply designated Washington and Jackson Parks as the "Upper Division" and "Lower Division" of a unified park plan called South Park; they were later named after presidents George Washington and Andrew Jackson.

4. Ibid., 213.

5. South Parkway's name was changed from Grand Boulevard in the mid- to late 1920s and, much later, changed again to Martin Luther King Jr. Drive; for the sake of clarity I refer to the street as South Parkway throughout. Only months after Olmsted and Vaux completed their report, the Great Chicago Fire swept through the city and burned more than 2,000 acres. Although the fire did not come close to the land designated for the South Park, damage from it in combination with the financial panic that seized the nation two years later severely constrained the city's financial ability to carry out Olmsted and Vaux's vision. The chairman of the horticultural committee later remarked that the discrepancy between the plan and its realization "was a case of 'champagne appetite and beer purse.'" Washington Park (unlike Jackson Park) escaped any alterations stemming from the 1893 World's Fair, however, and the Chicago Park District noted in 1941 that "the general contour of the park and its original acreage has been preserved,"

despite numerous landscaping changes and construction projects undertaken over the course of seven decades. Chicago South Park Commissioners, *Annual Report of the South Park Commissioners for the Year 1908–1909* (Chicago, 1909), 61; Chicago Park District, *Historical Register of the Twenty-Two Superseded Park Districts* (Chicago, 1941), 416.

6. According to the U.S. Census, Chicago's African American population was only 3,691 (barely 1 percent of the city's total population and mostly concentrated on the north side) in 1870, just five years after the Civil War. Although Olmsted and Vaux anticipated that the South Park would soon "be in the center of a really populous and wealthy district" and hence used most often by those classes, the design also accounted for its "holiday use by the whole body of citizens." Olmsted and Vaux, "Report," 207. On the recreation of wealthy whites in Washington Park, see chapter 3 in Robin Faith Bachin, *Building the South Side: Urban Space and Civic Culture in Chicago, 1890–1919* (Chicago: University of Chicago Press, 2004); Glen E. Holt, Dominic A. Pacyga, and Chicago Historical Society, *Chicago, a Historical Guide to the Neighborhoods: The Loop and South Side* (Chicago: Chicago Historical Society, 1979), 87–88; and Parks / Illinois-Chicago / Washington Park / Folder 1, MVF.

7. Quoted in Edgar Marquess Branch, *Studs Lonigan's Neighborhood and the Making of James T. Farrell* (Newton, MA: Arts End Books, 1996), 52. On how Chicago's growing African American population changed South Side neighborhoods' demographics in this period, see Holt et al., *Chicago,* 174.

8. While there is a rich African American history on Chicago's West Side that includes Union, Stanton, and Seward Parks among others, this book focuses on the larger South Side community. At Jackson Park, farther east and along Lake Michigan, the report estimated a daily attendance of African Americans of only 940, accounting for just 2 percent of the total attendance. Chicago Commission on Race Relations, *The Negro in Chicago: A Study of Race Relations and a Race Riot* (Chicago: University of Chicago Press, 1922), 275–276.

9. Olmsted and Vaux believed that fresh air and better drainage would create a "fresh and healthy" environment. Although the passage about the "restful, dreamy nature of the South" refers specifically to the tropical plantings best-suited to Jackson Park's lakeshore, Olmsted and Vaux go on to say that such objectives would "be admirably fitted to the general purposes of any park, and which certainly could nowhere be more grateful than in the borders of your city." Olmsted and Vaux's design explicitly attempted to emulate the "wooded lagoons of the tropics," but the mangroves, bamboo, and palms they reference were also native to the American South. Although he had been an abolitionist, Olmsted's ideas about the restful virtues of tropical environments may have also been influenced by his tours of the American South in the 1850s. Olmsted and Vaux, "Report," 213, 207. For Olmsted's accounts of the American South, see Frederick Law Olmsted, *A Journey in the Back Country* (New York: Schocken Books, 1970; 1860); and Frederick Law Olmsted, *A Journey in the Seaboard*

Slave States in the Years 1853–1854 (New York: G. P. Putnam's Sons, 1904). As Lawrence Buell put it, Olmsted's designs sought "an urbanism that would retain a measure of rural healthfulness." Lawrence Buell, *Writing for an Endangered World: Literature, Culture, and Environment in the U.S. and Beyond* (Cambridge: Belknap Press of Harvard University Press, 2001), 101.

10. On the Southern origins of Chicago's African American population, see Harold Foote Gosnell, *Negro Politicians: The Rise of Negro Politics in Chicago* (Chicago: University of Chicago Press, 1967), 18; and St. Clair Drake and Horace Cayton, *Black Metropolis: A Study of Negro Life in a Northern City* (Chicago: University of Chicago Press, [1945] 1993), 99. By the turn of the twentieth century there were already nearly seven miles of curving roads in Washington Park that connected to the city's rectilinear grid of streets. Chicago South Park Commissioners, *Annual Report of the South Park Commissioners for the Year 1896–1897* (Chicago, 1897), 18.

11. On the long history of conflicted African American relationships with nature due to the legacy of slavery, sharecropping, and lynching, see Kimberly K. Smith, *African American Environmental Thought: Foundations* (Lawrence: University Press of Kansas, 2007); chapter 2 in James R. Grossman, *Land of Hope: Chicago, Black Southerners, and the Great Migration* (Chicago: University of Chicago Press, 1989); Robert Bone, *Down Home: A History of Afro-American Short Fiction from its Beginnings to the End of the Harlem Renaissance* (New York: Putnam, 1975), 126–133, 286–287; Melvin Dixon, *Ride out the Wilderness: Geography and Identity in Afro-American Literature* (Urbana: University of Illinois Press, 1987); and Michael Bennett, "Anti-Pastoralism, Frederick Douglass, and the Nature of Slavery," in *Beyond Nature Writing: Expanding the Boundaries of Ecocriticism,* ed. Karla Armbruster and Kathleen R. Wallace (Charlottesville: University Press of Virginia, 2001), 195–210.

12. On environmental injustice in Chicago in this era, see chapter 2 in David Pellow, *Garbage Wars: The Struggle for Environmental Justice in Chicago* (Cambridge, MA: MIT Press, 2002); and Sylvia Hood Washington, *Packing Them In: An Archaeology of Environmental Racism in Chicago, 1865–1954* (Lanham, MD: Lexington Books, 2005).

13. On the politics of respectability and race uplift in this era, see Victoria W. Wolcott, *Remaking Respectability: African American Women in Interwar Detroit* (Chapel Hill: University of North Carolina Press, 2001), 1–10; Evelyn Brooks Higginbotham, *Righteous Discontent: The Women's Movement in the Black Baptist Church, 1880–1920* (Cambridge, MA: Harvard University Press, 1993), 185–230; and Kevin Kelly Gaines, *Uplifting the Race: Black Leadership, Politics, and Culture in the Twentieth Century* (Chapel Hill: University of North Carolina Press, 1996). White resistance to black leisure at public beaches in Chicago bore striking similarities to racial conflict over leisure in the Jim Crow South. Andrew Kahrl suggests that, in the South, much of the white hostility stemmed precisely from black middle-class respectability on display, which disrupted white notions of black vice and leisure seeking, hence threatening constructions of racial superiority. Andrew Kahrl, *The Land*

Was Ours: African American Beaches from Jim Crow to the Sunbelt South (Cambridge, MA: Harvard University Press, 2012). For the mores governing white behavior in Washington Park and other city parks, see Bachin, *Building the South Side*, 130–138. On Jane Addams, women's activism in Chicago, and the playground movement, see Maureen A. Flanagan, *Seeing with Their Hearts: Chicago Women and the Vision of the Good City, 1871–1933* (Princeton, NJ: Princeton University Press, 2002); Mary Jo Deegan, *Jane Addams and the Men of the Chicago School, 1892–1928* (New Brunswick, NJ: Transaction Books, 1988); Anne Meis Knupfer, *The Chicago Black Renaissance and Women's Activism* (Urbana: University of Illinois Press, 2006); and Dominick Cavallo, *Muscles and Morals: Organized Playgrounds and Urban Reform, 1880–1920* (Philadelphia: University of Pennsylvania Press, 1981).

14. Olmsted and Vaux, "Report," 211. Yet perhaps because of the park commissioners' constrained budget, landscape architects actually sought to preserve this "native growth" of oak trees in the northwest portion of Washington Park by mulching and spreading black soil around them. By 1875, however, the trees were "dying out fast," leading the landscapers to replace many of the original "common scrub oak" grove "with trees of a more lasting growth." Park developers left only a few of the dead oaks "covered with vines and creeping plants" that they hoped would "give a fine effect in the summer season." Chicago South Park Commissioners, *Annual Report of the South Park Commissioners for the Year 1872–1873* (Chicago, 1873), 14; Chicago South Park Commissioners, *Annual Report of the South Park Commissioners for the Year 1873–1874* (Chicago, 1874), 7, 14; Chicago South Park Commissioners, *Annual Report of the South Park Commissioners for the Year 1875–1876* (Chicago, 1876), 7; Chicago South Park Commissioners, *1908–1909*, 61.

15. Chicago South Park Commissioners, *1908–1909*, 56–57. On Olmsted and Vaux's use of exotics, see Bachin, *Building the South Side*, 133; Colin Fisher, *Urban Green: Nature, Recreation, and the Working Class in Industrial Chicago* (Chapel Hill: University of North Carolina Press, 2015), 10–12; and Daniel M. Bluestone, *Constructing Chicago* (New Haven, CT: Yale University Press, 1991), 37–52. On Washington Park's wide variety of plantings, see Chicago South Park Commissioners, *1872–1873*, 14; Chicago South Park Commissioners, *1873–1874*, 14; Chicago South Park Commissioners, *Annual Report of the South Park Commissioners for the Year 1874–1875* (Chicago, 1875), 11; Chicago South Park Commissioners, *Annual Report of the South Park Commissioners for the Year 1883–1884* (Chicago, 1884), 13; and Chicago South Park Commissioners, *Annual Report of the South Park Commissioners for the Year 1893–1894* (Chicago, 1894), 7. It was not until Jens Jensen's experimentation of the late 1880s and 1890s that serious attention was given to designing parks around the native vegetation, waterways, and land formations of the prairie. Chicago Historical Society, *Prairie in the City: Naturalism in Chicago's Parks, 1870–1940* (Chicago: Chicago Historical Society, 1991), 24–28.

16. Chicago South Park Commissioners, *Annual Report of the South Park Commissioners for the Year 1921–1922* (Chicago, 1922), 61. See also Chicago South Park

Commissioners, *Annual Report of the South Park Commissioners for the Year 1888–1889* (Chicago, 1889), 8; Chicago South Park Commissioners, *Annual Report of the South Park Commissioners for the Year 1900–1901* (Chicago, 1901), 13; and Chicago South Park Commissioners, *Annual Report of the South Park Commissioners for the Year 1919–1920* (Chicago, 1920), 56.

17. Although the general layout of Washington Park remains much like Olmsted and Vaux's design to this day, its infrastructure did change as buildings were erected and demolished, and plantings added and removed. The following descriptions are based in part on the 1913 map of Washington Park, at the very beginning of the Great Migration. See also "The Gardener at Work," *Chicago Tribune,* May 9, 1915, p. D9; Genevieve Forbes, "Purple Martin Here; Heralds Exit of Cold," *Chicago Tribune,* May 13, 1924, p. 11; "Spring's Here for Sure; Purple Martins Are Back," *Chicago Tribune,* April 20, 1932, p. 1; "Children and Ducks Find Relief from Heat Together," *Chicago Tribune,* August 18, 1925, p. 36; "Park Duck Pond Turned into Wading Pool," *Chicago Tribune,* July 29, 1930, p. 5; and "Time Looks On," *Chicago Defender (National Edition),* July 30, 1932, p. 20.

18. Olmsted and Vaux, "Report," 210. Despite this natural advantage, at Washington Park's northern end the "South Open Green" still required extensive labor to transform it into an expansive lawn. See Chicago South Park Commissioners, *Report of the South Park Commissioners to the Board of County Commissioners of Cook County for Nine Months from March 1st to December 1st, 1872* (Chicago, 1872), 7; Chicago South Park Commissioners, *1873–1874,* 6; and Chicago South Park Commissioners, *Annual Report of the South Park Commissioners for the Year 1886–1887* (Chicago, 1887), 8.

19. Edward Franklin Frazier, "Recreation and Amusement among American Negroes, A Research Memorandum," in Carnegie-Myrdal Study of the Negro in America research memoranda collection, ed. Carnegie Corporation of New York et al. (1940), 18–19. On cricket in Washington Park, see "International Cricketers Defeat Crack White Club," *Chicago Defender (National Edition),* June 7, 1924, p. 10; and "Washington Park Cricket Beats out International," *Chicago Defender (National Edition),* August 15, 1925, p. 8.

20. Chicago South Park Commissioners, *Annual Report of the South Park Commissioners for the Year 1913–1914* (Chicago, 1914), 60. See also Chicago South Park Commissioners, *Annual Report of the South Park Commissioners for the Year 1907–1908* (Chicago, 1908), 45. An 1850s Chicago city ordinance that had forbidden and issued fines for playing baseball or cricket on park grounds (because those sports had once been deemed unsuitable for the type of refined leisure parks were intended to foster) was already long stricken from the books. Olmsted and Vaux's original pastoral vision for the meadow included "athletic sports, such as baseball, football, cricket, and running games," as well as "sheep and cows . . . grazing upon [the meadow] and boys and men playing here and there, as on a village green." Olmsted and Vaux, "Report," 217–221. On Olmsted's legacy and the evolving uses of park space in this period, see Galen Cranz, *The Politics of Park Design:*

A History of Urban Parks in America (Cambridge: MIT Press, 1982); chapter 3 in Bachin, *Building the South Side;* Roy Rosenzweig and Elizabeth Blackmar, *The Park and the People: A History of Central Park* (Ithaca, NY: Cornell University Press, 1992); chapter 2 in Matthew Gandy, *Concrete and Clay: Reworking Nature in New York City* (Cambridge, MA: MIT Press, 2002); chapter 4 in Matthew W. Klingle, *Emerald City: An Environmental History of Seattle* (New Haven, CT: Yale University Press, 2007); and Elizabeth Halsey and Chicago Recreation Commission, *The Development of Public Recreation in Metropolitan Chicago* (Chicago: Chicago Recreation Commission, 1940), 8, 114–116.

21. Chicago South Park Commissioners, *Annual Report of the South Park Commissioners for the Year 1909–1910* (Chicago, 1910), 34. On the construction of baseball diamonds on the meadow in the 1880s and the sport's continued popularity, see Chicago South Park Commissioners, *Annual Report of the South Park Commissioners for the Year 1876–1877* (Chicago, 1877), 26; Chicago South Park Commissioners, *Annual Report of the South Park Commissioners for the Year 1885–1886* (Chicago, 1886), 11; Chicago South Park Commissioners, *Annual Report of the South Park Commissioners for the Year 1887–1888* (Chicago, 1888), 14; and Chicago South Park Commissioners, *1888–1889,* 15.

22. "Sports", Box 40, Folder 3, 6, IWP. See also Frederic H. H. Robb, *The Negro in Chicago: 1779–1929, Vols. 1–2* (Chicago: Washington Intercollegiate Club; International Negro Student Alliance, 1929), 142; and "Y.M.C.A. News," *Chicago Whip*, October 23, 1920, p. 3. At least in the early years, "as an incentive to its colored employes [*sic*] to join the Y.M.C.A., [Armour gave] an annual membership to each worker at the end of his first year of service." Kate J. Adams, *Humanizing a Great Industry* (Chicago: Armour and Company, 1919), 21. These industrial leagues embodied "welfare capitalism" in Chicago's Black Belt; for more on this general trend, see chapter 2 in Lizabeth Cohen, *Making a New Deal: Industrial Workers in Chicago, 1919–1939* (New York: Cambridge University Press, [1990] 2008), 159–211. On the Sunday School league, which had twenty teams by 1925, and other leagues that pitted African American teams against white teams in Washington Park, see Nathan M. Jackson, "Church Sports Gains," *Chicago Defender (National Edition),* June 4, 1910, p. 4; "Games Today," *Chicago Defender (National Edition),* July 3, 1915, p. 7; David Kellum, "Constant Disputes Hurt Sunday School League Play," *Chicago Defender (National Edition),* July 26, 1924, p. 9; and "Sunday School League Is Divided into Three Parts," *Chicago Defender (National Edition),* April 25, 1925, p. 11. Such leagues were common in major cities with significant African American populations. For their popularity in Washington, DC, for instance, see William Henry Jones, *Recreation and Amusement among Negroes in Washington, D.C.: A Sociological Analysis of the Negro in an Urban Environment* (Washington, DC: Howard University Press, 1927), 69. Sheep grazed in the park's early years, from 1877–1890, and then were reintroduced from 1916–1920. Chicago Park District, *Historical Register,* 400.

23. On the popularity of African American baseball near Birmingham, Alabama, and the industrial leagues there, see Peter M. Rutkoff and William B. Scott,

Fly Away: The Great African American Cultural Migrations (Baltimore: Johns Hopkins University Press, 2010), 114–122; and Charles Spurgeon Johnson, *Shadow of the Plantation* (Chicago: University of Chicago Press, 1934), 181.

24. Rutkoff and Scott, *Fly Away*, 114; Colin Fisher, "African Americans, Outdoor Recreation, and the 1919 Chicago Race Riot," in *To Love the Wind and the Rain: African Americans and Environmental History*, ed. Dianne D. Glave and Mark Stoll (Pittsburgh: University of Pittsburgh Press, 2006), 71; "With the Picnickers," *Chicago Defender (National Edition)*, July 27, 1912, p. 1; "Walter's A. M. E. Zion Church," *Chicago Defender (National Edition)*, August 22, 1914, p. 2; "News of the Churches," *Chicago Defender (National Edition)*, July 10, 1915, p. 6; "On the Bridle Path," *Chicago Defender (National Edition)*, June 13, 1925, p. 2; and Charles Davis and Clarice Durham, interview with the author, January 20, 2010.

25. Olmsted and Vaux, "Report," 224. Indeed, this is precisely the way the main character in Alden Bland's 1947 novel *Behold a Cry*, set in 1918–1919, experiences the lagoon. Alden Bland, *Behold a Cry* (New York: C. Scribner's Sons, 1947), 142–143.

26. "Skating in Washington Park," *Chicago Defender (National Edition)*, January 13, 1912, p. 5. See also "Trying Out those Steel Blades," *Chicago Defender (National Edition)*, January 31, 1925, p. 1; and Chicago South Park Commissioners, *1873–1874*, 21; Chicago South Park Commissioners, *1907–1908*, 43; Chicago South Park Commissioners, *1908–1909*, 103.

27. W. L. Bliss, "Parks Offer Attractive Program to the Negroes: Stanton, Seward, Union and Washington Parks Do Good Work," *Chicago Park District Recreation News* 2, no. 2 (February 1938), 3.

28. "Cops Junior Relay Honors," *Chicago Defender (National Edition)*, January 30, 1926, p. 9. See also "In Silver Skate Derby," *Chicago Defender (National Edition)*, January 28, 1928, p. A10; and "After the Storm King's Rule," *Chicago Defender (National Edition)*, January 22, 1927, p. 4.

29. Frazier, "Recreation and Amusement," 19. See also Forrester B. Washington, "Recreational Facilities for the Negro," *Annals of the American Academy of Political and Social Science* (November 1928), 272; Rutkoff and Scott, *Fly Away*, 114; Johnson, *Shadow of the Plantation*, 101, 181; Arna Bontemps, *The Old South; "A Summer Tragedy" and Other Stories of the Thirties* (New York: Dodd, Mead, 1973), 13–14; Sara Brooks and Thordis Simonsen, *You May Plow Here: The Narrative of Sara Brooks* (New York: Norton, 1986), 89–90.

30. Timuel Black, interviews with the author, January 21 and July 27, 2010. On fishing and the maintenance of the lagoons, see Chicago South Park Commissioners, *Annual Report of the South Park Commissioners for the Year 1914–1915* (Chicago, 1915), 60; Chicago South Park Commissioners, *1909–1910*, 34; Larry St. John, "Woods and Waters," *Chicago Tribune*, August 1, 1917, p. 19; and Drake and Cayton, *Black Metropolis*, 603.

31. Perhaps in part because of these trends, Woodson also claimed, "Urban recreation [had] become the dominant factor in rural recreation" and activities like "hunting, fishing and the popular picnic in the nearby woods," had by

1930 "been replaced . . . by the radio, moving pictures, and the like." Carter Godwin Woodson, *The Rural Negro* (Washington, DC: Association for the Study of Negro Life and History, 1930), 138–139. Woodson perhaps inadvertently overstates the case to emphasize this trend: although rural life was unquestionably changing, rural recreation in nature was never fully replaced. The penetration of urban entertainment into rural spaces was simply another instance of the rise of hybrid cultures that developed in both North and South because of improved transportation and communication networks that flattened regional and urban/rural differences. On African American recreation in the South, see Kahrl, *The Land Was Ours;* Victoria W. Wolcott, *Race, Riots, and Roller Coasters: The Struggle over Segregated Recreation in America* (Philadelphia: University of Pennsylvania Press, 2012); and William E. O'Brien, *Landscapes of Exclusion: State Parks and Jim Crow in the American South* (Amherst: University of Massachusetts Press, 2016).

32. Chicago Commission, *The Negro in Chicago,* 290.

33. James T. Farrell, *Studs Lonigan: A Trilogy* (New York: Library of America, 2004), 221, 451. Perhaps no fictional character embodies the racial and spatial significance of Washington Park better than James T. Farrell's Studs Lonigan; again and again Chicago's parks appear in the Studs Lonigan trilogy. A thinly veiled composite of his boyhood friends and Farrell himself (who had grown up just across the street from Washington Park and fondly recalled playing baseball there), Studs embodies Farrell's memory that, in real life, "to me this park had once been the world of nature. It was where I located dreams and hopes." Branch, *Studs Lonigan's Neighborhood,* 57. For critical interpretations of the park's significance in the novels, see Charles Fanning and Ellen Skerrett, "James T. Farrell and Washington Park: The Novel as Social History," *Chicago History* 8, no. 2 (Summer 1979), 80–91; Robert Butler, "Farrell's Ethnic Neighborhood and Wright's Urban Ghetto: Two Visions of Chicago's South Side," *MELUS* 18, no. 1 (Spring 1993), 103–111; Robert Butler, "Parks, Parties, and Pragmatism: Time and Setting in James T. Farrell's Major Novels," *Essays in Literature* 10, no. 2 (Fall 1983), 241–253; and Fisher, *Urban Green,* 64–66.

34. For examples of interracial violence in Washington Park, see Chicago Commission, *The Negro in Chicago,* 286–292; "Race Girls Brutally Assaulted by Whites in Washington Park," *Chicago Defender (National Edition),* June 8, 1918, p. 11; and "Boys Attack Men in South Side Park," *Chicago Defender (National Edition)* June 12, 1920, p. 1. For the history of African American recreation in the city's green spaces, see Fisher, *Urban Green,* 90–91.

35. Frazier, "Recreation and Amusement," 45–46; Thomas Jackson Woofter and Institute of Social and Religious Research, *Negro Problems in Cities: A Study* (Garden City, NY: Doubleday, Doran & Co, 1928), 231–232.

36. Hughes toured the South in the midst of the epic Mississippi Valley flooding, which exacerbated racial tensions across the South. Langston Hughes, *The Big Sea, an Autobiography* (New York: Hill and Wang, 1963), 286.

37. Ibid., 33; "Beaches Free to All," *Chicago Defender (National Edition)*, August 4, 1917, p. 3.

38. Joseph Dean Lohman and Chicago Park District, *The Police and Minority Groups: A Manual Prepared for Use in the Chicago Park District Police Training School* (Chicago: Chicago Park District, 1947), 72.

39. Chicago Commission, *The Negro in Chicago*, 572; William M. Tuttle, *Race Riot: Chicago in the Red Summer of 1919* (Urbana: University of Illinois Press, 1996; 1970), 237–241; "No Disorders July 4," *Chicago Defender (National Edition)*, July 5, 1919, p. 17; "Hope Presbyterian Church," *Chicago Defender (National Edition)*, July 11, 1914, p. 3; and "Personal Mention," *Chicago Defender (National Edition)*, July 13, 1912, p. 2. Migrants likely would have been familiar with similar celebrations of such national holidays in the South. Rutkoff and Scott, *Fly Away*, 113, 226.

40. "Ruffianism in the Parks," *Chicago Defender (National Edition)*, July 12, 1919, p. 20. Both whites and blacks—and especially the *Defender* (which was unsurprising given its class politics)—tended to blame the violence on lower-class whites who lived on the western edge of the Black Belt, much farther from Washington and Jackson Parks than the middle- and upper-class whites who lived nearby. See, for example "South Siders Ask for More Park Police," *Chicago Defender (City Edition)*, August 28, 1926, p. 10; "See Need for More South Park Police," *Chicago Defender (City Edition)*, August 6, 1927, p. 5; "Ruffianism in the Parks"; and Thomas Romayne, "'Southern Gentleman,'" *Chicago Defender (National Edition)*, August 17, 1929, p. A2. The *Broad Ax*, meanwhile, linked the bombings of African American homes to its vociferous denunciation of discriminatory housing policies perpetuated by the white middle and upper classes. See, for instance, "The Grand Boulevard Branch of the Kenwood and Hyde Park Property Owners Association," *Broad Ax*, January 10, 1920, p. 1. On black Chicagoans preparing for violence that summer, see "Clubs and Fraternal," *Chicago Defender (National Edition)*, July 5, 1919, p. 12; and Fisher, "African Americans," 72.

41. Bland, *Behold a Cry*, 68. Bland places his main character, Ed, and his two sons, at ground zero of the riot's inception at 29th Street beach. After the three characters witness the boy's drowning and the beginning of violence, Ed is beaten badly in the ensuing riot.

42. "Bloody Anarchy, Murder, Rapine, Race Riots, and All Forms of Lawlesness," *Broad Ax*, August 2, 1919, p. 2.

43. For the best accounts of the riot, see Chicago Commission, *The Negro in Chicago*; Cameron McWhirter, *Red Summer: The Summer of 1919 and the Awakening of Black America* (New York: Henry Holt & Co., 2011), 114–148; and Tuttle, *Race Riot*, 3–10. Somewhat tragically, the *Chicago Whip* had relayed the South Park Commissioners' entreaty to black Chicagoans urging them to bring their children to 26th Street beach earlier that month, assuring readers that "they will get courteous expert attention from the trained life guard" who was African American, and they should "make this beach the

Atlantic City of the second ward." "26th Street Beach in Full Bloom," *Chicago Whip*, July 3, 1919, p. 7.

44. Farrell, *Studs Lonigan: A Trilogy*, 244.

45. Ibid., 244–245. Studs and his young working-class Irish friends are a fictional equivalent to the sorts of real-life gangs that participated in the 1919 riot and that were studied by Chicago sociologists like Frederic Thrasher. The most notable of these real-life gangs in the riot was the predominantly Irish "Ragen's Colts." See Frederic Thrasher, *The Gang: A Study of 1,313 Gangs in Chicago* (Chicago: University of Chicago Press, 1927); Chicago Commission, *The Negro in Chicago*, 12–14, 55; and Tuttle, *Race Riot*, 32–33, 54–55.

46. "Segregation by Agreement," *Chicago Whip*, November 15, 1919, p. 8.

47. "18th Annual Report of the Juvenile Protective Association of Chicago, 1918–1919," Box 9, Folder 126, 25, JPA. The Juvenile Protective Association's 1919 report on the riot was found under the heading "Protection of Colored Children," but the JPA's history regarding race is somewhat vexed. Although the group spoke out against racial injustice in the city and collaborated with African American social organizations, it also investigated and targeted "black & tan" dance halls in the Black Belt—and the social mixing of races there—as centers of vice. See Louise de Koven Bowen, "The Colored People of Chicago: An Investigation made for the Juvenile Protective Association," 1913, Box 10, Folder 128, JPA; Paul Gerard Anderson, "The Good to Be Done: A History of Juvenile Protective Association of Chicago, 1898–1976" (Ph.D. diss., University of Chicago), 240–286, 412–419; "Women's Civic League," *Chicago Defender (National Edition)*, March 28, 1914, p. 6; Arvarh E. Strickland, *History of the Chicago Urban League* (Urbana: University of Illinois Press, 1966), 30; "Illinois Home Aid Society Issues Plea," *Chicago Defender (National Edition)*, December 23, 1922, p. 5; "Reformers Play up Race Issue in Vice Probe," *Chicago Defender (National Edition)*, January 20, 1923, p. 2; A. L. Jackson, "The Onlooker," *Chicago Defender (National Edition)*, January 20, 1923, p. 12; "Girls Are Girls," *Chicago Defender (National Edition)*, February 9, 1924, p. 5; and Kevin J. Mumford, *Interzones: Black/White Sex Districts in Chicago and New York in the Early Twentieth Century* (New York: Columbia University Press, 1997).

48. Dempsey Travis, *An Autobiography of Black Chicago* (Chicago: Urban Research Institute, 1981), 26.

49. The report listed Washington Park and several other city parks, playgrounds, and beaches as points of interracial conflict. Chicago Commission, *The Negro in Chicago*, 289. See also McWhirter, *Red Summer*, 120–125; and "Rowdies in Park Slug Richard Hudlin," *Chicago Defender (City Edition)*, May 30, 1925, p. 1.

50. "Washington Park Gang Beats Another Victim," *Chicago Defender (National Edition)*, June 10, 1922, p. 1.

51. Chicago Commission, *The Negro in Chicago*, 292.

52. "Washington Park Gang Beats Another Victim." On this more assertive "New Negro" mentality in Chicago, see Davarian L. Baldwin, *Chicago's New*

Negroes: Modernity, the Great Migration, & Black Urban Life (Chapel Hill: University of North Carolina Press, 2007).

53. Among many other studies of the "Talented Tenth," see chapter 2 in Gaines, *Uplifting the Race.*

54. "The Home of Mr. and Mrs. Oscar De Priest," *Broad Ax,* April 9, 1921, p. 1. See also "De Priest Vows Revenge on Bomb Squad," *Chicago Whip,* April 9, 1921, p. 1. On Farrell's youth in the neighborhood and his fictionalization of Binga's house bombing, see Robert K. Landers, *An Honest Writer: The Life and Times of James T. Farrell* (San Francisco: Encounter Books, 2004), 28, 39, 79; and Farrell, *Studs Lonigan: A Trilogy,* 330. As the Black Belt extended southward and ever nearer Washington Park in the 1920s, more prosperous African Americans were almost always at the southern reaches of the expansion where the housing stock was better, because these were neighborhoods where the white middle and upper classes had lived. On this expansion and the resulting bombing of Binga's home and others, see Chicago Commission on Race Relations, *The Negro in Chicago,* 122–129, 184–194; Drake and Cayton, *Black Metropolis,* 63–64, 178–179, 603–605; Edward Franklin Frazier, *The Negro Family in Chicago* (Chicago: University of Chicago Press, 1932), 98–101; Jeffrey Helgeson, "Striving in Black Chicago: Migration, Work, and the Politics of Neighborhood Change 1935–1965" (Ph.D. diss., University of Illinois at Chicago), 49–50; Thomas Lee Philpott, *The Slum and the Ghetto: Immigrants, Blacks, and Reformers in Chicago, 1880–1930* (Belmont, CA: Wadsworth Publishing, 1991), 163–182; and Bachin, *Building the South Side,* 252–254.

55. "Bomb Rips Front Porch from Jesse Binga's Dwelling," *Chicago Defender (National Edition),* September 3, 1921, p. 3.

56. Chicago Commission, *The Negro in Chicago,* 293.

57. Gunnar Myrdal, *An American Dilemma: The Negro Problem and Modern Democracy* (New York: Harper & Brothers, 1944), 624. Racially restrictive covenants prevented African Americans from settling in the neighborhood immediately south of Washington Park until 1940–1941. See Chapter 3 for a more complete discussion of the landmark *Hansberry* v. *Lee* Supreme Court case and the collapse of covenants in the Washington Park subdivision. Drake and Cayton, *Black Metropolis,* 182–190; Lohman and Chicago Park District, *The Police and Minority Groups,* 67–68. For more on the environmental implications of racially restrictive covenants in Chicago and other cities, see chapter 8 in Dorceta Taylor, *Toxic Communities: Environmental Racism, Industrial Pollution, and Residential Mobility* (New York: New York University Press, 2014).

58. See "'Help Keep Chicago Clean,'" *Broad Ax,* April 15, 1916, p. 1; Louis B. Anderson and Robert R. Jackson, "The Colored Preachers Are Urged to Assist to Help Us Clean up the Second Ward," *Broad Ax,* May 11, 1918, p. 2; "Y.M.C.A. News," *Chicago Whip,* June 26, 1920, p. 4; Chicago Commission, *The Negro in Chicago,* 194; St. Clair Drake and United States Work Projects Administration, *Churches and Voluntary Associations in the Chicago Negro Community* (Chicago, 1940), 145–146; and chapter 6 in Washington, *Packing Them In.* South Side victory gardens planted during World War I were part of a city-

wide effort. See J. Seymour Currey, *Illinois Activities in the World War: Covering the Period from 1914 to 1920* (Chicago: Thomas B. Poole, 1921), 797–799; "The Colored People Are Becoming Greatly Interested in the Community Gardens in All Parts of the City," *Broad Ax,* April 21, 1917, p. 4; "Frederick Douglass Center Garden," *Broad Ax,* May 26, 1917, p. 4; and "Keep Chickens at Home," *Broad Ax,* June 9, 1917, p. 4.

59. Jennie E. Lawrence, "Voice of the People—Terrorizing Negro Girls," *Chicago Tribune,* August 1, 1929, p. 14. On that summer's heat and the popularity of Chicago's lakefront, see "Three Drown as Thousands Jam Beaches," *Chicago Tribune,* July 22, 1929, p. 3; "Mercury Climbs to 91; Hottest Day of Summer," *Chicago Tribune,* July 25, 1929, p. 3; "Heat Wave to Continue Today; Youth Drowned," *Chicago Tribune,* July 27, 1929, p. 2; "Heat at Peak; Relief Today," *Chicago Tribune,* July 28, 1929, p. 1; "Oak Street Beach Mass of Humanity on Hottest Day of Year in Chicago," *Chicago Tribune,* July 28, 1929, p. 3; "Record Crowds Swarm Beaches as Heat Breaks," *Chicago Tribune,* July 29, 1929, p. 3; "Sultry Sunday Draws Record Beach Crowds," *Chicago Tribune,* August 12, 1929, p. 7; and "Mercury 93; 4 Die in Heat; Relief on Way," *Chicago Tribune,* August 23, 1929, p. 1.

60. Ralph Watson, "Voice of the People—Color at the Beach," *Chicago Tribune,* August 1, 1929, p. 14.

61. Lawrence, "Voice of the People—Terrorizing Negro Girls."

62. Romayne, "Southern Gentleman." A less hostile letter writer also invoked the 1919 riot. Alfred P. Williams, "Trouble at Jackson Park Beach," *Chicago Defender (National Edition),* August 10, 1929, p. A2.

63. H. D. O., "Voice of the People—Witness of the Trouble," *Chicago Tribune,* August 3, 1929, p. 8; and G. H. Shafer, "Voice of the People—Segregated Swimming," *Chicago Tribune,* August 3, 1929, p. 8.

64. "Racial Conflict at the Beaches," *Chicago Tribune,* August 5, 1929, p. 14.

65. Romayne, "Southern Gentleman."

66. "Racial Conflict at the Beaches."

67. "Arrest Youth at Beach for Disorderly Conduct," *Chicago Defender (National Edition),* July 27, 1929, p. 1. 29th Street beach effectively became 31st Street beach in 1925 after South Park Commissioners' negotiations and land deals with the Illinois Central Railroad. Despite expanded access to Lake Michigan, the South Park Commissioners noted—and capitulated to—resistance to African American bathing at the lakefront south of 33rd Street as late as 1929. See Chicago South Park Commission, *Official Proceedings of the South Park District,* Vol. 32 (1924), 346, CPD; Chicago South Park Commission, *Official Proceedings of the South Park District,* Vol. 33 (1925), 104, 323–328, CPD; and Chicago South Park Commission, *Official Proceedings of the South Park District,* Vol. 37 (1929), 357, CPD. On black Chicago's population growth, see Drake and Cayton, *Black Metropolis,* 8–9.

68. Race relations at Jackson Park had been tense for years, but became increasingly uneasy as black residential neighborhoods crept nearer and more African Americans began using the park. See Wolcott, *Race, Riots,*

and Roller Coasters, 28–29. For racial discrimination and conflict in Jackson Park beach as early as 1920, see Nettie George Speedy, "Prejudice and Diplomacy Work Ill to Golfers," *Chicago Defender (National Edition)*, August 5, 1922, p. 2; "Park Board Denies Part in Beach Segregation," *Chicago Defender (National Edition)*, July 25, 1925, p. 4; and "Breeding Trouble," *Chicago Defender (National Edition)*, July 18, 1925, p. A9.

69. Just Me, "More about Beaches," *Chicago Defender (National Edition)*, August 10, 1929, p. A2. On longstanding complaints about these inadequate facilities, see also Chicago Commission, *The Negro in Chicago*, 272, 287; Shafer, "Voice of the People—Segregated Swimming"; "Voice of the People—Negro Beaches," *Chicago Tribune*, August 6, 1929, p. 14; A Friend of the Negro, "Voice of the People—A Question of Propriety," *Chicago Tribune*, August 9, 1929, p. 10; Mrs. L. R. F., "For Separate Beaches," *Chicago Defender (National Edition)* August 10, 1929, p.A2; "Under the Lash of the Whip," *Chicago Whip*, July 1, 1922, p. 8; and "Promises Negro Bathers They'll Get Protection," *Chicago Tribune*, August 15, 1929, p. 6. They were even fictionalized in Alden Bland's Great Migration novel, *Behold a Cry*. Bland, *Behold a Cry*, 68.

70. Mrs Edward Smith, "How they Fool Us," *Chicago Defender (National Edition)*, October 2, 1926, p. A2; Eddy W. Jefferson, "Voice of the People—Improve the Negro Beaches," *Chicago Tribune*, August 3, 1929, p. 8; and Williams, "Trouble at Jackson Park Beach." On similar racial inequalities across the South, see chapter 4 in Kahrl, *The Land Was Ours*; and O'Brien, *Landscapes of Exclusion*.

71. "Aldermen on So. Side Lie down on Job," *Chicago Defender (City Edition)*, August 14, 1926, p. 1.

72. "For Better Beaches for Chicagoans," *Chicago Defender (National Edition)*, July 27, 1929, p. 2. In the wake of the near-riot in July and protests from the community, the South Park police renewed their commitment to protect black bathers. "Promises Negro Bathers They'll Get Protection"; "Colored Leaders Ask Equal Rights at City Beaches," *Chicago Tribune*, August 12, 1929, p. 7.

73. Herbert A. Turner, "Voice of the People—Racial Conflict at the Beaches," *Chicago Tribune*, August 7, 1929, p. 14. For similar arguments, see J. H. Scott, "Voice of the People—Legal and Economic Rights," *Chicago Tribune*, August 8, 1929, p. 12; Lawrence, "Voice of the People—Terrorizing Negro Girls"; Julius J. Hyde, "Voice of the People—the Legal Rights of Negroes," *Chicago Tribune*, August 7, 1929, p. 14; and Florida M. Thomas, "Voice of the People—Equality, Freedom," *Chicago Tribune*, August 6, 1929, p. 14. For a range of arguments in support of separate bathing facilities, see Williams, "Trouble at Jackson Park Beach"; A Friend of the Negro, "Voice of the People—A Question of Propriety"; Mrs. L. R. F., "For Separate Beaches"; Shafer, "Voice of the People—Segregated Swimming"; H. D. O., "Voice of the People—Witness of the Trouble,"; Jimmie Farrell, "Voice of the People—Dividing the Parks," *Chicago Tribune*, August 3, 1929, p. 8; and "Voice of the People—Negro Beaches."

74. Romayne, "Southern Gentleman." For a similar argument, see also Thomas, "Voice of the People—Equality, Freedom."

75. "The Foolish Question Hovering over Lake Michigan," *Chicago Defender (City Edition),* August 17, 1929, p. 1.

76. Drake and Cayton, *Black Metropolis,* 63.

77. "The Tribune Speaks," *Chicago Defender (National Edition),* August 10, 1929, p. A2.

78. Romayne, "Southern Gentleman."

79. Jefferson, "Voice of the People—Improve the Negro Beaches."

80. Farrell, "Voice of the People—Dividing the Parks." Although I cannot say with absolute certainty that the "Jimmie Farrell" who wrote the letter was James T. Farrell, it seems quite likely given the author's interest in race conflict on the South Side and that he was, at the time, a twenty-five-year-old living on Chicago's South Side. The similarity in language and perspective to a letter Farrell sent a friend in August 1927 is also striking. See Branch, *Studs Lonigan's Neighborhood,* 52. Farrell's Studs Lonigan trilogy fictionalizes the author's family's moves ever southward. See, in particular, Farrell, *Studs Lonigan: A Trilogy,* 552, 574, 693–695, 705–715, 718–721, 798–799.

81. "Racial Conflict at the Beaches." Another letter described African American use of the park as appropriation rather than inheritance. A Friend of the Negro, "Voice of the People—A Question of Propriety," 10. The boulevards referenced are almost certainly Garfield (55th Street) and South Parkway, which by this time were in the heart of the Black Belt.

82. "Hon. A. H. Roberts Has Introduced," *Broad Ax,* April 19, 1919, p. 5.

83. Just a Spectator an Old Residenter, "An Armory in Washington Park," *Chicago Defender (National Edition),* March 3, 1928, p. 14. The armory was ultimately built, following a longstanding trend of eliminating green space in favor of buildings in a range of parks citywide. On the park as African American space, see also "Sports"; R. A. F., "Opposed to a Near South Side Park," *Chicago Tribune,* March 29, 1923, p. 8; "The Inquiring Reporter," *Chicago Defender (National Edition),* July 23, 1927, p. 3.

84. "This Is Progress," *Chicago Defender (National Edition),* August 10, 1929, p. A2.

85. "BVD's Are again Seen on Tennis Courts in Park," *Chicago Defender (National Edition),* June 17, 1922, p. 8.

86. "Washington Park Becomes Pest-Bound," *Chicago Defender (National Edition),* August 30, 1924, p. 4. See also "Fay Says," *Chicago Defender (National Edition),* July 16, 1927, p. 10; Robb, *The Negro in Chicago,* 85; Baldwin, *Chicago's New Negroes,* 36; and Grossman, *Land of Hope,* 153–155.

87. Mahalia Jackson and Evan McLeod Wylie, *Movin' on Up* (New York: Hawthorn Books, 1966), 17.

88. On baptisms and Baptists in Chicago, see St. Clair Drake, "Negro Churches and Associations in Chicago: A Research Memorandum," in *The Carnegie-Myrdal Study,* 223, 365; "Fifty Baptized in Lake Michigan," *Chicago Whip,* July 2, 1921, p. 5; and Wallace D. Best, *Passionately Human, No Less Divine: Religion and Culture in Black Chicago, 1915–1952* (Princeton, NJ: Princeton University Press, 2005). On baptisms in the South, see Allison Davis, "The Negro Church and Associations in the Lower South: A Research Memo-

randum," in *The Carnegie-Myrdal Study*, 82–83; John Dollard, *Caste and Class in a Southern Town* (New Haven, CT: Yale University Press, 1937), 236–238; William E. Montgomery, *Under Their Own Vine and Fig Tree: The African-American Church in the South, 1865–1900* (Baton Rouge, LA: Louisiana State University Press, 1993), 294–296; Michael Angelo Gomez, *Exchanging Our Country Marks: The Transformation of African Identities in the Colonial and Antebellum South* (Chapel Hill: University of North Carolina Press, 1998), 272–274; and Albert J. Raboteau, *Slave Religion: The "Invisible Institution" in the Antebellum South* (New York: Oxford University Press, 1978), 227–228.

89. "Sunday Circus in Lake Michigan," *Chicago Defender (National Edition)*, July 26, 1924, p. 8. Like the churches housing mixed-class and mixed "new settler" / "old settler" congregations that Wallace Best examines in his study of migration-era African American religion in Chicago, city parks and beaches were venues where diverse elements of the African American community interacted and sometimes conflicted. See Best, *Passionately Human, No Less Divine*, 25–31.

90. Kellum, "Constant Disputes Hurt Sunday School League Play." Despite a few teams that had both white and black players, teams and spectators were more commonly segregated; black teams played black teams and white teams played white teams while spectators self-segregated. Chicago Commission, *The Negro in Chicago*, 286. On the racial and cultural implications of baseball on the South Side, see chapter 6 in Baldwin, *Chicago's New Negroes*, 206; and Bachin, *Building the South Side*, 264–268.

91. Fay, "Sport Editorial: Stop It at Once," *Chicago Defender (National Edition)*, June 4, 1927, p. 9.

92. Frank A. Young, "State Street Is a Breeding Spot for Evil," *Chicago Defender (National Edition)*, April 19, 1913, p. 1.

93. "Washington Park Becomes Pest-Bound."

94. "Lip Slobbering in Theaters Is Given the Razz," *Chicago Defender (National Edition)*, September 16, 1922, p. 8.

95. See "21st Annual Report of the Juvenile Protective Association of Chicago" (1921), 11, and "27th Annual Report of the Juvenile Protective Association of Chicago" (1927), 13, Box 9, Folder 126, JPA. On the implications of class intermingling at Washington Park, see Chicago South Park Commissioners, *1887–1888*, 14; and Bachin, *Building the South Side*, 135–136.

96. "Best Citizens," *Chicago Defender (National Edition)*, July 9, 1921, p. 4. Perhaps unbeknownst to the *Defender* editorialist, the "hitch your wagon to a star" trope originated with one of the giants of the American environmental movement, Ralph Waldo Emerson. A commonplace by the 1920s, Emerson published the idea in the April 1862 issue of *The Atlantic Monthly* in an article titled "American Civilization." Thanks are due to Lawrence Buell for this insight. On the Stroll, see chapter 1 in Baldwin, *Chicago's New Negroes*.

97. Arising from a decades-long movement rooted in the black church, these "politics of respectability" were, as historian Evelyn Brooks Higginbotham

has written, "middle-class ideals [promoted] among the masses of blacks in the belief that such ideals ensured the dual goals of racial self-help and respect from white America." Agreement over the ideal middle-class respectable behavior at public parks could serve as a "bridge discourse" between white and black reformers, but black reformers worried that failing to live up to those standards reflected poorly on the race as a whole. This also helps explain why publications like the *Defender* were so keen to blame race violence on the white working classes rather than on more ostensibly "respectable" whites. See Higginbotham, *Righteous Discontent*, 14, 187, 197. These "middle-class ideals" also dovetailed with anxieties that unwelcome behavior might confirm racist white convictions that African Americans were an inferior, "primitive" race. See Chapter 2 for an elaboration of these ideas.

98. "BVD's Are again Seen on Tennis Courts in Park." The *Broad Ax* was even more critical, calling migrant behavior along South Parkway "little better than hottentots" and urging, "For the love of Douglass, Washington and the culture and refinement of our race, let us keep our fronts clean always, grow grass, keep it trimmed, cultivate flowers and above all things keep windows washed, and front curtains clean, and avoid making boisterous noise." Before the 1919 riot, they even went so far as to blame both "bulldozing Whites who entertain the idea that they own the whole earth, and . . . many loud mouthed Negroes who are always walking around with chips on their backs looking for trouble" for racial unrest at the city's beaches. "Living on the Boulevards," *Broad Ax*, January 31, 1920, p. 1; "Trash," *Broad Ax*, December 7, 1918, p. 8; and "Beach Race Rioters Fined," *Broad Ax*, August 5, 1916, p. 1. Although the *Chicago Whip* generally took a less harshly critical view of this behavior than either the *Broad Ax* or the *Defender* (the latter of which the *Whip* accused of blaming the victim), it too was quite concerned with white perceptions of black behavior in these green spaces and pointed to those perceptions as a reason to participate in annual spring cleanup campaigns. "Living on the Boulevards," *Chicago Whip*, October 4, 1919, p. 12; "Under the Lash of the Whip," *Chicago Whip*, September 4, 1920, p. 2; and Dr. Troy Smith, "Health Hints," *Chicago Whip*, April 16, 1921, p. 8.

99. "Washington Park Becomes Pest-Bound." See also "Keep Parkway Clean!" *Chicago Defender (City Edition)*, May 22, 1926, p. 8; and "Keep off the Grass," *Chicago Defender (City Edition)*, June 11, 1927, p. 5.

100. "Washington Park Becomes Pest-Bound."

101. Farrell, "Voice of the People—Dividing the Parks."

102. "Racial Conflict at the Beaches."

103. "History of Washington Park: Document #6a" (1927), 3, VMP, Volume 5, Part 1; and "History of Washington Park: Document #6" (1927), 2, VMP, Volume 5, Part 1.

104. Edith Abbott, Sophonisba Preston Breckinridge, and the University of Chicago School of Social Service Administration, *The Tenements of Chicago*,

1908–1935 (Chicago: University of Chicago Press, 1936), 122–123, 178. See also Philpott, *The Slum and the Ghetto,* 158; and Frederick Douglass Opie, *Hog & Hominy: Soul Food from Africa to America* (New York: Columbia University Press, 2008), 57. These sorts of farm-like artifacts in the city persisted through the 1930s, when the poverty of the Great Depression put a premium on one's ability to be self-sufficient: Charles Davis's relatives kept chickens in their backyard early in the decade, for instance. That said, Davis remembered the practice being relatively rare. Isabel Wilkerson, *The Warmth of Other Suns: The Epic Story of America's Great Migration* (New York: Random House, 2010), 269; Davis and Durham, interview with the author, January 20, 2010.

105. Abbott, *The Tenements of Chicago,* 122–123, 178. See also Chicago Commission, *The Negro in Chicago,* 101, 172, 184; and Jeffrey Helgeson, *Crucibles of Black Empowerment: Chicago's Neighborhood Politics from the New Deal to Harold Washington* (Chicago: University of Chicago Press, 2014), 1. The situation was similar in Washington, DC. See James Borchert, *Alley Life in Washington: Family, Community, Religion, and Folklife in the City, 1850–1970* (Urbana: University of Illinois Press, 1980), 86–96. Although there were far fewer spatial constraints in the rural South, similar economic constraints also prevented many sharecroppers from gardening, despite entreaties from reformers such as Booker T. Washington and George Washington Carver at the Tuskegee Institute. Johnson, *Shadow of the Plantation,* 100–115; Woodson, *The Rural Negro,* 5; Dorothy Dickins, "A Nutritional Investigation of Tenants in the Yazoo-Mississippi Delta," *Mississippi Agricultural Experiment Station Bulletin* 254 (August 1928); Mark D. Hersey, *My Work Is That of Conservation: An Environmental Biography of George Washington Carver* (Athens: University of Georgia Press, 2011), 131, 147, 202–203; Dianne D. Glave, "Rural African American Women, Gardening, and Progressive Reform in the South," in *To Love the Wind and the Rain: African Americans and Environmental History,* ed. Dianne D. Glave and Mark Stoll (Pittsburgh: University of Pittsburgh Press, 2006), 37–50; Smith, *African American Environmental Thought,* 87–95; and Kevin C. Armitage, *The Nature Study Movement: The Forgotten Popularizer of America's Conservation Ethic* (Lawrence: University Press of Kansas, 2009), 111–143.

106. "A Park for South Side," *Chicago Defender (City Edition),* February 12, 1927, p. 7. See also Dr. W. A. Driver, "Talks on Health, Cleanliness Proper Living Sanitation, etc." *Broad Ax,* April 10, 1915, p. 4.

107. "A Park for South Side," *Chicago Defender (City Edition),* January 15, 1927, p. 5. See also Davis and Durham, interview with the author, July 28, 2010; Division of Playgrounds and Sports, South Park Commissioners, "A Survey of the Madden Park Community" (Chicago Park District Archives, 1930), 28; Frazier, *The Negro Family in Chicago,* 99–139.

108. L. B. Sidway, "Early History of the South Parks," in Chicago South Park Commissioners, *1908–1909,* 70.

109. Chicago Commission, *The Negro in Chicago,* 102.
110. Ibid., 273.; Chicago Park District, *Historical Register,* 354. See also "History of Douglas: Document #13," 6–7, VMP, Volume 4, Part 2; Earl Richard Moses, "Community Factors in Negro Delinquency" (master's thesis, University of Chicago, 1932). Fighting for small neighborhood parks was also part and parcel of the white Progressive agenda, which in Chicago stretched back to the late 1890s. Bachin, *Building the South Side,* 138–159.
111. "Recreational Park and Beach for South Side," *Chicago Whip,* November 18, 1922, p. 3.
112. Chicago Commission, *The Negro in Chicago,* 272–273. On cost differences between playgrounds, small parks, and large parks, see also Chicago South Park Commissioners, *1914–1915,* 67; Chicago South Park Commissioners, *Annual Report of the South Park Commissioners for the Year 1915–1916* (Chicago, 1916), 13; and Chicago South Park Commissioners, *1921–1922,* 30.
113. "Dedicate Beautiful Playground," *Chicago Defender (National Edition),* October 23, 1926, p. 3; "New Playground Is Dedicated," *Chicago Tribune,* October 17, 1926, p. 20; and "Alderman Jackson Gives Voters Proof in Record," *Chicago Defender (City Edition),* January 29, 1927, Part 2, p. 8. Jackson and fellow alderman Louis B. Anderson had long track records of advocating for expanded recreational space in the Black Belt. See "Platform of Louis B. Anderson," *Broad Ax,* February 10, 1917, p. 4; "Major Robert R. Jackson's Platform. It Is Worth Any One's Time to Carefully Read and Study it," *Broad Ax,* March 23, 1918, p. 1; "Alderman Jackson and Alderman Anderson Secure Largest Playground in Chicago," *Broad Ax,* April 10, 1920, p. 2; "Ald. Jackson Gets Street Beaches for Children," *Chicago Whip,* December 2, 1922, p. 3; and "Ald. Jackson Endorsed for Re-Election," *Chicago Defender (National Edition),* December 1, 1934, p. 3.
114. "A Park for South Side," *Chicago Defender (City Edition),* January 22, 1927, p. 8. On how little resemblance playgrounds bore to "natural" environments, see Cavallo, *Muscles and Morals,* 26. For an alternative perspective on how playgrounds worked in tandem with more "natural" spaces, see Fisher, *Urban Green,* 22–28.
115. Chicago Commission, *The Negro in Chicago,* 272. See also Chicago South Park Commissioners, *Annual Report of the South Park Commissioners for the Year 1918–1919* (Chicago, 1919), 67; Robert Ezra Park et al., *The City* (Chicago: University of Chicago Press, 1925), 111–112; Cavallo, *Muscles and Morals,* 2–4.
116. Chicago South Park Commission, *Official Proceedings,* Vol. 33, 71, CPD. For the details of this battle, see Chicago South Park Commission, *Official Proceedings,* Vol. 25 (1918), 1, CPD; Chicago South Park Commission, *Official Proceedings of the South Park District,* Vol. 26 (1919), 79, CPD; Chicago South Park Commission, *Official Proceedings of the South Park District,* Vol. 30 (1923), 134, CPD; and Chicago South Park Commission, *Official Proceedings of the South Park District,* Vol. 31 (1924), 34, 104, 178, 231, 384, CPD. The history of fighting for park space in Chicago dated back at least

to an 1896 campaign led in part by Reverend Reverdy Ransom. Bachin, *Building the South Side,* 139.

117. On the mass meeting, where citizens demanded that the South Park board finally build a park in the Black Belt using funds from a $3 million bond issue in 1923 that had been supported by the black community, see Chicago South Park Commission, *Official Proceedings,* Vol. 33, 254, CPD; and "Playground, Park Assured South Side," *Chicago Defender (City Edition),* May 23, 1925, p. 10. On Ida B. Wells's petition and continued activism in 1926, see Chicago South Park Commission, *Official Proceedings of the South Park District,* Vol. 34 (1926), 310, CPD; Chicago South Park Commission, *Official Proceedings of the South Park District,* Vol. 35 (1927), 5, CPD; Chicago Park District, *Historical Register,* 354; and "See Slight Prospect of Playgrounds: Citizens Urge S. Park Board to Act," *Chicago Defender (City Edition),* July 24, 1926, p. 5.

118. "10th Annual Report" (1926), 8, Series I, Box 1, Folder 6, CUL.

119. Chicago Park District, *Historical Register,* 354. See also Chicago South Park Commission, *Official Proceedings of the South Park District,* Vol. 35, 74, CPD; and "South Side Citizens Show They Really Want a Park," *Chicago Defender (City Edition),* October 30, 1926, p. 5.

120. "Do You Want a Park?" *Chicago Defender (City Edition),* November 13, 1926, p. 2.

121. A South Side Citizen, "This Is to Be a Community Park, Not a Race Park," *Chicago Defender (National Edition),* November 20, 1926, p. A2.

122. Ibid. On the racial composition of nearby neighborhoods, see the map in Chicago Commission, *The Negro in Chicago,* 120–121; and Holt, *Chicago, a Historical Guide,* 54.

123. "Vote 'Yes' on New Park Bond Issues," *Chicago Defender (City Edition),* June 4, 1927, p. 2.

124. "Board Votes for Location Citizens Pick: *Defender* Wins Fight for Recreation Spot," *Chicago Defender (City Edition),* May 28, 1927, p. 1.

125. "A Park for South Side," *Chicago Defender (City Edition),* February 5, 1927, p. 2. This article was one of several similar articles that outlined myriad reasons to establish a new park and ran from January–May 1927 in the *Defender*'s City Edition. On the culmination of the battle for Madden Park and its long path to improvement, see "Madden Park Women Fete 200 Billikens," *Chicago Defender (National Edition),* October 4, 1930, p. 15; and Chicago Park District, *Historical Register,* 355. Madden, who died in office in 1928, had supported anti-lynching legislation, was integral in getting African Americans jobs in the Chicago Post Office, and according to the *Defender* "fought for every measure that meant added protection and security for the Race, and . . . desperately against whatever he found to be detrimental." "All America Mourns for M. B. Madden," *Chicago Defender (National Edition),* May 5, 1928, p. 1. See also "Name Park in Honor of Late Martin B. Madden," *Chicago Defender (National Edition),* May 5, 1928, p. 1;

and Thomas Robert Bullard, "From Businessman to Congressman: The Careers of Martin B. Madden" (Ph.D. diss., University of Illinois at Chicago), 206–217.

126. Dr. A. Wilberforce Williams, "Keep Healthy," *Chicago Defender (National Edition)*, August 2, 1913, p. 7. Williams perhaps paraphrased William Wordsworth, who wrote in "The Tables Turned" in 1798, "Let Nature be your teacher."

2. Black Chicagoans in Unexpected Places

1. "Binga's Guard Tries Gun Play after Bombing," *Chicago Tribune*, August 26, 1921, p. 13. On the rash of bombings in the Black Belt, see "More than Forty Death Dealing Bombs," *Broad Ax* May 14, 1921, p. 1; and St. Clair Drake and Horace Cayton, *Black Metropolis: A Study of Negro Life in a Northern City* (Chicago: University of Chicago Press, [1945] 1993), 177–179.

2. "Bomb Rips Front Porch from Jesse Binga's Dwelling," *Chicago Defender (National Edition)*, September 3, 1921, p. 3. Binga had moved into his home opposite Washington Park in 1916. "Mr. and Mrs. Jesse Binga Entertained Their Friends on New Year's Day at Their Elegant New Home, 5922 Grand Blvd." *Broad Ax*, January 6, 1917, p. 1. On De Priest's home bombing that April, see "De Priest Vows Revenge on Bomb Squad," *Chicago Whip*, April 9, 1921, p. 1; and "The Home of Mr. and Mrs. Oscar De Priest," *Broad Ax*, April 9, 1921, p. 1. Idlewilders hailing from other cities, such as Dr. Alexander Turner of Detroit, were also victims of race violence in their city homes. See "They Romp and Play the Livelong Day at Idlewild," *Chicago Defender (National Edition)*, August 28, 1926, p. 2; and Kevin Boyle, *Arc of Justice: A Saga of Race, Civil Rights, and Murder in the Jazz Age* (New York: H. Holt, 2004), 152–153.

3. W. E. B. Du Bois, "Hopkinsville, Chicago, and Idlewild," *Crisis* 22, no. 4 (August 1921), 158, 160. Du Bois exhibited similar reverence for the natural environment well beyond the bounds of his Idlewild boosterism. See, for example, W. E. B. Du Bois, "Criteria of Negro Art," *Crisis* 32 (October 1928), 297; W. E. B. Du Bois, *The Souls of Black Folk* (New York: W. W. Norton, [1903] 1999), 81; Kimberly K. Smith, *African American Environmental Thought: Foundations* (Lawrence: University Press of Kansas, 2007), 154–156; and Scott Hicks, "W. E. B. Du Bois, Booker T. Washington, and Richard Wright: Toward an Ecocriticism of Color," *Callaloo* (Winter 2006), 202–222. On Binga and his wife's regular retreats to Idlewild, see Susie J. Bantom, "Idlewild," *Lake County Star*, August 29, 1924, p. 3; Susie J. Bantom, "Idlewild," *Lake County Star*, August 20, 1926, p. 3; and Susie J. Bantom, "Idlewild," *Lake County Star*, January 27, 1928, p. 4.

4. See, for example, "Notice," *Chicago Defender (National Edition)*, June 15, 1918, p. 6; "Excursion to Idlewild," *Chicago Defender (National Edition)*, June 28,

1919, p. 19; and Monroe Tabor, "Letters," *Chicago Defender (National Edition)*, August 12, 1922, p. 7.

5. Du Bois, "Hopkinsville," 158. Although black Chicagoans regularly expressed sentiments similar to those of white environmentalists, there is little acknowledgment of the preservation or conservation movements of the period in the African American press. On how modernization and industrialization spurred different relationships with nature, the classic study remains Roderick Nash, *Wilderness and the American Mind* (New Haven, CT: Yale University Press, [1965] 2001). See also T. J. Jackson Lears, *No Place of Grace: Antimodernism and the Transformation of American Culture, 1880–1920* (Chicago: University of Chicago Press, [1981] 1994), 4–5; Leo Marx, *The Machine in the Garden: Technology and the Pastoral Ideal in America* (New York: Oxford University Press, 1964), 9; and Kevin C. Armitage, *The Nature Study Movement: The Forgotten Popularizer of America's Conservation Ethic* (Lawrence: University Press of Kansas, 2009), 26.

6. Here I borrow from Philip Deloria's *Indians in Unexpected Places*, in which he explores many different places where Native Americans confronted and contested the "broad cultural expectations [that] are both the products and the tools of domination." Philip Joseph Deloria, *Indians in Unexpected Places* (Lawrence: University Press of Kansas, 2004), 4.

7. Booker T. Washington, *Up from Slavery* (New York: Norton, [1901] 1996), 121. On Washington and the environment, see Hicks, "W. E. B. Du Bois," 202–222. On African Americans' historical associations of the South's wild, rural landscapes with both freedom and racial violence, see chapter 8 in Walter Johnson, *River of Dark Dreams: Slavery and Empire in the Cotton Kingdom* (Cambridge, MA: Belknap Press of Harvard University Press, 2013); Elizabeth D. Blum, "Power, Danger, and Control: Slave Women's Perceptions of Wilderness in the Nineteenth Century," *Women's Studies* 31, no. 2 (2002), 247–265; and Melvin Dixon, *Ride out the Wilderness: Geography and Identity in Afro-American Literature* (Urbana: University of Illinois Press, 1987).

8. "Idlewild Host to Prominent Persons," *Chicago Defender (National Edition)*, August 14, 1926, p. 5.

9. Ronald J. Stephens, *Idlewild: The Rise, Decline, and Rebirth of a Unique African American Resort Town* (Ann Arbor: University of Michigan Press, 2013), 64. Abbott undoubtedly admired Washington; when Washington died in 1915, Abbott helped commission a book project commemorating his life. On Abbott's ties to Washington's accommodationism, see James R. Grossman, *Land of Hope: Chicago, Black Southerners, and the Great Migration* (Chicago: University of Chicago Press, 1989), 81–82.

10. Robert Bone and Richard Courage call this hybrid racial ideology " 'Bookerism sui generis,' " in which these black Chicagoans "took the best of Washington and left the rest." Robert Bone and Richard A. Courage, *The Muse in Bronzeville: African American Creative Expression in Chicago, 1932–1950*

(New Brunswick, NJ: Rutgers University Press, 2011), 60–61. See also Touré F. Reed, *Not Alms but Opportunity: The Urban League & the Politics of Racial Uplift, 1910–1950* (Chapel Hill: University of North Carolina Press, 2008), 4–11; Kevin Kelly Gaines, *Uplifting the Race: Black Leadership, Politics, and Culture in the Twentieth Century* (Chapel Hill: University of North Carolina Press, 1996); and Stephens, *Idlewild*, 30–53.

11. Grossman, *Land of Hope*, 130.

12. Du Bois, "Hopkinsville," 160.

13. "Washington Park Gang Beats Another Victim," *Chicago Defender (National Edition)*, June 10, 1922, p. 1.

14. "Vacation Days," *Crisis* 4, no. 4 (August 1912), 186–188.

15. On black primitivist ideology and its relationship to Booker T. Washington and the Chicago School of Sociology, see especially chapters 4 and 5 in Aldon D. Morris, *The Scholar Denied: W. E. B. Du Bois and the Birth of Modern Sociology* (Oakland: University of California Press, 2015); Fred H. Matthews, *Quest for an American Sociology: Robert E. Park and the Chicago School* (Montreal: McGill-Queen's University Press, 1977); Reed, *Not Alms but Opportunity*, 20–25; and Daryl Michael Scott, *Contempt and Pity: Social Policy and the Image of the Damaged Black Psyche, 1880–1996* (Chapel Hill: University of North Carolina Press, 1997), 45. On black primitivist thought and its cultural consequences more generally in this period, see chapters 4–6 in Smith, *African American Environmental Thought*; chapters 1 and 6 in Davarian L. Baldwin, *Chicago's New Negroes: Modernity, the Great Migration, & Black Urban Life* (Chapel Hill: University of North Carolina Press, 2007); and Jeffrey Myers, *Converging Stories: Race, Ecology, and Environmental Justice in American Literature* (Athens: University of Georgia Press, 2005), 87–110.

16. "Vacation Time," *Chicago Defender (National Edition)*, July 26, 1924, p. 12. For nearly identical perspectives, see also "Outdoors for the Children," *Broad Ax*, June 3, 1916, p. 4; and "Summer Hints," *Broad Ax*, July 22, 1916, p. 4.

17. Daniel Hudson Burnham et al., *Plan of Chicago* (Chicago: Great Books Foundation, [1909] 2009), 53.

18. " 'Nosey' Sees All Knows All," *Chicago Whip*, September 2, 1922, p. 5. On Idlewild's early development, see Pehyun Wen, "Idlewild: A Negro Village in Lake County, Michigan" (master's thesis, University of Chicago, 1972), 73–77; Stephens, *Idlewild*, 15–16; and Joseph John Jones, "The Making of a National Forest: The Contest over the West Michigan Cutover, 1888–1943" (Ph.D. diss., Michigan State University, 2007), 166–167.

19. For Lake County's black population, see Jones, "The Making of a National Forest," 185. On East Coast African American resorts, see Mark S. Foster, "In the Face of 'Jim Crow': Prosperous Blacks and Vacations, Travel and Outdoor Leisure, 1890–1945," *Journal of Negro History* 84, no. 2 (Spring 1999), 136; and Andrew Kahrl, "The Political Work of Leisure: Class, Recreation, and African American Commemoration at Harpers Ferry, West

Virginia, 1881–1931," *Journal of Social History* 42, no. 1 (Fall 2008), 57–77. On the West Michigan Resort, see J. Fenton Johnson, "The West Michigan Resort," *Chicago Defender (National Edition)*, July 22, 1911, p. 7; A. T. Stewart, "Open Letter to the Editor," *Chicago Defender (National Edition)*, September 13, 1913, p. 5; "Dr. A. Wilberforce Williams Talks on Preventive Measures First Aid Remedies Hygienics and Sanitation," *Chicago Defender (National Edition)*, June 26, 1915, p. 8; "Resort Is Closed; A. L. M'Bride Is Peeved," *Chicago Defender (National Edition)*, July 17, 1915, p. 1; and Helen Buckler, *Doctor Dan, Pioneer in American Surgery* (Boston: Little, Brown, 1954), 259.

20. "The Dedication of Idlewild," *Chicago Defender (National Edition)*, June 10, 1916, p. 4.

21. "Notice"; "Excursion to Idlewild"; "Idlewild Concert," *Chicago Defender (National Edition)*, January 29, 1921, p. 12; Lewis Walker and Benjamin C. Wilson, *Black Eden: The Idlewild Community* (East Lansing: Michigan State University Press, 2002), 23–24; Wen, "Idlewild," 78; and John Fraser Hart, "A Rural Retreat for Northern Negroes," *Geographical Review* 50, no. 2 (April 1960), 158. On the class politics of the AME church in Chicago, see Wallace D. Best, *Passionately Human, No Less Divine: Religion and Culture in Black Chicago, 1915–1952* (Princeton, NJ: Princeton University Press, 2005), 120–128.

22. "Heard in Idlewild," *Lake County Star*, May 10, 1929, p. 4; Susie J. Bantom, "Idlewild," *Lake County Star*, June 13, 1924, p. 2; Susie J. Bantom, "Idlewild," *Lake County Star*, August 14, 1925, p. 3; Susie J. Bantom, "Idlewild," *Lake County Star*, February 12, 1926, p. 3; Susie J. Bantom, "Idlewild," *Lake County Star*, August 12, 1927; "Success of 'Idlewild,' Michigan's Famous Summer Resort, Suggests Growth of Negro Leisure Class," *Pittsburgh Courier*, October 11, 1930, p. 2; Walker and Wilson, *Black Eden*, 29; "Idlewild, Mich.," *Chicago Defender (National Edition)*, August 19, 1922, p. 3; "Lake Ivanhoe: The Resort Beautiful," *Chicago Defender (City Edition)*, May 30, 1925, p. 8; Edith Spurlock Sampson, "Chicago Society," *Pittsburgh Courier*, May 28, 1927, p. 6; "Chicago Society," *Pittsburgh Courier*, May 31, 1930, p.A9; "Spend a Real Vacation and Week Ends at the Homestead," *Chicago Defender (National Edition)*, October 28, 1922, p. 4; "Val-Du-Lakes, Michigan, Has New Summer Resort," *Chicago Defender (National Edition)*, May 31, 1924, p. 11; "National Notes," *Chicago Defender (National Edition)*, August 20, 1938, p. 15; and "Michigan Resort Is Destroyed by Fire," *Chicago Defender (National Edition)*, March 26, 1927, p. 4.

23. "City News in Brief," *Chicago Defender (National Edition)*, August 5, 1922, p. 4; "Among the Prominent Visitors," *Chicago Defender (National Edition)*, August 24, 1918, p. 13; Wen, "Idlewild," 81; "They Romp and Play"; "Y.M.C.A. News," *Chicago Defender (National Edition)*, September 11, 1920, p. 2; "Bryants on Auto Tour," *Chicago Defender (National Edition)*, August 14, 1920, p. 8; "Michigan News," *Chicago Defender (National Edition)*, July 27, 1929, p. A8; Mrs Bertha M. Lewis, "Chicago Society," *Pittsburgh Courier*, January 16, 1926, p. 5; "Idlewild Resort Party," *Chicago Defender (National Edition)*, January 21,

1922, p. 4; Stephens, *Idlewild*, 19, 53–58; "Lake-Side Wedding," *Chicago Whip*, August 21, 1920, p. 4; Susie J. Bantom, "Idlewild," *Lake County Star*, February 5, 1926, p. 3; Susie J. Bantom, "Idlewild," *Lake County Star*, August 15, 1924, p. 3; Susie J. Bantom, "Idlewild," *Lake County Star*, August 8, 1930, p. 4; Susie J. Bantom, "Idlewild," *Lake County Star* September 2, 1927; "Y.W.C.A." *Chicago Defender (National Edition)*, August 21, 1920, p. 8; and Anderson marriage quote in "Attorney Violette N. Anderson United in Marriage to Dr. A. E. Johnson," *Broad Ax*, August 21, 1920, p. 3.

24. "Idlewild Is Newest Summer Resort Here," *Lake County Star*, December 31, 1915, p. 1.

25. Bantom, "Idlewild," February 5, 1926. See also "Your Stutz," *Chicago Defender (National Edition)*, June 9, 1923, p. 8.

26. "Vacation Time."

27. Timuel Black, *Bridges of Memory: Chicago's First Wave of Black Migration* (Evanston, IL: Northwestern University Press, 2003), 28.

28. "Washington Park Becomes Pest-Bound," *Chicago Defender (National Edition)*, August 30, 1924, p. 4. On the ways in which this intraracial class exclusion played out in Southern resort towns, see chapter 3 in Andrew Kahrl, *The Land Was Ours: African American Beaches from Jim Crow to the Sunbelt South* (Cambridge, MA: Harvard University Press, 2012). On Idlewild lot prices, see "Excursion to Idlewild"; "Excursion to Beautiful Idlewild, Mich.," *Chicago Defender (National Edition)*, July 12, 1919, p. 16; "Visitors Go to Idlewild," *Chicago Defender (National Edition)*, August 14, 1920, p. 8; "Excursion to Idlewild," *Chicago Defender (National Edition)*, August 3, 1918, p. 12; "Idlewild Excursion," *Chicago Defender (National Edition)*, August 2, 1924, p. 4; "Beautiful Idlewild," *Chicago Defender (National Edition)*, July 20, 1918, p. 8; "Beautiful Idlewild," *Chicago Defender (National Edition)*, November 1, 1919, p. 17; "Real Estate for Sale at Bell's Idlewild, Mich; Stop, Look, and Listen," *Chicago Defender (National Edition)*, October 2, 1920, p. 11; and "Idlewild Lot Sale," *Chicago Defender (National Edition)*, May 7, 1921, p. 15. On black working-class wages in Chicago, see Leila Houghteling and Ethel Austin Martin, *The Income and Standard of Living of Unskilled Laborers in Chicago* (Chicago: University of Chicago Press, 1927), 25, 94, 112; Eva Gertrude Boggs, "Nutrition of Fifty Colored Families in Chicago" (master's thesis, University of Chicago, 1929), 11–12; Alma Herbst, *The Negro in the Slaughtering and Meat-Packing Industry in Chicago* (New York: Houghton Mifflin Company, 1932), 86–87; and Chicago Commission on Race Relations, *The Negro in Chicago: A Study of Race Relations and a Race Riot* (Chicago: University of Chicago Press, 1922), 163–183, 365–367.

29. Bantom, "Idlewild," September 2, 1927. On these "politics of respectability," see Evelyn Brooks Higginbotham, *Righteous Discontent: The Women's Movement in the Black Baptist Church, 1880–1920* (Cambridge, MA: Harvard University Press, 1993), 185–229; and Victoria W. Wolcott, *Remaking Respecta-*

bility: African American Women in Interwar Detroit (Chapel Hill: University of North Carolina Press, 2001), 1–10.

30. Johnson, "The West Michigan Resort"; "Vacation Time." The editor paraphrased Tennyson's "Locksley Hall," published in 1842.

31. Susie J. Bantom, "Idlewild," *Lake County Star*, November 28, 1924, p. 3.

32. Du Bois, "Hopkinsville," 160; Walker and Wilson, *Black Eden*, 22.

33. "Real Estate for Sale."

34. "Idlewild the Scene of Activity Preparing for Season's Opening," *Lake County Star*, June 2, 1916.

35. Stephens, *Idlewild*, 17–18.

36. Du Bois, "Hopkinsville," 160.

37. Susie J. Bantom, "Idlewild," *Lake County Star*, March 4, 1927, p. 4. See also Bantom, "Idlewild," November 28, 1924; and "YWCA News," *Chicago Whip*, June 12, 1920, p. 4. On uplift ideology's critical deficiencies, see Gaines, *Uplifting the Race*.

38. "Idlewild the Scene of Activity." See also "Heard among Resorts and Resorters," *Lake County Star*, July 7, 1916.

39. "And This Is Civilization," *Chicago Defender (National Edition)*, September 7, 1929, p. A2. On *The Negro Motorist Green Book* and sundown towns, see the New York Public Library Digital Collections, "The Green Book," digitalcollections.nypl.org/collections/the-green-book (accessed February 5, 2016); and James W. Loewen, *Sundown Towns: A Hidden Dimension of American Racism* (New York: W. W. Norton, 2005).

40. Quote in Susie J. Bantom, "Idlewild," *Lake County Star*, November 20, 1925, p. 3. See also Susie J. Bantom, "Idlewild," *Lake County Star*, July 9, 1926, p. 4; Wen, "Idlewild," 78; Du Bois, "Hopkinsville," 160; "Notes from Idlewild, Michigan," *Broad Ax*, July 15, 1922, p. 3; Benjamin C. Wilson, *The Rural Black Heritage between Chicago and Detroit, 1850–1929: A Photograph Album and Random Thoughts* (Kalamazoo: New Issues Press, Western Michigan University, 1985), 168; Foster, "In the Face of 'Jim Crow,'" 139–140. There were also Idlewild real estate offers that seemed—and probably were—too good to be true. See "Get a Home in Idlewild Mich. FREE," *Chicago Whip*, November 18, 1922, p. 4.

41. Susie J. Bantom, "Idlewild," *Lake County Star*, August 13, 1926, p. 3. On (African) American automobility and nature in this period, see chapter 4 in Cotten Seiler, *Republic of Drivers: A Cultural History of Automobility in America* (Chicago: University of Chicago Press, 2008); chapter 6 in Christopher W. Wells, *Car Country: An Environmental History* (Seattle: University of Washington Press, 2012); chapter 3 in Lawrence M. Lipin, *Workers and the Wild: Conservation, Consumerism, and Labor in Oregon, 1910–30* (Urbana: University of Illinois Press, 2007); and Paul Sutter, *Driven Wild: How the Fight against Automobiles Launched the Modern Wilderness Movement* (Seattle: University of Washington Press, 2002).

42. "Your Summer Outings at Beautiful Woodland Park Will Pay You Health Dividends," *Chicago Defender (National Edition)*, April 21, 1923, p. 20. See also "Think of Buying a Lot in Beautiful Woodland Park," *Chicago Defender (National Edition)*, May 5, 1923, p. 12; "Think of Buying a Lot in Beautiful Woodland Park," *Chicago Defender (National Edition)*, May 12, 1923, p. 3; "Woodland Park," *Chicago Defender (National Edition)*, June 2, 1923, p. 3; and "Woodland Park," *Chicago Defender (National Edition)*, Aug 18, 1923, p. 3. Woodland Park's lot prices were more affordable than Idlewild's. Jones, "The Making of a National Forest," 219; Stephens, *Idlewild*, 25–26.

43. "Your Summer Outings."

44. "Let Your Dreams Come True," *Chicago Defender (National Edition)*, November 4, 1922, p. 20.

45. Du Bois, "Hopkinsville," 160. On these broader trends, see Sutter, *Driven Wild*, 14–21.

46. Quote in Susie J. Bantom, "Idlewild," *Lake County Star*, July 30, 1926, p. 3. See also Bantom, "Idlewild," August 20, 1926; "Heard among Resorts and Resorters," *Lake County Star*, August 4, 1916; Walker and Wilson, *Black Eden*, 38. For a well-researched biography of Major N. Clark Smith, see Marian M. Ohman, "Major N. Clark Smith in Chicago," *Journal of the Illinois State Historical Society* 96, no. 1 (Spring 2003), 49–79.

47. Walker and Wilson, *Black Eden*, 51–52, 245–247. For similar promotional language concerning nature tourism in Michigan, see "Advertising the Wild," in Sutter, *Driven Wild;* James Kates, *Planning a Wilderness: Regenerating the Great Lakes Cutover Region* (Minneapolis: University of Minnesota Press, 2001), 89–113; Aaron Alex Shapiro, "'One Crop Worth Cultivating': Tourism in the Upper Great Lakes, 1910–1965" (Ph.D. diss., University of Chicago, 2005), 184.

48. "Beautiful Idlewild," July 20, 1918; Du Bois, "Hopkinsville," 159. The idea that children were somehow closer to the natural environment—and that the natural environment could somehow make adults more childlike—was closely tied to recapitulation theory, which was itself closely connected to primitivist ideology. See Armitage, *The Nature Study Movement;* Gail Bederman, *Manliness & Civilization: A Cultural History of Gender and Race in the United States, 1880–1917* (Chicago: University of Chicago Press, 1995), 77–120.

49. Du Bois, "Hopkinsville," 160.

50. "Idlewild the Scene of Activity."

51. Quoted in Wen, "Idlewild," 81. See also "Plan Chautauqua and Camp Meeting," *Lake County Star*, January 31, 1919, p. 1; "At Idlewild, Mich.," *Chicago Defender (National Edition)*, August 5, 1922, p. 4; Walker and Wilson, *Black Eden*, 20; Ronald J. Stephens, *Idlewild: The Black Eden of Michigan* (Chicago: Arcadia Publishing, 2001), 22; and Stephens, *Idlewild*, 20–22.

52. "Attorney B. F Moseley Becomes Mayor of Idlewild Michigan," *Broad Ax*, October 30, 1915, p. 1; "'Nosey' Sees All Knows All," *Chicago Whip*, Sep-

tember 16, 1922, p. 5. See also " 'Nosey' Sees All Knows All," *Chicago Whip,* September 9, 1922, p. 5.

53. Bantom, "Idlewild," February 5, 1926.

54. "Announcing the Opening of Idlewild's Purple Palace," *Lake County Star,* August 3, 1928, p. 2. See also "Purple Palace," *Lake County Star,* August 9, 1929, p. 3.

55. Grace, "Idlewild is Ideal!" *Pittsburgh Courier,* August 31, 1929, p. 7.

56. Alexander O. Taylor, "Idlewild Special," *Chicago Defender (National Edition),* August 30, 1919, p. 2. On religious practice at Idlewild and in Chicago, see "Idlewild, Mich.," *Chicago Defender (National Edition),* August 19, 1922, p. 3; Stephens, *Idlewild,* 43; and Best, *Passionately Human,* 123–136. On political activity at Idlewild, see James H. Peyton, "Michigan," *Chicago Defender (National Edition),* September 1, 1928, p. A9; and Ronald J. Stephens, "Garveyism in Idlewild, 1927 to 1936," *Journal of Black Studies* 34, no. 4 (March 2004) 462–488.

57. Susie J. Bantom, "Idlewild," *Lake County Star,* July 17, 1925, p. 3. See also Taylor, "Idlewild Special"; "Idlewild, Mich.," August 19, 1922; and Susie J. Bantom, "Idlewild," *Lake County Star,* November 7, 1924, p. 4.

58. Quoted in Helen M. Chesnutt, *Charles Waddell Chesnutt, Pioneer of the Color Line* (Chapel Hill: University of North Carolina Press, 1952), 292.

59. Taylor, "Idlewild Special."

60. Chesnutt, *Charles Waddell Chesnutt,* 296–297. On Dan Jackson and hunting at Idlewild, see Lewis, "Chicago Society"; "Idlewild Resort Party"; "Prepare NOW," *Chicago Defender (National Edition),* November 25, 1922, p. 2; Robert M. Lombardo, "The Black Mafia: African-American Organized Crime in Chicago 1890–1960," *Crime, Law & Social Change* 38 (2002), 33–65.

61. Quoted in Jones, "The Making of a National Forest," 40. On Lake County's environmental history, see Stephens, *Idlewild,* 16; Walker and Wilson, *Black Eden,* 2, 8; Bert Hudgins, *Michigan: Geographic Backgrounds in the Development of the Commonwealth,* (Detroit, 1953), 29, 63; Hart, "A Rural Retreat," 149; William Cronon, *Nature's Metropolis: Chicago and the Great West* (New York: W. W. Norton, 1992), 184; Wen, "Idlewild," 65–70; and Kates, *Planning a Wilderness,* 1–31. On the idea of "wilderness" and these rural landscapes, see William Cronon, "The Trouble with Wilderness; Or, Getting Back to the Wrong Nature," in *Uncommon Ground: Rethinking the Human Place in Nature* (New York: W. W. Norton, 1996), 69–90; Nash, *Wilderness;* Sutter, *Driven Wild.*

62. See Wilson, *The Rural Black Heritage,* 240; Wen, "Idlewild," 77, 82; Hart, "A Rural Retreat," 150; Hudgins, *Michigan,* 67.

63. "Idlewild, Mich.," *Chicago Defender (National Edition),* July 29, 1922, p. 4; John C. Hudson and Center for American Places, *Chicago: A Geography of the City and Its Region* (Chicago: University of Chicago Press, 2006), 37–38; and Hudgins, *Michigan,* 32, 76, 94.

64. Quote in Chicago Council of Social Agencies, "Summer Camps and Outings in and Near Chicago," 3, Box 217a, Folder 1, WC. See also Chicago

Council of Social Agencies, "Camps Operated by Social Service Agencies of the Chicago District 1929," Box 217a, Folder 1, WC; and "39th Annual Report" (1915), 35, Series I, Box 58, Folder 624, YWCAM.

65. "Vacation Time," 12. On similar camping trends and motivations among whites, see Abigail Ayres Van Slyck, *A Manufactured Wilderness: Summer Camps and the Shaping of American Youth, 1890–1960* (Minneapolis: University of Minnesota Press, 2006); Leslie Paris, *Children's Nature: The Rise of the American Summer Camp* (New York: New York University Press, 2008); David I. Macleod, *Building Character in the American Boy: The Boy Scouts, YMCA, and their Forerunners, 1870–1920* (Madison: University of Wisconsin Press, 1983); Philip Joseph Deloria, *Playing Indian* (New Haven: Yale University Press, 1998), 102; and Armitage, *The Nature Study Movement*, 27.

66. Quoted in Wilson, *The Rural Black Heritage*, 168.

67. Roland B. Davis, "Playgrounds," *Chicago Defender (City Edition)*, February 12, 1927, Part 2, p. 12; "44th Annual Report" (1920), 30, Series I, Box 58, Folder 624, YWCAM; Henry Louis Gates and Evelyn Brooks Higginbotham, *The African American National Biography* (New York: Oxford University Press, 2008); William C. Graves to Julius Rosenwald, Box 45, Folder 16, JR; "Executive Committee" (1923), Series I, Box 46, Folder 559, YWCAM; Frederic H. H. Robb, *The Negro in Chicago: 1779–1929, Vols. 1–2* (Chicago: Washington Intercollegiate Club; International Negro Student Alliance, 1929), 141; "George Arthur, Chicago 'Y' Secretary, Dies," *Chicago Defender (National Edition)*, June 7, 1941, p. 12.

68. On the Wabash YMCA's founding and philanthropic contributors to Chicago's black YWCA, see Nina Mjagkij, *Light in the Darkness: African Americans and the YMCA, 1852–1946* (Lexington: University Press of Kentucky, 1994), 78–79; George Robert Arthur, *Life on the Negro Frontier: A Study of the Objectives and the Success of the Activities Promoted in the Young Men's Christian Associations Operating in "Rosenwald" Buildings* (New York: Association Press, 1934), 39; Booker T. Washington, "A Remarkable Triple Alliance: How a Jew Is Helping the Negro through the Y.M.C.A.," *Outlook* 108 (September–December 1914), 486; "Y.M.C.A. Bldg. Dedicated with Imposing Ceremonies," *Chicago Defender (National Edition)*, Jun 21, 1913, p. 1; and "51st Annual Report" (1927), 10, Series I, Box 58, Folder 624, YWCAM. On race pride and critics of the Y's segregation policy, see Mjagkij, *Light in the Darkness*, 198; Judith Weisenfeld, *African American Women and Christian Activism: New York's Black YWCA, 1905–1945* (Cambridge, MA: Harvard University Press, 1997), 4–36, 111; Baldwin, *Chicago's New Negroes*, 34–37; Boys' Club Federation, "A Special Study of the Boy Situation in Chicago, Ill." (1929), 33, Box 1, Folder 12, CBGC; Reed, *Not Alms but Opportunity;* Higginbotham, *Righteous Discontent;* Robb, *The Negro in Chicago*, 141; and Timuel Black, interview with the author, January 21, 2010.

69. Richard E. Saxton, "Boy Scout News," *Chicago Defender (National Edition)*, January 17, 1925, p. A2; Boys' Club Federation, "A Special Study," 33; "Em-

erson James Gets Scout Post," *Chicago Defender (National Edition)*, January 23, 1937, p. 17; Herbert Brady, "Boy Scout News," *Chicago Defender (National Edition)*, July 18, 1925, p. A8; Best, *Passionately Human*, 46; Robb, *The Negro in Chicago*, 147; Mason W. Fields, "Boy Scouts, like Billikens, Celebrate Anniversary Week," *Chicago Defender (City Edition)*, February 6, 1926, p. 5; and Chicago Council of Social Agencies, *Report of South Side Survey, April, 1931, Chicago, Illinois*, Box 145, Folder 2, WC. More generally on the relationship between the YMCA and Boy Scouts, see Macleod, *Building Character*, 146, 158–165.

70. "City News in Brief," *Chicago Defender (National Edition)*, July 29, 1922, p. 4; "Summer Musicales Please Audiences at Wabash 'Y'," *Chicago Defender (National Edition)*, July 8, 1922, p. 5; and "What Y.M.C.A. Means to Chicagoans," *Chicago Defender (National Edition)*, October 14, 1922, p. 15.

71. "What Y.M.C.A. Means to Chicagoans." See also Arthur, *Life on the Negro Frontier*, 124; Mjagkij, *Light in the Darkness*, 55–57; and Macleod, *Building Character*, 176–177.

72. Henry William Gibson, *Camping for Boys* (New York: Association Press, 1911), 11, 87, 231–239. On nature study and the centrality of Gibson's manual to youth camping in this era, see Van Slyck, *A Manufactured Wilderness*, xxx; Robert H. MacDonald, *Sons of the Empire: The Frontier and the Boy Scout Movement, 1890–1918* (Toronto: University of Toronto Press, 1993); and Paris, *Children's Nature*, 118.

73. "Spring," *Chicago Defender (National Edition)*, May 16, 1914, p. 8; "Vacation Time." Cowper wrote that "God made the country, and man made the town."

74. "44th Annual Report," 30. On the founding of Chicago's African American YWCA and the origins of its camp, which was first considered in the fall of 1919, just months after the race riot, see "45th Annual Report" (1921), 27, Series I, Box 58, Folder 624, YWCAM; "Minutes of the November Board Meeting" (1919), Series I, Box 45, Folder 555, YWCAM; and "Minutes" (1918), Series I, Box 45, Folder 554, YWCAM. On black YWCA camps established by chapters in New York and Detroit, two other Great Migration destinations, see Weisenfeld, *African American Women*, 186–187; "At the 'Y's,'" *Chicago Defender (National Edition)*, July 16, 1927, p. A5; and Wolcott, *Remaking Respectability*, 70.

75. "Minutes of Metropolitan Board" (1926), Series I, Box 47, Folder 562, YWCAM. See also "Industrial Department," Series I, Box 54, Folder 607, YWCAM; and "44th Annual Report," 30.

76. "46th Annual Report" (1922), 18, Series I, Box 58, Folder 624, YWCAM. See also "News of the Chicago Women's Clubs," *Chicago Tribune*, June 17, 1923, p. B9; and "Y.W.C.A. News," *Chicago Defender (National Edition)*, July 2, 1921, p. 5.

77. "Executive Committee"; "Report of Business Secretary" (1923), Series I, Box 46, Folder 559, YWCAM; "Y.W.C.A. News"; "45th Annual Report," 27; "47th

Annual Report" (1923), 36, Series I, Box 58, Folder 624, YWCAM; "49th Annual Report" (1925), 10, Series I, Box 58, Folder 624, YWCAM; Indiana
Avenue YWCA to Julius Rosenwald (1925), Box 45, Folder 16, JR; "48th Annual Report" (1924), 20, Series I, Box 58, Folder 624, YWCAM; "Summer
Executive Committee" (1924), Series I, Box 46, Folder 560, YWCAM; "Minutes of the Board of Directors" (1920), Series I, Box 46, Folder 556, YWCAM;
"1923 Statistics" (1923), Series I, Box 46, Folder 559, YWCAM; "Y.W.C.A.
Notes," *Chicago Whip*, July 17, 1920, p. 4; and Robb, *The Negro in Chicago*, 151.

78. Quoted in "44th Annual Report," 30. See also "47th Annual Report," 13;
Chicago Council of Social Agencies, "Summer Camps and Outings," 22;
"Y.W.C.A News," *Chicago Defender (National Edition)*, April 30, 1921, p. 5;
"Y.W.C.A. Notes"; and Indiana Avenue YWCA to Julius Rosenwald. Armour had its own camp in Round Lake, Illinois, though there is no evidence that African American workers could attend. Kate J. Adams, *Humanizing a Great Industry* (Chicago: Armour and Company, 1919), 23–24. On
the industrial picnic, which was first held in 1922, see "Y.M.C.A. News,"
Chicago Whip, July 1, 1922, p. 5; "Y.M.C.A. News," *Chicago Whip*, July 8,
1922, p. 3; "Summer Musicales"; and Robb, *The Negro in Chicago*, 142. On
the YMCA and welfare capitalism more generally, see Grossman, *Land of
Hope*, 228–229; Lizabeth Cohen, *Making a New Deal: Industrial Workers in Chicago, 1919–1939* (Cambridge: Cambridge University Press, [1990] 2008),
159–211; Rick Halpern, *Down on the Killing Floor: Black and White Workers in
Chicago's Packinghouses, 1904–54* (Urbana: University of Illinois Press, 1997),
59–60; James R. Barrett, *Work and Community in the Jungle: Chicago's Packinghouse Workers, 1894–1922* (Urbana: University of Illinois Press, 1987), 213;
and Sutter, *Driven Wild*, 23.

79. "42nd Annual Report" (1919), 1, Series I, Box 58, Folder 624, YWCAM;
"Y.W.C.A. Summer Camps Will Soon Be Open, Girls!" *Chicago Tribune*,
June 5, 1921, p. G3. This white camp on Lake Michigan was called Forest
Beach camp and was located near New Buffalo, Michigan. Camp Millhurst,
for girls aged twenty and under, was located on the Fox River near Plano,
Illinois.

80. "44th Annual Report," 30; and "This Week: The Y.W.C.A. Camp," *Chicago
Defender (National Edition)*, August 6, 1921, p. 15. On uncertainty over the
camp's permanence and the general lack of funds, see "45th Annual Report," 27; and "47th Annual Report," 36.

81. "45th Annual Report," 27.

82. "44th Annual Report," 30. On swimming at Camp Hammond, see "45th Annual Report," 27; "46th Annual Report," 18; and "47th Annual Report," 36.

83. "Adjourned Session of the December Board Meeting" (1925), 5, Series I,
Box 47, Folder 561, YWCAM.

84. "Minutes of Finance Committee" (1925), Series I, Box 47, Folder 561,
YWCAM; and "50th Annual Report" (1926), 11, Series I, Box 58, Folder
624, YWCAM.

85. Mrs. Edgar J. Goodspeed to Mr. Stern, June 4, 1927, Box 45, Folder 16, JR.

86. Mrs. William L. Hodgkins to Mr. Edwin R. Embree, President, Julius Rosenwald Fund, 1929, Box 45, Folder 16, JR; Robb, *The Negro in Chicago,* 150–152.

87. "Y.M.C.A. Camp Opened at Cedar Lake, Indiana," *Chicago Defender (National Edition),* July 15, 1922, p. 5; "City News in Brief." On these early camping excursions, reported by both the *Defender* and the *Whip,* see "Boys' Division of the Wabash Avenue Y.M.C.A.," *Chicago Defender (National Edition),* July 20, 1918, p. 10; "Wabash 'Y' Promotes Cherry Pickers Camp," *Chicago Defender (National Edition),* June 3, 1922, p. 5; "Y.M.C.A. News," *Chicago Defender (National Edition),* July 12, 1919, p. 15; "Chicago Boys Win Cherry Picking Championship," *Chicago Defender (National Edition),* August 6, 1921, p. 1; "Y.M.C.A. News," *Chicago Whip,* August 12, 1922, p. 5; and "Y.M.C.A. News," *Chicago Defender (National Edition),* January 6, 1923, p. 4.

88. "A Southern Christian Drove Them Out," *Chicago Defender (National Edition),* July 22, 1922, p. 3; "Boy Scouts Driven from Cedar Lake Camp," *Chicago Defender (National Edition),* July 22, 1922, p. 1; and "Y.M.C.A. Breakfast Club Grows in Public Favor," *Chicago Defender (National Edition),* August 26, 1922, p. 5.

89. "YWCA News," *Chicago Defender (National Edition),* May 3, 1924, p. 10.

90. "A Deserved Honor," *Chicago Defender (National Edition),* June 2, 1928, p. A2. On camps owned by black churches in rural Massachusetts and New York in this period, see Paris, *Children's Nature,* 73.

91. Quotes in "Report of the New Camp Project" (1926), Box 6, Folder 64, YMCAW; and Robb, *The Negro in Chicago,* 143. See also Wen, "Idlewild," 59–60; "Report of Boys Work Committee" (1926), Box 6, Folder 64, YMCAW; and "Activities Report—1925 Wabash Avenue YMCA" (1926), 1, Box 6, Folder 64, YMCAW. More generally on class status and camping in this period, see Macleod, *Building Character,* xv; Van Slyck, *A Manufactured Wilderness,* 4; and Paris, *Children's Nature,* 19.

92. Robb, *The Negro in Chicago,* 153. On Camp Wabash's budget, see "Report of the Executive Secretary to the Committee of Management—Wabash Avenue Department" (1928), Box 6, Folder 65, YMCAW; and "Report of Acting Executive Secretary—Wabash Avenue Department" (1928), 3, Box 6, Folder 65, YMCAW. On the importance of African American YMCA summer camps nationwide, see the International Committee of YMCAs, "What the 'Y' Means to Colored Men and Boys," Box 92, Folder 7, YMCAM.

93. "Report of Boys Work Committee." On the Indiana Dunes hikes, see "Report of the Physical Section Month of May 1926," Box 6, Folder 64, YMCAW; "Boys' Division," 10; "Y.M.C.A. News," *Chicago Defender (National Edition),* August 31, 1918, p. 11; and "Y.M.C.A. News," *Chicago Defender (National Edition),* September 6, 1919, p. 17.

94. Herbert Brady, "Boy Scout News," *Chicago Defender (National Edition),* July 4, 1925, p. A9.

95. Ibid.

96. Robb, *The Negro in Chicago*, 143. On masculinity and manhood in this period, see Bederman, *Manliness & Civilization;* Macleod, *Building Character;* MacDonald, *Sons of the Empire;* and Jeffrey P. Hantover, "The Boy Scouts and the Validation of Masculinity," *Journal of Social Issues* 34, no. 1 (1978), 184–195.

97. Richard E. Saxton, "Boy Scout News," *Chicago Defender (National Edition)*, January 3, 1925, p. 19; and Brady, "Boy Scout News."

98. "Committee of Management of the Wabash Avenue Department" (1927), Box 6, Folder 65, YMCAW; "Committee of Management of the Wabash Avenue Department" (1928), Box 6, Folder 65, YMCAW; Van Slyck, *A Manufactured Wilderness*, 4; and Paris, *Children's Nature*, 184–187.

99. Ben Gaines, interview with the author, July 27, 2010; and Brady, "Boy Scout News." On the universality of camps located near bodies of water, see Van Slyck, *A Manufactured Wilderness*, 11; and Paris, *Children's Nature*, 114.

100. "Boy Scout News," *Chicago Defender (National Edition)*, August 21, 1926, p. A3; *Scoutcraft: Summer Camp News* (1929), 6, www.fortdearborn.org /Activities/Current/1929%20Owasippe%20Manual.pdf (accessed August 3, 2010).

101. Herbert B. Brady, "Boy Scout News," *Chicago Defender (National Edition)*, January 2, 1926, p. A6.

102. Burnham, *Plan of Chicago*, 54; Brady, "Boy Scout News." On Scouts, nature study, and conservationism and preservationism more broadly, see Armitage, *The Nature Study Movement*, 86–87; and Macleod, *Building Character*, 240–246, 278–279.

103. Herbert Everett Brady, "Boy Scout News," *Chicago Defender (National Edition)*, September 26, 1925, p. A5; "Boy Scout News," *Chicago Defender (National Edition)*, May 8, 1926, p. A6; "Boy Scout News," *Chicago Defender (National Edition)*, July 24, 1926, p. A3; "Chicago Y.M.C.A. News," *Chicago Whip*, November 22, 1919, p. 7; and "Boy Scout News," *Chicago Defender (National Edition)*, October 31, 1925, p. A8.

104. Burnham, *Plan of Chicago*, 48, 53. On Burnham's plan, the City Beautiful Movement in Chicago, and broader cultural trends with respect to the environment, see Carl S. Smith, *The Plan of Chicago: Daniel Burnham and the Remaking of the American City* (Chicago: University of Chicago Press, 2006); Robin Faith Bachin, *Building the South Side: Urban Space and Civic Culture in Chicago, 1890–1919* (Chicago: University of Chicago Press, 2004), 169–171; Chicago (Ill.). Special Park Commission, Dwight Heald Perkins, and John J. Bradley, *Report of the Special Park Commission to the City Council of Chicago on the Subject of a Metropolitan Park System* (Chicago: W. J. Hartman, 1905), 63; and Nash, *Wilderness and the American Mind*, 161–181.

105. Burnham, *Plan of Chicago*, 53.

106. "Vacation Time." See also "Camp Sanitation," *Broad Ax*, July 1, 1922, p. 2. On Forest Preserves attendance, see Volume 1 of Chicago Recreation Commission et al., *The Chicago Recreation Survey, 1937* (Chicago, 1937), 166.

107. Julius N. Avendorph, Dr. D. Herbert Anderson, and Dr. J. Norman Croker, "Citizens Indorse [sic] Peter Reinberg," *Chicago Defender (National Edition)*, November 2, 1918, p. 13.

108. "City News in Brief," *Chicago Defender (National Edition)*, June 4, 1921, p. 4; "Clubs," *Chicago Defender (National Edition)*, July 22, 1922, p. 5; "Funeral Group Takes Day Off," *Chicago Defender (National Edition)* August 18, 1928, p. A12; and "'Y' Workers Spend Day at 'House in the Woods,'" *Chicago Defender (National Edition)*, September 23, 1922, p. 5. Avendorph, for instance, was founder of the Appomattox Club that often picnicked in green spaces in and around Chicago; historian Wallace Best has described the Appomattox Club as "run on a 'pretentious scale,' providing social life and recreation for an exclusive list of members." Best, *Passionately Human*, 35.

109. "Beautiful Mount Glenwood," *Chicago Defender (National Edition)*, March 11, 1922, p. 2; "Beautiful Mt. Glenwood: The Coming Cemetery of Chicago and Cook County," *Chicago Whip*, February 25, 1922, p. 5; and "Decoration Day at Mt. Glenwood," *Chicago Defender (National Edition)*, June 4, 1910, p. 1.

110. M. S. Szymczak, "Co-Operation Appreciated," *Chicago Defender (National Edition)*, September 8, 1928, p. A2.

111. "Idlewild is Ideal!" On Idlewild as a center of race pride, see Wen, "Idlewild," 63; Foster, "In the Face of 'Jim Crow,'" 135; and Robert B. Stepto, *Blue as the Lake: A Personal Geography* (Boston: Beacon Press, 1998), 7.

112. "Idlewild is Ideal!"

113. Albert Barnes, "Negro Art and America," in *The New Negro: An Interpretation*, ed. Alain LeRoy Locke (New York: A. and C. Boni, 1925), 20, 24, 23.

114. "Idlewild is Ideal!" Similar language was nearly ubiquitous in this period; see, for example, "The Promoters of Beautiful Idlewild Offer a New Opportunity," *Chicago Defender (National Edition)*, October 21, 1922, p. 20; "Lake Ivanhoe"; and "Are You Ready to Join the Crowd Going to Lake Ivanhoe?" *Chicago Defender (City Edition)*, August 14, 1926, p. 8.

115. "Spring."

3. Playgrounds and Protest Grounds

1. "Thousands Cheer Bud's 'Gang' in Parade," *Chicago Defender (National Edition)*, August 23, 1930, p. 15. The *Defender* unsurprisingly heavily promoted its own parade; for additional promotion and coverage of the 1930 parade—which was fairly typical of subsequent years—see "Expect 10,000 at Picnic Saturday, Aug. 16," *Chicago Defender (National Edition)*, August 2, 1930, p. 15; "Big Bathing Beauty Contest for Kiddies," *Chicago Defender (National Edition)*, August 9, 1930, p. 15; "Grownups to Help Bud Billiken with Picnic," *Chicago Defender (National Edition)*, August 9, 1930, p. 15; "Boy Scouts Lead Bud's Big Parade," *Chicago Defender (National Edition)*, August 23, 1930, p. 15; "12,000 Children Attend Bud Billiken Picnic," *Chicago Defender (National Edition)*,

August 23, 1930, p. 4; and "Not a Child Hurt at Bud's Picnic," *Chicago Defender (National Edition)*, August 30, 1930, p. 15. Reportedly drawing 4,000 marchers, the Billiken Club's first parade was actually on a rainy November day in 1928 and ended with a gathering at the Regal Theater a few blocks north of Washington Park. "4000 at Party," *Chicago Defender (National Edition)*, November 24, 1928, p. A3. There appears to have been no parade in 1929, however, and 1930 was the first year the parade culminated in a picnic at Washington Park in August—a practice that, more than eighty years later, continues to this day. Other historical accounts have asserted that the first official parade and picnic occurred in 1929, but contemporary *Defender* articles clearly state that the inaugural event took place in 1930.

2. On the genesis of the club and its name, see Stephan Benzkofer, "A Can't-Miss Part of Summer," *Chicago Tribune*, http://articles.chicagotribune.com /2012–08–05/site/ct-per-flash-billikenparade-0805–20120805_1_lucius -harper-chicago-defender-picnic-and-parade (accessed July 3, 2015); Miriam Forman-Brunell, *Made to Play House: Dolls and the Commercialization of American Girlhood, 1830–1930* (Baltimore: Johns Hopkins University Press, 1998), 91; and Peter M. Rutkoff and William B. Scott, *Fly Away: The Great African American Cultural Migrations* (Baltimore: Johns Hopkins University Press, 2010), 224.

3. On the 1931 parade, see "Crowd of 35,000 Attends Bud Billiken's Big Picnic," *Chicago Defender (National Edition)*, August 22, 1931, p. 1; Nahum Daniel Brascher, "35,000 Cheer Amos 'N' Andy at Bud's Picnic," *Chicago Defender (National Edition)*, August 22, 1931, p. 16; "Show Movies of Bud's Picnic," *Chicago Defender (National Edition)*, August 29, 1931, p. 16; and Rutkoff and Scott, *Fly Away*, 222.

4. "250,000 Hail Joe Louis at Billiken Picnic," *Chicago Defender (National Edition)*, August 19, 1939, p. 1. On participants drawn from well beyond the South Side, see Goldie M. Walden, "Children at Picnic Return Home Safely," *Chicago Defender (National Edition)*, August 24, 1935, p. 5. Although it is possible (and even probable) that the *Defender* inflated its attendance estimates in order to promote its own event, it seems clear that a substantial portion of Chicagoland's African American community participated in the parade and picnic.

5. Quoted in Rutkoff and Scott, *Fly Away*, 229–230. In 1940 and 1941, as the Allies waged war against the totalitarian Axis Powers in Europe and American involvement seemed more and more likely, the annual Bud Billiken Day events "stress[ed] Americanism" and American flags were distributed to all the marchers. "To Stress Americanism in Bud Billiken's Parade," *Chicago Defender (National Edition)*, July 6, 1940, p. 21; "'God Bless America' Is Patriotic Theme," *Chicago Defender (National Edition)*, July 20, 1940, p. 19; "Patriotic Parade to Feature Big Celebration Aug. 2," *Chicago Defender (National Edition)*, August 2, 1941, p. 19; and "150,000 Set Record at Bud Billiken Picnic," *The Chicago Defender (National Edition)* August 9, 1941, p. 1.

6. Rutkoff and Scott trace these sorts of African American celebrations back even further to "the Pinkster Day celebrations in eighteenth-century New York" that "Americanized West African traditions." Rutkoff and Scott, *Fly Away*, 223, 227, 228.

7. Ibid., 226.

8. Jimmy Ellis, interview with the author, July 26, 2010. See also "Put Your Bike in Our Parade," *Chicago Defender (National Edition)*, August 8, 1936, p. 15.

9. St. Clair Drake and Horace Cayton, *Black Metropolis: A Study of Negro Life in a Northern City* (Chicago: University of Chicago Press, [1945] 1993), 84. For James T. Farrell's fictionalized account of Binga's precipitous fall in the third novel of his Studs Lonigan trilogy, see James T. Farrell, *Studs Lonigan: A Trilogy* (New York: Library of America, 2004), 929. On not only Binga's but also the entire South Side's dire financial straits, see also Christopher Robert Reed, *The Depression Comes to the South Side: Protest and Politics in the Black Metropolis, 1930–1933* (Bloomington: Indiana University Press, 2011), 18–21.

10. "Thousands Cheer."

11. "Billikens to Aid in City Crime Drive," *Chicago Defender (National Edition)*, May 3, 1930, p. A12. On Scout participation, see "Chicago Prepares for Bud's Big Outing," *Chicago Defender (National Edition)*, July 30, 1932, p. 16; "Heads Scouts," *Chicago Defender (National Edition)*, July 30, 1932, p. 16; "W. T. Brown Jr. Offers 2,000 Paper Caps to Marchers," *Chicago Defender (National Edition)*, July 15, 1933, p. 16; "50,000 Hail the Chicago Defender Billikens," *Chicago Defender (National Edition)*, August 26, 1933, p. 3; "Picnic Invitations Will be Ready for You Next Week," *Chicago Defender (National Edition)*, July 4, 1936, p. 15; "How 80,000 Enjoyed Chicago Defender Bud Billiken Picnic," *Chicago Defender (National Edition)*, August 29, 1936, p. 17; and "Heads Scouts," *Chicago Defender (National Edition)*, July 24, 1937, p. 12. Much like its promotion of the Great Migration that built black Chicago into a Land of Hope for migrants who had escaped the Jim Crow South while also helping sell newspapers, the *Defender*'s promotion of Bud Billiken Day was at once somewhat selflessly community conscious and self-serving: it pitched the black cultural elite's institutions as the best bet for countering the Great Depression's ill effects while also hoping to boost flagging sales. A representative plea to readers in the 1930s, for instance, encouraged Bud Billiken Club members both to "be better boys and girls, resolving to be obedient to our parents and teachers" and to "urge both your parents and friends to BUY The Chicago Defender." "Our Plans for 1937," *Chicago Defender (National Edition)*, January 9, 1937, p. 12. See also "Rules of Bud Billiken Club," *Chicago Defender (National Edition)*, August 17, 1929, p. A3; Rutkoff and Scott, *Fly Away*, 223; and "Join the Bud Billiken Club," *Chicago Defender (National Edition)*, April 9, 1921, p. 5.

12. In 1936, for instance, the *Defender* noted that "Dr. William H. Benson, district executive, . . . rushed to Chicago from Camp Owassippe, Mich., to be

here for the outing." "Billiken Marchers Cheered as They Move Along," *Chicago Defender (National Edition)*, August 22, 1936, p. 18.

13. Quoted in Anne Meis Knupfer, *The Chicago Black Renaissance and Women's Activism* (Urbana: University of Illinois Press, 2006), 99; Drake and Cayton, *Black Metropolis*, 380. On evictions and unemployment in the Black Belt, see ibid., 217–218; "Chicago," 16–17, Box 37, Folder 2, IWP; and Harold Foote Gosnell, *Negro Politicians: The Rise of Negro Politics in Chicago* (Chicago: University of Chicago Press, 1967), 347.

14. Claude M. Lightfoot, *Chicago Slums to World Politics: Autobiography of Claude M. Lightfoot* (New York: New Outlook Publishers, 1980), 33; St. Clair Drake and United States Work Projects Administration, *Churches and Voluntary Associations in the Chicago Negro Community* (Chicago, 1940), 3.

15. On the tangle of black politics on the South Side during the Great Depression, see chapters 1 and 2 in Jeffrey Helgeson, *Crucibles of Black Empowerment: Chicago's Neighborhood Politics from the New Deal to Harold Washington* (Chicago: University of Chicago Press, 2014). On African Americans' contested collective identity more generally, see Robin D. G. Kelley, *Race Rebels: Culture, Politics, and the Black Working Class* (New York: Free Press, 1994), 52.

16. Drake and Cayton, *Black Metropolis*, 603. See also Randi Storch, *Red Chicago: American Communism at its Grassroots, 1928–35* (Urbana: University of Illinois Press, 2007), 46. On the attraction of free activities in Washington Park, see Charles Davis and Clarice Durham, interview with the author, January 20, 2010.

17. Drake and Cayton, *Black Metropolis*, 380, 603.

18. Ibid., 380. *Black Metropolis* emphasizes Washington Park's expansiveness (and, by extension, its cultural significance), alternately stating its size as two or four square miles. At 371 acres, the park is actually much closer to half a square mile in size; the entirety of Chicago's Black Belt at this time measured about four square miles.

19. Jimmy Ellis, interview with the author, July 26, 2010.

20. Timuel Black, interview with the author, July 27, 2010.

21. Louis Caldwell interview transcript, 3, TB; Davis and Durham, interview with the author, January 20, 2010; Chicago Recreation Commission et al., *The Chicago Recreation Survey, 1937* (Chicago, 1937), 209–210. The busy tennis courts—as well as 31st Street beach and Washington and Jackson Parks more generally—play an incidental role in Waters Turpin's novel *O Canaan!* One character tells another, " 'There's no telling when we'll get on!' " Waters E. Turpin, *O Canaan! A Novel* (New York: Doubleday, Doran & Company, Inc., 1939), 265.

22. Edward Franklin Frazier, "Recreation and Amusement among American Negroes, A Research Memorandum," in Carnegie-Myrdal Study of the Negro in America research memoranda collection, ed. Carnegie Corporation of New York et al. (1940), 106; "Outdoor Baptism Attracts Thousands," *Chicago Defender (National Edition)*, August 13, 1938, p. 7; Marcia Winn, "40

Wash Their Sins away in a Park Lagoon," *Chicago Tribune,* August 8, 1938, p. 16; "Baptizing in Washington Park," *Chicago Tribune,* August 14, 1938, p. H6; W. L. Bliss, "Parks Offer Attractive Program to the Negroes: Stanton, Seward, Union and Washington Parks Do Good Work," *Chicago Park District Recreation News* 2, no. 2 (February 1938), 3.

23. Rutkoff and Scott, *Fly Away,* 231. Although Bud Billiken Day organizers made a point of welcoming all races to the parade and picnic, white participation was virtually nonexistent. See "Thousands Cheer"; G. W. Wilhoite, "Liked Mixing of Races," *Chicago Defender (National Edition),* September 4, 1932, p. 16.

24. Emphasis mine. Horace Cayton, *Long Old Road* (New York: Trident Press, [1964] 1965), 176.

25. Black, interview with the author, July 27, 2010. Indeed, photographic evidence at the Chicago Park District shows that at least some white people continued to play baseball in Washington Park into the 1930s, but this appears to have been the exception rather than the rule. On park demographics, see also Chicago Park District, *Historical Register of the Twenty-Two Superseded Park Districts* (Chicago, 1941), 415; and Edith Margo, "South Side Sees Red," *Left Front* (June / July 1933), 3.

26. Drake and Cayton, *Black Metropolis,* 106. Indeed, for the most part, *Black Metropolis* follows the 1922 Chicago Commission on Race Relations report in identifying racial conflict at parks and beaches as "primary tension points" between black and white Chicagoans; the study sees the "playground" of Washington Park as the exception rather than the rule. This view has dominated historical interpretations since. Ibid., 103–106; Allan H. Spear, *Black Chicago: The Making of a Negro Ghetto, 1890–1920* (Chicago: University of Chicago Press, 1967), 205; and Dorceta E. Taylor, *The Environment and the People in American Cities, 1600–1900s: Disorder, Inequality, and Social Change* (Durham, NC: Duke University Press, 2009), 332–335. An exception is Colin Fisher, *Urban Green: Nature, Recreation, and the Working Class in Industrial Chicago* (Chapel Hill: University of North Carolina Press, 2015).

27. Davis and Durham, interview with the author, January 20, 2010. See also Colin Fisher, "African Americans, Outdoor Recreation, and the 1919 Chicago Race Riot," in *To Love the Wind and the Rain: African Americans and Environmental History,* ed. Dianne D. Glave and Mark Stoll (Pittsburgh: University of Pittsburgh Press, 2006), 73.

28. Jimmie Farrell, "Voice of the People—Dividing the Parks," *Chicago Tribune,* August 3, 1929, p. 8; Chicago Park District, *Historical Register,* 354; Chicago Recreation Commission, "Recreation in Chicago," Box 40, Folder 265, MB. On the broader effect of New Deal agencies for black workers in Chicago, see chapter 2 in Lionel Kimble Jr., *A New Deal for Bronzeville: Housing, Employment & Civil Rights in Black Chicago, 1935–1955* (Carbondale: Southern Illinois University Press, 2015).

29. Historian Earl Lewis has called this sort of segregated community-building "congregation," in which African American communities productively

assert "the power to redefine aspects of their own existence." Earl Lewis, *In Their Own Interests: Race, Class, and Power in Twentieth-Century Norfolk, Virginia* (Berkeley: University of California Press, 1991), 91. Historian Matthew Lassiter avoids using the de facto / de jure distinction in part to break down "artificial binaries between South and North." Although this book also seeks to break down such binaries, the distinction remains useful in describing racially separate recreational spaces that largely stemmed from segregated residential patterns. Matthew D. Lassiter, "De Jure / De Facto Segregation: The Long Shadow of a National Myth," in *The Myth of Southern Exceptionalism*, ed. Matthew D. Lassiter and Joseph Crespino (New York: Oxford University Press, 2010), 28.

30. "Washington Park Gang Beats Another Victim," *Chicago Defender (National Edition)*, June 10, 1922, p. 1; and Davis and Durham, interview with the author. Although violence largely abated, there were isolated examples of white-on-black violence in Washington Park in the 1930s. See, for instance, "Act to Curb Attacks upon Young Girls," *Chicago Defender (National Edition)*, May 21, 1932, p. A1. On the shifting discourse of respectability in the Depression more generally, see Victoria W. Wolcott, *Remaking Respectability: African American Women in Interwar Detroit* (Chapel Hill: University of North Carolina Press, 2001), 207, 226. On baptisms in public parks and beaches in Chicago, see "Sunday Circus in Lake Michigan," *Chicago Defender (National Edition)*, July 26, 1924, p. 8; St. Clair Drake, "Negro Churches and Associations in Chicago: A Research Memorandum," in *The Carnegie-Myrdal Study*, 365; "Crowd of 20,000 Witness Chicago Baptising," *Chicago Defender (National Edition)*, August 20, 1938, p. 1; "Outdoor Baptism"; Winn, "40 Wash"; "Baptizing in Washington Park"; and Davis and Durham, interview with the author, January 20, 2010.

31. "Parade to Feature Bud's Grand Picnic," *Chicago Defender (National Edition)*, July 16, 1932, p. 16.

32. Jimmy Ellis, interview with the author.

33. Lightfoot, *Chicago Slums*, 34.

34. Edith Margo, "South Side Sees Red," *Left Front* (January / February 1934), 4–6; Drake and Cayton, *Black Metropolis*, 84–85; Reed, *The Depression Comes to the South Side*, 77–83; Christopher Robert Reed, "A Study of Black Politics and Protest in Depression-Decade Chicago: 1930–1939" (Ph.D. diss., Kent State University), 162–172; and Lizabeth Cohen, *Making a New Deal: Industrial Workers in Chicago, 1919–1939* (New York: Cambridge University Press, [1990] 2008), 153. Another notable protest campaign was a "Don't Buy Where You Can't Work" boycott begun in late 1929 by the Chicago NAACP and the *Whip*, which inspired similar campaigns across the country. See Drake and Cayton, *Black Metropolis*, 84; Reed, *The Depression Comes to the South Side*, 67–76; Reed, "A Study of Black Politics," 146–162; Cheryl Lynn Greenberg, *"Or Does it Explode?" Black Harlem in the Great Depression* (New York: Oxford Uni-

versity Press, 1991), 114–139; and Mark Naison, *Communists in Harlem during the Depression* (Urbana: University of Illinois Press, [1983] 2005), 50.

35. Michael Gold, "The Negro Reds of Chicago (Installment 1)," *The Daily Worker*, September 28, 1932, p. 4. On Gold, see Morris Dickstein, *Dancing in the Dark: A Cultural History of the Great Depression* (New York: W. W. Norton, 2009), 19; and Alan M. Wald, *Exiles from a Future Time: The Forging of the Mid-Twentieth-Century Literary Left* (Chapel Hill: University of North Carolina Press, 2002), 39–70.

36. Margo, "South Side Sees Red" (1933), 3.

37. "18th Annual Report" (1932), 24, Series I, Box 1, Folder 10, CUL; Drake, *Negro Churches*, 548. On Chicago's black Communist enrollment and less official affiliations, see Storch, *Red Chicago*, 39, 241; Drake and Cayton, *Black Metropolis*, 735; "Communism?" *Chicago Defender (National Edition)*, August 8, 1931, p. 1; "Editorial," *Chicago Defender (National Edition)*, August 22, 1931, p. 15; Paul Clinton Young, "Race, Class, and Radicalism in Chicago, 1914–1936" (Ph.D. diss., University of Iowa), 164; and "Reds Riot; 3 Slain by Police," *Chicago Tribune*, August 4, 1931, p. 1. On black communism beyond Chicago, see Storch, *Red Chicago;* Naison, *Communists in Harlem;* Greenberg, *"Or Does it Explode?";* and Robin D. G. Kelley, *Hammer and Hoe: Alabama Communists during the Great Depression* (Chapel Hill: University of North Carolina Press, 1990).

38. Horace Cayton, "The Black Bugs," *The Nation* (September 9, 1931), 256. No doubt influenced by his acrimonious split with the Communist Party, Richard Wright was far more critical of communist organizing on the South Side; Cayton's account seems more reliable. See Richard Wright, *Black Boy (American Hunger): A Record of Childhood and Youth* (New York: HarperPerennial Modern Classics, [1945] 2006), 294–295, 331; Bill Mullen, *Popular Fronts: Chicago and African-American Cultural Politics, 1935–46* (Urbana: University of Illinois Press, 1999), 19–43; and Ralph Ellison, "Remembering Richard Wright," in *Going to the Territory* (New York: Random House, 1986), 213.

39. Drake and Cayton, *Black Metropolis*, 735; Drake, *Negro Churches*, 548. See also Reed, *The Depression Comes to the South Side*, 24–34.

40. Hazel Rowley, *Richard Wright: The Life and Times* (Chicago: University of Chicago Press, 2008), 96; Michael Gold, "The Negro Reds of Chicago (Installment 2)," *The Daily Worker*, September 29, 1932, p. 4; Davis and Durham, interview with the author, January 20, 2010; Timuel Black, interview with the author, January 21, 2010; Harold D. Lasswell and Dorothy Blumenstock, *World Revolutionary Propaganda. A Chicago Study* (New York: A. A. Knopf, 1939), 44, 82, 170–172. On Unemployed Councils beyond Chicago, see Robert H. Zieger, *American Workers, American Unions* (Baltimore: Johns Hopkins University Press, [1986] 1994), 15–19; Fraser M. Ottanelli, *The Communist Party of the United States: From the Depression to World War II* (New Brunswick, NJ: Rutgers University Press, 1991), 28–36; Kimberley L. Phil-

lips, *Alabama North: African-American Migrants, Community, and Working-Class Activism in Cleveland, 1915–45* (Urbana: University of Illinois Press, 1999), 209–210; and "Cause of Communist Riot," *Chicago Defender (National Edition)*, October 17, 1931, p. 20. The Scottsboro Boys case captivated the nation from 1931 to 1937 and was the touchstone connection for communists with African Americans. On the importance of the Scottsboro case in Chicago and beyond, see Drake and Cayton, *Black Metropolis,* 734–737; Dempsey Travis, *An Autobiography of Black Chicago* (Chicago: Urban Research Institute, 1981), 49; Naison, *Communists in Harlem during the Depression,* 57–94; and Storch, *Red Chicago.*

41. "Chicago"; "Reds Riot"; and "Officials Pledge Efforts to End Communist Strike," *Chicago Tribune,* August 8, 1931, p. 4. On the protests' popularity, see Gold, "The Negro Reds of Chicago (Installment 2)," 4; Storch, *Red Chicago,* 46; Naison, *Communists in Harlem,* 17; and Lightfoot, *Chicago Slums,* 42.

42. Lightfoot, *Chicago Slums,* 33.

43. Wright, *Black Boy,* 288, 294–295. Even though the black neighborhoods surrounding Washington Park were more economically sound than the tenements farther north, the deep cut of the Depression led to many evictions in what were considered more middle-class neighborhoods. One *Defender* letter writer cynically suggested that "Washington park offer[ed] sufficient space to accommodate [the] great army of the unwashed . . . out of sight," and that the Park District should remove benches along the more visible boulevards so that the "bums and morons" could not "loaf on the main thoroughfare." Stephens D. Williams, "Objects to Benches," *Chicago Defender (National Edition),* July 30, 1938, p. 16.

44. Gold, "The Negro Reds of Chicago (Installment 2)," 4.

45. Lasswell and Blumenstock, *World Revolutionary Propaganda,* 46, 170–174.

46. Margo, "South Side Sees Red" (1933), 2.

47. Frederick Law Olmsted and Calvert Vaux, "Report Accompanying Plan for Laying Out the South Park," in *The Papers of Frederick Law Olmsted. Supplementary Series* (Baltimore: Johns Hopkins University Press, 1997), 216. Nearly one-third of communist protests were held outdoors between 1930 and 1934, excluding outdoor picnics and parades. Lasswell and Blumenstock, *World Revolutionary Propaganda,* 45. These gatherings likely moved indoors in the colder months. See Wilson T. Seney, "A Study of the Activities of the Communist Party in Organizing Unrest among the Negroes of Chicago" (1931), Box 183, Folder 1, EWB.

48. Alternative accounts state that the "Negro Bug Club" possibly began as early as 1927. Yvonne Watkins Kyler, "The Forum Movement of the Thirties: Focusing on the Washington Park Forum as a Microcosm of Black Dissent and Marginality" (master's thesis, Northeastern Illinois University, 1973), 32–34, 81–82; and Reed, "A Study of Black Politics," 174. For James T. Farrell's fictionalization of the Bug Club, see Farrell, *Studs Lonigan: A Trilogy,* 452–458. On Chicago's parks long being an organizing ground for labor

activists and political radicals, see Robin Faith Bachin, *Building the South Side: Urban Space and Civic Culture in Chicago, 1890–1919* (Chicago: University of Chicago Press, 2004), 165–166.

49. Richard Wright, "Uncle Tom's Children," in *Early Works* (New York: Library of America, 1991), 405. One is tempted to see Erlone, the surname of the main white communist character in *Native Son*, as a subtle reference to the vernacular version of "alone" that Wright used in "Fire and Cloud," perhaps indicating the failure of communist organizing that ultimately leaves both races "erlone." On "Fire and Cloud" and Wright's later, more mixed portrayals of the Communist Party in *Native Son*, see ibid., 397–398; Richard Wright, *Native Son* (New York: HarperCollins, [1940] 1998), 69–77; Rowley, *Richard Wright*, 89, 117; and Michel Fabre, *The Unfinished Quest of Richard Wright* (Urbana: University of Illinois Press, [1973] 1993), 134.

50. On communists' interracial organizing and parades, see Storch, *Red Chicago*, 101, 114; Lightfoot, *Chicago Slums*, 42; Drake and Cayton, *Black Metropolis*, 735–737; Wright, *Black Boy*, 339; and Rick Halpern, *Down on the Killing Floor: Black and White Workers in Chicago's Packinghouses, 1904–54* (Urbana: University of Illinois Press, 1997), 101–112. James T. Farrell fictionalizes such a parade in the last novel of his *Studs Lonigan* trilogy. See Farrell, *Studs Lonigan: A Trilogy*, 584, 864, 933–947. On communist organizing in the South, see Kelley, *Hammer and Hoe*, 369.

51. Quoted in Halpern, *Down on the Killing Floor*, 110–112. See also Travis, *An Autobiography*, 48.

52. Quoted in Storch, *Red Chicago*, 113. See also Cohen, *Making a New Deal*, 266.

53. Storch, *Red Chicago*, 97.

54. Travis, *An Autobiography*, 48–49.

55. Black, interviews with the author, January 21 and July 27, 2010.

56. Margo, "South Side Sees Red" (1933), 2. On Unemployed Councils' diversity, see also Reed, "A Study of Black Politics," 134.

57. Gold, "The Negro Reds of Chicago (Installment 2)," 4. On the African American version of communism, see also Kelley, *Race Rebels*, 105.

58. Margo, "South Side Sees Red" (1933), 2.

59. Cayton, "The Black Bugs," 255.

60. Young, *Race, Class, and Radicalism*, 216; Michael Gold, "The Negro Reds of Chicago (Installment 3)," *The Daily Worker*, September 30, 1932, p. 4. On African American religion and communism in Chicago and beyond, see Storch, *Red Chicago*, 97; and Kelley, *Hammer and Hoe*, 108.

61. Gold, "The Negro Reds of Chicago (Installment 3)," 4. Wright's "Fire and Cloud" culminates in just such an interracial fusion of communist organizing and African American religion. See Wright, *Uncle Tom's Children*, 406. It was likely this sort of inspirational ending that Wright would later regret; reflecting on *Native Son*, he famously said that he wanted to write something so "hard and deep" that no one could "weep over and feel good about." Wright, "How Bigger Was Born" in *Native Son*, 454.

62. Margo, "South Side Sees Red" (1933), 3. On the Communist Party's class politics in Chicago, see Drake, *Negro Churches*, 487–488.

63. Margo, "South Side Sees Red" (1934), 4. On the apparent inability of De Priest and local aldermen to deal with the Depression's widespread effects, see Reed, *The Depression Comes to the South Side*, 35–65.

64. "Negro Leaders Accuse Reds in Fatal Rioting," *Chicago Tribune*, August 4, 1931, p. 2; and Young, *Race, Class, and Radicalism*, 218. For elaboration on these contentious politics, see also Gold, "The Negro Reds of Chicago (Installment 2)," 4; Gosnell, *Negro Politicians*, 337; Lasswell and Blumenstock, *World Revolutionary Propaganda*, 140; Margo, "South Side Sees Red" (1933), 2; "'Reds' Ask Alderman's Aid," *Chicago Defender (National Edition)*, September 12, 1931, p. 20; Drake and Cayton, *Black Metropolis*, 342–355; William J. Grimshaw, *Bitter Fruit: Black Politics and the Chicago Machine, 1931–1991* (Chicago: University of Chicago Press, 1992), 47–68; and Reed, *The Depression Comes to the South Side*, 35–65. For more on Austin and Pilgrim Baptist, see Randall K. Burkett, "The Baptist Church in Years of Crisis: J. C. Austin and Pilgrim Baptist Church, 1926–1950," in *African-American Religion: Interpretive Essays in History and Culture*, ed. Timothy E. Fulop and Albert J. Raboteau (New York: Routledge, 1997), 312–339; and Wallace D. Best, *Passionately Human, No Less Divine: Religion and Culture in Black Chicago, 1915–1952* (Princeton, NJ: Princeton University Press, 2005), 106–109.

65. Drake and Cayton, *Black Metropolis*, 87. See also "Reds Riot"; Reed, "A Study of Black Politics," 173–175; "U.S. Acts to Curb 'Reds,'" *Chicago Defender (National Edition)*, August 8, 1931, p. 1; and Lightfoot, *Chicago Slums*, 38–39.

66. Margo, "South Side Sees Red" (1934), 6. At least two of the men were migrants, and their bodies were transported back to their final resting places in the South. Reed, *The Depression Comes to the South Side*, 91.

67. Storch, *Red Chicago*, 99. Storch seems to have accepted as fact this story from Michael Gold's and Edith Margo's accounts, which also implicate the NAACP in the "Chicago massacre." Although De Priest did have a dubious ethical history characteristic of Chicago's machine politics, whether or not these surreptitious meetings actually happened seems less certain, particularly given that Gold went so far as to call De Priest "a Judas to his race" and Margo later made the highly questionable and inflammatory accusation that De Priest "has consistently supported the Jim-Crowing, lynching system." Gold, "The Negro Reds of Chicago (Installment 1)," 4; Margo, "South Side Sees Red" (1934), 4–5. See also Gosnell, *Negro Politicians*, 339; Reed, "A Study of Black Politics," 17; and W. E. B. Du Bois, "Postscript," *Crisis* 36, no. 2 (February 1929), 57. On the wide range of protests in the wake of the "Chicago massacre," see Lasswell and Blumenstock, *World Revolutionary Propaganda*, 203–204; Storch, *Red Chicago*, 100–101; Gold, "The Negro Reds of Chicago (Installment 1)," 4; Lightfoot, *Chicago Slums*, 42; Young, *Race, Class, and Radicalism*, 215–216; "'Reds' in Mammoth Parade,"

Chicago Defender (National Edition), August 15, 1931, p. 22; and "Crowd Orderly at Funeral of Slain Rioters," *Chicago Tribune*, August 9, 1931, p. 11.

68. Lasswell and Blumenstock, *World Revolutionary Propaganda*, 198; Reed, "A Study of Black Politics," 178; and "Halt Evictions to Calm Unrest on South Side," *Chicago Tribune*, August 5, 1931, p. 1. On Abbott, Turner, and the more longstanding characterization of communist protests and other radical protests by the police and the middle and upper classes of both races, see Reed, *The Depression Comes to the South Side*, 87–89; "Reds Riot"; "Negro Leaders Accuse Reds"; "The Bugs again Alight in the Park," *Chicago Tribune*, July 24, 1921, p. 2; " 'Bugs' Buzz Once More in Park; Armistice On," *Chicago Tribune*, Jul 24, 1921, p. 2; Charles W. Mosher, "Voice of the People," *Chicago Tribune*, July 25, 1921, p. 6; "14,000 "Bug Club" Members Join in Court Fight," *Chicago Tribune*, August 3, 1921, p. 12; and Drake and Cayton, *Black Metropolis*, 105–106.

69. Drake and Cayton, *Black Metropolis*, 87. The reprieve only lasted a few weeks, however. By September, the *Defender* was again reporting on the arrests of communists as they attempted to put evicted families' belongings back in their homes. "Police Face 'Reds,' Ten," *Chicago Defender (National Edition)*, September 5, 1931, p. 20. See also Gosnell, *Negro Politicians*, 330; "Reds Riot"; Young, *Race, Class, and Radicalism*, 217–218; "Halt Evictions"; "Mayor Attacks Reds Preying on Unemployed," *Chicago Tribune*, August 7, 1931, p. 1; "Negro Leaders Accuse Reds"; and Storch, *Red Chicago*, 115.

70. Reed, *The Depression Comes to the South Side*, 44–45, 96–121. Drake and Cayton noted that "the high-water mark of unemployment among Negroes was probably reached in 1930 and 1931," but communist protests continued and became more mainstream later in the decade. Drake and Cayton, *Black Metropolis*, 217, 736–737. See also Storch, *Red Chicago*, 39; Reed, "A Study of Black Politics," 283; Lasswell and Blumenstock, *World Revolutionary Propaganda*, 38; and Mullen, *Popular Fronts*, 242. Research on the Communist Party outside of Chicago also suggests that with New Deal legislation addressing the plight of the unemployed, party interests turned elsewhere. See Greenberg, *"Or Does it Explode?"* 64; Naison, *Communists in Harlem*, 74–150; and Kelley, *Hammer and Hoe*, 32.

71. Division of Playgrounds and Sports, South Park Commissioners, "A Survey of the Madden Park Community" (1930), 4–5, CPD.

72. "Madden Park Woman's Club Honors President," *Chicago Defender (National Edition)*, January 25, 1930, p. 5; Earl Richard Moses, "Community Factors in Negro Delinquency" (master's thesis, University of Chicago, 1932), 135–136; "Madden Park Woman's Club Entertains Children," *Chicago Defender (National Edition)*, January 11, 1930, p. 5.

73. Chicago South Park Commission, *Official Proceedings of the South Park District*, Vol. 38 (1930), 354, CPD; "The Home of Mr. and Mrs. Oscar De Priest," *Broad Ax*, April 9, 1921, p. 1.

74. "Build Madden Park Now, Plea of Urban League," *Chicago Tribune*, December 13, 1931, p. H4. Already at this point in 1931, the Urban League was discussing "a model housing project for salaried and low wage tenants in the area immediately adjacent to the park"; a decade later, this vision would come to fruition in the Ida B. Wells Homes.

75. Chicago South Park Commission, *Official Proceedings of the South Park District*, Vol. 40 (1932), 115, 384, CPD; Chicago South Park Commission, *Official Proceedings of the South Park District*, Vol. 41 (1933), 2, 269, CPD.

76. The park was still "in course of construction" in 1932, but was already more functional than Jackson Playground. "Ald. Jackson Endorsed for Re-Election," *Chicago Defender (National Edition)*, December 1, 1934, p. 3; "Plan Softball Talks, Dancing for Field Day," *Chicago Tribune*, September 17, 1933, p .S3; "Salutes Old Glory," *Chicago Defender (National Edition)*, July 30, 1932, p. 20; "Play Ball!" *Chicago Defender (National Edition)*, September 4, 1932, p. 22; "Clear the Way!" *Chicago Defender (National Edition)*, December 3, 1932, p. 3; "'Scientist' Scans Skies for Eclipse," *Chicago Defender (National Edition)*, September 4, 1932, p. 22; "Chicago Defender's Soft Ball Meet Starts Sept. 5," *Chicago Defender (National Edition)*, September 3, 1932, p. 8; "Flashes A.C. Wins Chicago Defender Softball Tourney," *Chicago Defender (National Edition)*, September 10, 1932, p. 8; "Softball Meet in Final Rounds; 20 Teams Compete," *Chicago Defender (National Edition)*, October 1, 1932, p. 9; and "Defender Tourney Starts Labor Day," *Chicago Defender (National Edition)*, September 2, 1933, p. 8.

77. "200 Jobless Aid in Dressing up South Park Way," *Chicago Tribune*, October 30, 1932, p .F2; "New Park Leads Near South Side in Beauty Drive," *Chicago Tribune*, August 21, 1932, p. F3. On similar efforts undertaken by the Chicago Urban League, see Dorothy Crounse, Louise Gilbert, and Agnes Van Driel, "The Chicago Urban League" (1936), 71, Box 286, Folder 8, WC.

78. Chicago Park District, *Second Annual Report* (1936), 23, 21. On funding for parks in the Black Belt during the Depression, see John Thomas, "Seek Funds for Six Parks on Near South Side," *Chicago Defender (National Edition)*, October 5, 1935, p. 4; Emily Jefferson, "Park Benches," *Chicago Defender (National Edition)*, August 7, 1937, p. 16; Samuel Whitaks, "Those Tennis Courts," *Chicago Defender (National Edition)*, September 10, 1938, p. 16; and "Protest Condition of Washington Pk. Courts," *Chicago Defender (National Edition)*, August 19, 1939, p. 12.

79. Mrs Edward Smith, "How They Fool Us," *Chicago Defender (National Edition)*, October 2, 1926, p. A2. On the controversy over 31st Street beach's closing and segregated bathing at the World's Fair 12th Street beach, as well as the formation of Burnham Park, see Alex Rousseau Dawson, "What the People Say—We Will Swim, Mr. Castle," *Chicago Defender (National Edition)*, April 8, 1933, p. 14; "Defender Wins in Beach Fight," *Chicago Defender (National Edition)*, August 6, 1932, p. 1; Chicago Recreation Commission et al., *The Chicago Recreation Survey, 1937*, 208; Elizabeth Halsey and Chicago Recreation Commission, *The Development of Public Recreation in Metropolitan Chicago* (Chicago:

Chicago Recreation Commission, 1940), 63; and Bachin, *Building the South Side,* 175–179. According to Drake and Cayton, 31st Street marked the border between the "worst" and "mixed" areas of the Black Belt in 1930 (as "classified on the basis of median rentals, median education, and juvenile delinquency, illegitimacy, and insanity rates"). Drake and Cayton, *Black Metropolis,* 384. Chicago had long striven to live up to the ideas of Burnham, the visionary city planner who crafted the ambitious *Plan of Chicago* (the same plan that encouraged the creation of the city's Cook County Forest Preserves); he wrote, "The Lake front by right belongs to the people. It affords their one great unobstructed view, stretching away to the horizon, where water and clouds seem to meet." Daniel Hudson Burnham et al., *Plan of Chicago,* centennial ed. (1909; Chicago: Great Books Foundation, 2009), 50. The city did not fully succeed in "wrest[ing] its lake front from industry," as one historian has put it, until these New Deal-financed efforts. Halsey and Chicago Recreation Commission, *The Development of Public Recreation,* 3. On Burnham's plan, see Carl S. Smith, *The Plan of Chicago: Daniel Burnham and the Remaking of the American City* (Chicago: University of Chicago Press, 2006).

80. "2 Pools Costing $600,000 Will be Opened Tuesday," *Chicago Tribune,* July 4, 1937, p. SW2. See also Bliss, "Parks Offer Attractive Program," p. 3; "Three Swimming Pools for S. Side," *Chicago Defender (National Edition),* June 6, 1936, p. 21; "Dedicate New South Side Park Pools Tonight," *Chicago Tribune,* July 8, 1937, p. 14; and Benjamin J. Chlevin Jr., "Washington Park Swimming Pool" (March 6, 1945), CPD.

81. "New Park under Construction," *Chicago Defender (National Edition),* July 4, 1936, p. 22. On the Chicago Park District's work—with substantial help from the WPA—on South Side parks and beaches, see Chicago Park District, *Second Annual Report,* 39, 157–158; Chicago Park District, *Third Annual Report* (1937), 8; Chicago Park District, *Fourth Annual Report* (1938), 81; Chicago Park District, *Fifth Annual Report* (1939), 85; *Final Report: CWA Project 1340, a Consolidation of Projects* (1934), CPD; "Parks to Open Greatest Year of Recreation," *Chicago Tribune,* March 31, 1935, p. SW1; and "WPA Aids South Side Projects with $547,000," *Chicago Tribune,* February 14, 1937, p.S3.

82. Galen Cranz, *The Politics of Park Design: A History of Urban Parks in America* (Cambridge, MA: MIT Press, 1982), viii, 106. See also Jeff Wiltse, *Contested Waters: A Social History of Swimming Pools in America* (Chapel Hill: University of North Carolina Press, 2007), 93–95; and Susan Currell, *The March of Spare Time: The Problem and Promise of Leisure in the Great Depression* (Philadelphia: University of Pennsylvania Press, 2005), 16.

83. The superintendent was responding to a South Side citizen's request that a pool be constructed in Washington Park because he was afraid to take his children to the lake to swim. Chicago South Park Commission, *Official Proceedings of the South Park District* 19 (1912), 111, CPD.

84. Jimmy Ellis, interview with the author. See also "Youths to Have Water Carnival at Madden Park," *Chicago Tribune,* August 18, 1940, p. SW1; and

Wiltse, *Contested Waters*, 89. On controversies over infrastructure in Washington Park, see "Citizens Want Work on All Public Jobs," *Chicago Defender (National Edition)*, July 14, 1934, p. 12; "Advance Plans for Recreation in Park Project," *Chicago Defender (National Edition)*, June 1, 1935, p. 5; "Seek Seven Hundred Thousand to Build New Improvements at Washington Park," *Chicago Defender (National Edition)*, April 13, 1935, p. 5; "McKeough Gives Aid to Park Project," *Chicago Defender (National Edition)*, June 22, 1935, p. 4; Old Residenter, just a Spectator, "An Armory in Washington Park," *Chicago Defender (National Edition)*, March 3, 1928, p. 14; and "Protect the Parks," *Chicago Tribune*, March 11, 1930, p. 14.

85. James J. Gentry, "Bronzeville in Chicago," *Chicago Defender (National Edition)*, March 26, 1938, p. 18. On Jimmy Gentry, see Rutkoff and Scott, *Fly Away*, 322–323; and Elizabeth Schroeder Schlabach, *Along the Streets of Bronzeville: Black Chicago's Literary Landscape* (Urbana: University of Illinois Press, 2013), 19–20.

86. "Chicago's Congo," a meditation on African roots, civilization, and the urban landscape, is also the title of a Frank Marshall Davis poem published in 1935's *Black Man's Verse*. See Frank Marshall Davis and John Edgar Tidwell, *Black Moods: Collected Poems* (Urbana: University of Illinois Press, 2002), 5–17. For more on Davis, who moved to Chicago the same year as Richard Wright, see Robert Bone and Richard A. Courage, *The Muse in Bronzeville: African American Creative Expression in Chicago, 1932–1950* (New Brunswick, NJ: Rutgers University Press, 2011), 208–211. Davis's imagery is remarkably similar to that in James T. Farrell's *Young Lonigan,* published less than a decade earlier. Farrell, *Studs Lonigan: A Trilogy,* 97.

87. Originally published in Davis's 1937 collection *I Am the American Negro,* the full poem is more readily accessible in Davis and Tidwell, *Black Moods,* 68–73.

88. Jontyle Theresa Robinson et al., *The Art of Archibald J. Motley, Jr.* (Chicago: Chicago Historical Society, 1991), 111. Although neither "The Picnic" nor "Lawn Party" unambiguously telegraph their inspiration in South Side landscapes, Motley's well-documented fascination with the Black Belt's urban scenes in the same period makes it difficult to resist drawing connections to the Washington Park scene that Frank Marshall Davis so vividly conveyed in 1937. For representative contrasting images, see "Black Belt" (1934), "Saturday Night" (1935), "Nightlife" (1943), and "Bronzeville at Night" (1949) in Amy M. Mooney and Archibald John Motley, *Archibald J. Motley Jr.* (San Francisco: Pomegranate, 2004), 116. On Motley, see South Side Community Art Center, "South Side Community Art Center Fiftieth Anniversary" (1991), 11, Box 24, folder SSCAC, WM; Archibald John Motley et al., *Archibald Motley: Jazz Age Modernist* (Durham, NC: Nasher Museum of Art, 2014); and Bone and Courage, *The Muse in Bronzeville,* 71–74, 139–141.

89. Martin Bickham and Phillip Seman, "Planned Recreation for Chicago's Youth" (1936), 13–15, Box 189, Folder 1669, MB. On vacant lots utilized by

the Boys' Club, see also Volume 3 of Chicago Recreation Commission et al., *The Chicago Recreation Survey, 1937,* 56–57.

90. Edward J. Kelly, "My Hopes for the City-Planning of Recreation, Speech Delivered at the Chicago Recreation Conference, December 3, 1936," 1–3, Box 30, Folder 5, CAP.

91. Halsey and Chicago Recreation Commission, *The Development of Public Recreation,* 117.

92. "Citizens Demand Band Concerts in Public Parks," *Chicago Defender (National Edition),* July 14, 1934, p. 3. On WPA musicians in Madden Park, see "50 of WPA's Musicians Play Only Checkers," *Chicago Tribune,* December 21, 1935, p. 1.

93. Chicago Park District, *Third Annual Report,* 161.

94. Often this meant that park programming had little or nothing to do with the natural or landscaped environment, but officials were not unaware of the potential consequences of evolving park space usage. On this wide variety of programming, see V. K. Brown, "Let's Get off the Beaten Track," *Chicago Park District Recreation News* 2, no. 2 (February 1938), 5; Chicago Park District, *Fourth Annual Report,* 80; Chicago Park District, *Fifth Annual Report,* 84; Chicago Park District, *Sixth Annual Report* (1940), 92; and *Final Report: CWA Project 1340.*

95. Drake, *Negro Churches,* 485.

96. "Chicago Police Vs. the South Side," *Chicago Defender (National Edition),* September 23, 1939, p. 14. See also *Chicago Park District Recreation News* 3, no. 8 (August 1939), 5; Jimmy Ellis, interview with the author; "Swimmers Pass Test at Madden Park Pool," *Chicago Defender (National Edition),* September 11, 1937, p. 20.

97. "How Bigger Was Born" in Wright, *Native Son,* 453–454. For a less critical perspective on Wright's work at the Boys' Club, see Wright, *Black Boy,* 341.

98. "How Bigger Was Born" in Wright, *Native Son,* 453–454.

99. Chicago Park District, *Historical Register,* 354. On segregation in South Side parks, see also Chicago Park District, *Third Annual Report,* 115; Jimmy Ellis, interview with the author; "Chicago Police Vs. the South Side"; and Dorothy K. Toms, "Minutes of Meeting of the Executive Committee" (1939), 4, Box 168, Folder 1, WC. Similar segregation trends in recreational space were evident nationwide. See Wiltse, *Contested Waters,* 123; Lewis, *In Their Own Interests,* 83–84, 130. Exceptions to the rule in Chicago were Stanton and Seward Parks on the Near North Side and the YWCA's West Side pool (because each facility was surrounded by racially heterogeneous populations) in the late 1920s and 1930s. See Bliss, "Parks Offer Attractive Program"; "Metropolitan Board of Directors" (1937), Series I, Box 49, Folder 573, YWCAM; The Committee of Management of the West Side Branch of the Y.W.C.A. to the Metropolitan Board of the Y.W.C.A. of Chicago (1937), Series I, Box 49, Folder 573, YWCAM; "Record of Negro-White Relationships," Series I, Box 54, Folder 607, YWCAM; "Brief Notes on Meeting of

Group to Consider Interracial Policies of the Y.W.C.A." (1938), Series I, Box 54, Folder 607, YWCAM; and Mayor's Commission on Human Relations, *"Recreation for All: A Manual for Supervisors and Workers in Recreation"* (1946), 3–4, Box 171, Folder 5, WC.

100. Halsey, *The Development of Public Recreation,* 162; Bliss, "Parks Offer Attractive Program," 1, 3. On these African American programs in the parks, see "On Our Broadway," *Chicago Park District Recreation News* 3, no. 10 (October, 1939), 1; and Derek Vaillant, *Sounds of Reform: Progressivism and Music in Chicago, 1873–1935* (Chapel Hill: University of North Carolina Press, 2003), 275–276.

101. "Defender Wins in Beach Fight"; Chicago Recreation Commission, *Recreation in Chicago.* On 31st Street beach's inadequacy compared to Jackson Park beach, see Chicago Recreation Commission et al., *The Chicago Recreation Survey, 1937,* 208; Halsey, *The Development of Public Recreation,* 172–173; James J. Gentry, "Bronzeville in Chicago," *Chicago Defender (National Edition),* July 17, 1937, p. 11; and Dawson, "What the People Say."

102. Olmsted and Vaux, *Report Accompanying Plan,* 213.

103. I am indebted to Nick Donofrio for suggesting this reading at a presentation of this work at Harvard's American Literature Colloquium. See also Robinson et al., *The Art of Archibald J. Motley, Jr.,* 122.

104. Ibid., 33.

105. For an image of the painting, see Mooney and Motley, *Archibald J. Motley Jr.,* 106. Although Motley makes the races of other characters in the painting difficult to determine, it seems doubtful that any of the others—all of them in groups save for a park policeman—are African American. Instead, many of the characters seem drawn from the Italian American neighborhood in which Motley grew up. "Oral History Interview with Archibald Motley, 1978 Jan. 23–1979 Mar. 1," Archives of American Art, Smithsonian Institution.

106. "How Bigger Was Born" in Wright, *Native Son,* 453–454. References to the Scottsboro Boys trials indicate that the action of the novel almost certainly takes place in 1937 or 1938, just after Washington Park's massive new swimming pool opened, but the pool and other features of the park are absent from the novel. See Wright, *Native Son,* 75.

107. Ibid., 75, 78, 411.

108. On the influence of the Chicago School on Wright and others in the Chicago Renaissance, see Richard Wright, "Introduction by Richard Wright," in *Black Metropolis,* xvii–xxxiv; Lawrence Buell, *Writing for an Endangered World: Literature, Culture, and Environment in the U.S. and Beyond* (Cambridge, MA: Belknap Press of Harvard University Press, 2001), 142; and Carla Cappetti, *Writing Chicago: Modernism, Ethnography, and the Novel* (New York: Columbia University Press, 1993), 13.

109. Wright, *Native Son,* 228, 279, 392.

110. See "How Bigger Was Born" in ibid., 439.

111. For an expansion of this comparison and connections between Farrell and Wright, see Robert Butler, "Farrell's Ethnic Neighborhood and Wright's Urban Ghetto: Two Visions of Chicago's South Side," *MELUS* 18, no. 1 (Spring 1993), 103–111; Rowley, *Richard Wright,* 120; and Fabre, *The Unfinished Quest,* 135–138.

112. Drake and Cayton, *Black Metropolis,* 88. On the progress of the Wells Homes, see Helgeson, *Crucibles of Black Empowerment,* 70–79; Preston H. Smith, *Racial Democracy and the Black Metropolis: Housing Policy in Postwar Chicago* (Minneapolis: University of Minnesota Press, 2012), 25–39; Kimble Jr., *A New Deal for Bronzeville,* 28–33; Al Chase, "U.S. Announces Second Housing Project Here," *Chicago Tribune,* October 26, 1934, p. 31; "South Siders in Fight for Housing Plan," *Chicago Defender (National Edition),* August 24, 1935, p. 18; and "Last Brick Laid in $9,000,000 Negro Housing Project," *Chicago Tribune,* August 17, 1940, p. 12. For a pithy overview of the rationale that underlay the origins of public housing in the United States, see Edward G. Goetz, *New Deal Ruins: Race, Economic Justice, and Public Housing Policy* (Ithaca, NY: Cornell University Press, 2013), 25–37.

113. D. Bradford Hunt, *Blueprint for Disaster: The Unraveling of Chicago Public Housing* (Chicago: University of Chicago Press, 2009), 62. On applications to the Wells Homes, see ibid., 39–40.

114. Chicago Park District, *Historical Register,* 355. From the very earliest planning stages, the Wells Homes were reported on as segregated African American housing. See, for example, Chase, "U.S. Announces"; "Finish Plans for South Side Negro Housing," *Chicago Tribune,* September 11, 1938, p. C20; and "Last Brick Laid."

115. Chicago Housing Authority, "Flowers Grow Where Slums Once Stood" (1946), Box 58, Folder 14, SCD.

116. Lorraine Hansberry, *A Raisin in the Sun* (1959; New York: Vintage Books, 1995), 52–53. Although the play did not debut until 1959 and is set in post–World War II Chicago, given that it was inspired in large part by her own family's battle against restrictive covenants on the South Side of Chicago in the 1930s (when Hansberry herself was in grade school), I would argue that it can be read in part as a meditation on Hansberry's parents' generation—those African Americans who migrated to Chicago's South Side during the first Great Migration, before World War II.

117. If there was any doubt that Hansberry intended this identification with the land, when her daughter expresses surprise that Lena would pack up "that raggedy-looking old thing" to move to their new home, Lena responds with an impassioned, "It expresses ME!" Ibid., 121.

118. Quoted in J. S. Fuerst and D. Bradford Hunt, *When Public Housing Was Paradise: Building Community in Chicago* (Westport, CT: Praeger, 2003), 47.

119. Quoted in ibid., 11. See also "Neighborhood Cleanup," *Chicago Defender (National Edition),* May 5, 1934, p. A2.

120. Quoted in Fuerst and Hunt, *When Public Housing was Paradise*, 79. See also John Henry Lewis, "Social Services in Negro Churches" (master's thesis, University of Chicago), 24, 31; and Hunt, *Blueprint for Disaster*, 60–61.

121. Chicago Park District, *Historical Register*, 355.

122. Drake and Cayton, *Black Metropolis*, 380.

123. Chicago (Ill.). Michigan Boulevard Garden Apartment Building Corporation, *Five-Year Report* (Chicago: The Corporation, 1935), 1, 3. For a class comparison of residents of the Wells Homes and the Michigan Boulevard Garden Apartments (the latter would eventually house such famous African Americans as Gwendolyn Brooks, Nat King Cole, Joe Louis, and Quincy Jones), see Drake and Cayton, *Black Metropolis*, 660–663; and Smith, *Racial Democracy and the Black Metropolis*, xiii. Although the Michigan Boulevard Garden Apartments were the realization of an idea Rosenwald had had as early as 1914 (at the very beginning of the Great Migration), they were eventually modeled after Harlem's Dunbar Apartments that opened in 1928 and were financed by John D. Rockefeller. Thomas Lee Philpott, *The Slum and the Ghetto: Immigrants, Blacks, and Reformers in Chicago, 1880–1930* (Belmont, CA: Wadsworth Publishing, 1991), 208–209, 260–268; Touré F. Reed, *Not Alms but Opportunity: The Urban League & the Politics of Racial Uplift, 1910–1950* (Chapel Hill: University of North Carolina Press, 2008), 48–56.

124. Chicago (Ill.). Michigan Boulevard Garden Apartment Building Corporation, *Seven-Year Report* (Chicago: The Corporation, 1937), 10.

125. Michigan Boulevard Garden Apartment Building Corporation, *Five-Year Report*, 20, 24. On the environmental aesthetics of the Michigan Boulevard Garden Apartments and its residents, see also Dorceta Taylor, *Toxic Communities: Environmental Racism, Industrial Pollution, and Residential Mobility* (New York: New York University Press, 2014), 204–212. For a similar garden-living ideal promoted among the urban white working classes in the early 1940s—which effectively sought to bring the suburban single-family home (rather than apartment living) to the city—see Robert O. Self, *American Babylon: Race and the Struggle for Postwar Oakland* (Princeton, NJ: Princeton University Press, 2003), 28–34. The pastoral garden ideal has deep roots in American culture; the landmark study remains Leo Marx, *The Machine in the Garden: Technology and the Pastoral Ideal in America* (New York: Oxford University Press, 1964).

126. Robert R. Taylor, *A Description and Evaluation of the Social and Community Features at the Michigan Boulevard Garden Apartments* (Chicago: National Association of Housing Officials, 1934), 3.

127. Turpin, *O Canaan! A Novel*, 288.

128. Hansberry's father was born in 1895 in Mississippi and moved to Chicago as a young man; his wife and Lorraine's mother, Nannie Louise Perry, was born in Tennessee.

129. Robert Nemiroff and Lorraine Hansberry, *To Be Young, Gifted, and Black* (New York: Signet Classics, [1969] 2011), 50.

130. Joseph Dean Lohman and Chicago Park District, *The Police and Minority Groups: A Manual Prepared for Use in the Chicago Park District Police Training School* (Chicago: Chicago Park District, 1947), 67–68. See also Drake and Cayton, *Black Metropolis,* 184–189; Frederick Burgess Lindstrom, "The Negro Invasion of the Washington Park Subdivision"; and Drake, *Churches and Voluntary Associations,* 173.

131. Nemiroff and Hansberry, *To Be Young, Gifted, and Black,* 51.

132. *Brief of Petitioners, in the Supreme Court of the United States,* October Term sess., 1940, 7. See also Drake and Cayton, *Black Metropolis,* 63.

133. W. E. B. Du Bois, "Postscript," *Crisis* 41, no. 4 (April 1934), 115. Du Bois employed only one concrete example of this self-segregation in his series of editorials, reaching back to the 1929–1930 "Don't Buy Where You Can't Work" campaign in Chicago that helped initiate a decade of mass protest in and around Washington Park on the South Side; he briefly endorsed the campaign in the March 1930 *Crisis*. Du Bois elaborated and clarified his ideas each month from January to June 1934, but the swift backlash nevertheless helped lead to his resignation from the NAACP effective July 1, 1934. See ibid., 117; W. E. B. Du Bois, "Postscript," *Crisis* 41, no. 1 (January 1934), 20; W. E. B. Du Bois, "Postscript," *Crisis* 41, no. 2 (February 1934), 53; and W. E. B. Du Bois, "Postscript," *Crisis* 37, no. 3 (March 1930), 102.

134. Du Bois, "Postscript" (April 1934), 115.

135. W. E. B. Du Bois, "Postscript," *Crisis* 41, no. 6 (June 1934), 182.

136. See Wolcott, *Remaking Respectability,* 167, 209–210.

4. Back to Nature in Hard Times

1. Susie J. Bantom, "Idlewild, Mich.," *Chicago Defender (National Edition),* August 30, 1930, p. 7.

2. Susie J. Bantom, "Idlewild," *Lake County Star,* August 8, 1930, p. 4. See also Susie J. Bantom, "Idlewild," *Lake County Star,* May 9, 1930, p. 2.

3. Bantom, "Idlewild, Mich."

4. W. E. B. Du Bois, "Hopkinsville, Chicago, and Idlewild," *Crisis* 22, no. 4 (August 1921), 158.

5. The *Defender* article puts Van Arsdale's age at fifteen in 1930, but his birth records indicate he was born on August 15, 1913. See Department of Commerce, Bureau of the Census, *Fifteenth Census of the United States: 1930. Chicago, Seventeenth Ward, Block 8, Enumeration District 16–652;* "W. Newman, Printer, Is Dead at 81," *Chicago Defender (National Edition),* August 6, 1938, p. 6; and Ancestry.com, *Cook County, Illinois, Birth Certificates Index, 1871–1922.*

6. For reminiscences of Hansberry's childhood trips to Tennessee, her mother's birthplace, see Robert Nemiroff and Lorraine Hansberry, *To Be Young, Gifted, and Black* (New York: Signet Classics, [1969] 2011), 25. The most tragic instance of black Chicagoans taking these sorts of trips down South, of course, was Emmett Till's 1955 trip to see his cousins in the Mississippi Delta. Till was murdered and his body dumped in the Tallahatchie River; his mother, whose own parents had migrated to the outskirts of Chicago from Mississippi in 1922, brought his body back to Chicago for burial.

7. Jimmy Ellis, interview with the author, July 26, 2010.

8. W. E. B. Du Bois, "Postscript," *Crisis* 41, no. 6 (June 1934), 182.

9. Susie J. Bantom, "Idlewild," *Lake County Star*, August 12, 1927.

10. Bantom, "Idlewild, Mich."

11. "Heard in Idlewild," *Lake County Star*, January 23, 1931, p. 4.

12. Susie J. Bantom, "Idlewild," *Lake County Star*, October 30, 1931, p. 2.

13. "Negro Leaders Accuse Reds in Fatal Rioting," *Chicago Tribune*, August 4, 1931, p. 2; Paul Clinton Young, "Race, Class, and Radicalism in Chicago, 1914–1936" (Ph.D. diss., University of Iowa, 2001), 218.

14. "'Reds' Ask Alderman's Aid," *Chicago Defender (National Edition)*, September 12, 1931, p. 20; Edith Margo, "South Side Sees Red," *Left Front* (June / July 1933), 3.

15. Helen Buckler, *Doctor Dan, Pioneer in American Surgery* (Boston: Little, Brown, 1954), 259; Ronald J. Stephens, *Idlewild: The Rise, Decline, and Rebirth of a Unique African American Resort Town* (Ann Arbor: University of Michigan Press, 2013), 76–81; Lewis Walker and Benjamin C. Wilson, *Black Eden: The Idlewild Community* (East Lansing: Michigan State University Press, 2002), 39–40; Pehyun Wen, "Idlewild: A Negro Village in Lake County, Michigan" (master's thesis, University of Chicago, 1972), 84; Bantom, "Idlewild, Mich."; "Heard in Idlewild," *Lake County Star*, August 30, 1935, p. 3; "Heard in Idlewild," *Lake County Star*, August 21, 1936, p. 2; Edythe G. McGruder, "Toronto," *Chicago Defender (National Edition)*, October 1, 1938, p. 22; Bert E. Grayson, "Travel Talks," *Chicago Defender (National Edition)*, October 30, 1937, p. 20; and "Joe Louis at Resort," *Lake County Star*, August 12, 1938, p. 1.

16. Susie J. Bantom, "Idlewild, Mich." *Chicago Defender (National Edition)*, June 7, 1930, p. 16. See also John Fraser Hart, "A Rural Retreat for Northern Negroes," *Geographical Review* 50, no. 2 (April 1960), 159; Walker and Wilson, *Black Eden*, 53–58; and Joseph John Jones, "The Making of a National Forest: The Contest over the West Michigan Cutover, 1888–1943" (Ph.D. diss., Michigan State University, 2007), 215–218. On automobility, nature tourism in the Upper Midwest, and other destinations for black Chicagoans, see chapter 6 in Christopher W. Wells, *Car Country: An Environmental History* (Seattle: University of Washington Press, 2012); Paul Sutter, *Driven Wild: How the Fight against Automobiles Launched the Modern Wilderness Movement* (Seattle: University of Washington Press, 2002); Aaron Alex Shapiro, "'One

Crop Worth Cultivating': Tourism in the Upper Great Lakes, 1910–1965" (Ph.D. diss., University of Chicago, 2005), 177–247; and "Chicagoans Get Relief from Heat," *Chicago Defender (National Edition)*, August 15, 1931, p. 22.

17. Du Bois, "Hopkinsville," 158.

18. Nettie George Speedy, "Society," *Chicago Defender (National Edition)*, August 8, 1931, p. 7.

19. Quote in "Activities at Resort Rival Elaborate Fetes of City," *Chicago Defender (National Edition)*, August 1, 1936, p. 6. See also Walker and Wilson, *Black Eden*, 36; Stephens, *Idlewild*, 85–88; Ronald J. Stephens, *Idlewild: The Black Eden of Michigan* (Chicago: Arcadia Publishing, 2001), 20, 43; "Success of 'Idlewild,' Michigan's Famous Summer Resort, Suggests Growth of Negro Leisure Class," *Pittsburgh Courier*, October 11, 1930, p. 2; and Ronald J. Stephens, "Garveyism in Idlewild, 1927 to 1936," *Journal of Black Studies* 34, no. 4 (March 2004), 471. On religion and class among black Chicagoans more broadly, see Wallace D. Best, *Passionately Human, No Less Divine: Religion and Culture in Black Chicago, 1915–1952* (Princeton, NJ: Princeton University Press, 2005), 123–136.

20. Robert B. Stepto, *Blue as the Lake: A Personal Geography* (Boston: Beacon Press, 1998), 10.

21. Grace, "Idlewild is Ideal!" *Pittsburgh Courier*, August 31, 1929, 7.

22. "Success of 'Idlewild,'"

23. Ruth Evans Shepard, "Social Stratification. Interview with Mrs. E. H. Wright" (1938), 7, Box 56, Folder 6, SCD.

24. "Idlewild, the Vacationers' Paradise," *Pittsburgh Courier*, June 29, 1940, p. 12. On Idlewild's advertising in this period, which was consistent with broader cultural trends, see also Stephens, *Idlewild*, 91–93; and Sutter, *Driven Wild*, 52.

25. "Idlewild—America's Distinctive National Resort," *Pittsburgh Courier*, June 15, 1940, p. 23. A resurgence of Woodland Park advertisements also emphasized the newly designated national forest. "Beautifully Wooded Lake Homesites," *Chicago Defender (National Edition)*, March 14, 1936, p. 4; and "Beautifully Wooded Lake Homesites," *Chicago Defender (National Edition)*, March 28, 1936, p. 4.

26. Stepto, *Blue as the Lake*, 201.

27. "Idlewild—America's Distinctive National Resort"; "Fisherman's Paradise," *Pittsburgh Courier*, May 11, 1940, p. 12.

28. "Idlewild: Keep Cool as a Penguin," *Pittsburgh Courier*, June 1, 1940, p. 12. For a representative sample of other ads run that summer, see "Idle Moments at Idlewild," *Pittsburgh Courier*, July 28, 1934, p. 1; "Full Speed Ahead for Vacation Days," *Pittsburgh Courier*, June 22, 1940, p. 12; and "Vacation Bound for America's Distinctive National Resort Idlewild," *Pittsburgh Courier*, July 6, 1940, p. 14.

29. Irene McCoy Gaines, "Idlewild Lot Owners Association: President's Annual Report" (1940), 2–3, Box 2, Folder 1, IMG.

30. "Success of 'Idlewild.' "

31. Susie J. Bantom, "Idlewild," *Lake County Star,* October 10, 1924, p. 4.

32. Susie J. Bantom, "Idlewild," *Lake County Star,* December 19, 1930, p. 4.

33. On these class tensions at Idlewild, see Walker and Wilson, *Black Eden,* 53–58; Stephens, *Idlewild,* 69, 88–94; and Jones, "The Making of a National Forest," 218–219. On similar class tensions at African American resorts in the South, see chapter 3 in Andrew Kahrl, *The Land Was Ours: African American Beaches from Jim Crow to the Sunbelt South* (Cambridge, MA: Harvard University Press, 2012). On Gaines, see Anne Meis Knupfer, *The Chicago Black Renaissance and Women's Activism* (Urbana: University of Illinois Press, 2006), 35, 94–95; and Stephens, *Idlewild,* 57–58. The desire to keep Idlewild "on a high plane"—and to cement that perception among local white communities—also helps explain why the local newspaper called the *Defender's* Bud Billiken Club "an organization of intellectual young men and women representing some of Chicago's finest families" when it bought land for a clubhouse, despite the fact that—as the annual parade and picnic revealed—the *Defender's* Billiken Club promoted middle-class values among all black Chicagoans. "Heard in Idlewild," *Lake County Star,* October 30, 1936, p. 2.

34. "Small Farms Woodland Park Acres," *Chicago Defender (National Edition),* September 30, 1922, p. 3; Hart, "A Rural Retreat," 159.

35. Hart, "A Rural Retreat," 159; Walker and Wilson, *Black Eden,* 53–58. These year-round settlements most closely approximate the working-class suburbs examined in Andrew Wiese, *Places of Their Own: African American Suburbanization in the Twentieth Century* (Chicago: University of Chicago Press, 2004).

36. Quoted in Hank DeZutter and Pamela Little DeZutter, "Black Eden," *Chicago Reader,* June 3, 1993. See also Jones, "The Making of a National Forest," 255; Wen, "Idlewild," 61; and Hart, "A Rural Retreat," 147, 163. On the "back to the land" movement in the Great Depression more generally, see chapter 5 in Dona Brown, *Back to the Land: The Enduring Dream of Self-Sufficiency in Modern America* (Madison: University of Wisconsin Press, 2011).

37. "Heard in Idlewild," *Lake County Star,* September 13, 1935, p. 2. See also "Heard in Idlewild," *Lake County Star,* August 20, 1937, p. 2.

38. Mumzie to Irene McCoy Gaines (May 25, 1935), Box 1, Folder 11, IMG. See also "Heard in Idlewild," *Lake County Star,* June 21, 1935, p. 3; "Heard in Idlewild," *Lake County Star,* August 16, 1935, p. 2; and Knupfer, *The Chicago Black Renaissance,* 94.

39. Mumzie to Irene McCoy Gaines (May 28, 1935), Box 1, Folder 11, IMG. On the longstanding tradition of gardening at Idlewild, see Walker and Wilson, *Black Eden,* 36–41; and Buckler, *Doctor Dan,* 259, 270.

40. Booker T. Washington, *Up from Slavery* (New York: Norton, [1901] 1996), 121. See also Booker T. Washington, *Working with the Hands: Being a Sequel*

to *"Up from Slavery,"* Covering the Author's Experiences in Industrial Training at *Tuskegee* (New York: Doubleday, Page & Company, 1904), 152–153. On the significance of Washington and gardening in the South, see Dianne D. Glave, "Rural African American Women, Gardening, and Progressive Reform in the South," in *To Love the Wind and the Rain: African Americans and Environmental History,* ed. Dianne D. Glave and Mark Stoll (Pittsburgh: University of Pittsburgh Press, 2006), 37–50; Kimberly K. Smith, *African American Environmental Thought: Foundations* (Lawrence: University Press of Kansas, 2007), 87–95; Scott Hicks, "W. E. B. Du Bois, Booker T. Washington, and Richard Wright: Toward an Ecocriticism of Color," *Callaloo* (Winter 2006), 202–222; and Kevin C. Armitage, *The Nature Study Movement: The Forgotten Popularizer of America's Conservation Ethic* (Lawrence: University Press of Kansas, 2009), 111–143.

41. Washington, *Up from Slavery,* 121.

42. "Report—Wabash" (1929), Box 6, Folder 65, YMCAW; "Report of the Executive Secretary to the Committee of Management" (1931), Box 6, Folder 65, YMCAW.

43. Frederic H. H. Robb, *The Negro in Chicago: 1779–1929, Vols. 1–2* (Chicago: Washington Intercollegiate Club; International Negro Student Alliance, 1929), 141.

44. "Camp Wabash" (1937), Box 8, Folder 93, YMCAW; "79 Girls Leave for Camp, Boys to Leave, July 27," *Chicago Defender (National Edition),* July 20, 1940, p. 16.

45. For reports on Camp Wabash's truck garden throughout the years, see Box 6, Folders 65–67, YMCAW; "79 Girls Leave for Camp." Camp Wabash's truck garden more closely approximated African Americans' working-class gardens than Idlewild's pleasure gardens. See Wiese, *Places of Their Own,* 77–88.

46. Chicago Council of Social Agencies, *Report of South Side Survey, April, 1931, Chicago, Illinois* (1931), 16, 26, Box 145, Folder 2, WC; Chicago Council of Social Agencies, *Classification of Chicago Social Agencies (Final Revision): Social Service Directory, 1930* (1930), Box 145, Folder 1, WC. On Camp Wabash's attendance and promotional campaigns, see "Wabash Y Camp Record Smashed," *Chicago Defender (National Edition),* September 6, 1930, p. 10; "'Y' Boys Go Camping," *Chicago Defender (National Edition),* August 29, 1931, p. 22; and "Camp Wabash," YMCAW.

47. "Report of Executive Secretary," YMCAW; "Report of the Women's Division to the Committee of Management" (1933), Box 6, Folder 66, YMCAW; "A Camp Benefit Tea" (1937), Box 8, Folder 94, YMCAW; "Glee Club on Vacation at Y Camp," *Chicago Defender (National Edition),* July 25, 1936, p. 7; "Chicagoan Drowns in Michigan," *Chicago Defender (National Edition),* July 11, 1931, p. 13; "To the Committee of Management," 2, YMCAW; and "Minutes of Meeting of the Board of Directors of Wabash Avenue Department YMCA" (1941), Box 6, Folder 67, YMCAW. Many of these girls

belonged to the Camp Fire Girls, a national organization that was growing in popularity on the South Side. See Marcia Chatelain, *South Side Girls: Growing Up in the Great Migration* (Durham, NC: Duke University Press, 2015), 130–142; "Campfire Girls," *Chicago Defender (National Edition),* March 30, 1935, p. 7; "Campfire Group Plans Its Fourth Annual Benefit," *Chicago Defender (National Edition),* March 30, 1935, p. 21; "Seen and Heard along the North Shore," *Chicago Defender (National Edition),* September 30, 1916, p. 11; "The Clotee Scott Settlement," *Chicago Defender (National Edition),* January 30, 1915, p. 3; and "CLUBS and SOCIETIES," *Chicago Defender (National Edition),* September 9, 1916, p. 5.

48. See Box 6, Folders 65–66, YMCAW; "Camp Wabash for Girls" (1938), Box 8, Folder 95, YMCAW; and "Three Smiling Winners," *Chicago Defender (National Edition),* August 18, 1934, p. 13.

49. See Box 6, Folders 65–66, YMCAW; Box 44, Folder 6, JR; "79 Girls Leave for Camp"; George Robert Arthur, *Life on the Negro Frontier: A Study of the Objectives and the Success of the Activities Promoted in the Young Men's Christian Associations Operating in "Rosenwald" Buildings* (New York: Association Press, 1934), 138.

50. Kathleen Allen, Director, Children's Clinic to Mr. Raymond S. Rubinow (August 25, 1930), Box 31, Folder 8, JR; "Report of Camp Wabash Season of 1932," YMCAW.

51. "Wire-Tappings," *Chicago Defender (National Edition),* July 30, 1932, p. 7.

52. George Arthur to Mr. N. W. Levin (July 20, 1935), Box 44, Folder 6, JR.

53. Chicago Council of Social Agencies, *Camps Operated by Social Service Agencies of the Chicago District 1929* (1929), 2, 15, Box 217a, Folder 1, WC; Chicago Camping Association, *1936 Camp Directory with Supplement* (1936), 10, Box 217a, Folder 1, WC; Chicago Council of Social Agencies, *Report of South Side Survey,* 26; Chicago Council of Social Agencies, *Classification of Chicago Social Agencies;* The Chicago Council Boy Scouts of America, "The March of Scouting: 1910–1935" (1935) Series I, Box 36, Folder 364, FPDCC; Chicago Council Boy Scouts of America, "Scouting Marches On!" (1936), Series I, Box 36, Folder 364, FPDCC; and "Scouts Enjoy Two Weeks of Camp Life," *Chicago Defender (National Edition),* September 20, 1930, p. 15. For statistics on the numbers of African American Boy and Girl Scouts, Sea Scouts, and Campfire Girls in the mid- to late 1930s, broken down by neighborhood, see Volume 4 of Chicago Recreation Commission et al., *The Chicago Recreation Survey, 1937* (Chicago, 1937).

54. Alfred C. Nichols Jr. to Mr. C. O. Sauers, Superintendent, Forest Preserves (October 19, 1931), Series I, Box 36, Folder 362, FPDCC.

55. Charles Davis and Clarice Durham, interviews with the author, January 20 and July 28, 2010. See also "Attendance Forest Preserves Camps" (1936), Series I, Box 36, Folder 364, FPDCC; "Recapitulation Attendance. Forest Preserves Camps" (1936), Series I, Box 36, Folder 364, FPDCC; and "Boy Scouts Launch City-Wide Campaign," *Chicago Defender (National Edition),*

March 30, 1935, p. 3. More broadly on class distinctions in camping groups, see David I. Macleod, *Building Character in the American Boy: The Boy Scouts, YMCA, and Their Forerunners, 1870–1920* (Madison: University of Wisconsin Press, 1983), 76.

56. "Report of Camp Wabash Season of 1932," YMCAW.

57. Southside Community Committee, *Won't You Send Her to Camp?* Box 98, Folder 3, CAP.

58. Iola Gaines, "Evaluation Report" (1945), 3, Box 98, Folder 3, CAP.

59. Forrester B. Washington, "Deluxe Summer Camp for Colored Children," *Opportunity: Journal of Negro Life* (October 1931), 303–307. Founded in 1931, the Detroit Urban League's Green Pastures Camp was quite similar to Camp Wabash. Although it is unclear exactly how much Green Pastures was influenced by Camp Wabash, the Detroit Urban League was certainly aware of the various Chicago camps, referring one inquiring correspondent to George Arthur and Camp Wabash. For more, see DUL, microfilm reels 4, 5, 6, and 24; Victoria W. Wolcott, *Remaking Respectability: African American Women in Interwar Detroit* (Chapel Hill: University of North Carolina Press, 2001), 222; and Arvarh E. Strickland, *History of the Chicago Urban League* (Urbana: University of Illinois Press, 1966), 30.

60. Quoted in DeZutter and DeZutter, "Black Eden"; Gaines, "Idlewild Lot Owners Association," 2. See also Ruth Evans Shepard, "Social Stratification. Interview with Mrs. Eliza Chilton Johnson" (1938), 4, Box 56, Folder 6, SCD; and "Minister's Wife Opens New Camp," *Chicago Defender (National Edition)*, July 6, 1935, p. 2.

61. "Lights and Shadows," *Chicago Defender (National Edition)*, September 24, 1938, p. 16.

62. Cora Watson et al., *Report of Value of City and Rural Beauty Conservation* (1930), Box 1, Folder 9, IMG.

63. "Advantages of Camping Are Cited," *Chicago Defender (National Edition)*, July 6, 1935, p. 10.

64. "Camp Wabash," YMCAW.

65. "Wire-Tappings."

66. Ibid. African Americans were not immune to the sorts of racial essentialism concerning Native Americans that was ingrained in YMCA and Boy Scout programs. Evidence is scant, but it appears that "playing Indian" did remain a facet of African American camping programs at least into the early 1930s, and one undated photo of Camp Wabash shows teepees at the campground. See photographs in Box 6, Folders 83, 89, and 91, YMCAW; "Report of Camp Wabash Season of 1932," YMCAW; and "Wire-Tappings." More broadly on "playing Indian," see Philip Joseph Deloria, *Playing Indian* (New Haven, CT: Yale University Press, 1998), 95–127; Leslie Paris, *Children's Nature: The Rise of the American Summer Camp* (New York: New York University Press, 2008), 191, 205–207; and Armitage, *The Nature Study Movement*, 72–87.

67. "Wire-Tappings."

68. Indeed, Dan Ryan Woods is about thirty blocks both south and west of where Davis and his family lived in 1935, at 57th Street and Michigan Avenue. Davis and Durham, interviews with the Author.

69. Sarah McGiffert, "Camp for Colored Children, Idlewild, Michigan" (1938), Box 1, Folder 12, IMG. See also Special, "Idlewild Summer Resort Closes its Best Season," *Chicago Defender (National Edition)*, September 3, 1938, p. 3; and "Billikens to Camp," *Chicago Defender (National Edition)*, July 29, 1939, p. 12.

70. South Side Community Committee, "Journal" (1942), 31, Box 98, Folder 1, CAP. See also Carl Davis, interview with the author, July 27, 2010.

71. Davis and Durham, interviews with the author. See also "Returns Home," *Chicago Defender (National Edition)*, September 12, 1936, p. 6.

72. Ben Gaines, interview with the author, July 27, 2010. Born in 1922, Gaines migrated to Chicago from rural Kentucky in 1945. By the time he served as counselor at Camp Wabash, it had been renamed Camp Arthur.

73. Timuel Black, interview with the author, July 27, 2010. Black was not completely sure that the camp he and his brother attended was Camp Wabash, but it seems highly unlikely it would have been a different camp given that he was certain it was an African American YMCA camp.

74. A. L. Foster, "Explains Origin of Social Service," *Chicago Defender (National Edition)*, May 4, 1935, p. 20; Chicago and Northern District Association of Colored Women, "Annual Report, 1937–1938" (1938), Box 1, Folder 12, IMG.

75. Chicago and Northern District Association of Colored Women, "Annual Report, 1937–1938." On the NACW's connection to environmental issues, see Elizabeth D. Blum, "Women, Environmental Rationale, and Activism during the Progressive Era," in *To Love the Wind and the Rain: African Americans and Environmental History*, ed. Dianne D. Glave and Mark Stoll (Pittsburgh: University of Pittsburgh Press, 2006), 77–92.

76. Dorothy K. Toms, "Minutes of Meeting of the Executive Committee" (1939), 5, Box 168, Folder 1, WC.

77. Ibid. On the array of camping opportunities, see "Minister's Wife Opens New Camp"; Hollis A. Woods, "Church Group Has Annual Winter Outing," *Chicago Defender (National Edition)*, March 23, 1940, p. 4; "Maywood, Ill.," *Chicago Defender (National Edition)*, July 6, 1935, p. 5; "Coleman's Camp to Hold Benefit Party April 18th," *Chicago Defender (National Edition)*, April 15, 1939, p. 16; "Camp Directory 1939" (1939), Box 217a, Folder 1, WC; Davis and Durham, interviews with the author; "Questionnaire about Interracial Practices in Y.W.C.A. Form A" (1943), Series I, Box 54, Folder 607, and YWCAM; Good Shepherd Community Center, "Summer Camp" (1938), 3, Box 98, Folder 1, CAP.

78. Julia P. Harvey, "Free and Low Fee Camping Services for the Chicago Area in 1940" (1941), Box 436, Folder 1, WC; "Memorandum to Present to Board

of Commissioners of Cook County in Regard Opening Camp Reinberg" (1945), Box 255, Folder 3, WC; Letter to Clayton F. Smith, President of Cook County Commissioners (February 4, 1944), Box 255, Folder 3, WC; "Report of the Executive Secretary to the Committee of Management—Wabash Avenue Department YMCA" (1930), Box 6, Folder 65, YMCAW; and Chicago Council of Social Agencies, "Preliminary Inquiry into Boys' Work in Chicago, Illinois" (1921), 24, Box 1, Folder 11, CBGC. On camping participation rates and turnover more generally, see Paris, *Children's Nature*, 62–63; and Macleod, *Building Character*, 278.

79. On race discrimination in New Deal agencies, see Mary Poole, *The Segregated Origins of Social Security: African Americans and the Welfare State* (Chapel Hill: University of North Carolina Press, 2006); Nancy J. Weiss, *Farewell to the Party of Lincoln: Black Politics in the Age of FDR* (Princeton, NJ: Princeton University Press, 1983); Harvard Sitkoff, *A New Deal for Blacks: The Emergence of Civil Rights as a National Issue: The Depression Decade* (New York: Oxford University Press, [1978] 2009); Nancy Grant, *TVA and Black Americans: Planning for the Status Quo* (Philadelphia: Temple University Press, 1990); Allen Francis Kifer, "The Negro under the New Deal, 1933–1941" (Ph.D. diss., University of Wisconsin–Madison, 1961); and John A. Salmond, *The Civilian Conservation Corps, 1933–1942: A New Deal Case Study* (Durham, NC: Duke University Press, 1967), 92–94.

80. Quote in A. L. Foster, "Memorandum to the Special Committee on Camp Reinberg of the Council of Social Agencies," Box 255, Folder 3, WC. Other YMCA branches with camping programs included Cincinnati, Columbus (OH), Dayton (OH), Harrisburg (PA), Indianapolis, Los Angeles, Montclair (NJ), Orange (NJ), and Pittsburgh. Arthur, *Life on the Negro Frontier*, 85, 259.

81. Foster, "Memorandum to the Special Committee."

82. "Special for Oak Leaves: The Story of Camp Algonquin" (1926), 2, Box 58, Folder 2, UCC; "A Summer at Camp Harlowarden" (1916), Box 59, Folder 2, UCC; "Glad Mothers and Babes Go to Algonquin," *Chicago Tribune,* June 22, 1917, p. 5. See also "10th Annual Report" (1926), 18, Series I, Box 1, Folder 6, CUL; "Algonquin Camp Filled to Limit after this Week," *Chicago Tribune*, July 6, 1915, p. 16; and "Camp Algonquin Faces Closure; Money Needed," *Chicago Tribune* July 29, 1917, p. A8. The rhetoric was characteristic of the way camp organizers often played on "primitive" Native American cultures in campgrounds. See Deloria, *Playing Indian,* 95–127; Paris, *Children's Nature*, 191, 205–207; and Armitage, *The Nature Study Movement,* 72–87.

83. "Needy Mothers, Children Get Trip to Farms," *Chicago Defender (National Edition)*, June 29, 1935, p. 4.

84. Stanley O'Carroll, "Report for the Summer Season of 1932. Camp Reinberg" (September 30, 1932), Series I, Box 17, Folder 169, FPDCC.

85. Quote in "Annual Report. Camp Reinberg. Palatine, Ill. Season of 1938" (1938), 2, Series V, Box 3, Folder 29, FPDCC; See also "Give Mothers and

Children Camp Outing," *The Chicago Defender (National Edition)*, July 14, 1934, p. 13; "Needy Mothers"; "Summer Outing Report 1938" (1938), Box 58, Folder 3, UCC; "Summary of Reports on Placements at Camp Algonquin and Harlowarden Year 1939" (1939), Box 58, Folder 3, UCC; "Summer Outing Report 1940" (1940), Box 58, Folder 3, UCC; "Revised Summer Outing Schedule Camp Algonquin—1936" (1936), Box 59, Folder 2, UCC; Elizabeth J. Mundie, "Minutes of the Meeting of the Conference Group on Camping for Negro girls" (1929), 1, Box 167, Folder 1, WC; Helen Lichtenfels, "Studies of Individual Camps" (1935), Box 59, Folder 2, UCC; O'Carroll, "Report for the Summer Season of 1932. Camp Reinberg"; Foster, "Explains Origin of Social Service"; "Special for Oak Leaves"; and "A Summer at Camp Harlowarden."

86. "Memorandum to Present to Board of Commissioners." See also Kathleen Allen, Director, Out-Patient Department to Mr. Raymond Rubinow (October 11, 1930), Box 31, Folder 8, JR.

87. "Camp Algonquin Summer 1929" (1929), 3, Box 59, Folder 3, UCC. See also "Comments and Suggestions regarding Camp Algonquin and Harlowarden" (October 6, 1939), Box 58, Folder 3, UCC. It also bears noting, however, that cultural and racial insensitivity was not exclusive to African Americans at Camp Algonquin. Another 1929 report noted, "The meat dish was often served on Friday and the Catholics, 85% of camp, refused to participate." "Notes regarding Camp Algonquin 1929" (1929), 2, Box 59, Folder 3, UCC.

88. "Mothers and Children off to Camp," *Chicago Defender (National Edition)*, July 30, 1932, p. 13.

89. "Camp Algonquin 1931" (1931), Box 58, Folder 3, UCC.

90. "Camp Algonquin: A Study by the Case Workers' Council of the United Charities of Chicago Presented May 4, 1937" (1937), 19, Box 58, Folder 3, UCC.

91. Ibid., 5.

92. Lea D. Taylor et al., "Report of the Special Committee of the Advisory Board, Cook County Bureau of Public Welfare, with Regard to Camp Reinberg" (November 27, 1934), Box 255, Folder 3, WC.

93. "Report from the Washington Park District Office, Cook County Bureau of Public Welfare, 3942 South Federal Street, Relative to Outings of its Clients at Camp Reinberg" (October 1, 1935), Box 255, Folder 3, WC. See also "Annual Report. Camp Reinberg. Palatine, Ill. Season of 1938," 2, FPDCC.

94. "Board of Directors" (February 8, 1923), Series I, Box 46, Folder 559, YWCAM.

95. Elsabelle Goss, "Compilation of Available Records Showing Inter-Racial Policies and Practices of the Chicago YWCA, 1927–1937" (February 25, 1938), Series I, Box 54, Folder 607, YWCAM.

96. Toms, "Minutes of Meeting of the Executive Committee," 4, WC.

97. "Metropolitan Board of Directors Executive Committee Meeting" (June 20, 1928), Series I, Box 47, Folder 564, YWCAM; "A Camp Experience in Interracial Living" (October 4, 1937), Series I, Box 54, Folder 607, YWCAM. Officials' actions were clearly informed by the conflict over interracial use of the YWCA pool on Chicago's West Side as it unfolded in the late 1920s and 1930s. See Series I, Box 49, Folder 573 and Box 54, Folder 607, YWCAM; Toms, "Minutes of Meeting of the Executive Committee," 3–4, WC; Mayor's Commission on Human Relations, "Recreation for All: A Manual for Supervisors and Workers in Recreation" (1946), 3–4, Box 171, Folder 5, WC.

98. "Board of Trustees Minutes" (January 25, 1934), Series I, Box 48, Folder 570, YWCAM; "A Camp Experience in Interracial Living," YWCAM; "President's Report to the Board of Trustees" (January 25, 1934), Series I, Box 48, Folder 570, YWCAM.

99. "A Camp Experience in Interracial Living," YWCAM.

100. "Girl Reserves of the YWCA: Then and Now" (1941), Series I, Box 6, Folder 76, YWCAM; "Index—Sagawau," Series I, Box 7, Folder 103, YWCAM.

101. "Index—Sagawau," YWCAM.

102. "Girl Reserves of the YWCA: Then and Now," YWCAM.

103. "Metropolitan Board of Directors" (May 22, 1936), Series I, Box 48, Folder 572, YWCAM. Camp Sagawau later expanded to more than twice that size. "Metropolitan Board of Directors" (May 24, 1935), Series I, Box 48, Folder 571, YWCAM; "Metropolitan Board of Directors" (January 24, 1936), Series I, Box 48, Folder 572, YWCAM; "A Camp Experience in Interracial Living," YWCAM.

104. As the same report put it, YWCA officials would pursue the "selection of Negroe [sic] campers at least for a while. This is to give white girls the opportunity to meet Negro girls with as good or better background than themselves." Ibid.

105. "Metropolitan Board of Directors" (May 22, 1936), YWCAM.

106. Goss, "Compilation of Available Records Showing Inter-Racial Policies," YWCAM; "A Camp Experience in Interracial Living," YWCAM.

107. "A Camp Experience in Interracial Living," YWCAM.

108. Goss, "Compilation of Available Records Showing Inter-Racial Policies," YWCAM.

109. "A Camp Experience in Interracial Living," YWCAM.

110. "Questionnaire about Interracial Practices in Y.W.C.A. Form B" (1943), Series I, Box 54, Folder 607, YWCAM; "Program Study Committee—Girl Reserve Department Presentation" (January 24, 1941), Series I, Box 49, Folder 577, YWCAM; "Questionnaire about Interracial Practices in Y.W.C.A. Form A," YWCAM. On the expansion of YWCA camping opportunities for South Side African American girls into the 1940s, see Knupfer, *The Chicago Black Renaissance*, 137–140.

111. Toms, "Minutes of Meeting of the Executive Committee," 3, YWCAM. See also Goss, "Compilation of Available Records Showing Inter-Racial Policies," YWCAM.

112. "Questionnaire about Interracial Practices in Y.W.C.A. Form B," YWCAM; "Camp Sagawau Open Soon to Girl Reserves," *Chicago Defender (National Edition)*, May 20, 1939, p. 17.

113. "Questionnaire about Interracial Practices in Y.W.C.A. Form B," YWCAM.

114. Du Bois, "Postscript," 182.

115. Cordella A. Winn, "Chicago—Interracial" (November 1937), Series I, Box 54, Folder 607, YWCAM.

116. Mayor's Commission on Human Relations, "Recreation for All," 6–7, WC.

117. "A Camp Experience in Interracial Living," YWCAM.

118. "Questionnaire about Interracial Practices in Y.W.C.A. Form B," YWCAM.

119. Barbara Abel to Mrs. Floy Steadry (July 20, 1937), Series I, Box 54, Folder 607, YWCAM.

120. "Index—Sagawau," YWCAM.

121. A. C. MacNeal to Mr. Charles G. Sauers, Gen'l. Supt. Forest Preserves (September 20, 1930), Series I, Box 8, Folder 68, FPDCC.

122. Charles G. Sauers to the Chicago Whip (September 23, 1930), Series I, Box 8, Folder 68, FPDCC.

123. A. L. Foster to Charles G. Sauers, General Superintendent, Forest Preserve District (July 29, 1933), Series I, Box 3, Folder 16, FPDCC.

124. A. L. Hornick to Charles C. Estes, Chief Construction Engineer, Forest Preserve District (July 15, 1937), Series I, Box 18, Folder 186, FPDCC. For more on how MacNeal effectively radicalized the NAACP in the 1930s following Herbert Turner's tenure, see Christopher Robert Reed, *The Depression Comes to the South Side: Protest and Politics in the Black Metropolis, 1930–1933* (Bloomington: Indiana University Press, 2011), 89–106.

125. Hornick to Charles C. Estes, FPDCC; Charles C. Estes to Mr. A. L. Hornick (July 19, 1937), Series I, Box 18, Folder 186, FPDCC.

126. Hornick to Charles C. Estes, FPDCC; Estes to Mr. A. L. Hornick, FPDCC.

127. "Game Warden Kills Woman," *Chicago Defender (National Edition)*, October 3, 1931, p. 1.

128. Foster to Charles G. Sauers, FPDCC; Charles G. Sauers to Chicago Urban League (August 5, 1933), Series I, Box 3, Folder 16, FPDCC.

129. Estes to Mr. A. L. Hornick, FPDCC.

130. Sauers to Chicago Urban League, FPDCC.

131. The area of the Cook County Forest Preserves continuously expanded over the course of its first two decades—from a modest beginning of 1,316 acres in 1916 they ballooned to 29,409 acres in 1925, expanding even further to 32,926 acres by 1937. Although citywide attendance figures were kept, there are no racial statistics for Forest Preserves visitors. See Volume 1 of Chicago Recreation Commission et al., *The Chicago Recreation Survey, 1937,* 163–166.

132. Robert S. Abbott to Mr. Charles G. Sauers, General Superintendent, Forest Preserve District (September 15, 1930), Series I, Box 1, Folder 1, FPDCC; MacNeal to Mr. Charles G. Sauers, FPDCC.

133. "Pollyanna Club Honors 300 at Annual Picnic," *Chicago Defender (National Edition)*, August 2, 1941, p. 18; "Climbers Club Gives Shower," *Chicago Defender (National Edition)*, August 7, 1937, p. 14; "Lovelies Enjoy Picnic in Forest Preserves," *Chicago Defender (National Edition)*, July 20, 1940, p. 4; "Singers Entertain Picnickers," *Chicago Defender (National Edition)*, June 28, 1941, p. 13; "Meharry Alumni and Auxiliary Sponsor Picnic," *Chicago Defender (National Edition)*, July 29, 1939, p. 18.

134. Quote in Ellis, Interview with the author. See also "Report of the Executive Secretary," 3, YMCAW; "Report of Executive Secretary," YMCAW; Davis and Durham, interviews with the author; Harry Keene, "Thousands Cheer Depriest at Big Republican Picnic," *Chicago Defender (National Edition)*, September 10, 1932, p. 3; "Ministers Plan Fete," *Chicago Defender (National Edition)*, July 13, 1935, p. 24; "President Speaks at Big Picnic," *Chicago Defender (National Edition)*, August 3, 1935, p. 24; "Newsies Follow through," *The Chicago Defender (National Edition)*, July 27, 1935, p. 2. On the industrial picnic in Hammond, which was first held in 1922 at the site of the YWCA's Camp Hammond, see chapter 2 and "Y.M.C.A. News," *Chicago Whip*, July 1, 1922, p. 5; "Y.M.C.A. News," *Chicago Whip*, July 8, 1922, p. 3; "Summer Musicales"; and Robb, *The Negro in Chicago*, 142.

5. Building Men and Building Trees

1. David L. Cohn, *God Shakes Creation* (New York: Harper & Brothers, 1935), 32–33.

2. United States Department of Labor. "A Chance to Work in the Forests: Questions and Answers for the Information of Men Offered the Opportunity to Apply for National Emergency Conservation Work. Bulletin Number 1" (April 17, 1933), microfilm reel 5, DUL. Each CCC company enrolled roughly 150 to 200 young men aged 17 to 28 (the eligible age range expanded from 18–23 in 1935 when the CCC itself expanded), except for the fraction of companies composed of World War I veterans who were older than the average CCC enrollee and hence even more likely to have been migrants with direct experience of the South beyond their early childhoods.

3. In this chapter, then, I answer environmental historian Richard White's call to examine humans' relationship with nature through work. See Richard White, "'Are You an Environmentalist or Do You Work for a Living?': Work and Nature," in *Uncommon Ground: Toward Reinventing Nature*, ed. William Cronon (New York: W. W. Norton & Co., 1995), 171–185; and Richard White, *The Organic Machine* (New York: Hill and Wang, 1995). Of all the landscapes in this book, the ones in this chapter most closely

resemble what environmental historian Thomas Andrews has called "workscapes," which refers to places "shaped by the interplay of human labor and natural processes"; it is a term that he believes "treats people as laboring beings who have changed and been changed in turn by a natural world that remains always under construction." Thomas G. Andrews, *Killing for Coal: America's Deadliest Labor War* (Cambridge, MA: Harvard University Press, 2008), 125.

4. Civilian Conservation Corps (U.S.) and Edgar G. Brown, *The Civilian Conservation Corps and Colored Youth* (Washington, DC: Office of the Director, 1939); Neil M. Maher, *Nature's New Deal: The Civilian Conservation Corps and the Roots of the American Environmental Movement* (New York: Oxford University Press, 2008), 3; Allen Francis Kifer, "The Negro under the New Deal, 1933–1941" (Ph.D. diss., University of Wisconsin–Madison), 56–64. On African American population figures and CCC enrollment rates (and racial quotas that resulted in an underrepresentation of African Americans in the South), see United States Bureau of the Census, *(Sixteenth) Census of the United States: 1940. Population, Volume II: Characteristics of the Population* (Washington, DC: U.S. Government Printing Office, 1943), 22, 479, 509; St. Clair Drake and Horace Cayton, *Black Metropolis: A Study of Negro Life in a Northern City* (Chicago: University of Chicago Press, [1945] 1993), 8–9, 99; Harold Foote Gosnell, *Negro Politicians: The Rise of Negro Politics in Chicago* (Chicago: University of Chicago Press, 1967), 18; James N. Gregory, *The Southern Diaspora: How the Great Migrations of Black and White Southerners Transformed America* (Chapel Hill: University of North Carolina Press, 2005), 26; Box 3, "Summary of Statistical Data," Statistical Reports on Enrollees, 1933–1942, RG 35, NACP; "Where Do You Live?," *Trojan*, August 1939, p. 10; "New Rookies—from Cass and Kent County," *Trojan*, October 9, 1936, p. 5; "New Rookies," *Trojan*, February 6, 1936, p. 3; Box 2, Folder A1 "Consolidated Reports on All Enrollment Periods (Beginning April 1935)," Statistical Reports on Enrollees, 1933–1942, RG 35, NACP; Box 2, Folder A3 "Quarterly Reports Fiscal Year 1938. Fiscal Year Report 1937," Statistical Reports on Enrollees, 1933–1942, RG35, NACP; "Camp Inspection Report" (May 9, 1939), Box 61, Folder Illinois SCS-7 Stockton Co. 610, Camp Inspection Reports, 1933–1942, RG 35, NACP; Harold G. Chafey, "Camp Inspection Report" (May 15–18, 1940), Box 58, Folder Illinois CP-3 Winnetka formerly SP-16, Camp Inspection Reports, 1933–1942, RG 35, NACP; Harold G. Chafey to Mr. J. J. McEntee, Director, CCC (December 23, 1940), 1, Box 62, Folder Illinois SCS-15 Carroll Co., Camp Inspection Reports, 1933–1942, RG 35, NACP; Harold G. Chafey, "Camp Inspection Report" (December 6, 1940), Box 61, Folder Illinois SCS-12 Mercer Co., Camp Inspection Reports, 1933–1942, RG 35, NACP; Gunnar Myrdal, *An American Dilemma: The Negro Problem and Modern Democracy* (New York: Harper & Brothers, 1944), 362; Harvard Sitkoff, *A New Deal for Blacks: The Emergence of Civil Rights as a National Issue: The Depression Decade* (New York: Oxford University Press, [1978] 2009), 39, 56; Kifer, "The Negro

under the New Deal," 22, 30–31, 67; John A. Salmond, *The Civilian Conservation Corps, 1933–1942: A New Deal Case Study* (Durham, NC: Duke University Press, 1967), 94, 99; George Philip Rawick, "The New Deal and Youth: The Civilian Conservation Corps, the National Youth Administration, and the American Youth Congress" (Ph.D. diss., University of Wisconsin–Madison, 1957), 140–143; and Richard Sterner, *The Negro's Share: A Study of Income, Consumption, Housing and Public Assistance* (New York: Harper & Brothers, 1943), 254–261. For studies on African Americans in the CCC outside the Midwest (of which there are few), see also Olen Cole, *The African-American Experience in the Civilian Conservation Corps* (Gainesville: University Press of Florida, 1999); and Michael Shane Hoak, "Men in Green: African Americans and the Civilian Conservation Corps, 1933–42" (master's thesis, William & Mary College, 2002).

5. On the working-class status of African American enrollees and CCC wages, see Helen Mabel Walker, *The CCC through the Eyes of 272 Boys: A Summary of a Group Study of the Reactions of 272 Cleveland Boys to their Experience in the Civilian Conservation Corps* (Cleveland: Western Reserve University Press, 1938), 13–14; Sam Davis, "Editorial," *Camp Carroll Volcano*, June 21, 1936, p. 2; and Brown, *The Civilian Conservation Corps and Colored Youth*, 5.

6. Washington complicates the more exclusively agrarian connotations of his exhortation by going on to say, "Up through commerce, education, and religion!" but his emphasis remains on labor in the natural environment. Booker T. Washington, *Working with the Hands; Being a Sequel to "Up from Slavery," Covering the Author's Experiences in Industrial Training at Tuskegee* (New York: Doubleday, Page & Company, 1904), 29. For a similar argument about "collective memory" in reference to African Americans' labor in the South's turpentine forests, see Cassandra Y. Johnson and Josh McDaniel, "Turpentine Negro," in *To Love the Wind and the Rain: African Americans and Environmental History*, ed. Dianne D. Glave and Mark Stoll (Pittsburgh: University of Pittsburgh Press, 2006), 51–62.

7. David Cade, "Social Stratification. Interview with Mrs. Bernice Ward" (April 20, 1938), 3, Box 56, Folder 6, SCD.

8. On the New Deal and race more generally, see Nancy J. Weiss, *Farewell to the Party of Lincoln: Black Politics in the Age of FDR* (Princeton, NJ: Princeton University Press, 1983); Ira Katznelson, *When Affirmative Action Was White: An Untold History of Racial Inequality in Twentieth-Century America* (New York: W. W. Norton, 2005); Mary Poole, *The Segregated Origins of Social Security: African Americans and the Welfare State* (Chapel Hill: University of North Carolina Press, 2006); and Sitkoff, *A New Deal for Blacks*. On environmental labor in the South, see (among many others), Mikko Saikku, *This Delta, this Land: An Environmental History of the Yazoo-Mississippi Floodplain* (Athens: University of Georgia Press, 2005); and Dianne D. Glave and Mark Stoll, eds., *To Love the Wind and the Rain: African Americans and Environmental History* (Pittsburgh: University of Pittsburgh Press, 2006).

9. United States Department of Labor, "A Chance to Work in the Forests," DUL. See also John Dancy to Spellman Lowe, CCC Company #670 (November 22, 1933), microfilm reel 5, DUL; M. O. Bousfield to John Dancy, Detroit Urban League (November 8, 1935), microfilm reel 7, DUL; Detroit Urban League, "Selectee's Enrolled in the C.C.C. from Urban League, April 1935," microfilm reel 7, DUL; and Kifer, "The Negro under the New Deal," 56–57.

10. Franklin D. Roosevelt, "Three Essentials for Unemployment Relief, March 21, 1933," in *The Public Papers and Addresses of Franklin D. Roosevelt*, ed. Samuel Irving Rosenman (New York: Random House, 1938), 81. On industrialization, unemployment, and the perceived moral perils of "spare time," see Chicago Recreation Commission et al., *Volume 5: The Chicago Recreation Survey, 1937* (Chicago, 1937), 44; and Susan Currell, *The March of Spare Time: The Problem and Promise of Leisure in the Great Depression* (Philadelphia: University of Pennsylvania Press, 2005), 19.

11. Franklin D. Roosevelt, "A Radio Address on the Third Anniversary of CCC, April 17, 1936," in *The Public Papers and Addresses of Franklin D. Roosevelt*, 171. For anecdotal evidence supporting FDR's claims of improved morale and health, see Spellman Lowe to John Dancy, Detroit Urban League (April 21, 1933), microfilm reel 5, DUL; Willie Wilkinson, 674 Co. Camp Pines, Grayling, Michigan to John Dancy, Detroit Urban League (February 20, 1935), microfilm reel 6, DUL. The CCC reshaped 118 million acres, including planting two billion trees and undertaking soil erosion projects on 40 million acres. Maher, *Nature's New Deal*, 3, 44.

12. On the ideological roots of the CCC and its influence (as well as other New Deal programs) on America's rural environment, see in particular Maher, *Nature's New Deal*; and Sarah T. Phillips, *This Land, this Nation: Conservation, Rural America, and the New Deal* (New York: Cambridge University Press, 2007).

13. Franklin D. Roosevelt, "Greetings to the Civilian Conservation Corps, July 8, 1933," in *The Public Papers and Addresses of Franklin D. Roosevelt*, 271.

14. "Welcome to Camp Aledo," *Camp Aledo Speaks*, January 1940, p. 1.

15. Chicago Commission on Race Relations, *The Negro in Chicago: A Study of Race Relations and a Race Riot* (Chicago: University of Chicago Press, 1922), 357; Walter A. Fogel and Wharton School Industrial Research Unit, *The Negro in the Meat Industry* (Philadelphia: University of Pennsylvania Press, 1970), 46, 51; Gregory, *The Southern Diaspora*, 22; James R. Grossman, *Land of Hope: Chicago, Black Southerners, and the Great Migration* (Chicago: University of Chicago Press, 1989), 181; and Peter Gottlieb, *Making Their Own Way: Southern Blacks' Migration to Pittsburgh, 1916–30* (Urbana: University of Illinois Press, 1987), 22–32.

16. Perhaps even more suggestively, the study contended that even if a family's primary home was in town, there was "probably no lower- or middle-class Negro family [in Indianola, Mississippi] of which some member has not at

some time made a crop. It is the accepted thing in these classes either to depend on farm work for the chief source of income, or else to eke out their livelihood by part-time work on a plantation." Hortense Powdermaker, *After Freedom: A Cultural Study in the Deep South* (New York: Viking Press, 1939), 113–114.

17. Drake and Cayton, *Black Metropolis,* 523. On manual labor and mechanization in Chicago's stockyards, see chapter 1 in James R. Barrett, *Work and Community in the Jungle: Chicago's Packinghouse Workers, 1894–1922* (Urbana: University of Illinois Press, 1987); and chapter 1 in Rick Halpern, *Down on the Killing Floor: Black and White Workers in Chicago's Packinghouses, 1904–1954* (Urbana: University of Illinois Press, 1997).

18. On migrants' evolving labor practices, see chapter 7 in Grossman, *Land of Hope.*

19. "The CCC Looks Back upon Six Years of Continuous Progress," *Chicago Defender (National Edition),* April 8, 1939, p. 6.

20. George S. Witherspoon, "Editorial," *Legionnaire Times,* March 1941. Given that this particular company was composed of World War I veterans roughly a generation older than the average "junior" enrollee, they were all the more likely to have migrated from the South as adults. Perhaps, then, they were even more apt to understand just how closely CCC labor resembled the sorts of manual labor on the land still so common across the South that had inspired the views of the long-dead Booker T. Washington.

21. "Forestry News: Moss Procurement," *Trojan,* April 15, 1939, p. 9.

22. John G. Sutton, "First Anniversary CCC Drainage Camps," *Gilman Gabber,* July 31, 1936.

23. "They 'Took' It," *Keyhole,* January 20, 1937, p. 4. See also "Factories Taking Enrollees away from Camps," *Trojan,* December 1939, p. 7.

24. Sutton, "First Anniversary."

25. Only 800 of 250,000 African American enrollees, for instance, received "business training in the capacity of store clerks and managers of the Post-Exchanges," and there had been only 147 African American educational advisors, 25 doctors and chaplains, four engineers, two commanding officers, and one historian. Brown, *The Civilian Conservation Corps and Colored Youth,* 4.

26. "CCC after 7 Years," *Chicago Defender (National Edition),* April 6, 1940, p. 13.

27. Roy S. Corey, "Narrative Report for the Month of August, of the Work Accomplished by S. P. 16 (Company 699)" (August 1934), Box 27 SP13-SP16, Folder Skokie Lagoons State Park, Illinois. SP 16, Project Reports on Civilian Conservation Corps Projects in State and Local Parks, 1933–1937, RG 79, NACP.

28. Nathaniel Carr, "My First Day on the Work Project," *Trojan* (August 1940), p. 6–10. See also Spellman Lowe to John Dancy, DUL; and Albert Shelton to John Dancy, Detroit Urban League (May 3, 1934), microfilm reel 6, DUL. On enrollees' workday schedules and classes, see "How the Enrollee Spends

His Time," *Trojan,* September 1939, p. 7–8; "CCC after 7 Years"; and Walker, *The CCC through the Eyes of 272 Boys,* 39.

29. Arthur Saunders, "The C.C.C. Blues," *Keyhole,* December 19, 1935, p. 2.

30. "Birth of Camp Aledo," *Keyhole,* November 28, 1935, p. 1. See also "History of Co. 2694," *Trojan,* December 1939, p. 8. On CCC companies' frequent moves, see "Camp Deer Grove Scene of Many Achievements in Last Two Years," *Deer Grove Ledger,* November 15, 1936, p. 1; "Camps Merge," *Gilman Gabber,* July 31, 1936; Frank Jackson, "Skokie Reunion," *Keyhole,* May 25, 1936, p. 2; "Camp Aledo Progresses Rapidly," *Keyhole,* August 19, 1936, p. 1; "Organization," *Camp Carroll Volcano,* June 7, 1937, p. 1.

31. Earl Icke, "Ye Ole Tymers," *Camp Carroll Volcano,* June 21, 1936, p. 1. See also "Organization," 1.

32. Earl C. Smith, "Accent on Accomplishment," *Camp Carroll Volcano,* August 7 1936, p. 3.

33. Icke, "Ye Ole Tymers"; "History of Co. 2694"; "Birth of Camp Aledo"; "First Year Ends at Camp Aledo," *Keyhole,* August 3, 1936, p. 1.

34. On the CCC's racial policies, see Maher, *Nature's New Deal,* 154; Hoak, "Men in Green," 11; Kifer, "The Negro under the New Deal," 21; Rawick, "The New Deal and Youth," 137–142; Cole, *The African-American Experience,* 26; and Albert W. Jernberg and Marya Tze Caraman, *My Brush Monkeys: A Narrative of the CCC* (New York: R. R. Smith, 1941), 78–80. On sundown towns, see James W. Loewen, *Sundown Towns: A Hidden Dimension of American Racism* (New York: W. W. Norton, 2005).

35. Quoted in Hoak, "Men in Green," 17.

36. "Drop Plan for Race CCC Camp Downstate," *Chicago Defender (National Edition),* July 10, 1937, p. 8. On similar white resistance motivated by racial fear (there is no evidence that African American enrollees exhibited violent or even inappropriate behavior in higher proportion than white enrollees) in the Midwest and beyond, see Rawick, "The New Deal and Youth," 148; Joseph M. Speakman, *At Work in Penn's Woods: The Civilian Conservation Corps in Pennsylvania* (University Park: Pennsylvania State University Press, 2006), 145–148; Kifer, "The Negro under the New Deal," 26; and Salmond, *The Civilian Conservation Corps,* 92.

37. "175 Negroes in First Forest Camp," *Lake County Star,* June 30, 1933. On this practice more broadly, see also Kifer, "The Negro under the New Deal," 31; Speakman, *At Work in Penn's Woods,* 135; Rawick, "The New Deal and Youth," 143–158; "Charge Jim Crow Plot in Ind. CCC," *Chicago Defender (National Edition),* December 11, 1937, p. 7.

38. "Relationship with the Civilian Population," *Gilman Gabber,* October 3, 1936.

39. "Fear Clash of Races in CCC Camp Protest," *Chicago Defender (National Edition),* January 21, 1939, p. 3.

40. Joseph Louer to Mr. Charles G. Sauers, Superintendent Forest Preserve District of Cook County (November 2, 1934), Series I, Box 23, Folder 238,

FPDCC; Charles G. Sauers to Joseph Louer (November 13, 1934), Series I, Box 23, Folder 238, FPDCC.

41. Chafey to Mr. J. J. McEntee, RG 35, NACP.

42. March 1937, Box 64, folder Illinois SCS-47 Annawan formerly D-6, Camp Inspection Reports, 1933–1942, RG 35, NACP.

43. "History of Co. 2694."

44. "CCC Enrollees Will Entertain Staff Officers," *Chicago Defender (National Edition)*, September 1, 1935, p. 4. See also "Social News: Departings"; Russell A. Sharpe, "Our Trip to Camp Bitely," *Trojan*, September 15, 1938; "CCC Doings," *Chicago Defender (National Edition)*, June 6, 1936, p. 4; "C.C.C. Celebration Is Set for Sunday," *Chicago Defender (National Edition)*, April 3, 1937, p. 3; "Largest CCC Camp Plans Celebration," *Chicago Defender (National Edition)*, April 2, 1938, p. 10; "Veteran CCC Company at Gilman, Ill.," *Chicago Defender (National Edition)*, October 12, 1935, p. 3; "Edgar G. Brown Pilot of CCC Stops in City," *Chicago Defender (National Edition)*, April 11, 1936, p. 3.

45. "699th Company CCC. Camp Skokie Valley. Glenview, Illinois. Subject: Inspection, 699Th Co., CCC, Camp Skokie Valley, SP-16(ILL), Glenview, Illinois" (February 4, 1937), Box 58, folder Illinois CP-3 Winnetka formerly SP-16, Camp Inspection Reports, 1933–1942, RG 35, NACP; "Supplementary Report. Company 2675, Camp P-85 (Ill.) Manito, Illinois" (March 9, 1939), Box 61, folder Illinois P-85 Pekin, Camp Inspection Reports, 1933–1942, RG 35, NACP; Harold G. Chafey, "Camp Inspection Report" (April 5, 1939), Box 61, Folder Illinois SCS-9, Camp Inspection Reports, 1933–1942, RG 35, NACP; William P. Hannon, "Camp Report" (December 13, 1935), Box 61, Folder Illinois SCS-12 Mercer Co., Camp Inspection Reports, 1933–1942, RG 35, NACP.

46. Corey, "Narrative Report for the Month of August," RG 79, NACP; "Ice Cream Tickets Ready on July 5," *Chicago Defender (National Edition)*, June 21, 1941, p. 19.

47. Earl C. Smith, "From E. C. Smith's Diary," *Camp Carroll Volcano*, August 21, 1936.

48. "Boxing Show," *Trojan*, December 1939, p. 9, 16, 18; "Enrollees Spend Holidays in Idlewild: Visit Friends at Camp Bitely CCC," *Trojan*, July 15, 1939, p. 6. See also Leroy Poorman, "Barrack 'C'," *Trojan*, October 9, 1936, p. 3; Alfred Gay, "Social News: 81 Enrollees Go on Leave," *Trojan*, January 15, 1939, p. 7; and "Society," *Trojan*, October 9, 1936, p. 4.

49. "Society"; "Social News: Departings," *Trojan*, March 27, 1937, p. 3; "Social News of Camp Walkerville," *Trojan*, February 6, 1937, p. 6; Ronald J. Stephens, *Idlewild: The Black Eden of Michigan* (Chicago: Arcadia Publishing, 2001), 62; Ronald J. Stephens, *Idlewild: The Rise, Decline, and Rebirth of a Unique African American Resort Town* (Ann Arbor: University of Michigan Press, 2013), 72–76.

50. "News Releases," *Trojan*, March–April–May, 1940, p. 11. On CCC sports, which could inspire more cordial relations with nearby white towns, see

"History of Co. 2694"; Lowe to John Dancy, DUL; Joseph W. Johnson, "Deer Grove Winner of Field Meet Trophy," *Deer Grove Ledger,* October 1, 1936, p. 1; John W. Webster, "Aledo—Here We Come," *Camp Carroll Volcano,* August 21, 1936, p. 2; "Camp Aledo's Championship Softball Team," *Keyhole,* September 23, 1936, p. 1; "Boxing Show"; and Brown, *The Civilian Conservation Corps and Colored Youth,* 5. For a much more thorough discussion of the role of sporting culture in discourses of race and manhood in Chicago, see chapter 6 in Davarian L. Baldwin, *Chicago's New Negroes: Modernity, the Great Migration, & Black Urban Life* (Chapel Hill: University of North Carolina Press, 2007).

51. Writers' Program of the Work Projects Administration in the State of Illinois, *Cavalcade of the American Negro* (Chicago: Diamond Jubilee Exposition Authority, 1940), 93. For the CCC, sports were also a type of welfare capitalism intended to keep workers happy. See chapter 4 in Lizabeth Cohen, *Making a New Deal: Industrial Workers in Chicago, 1919–1939* (New York: Cambridge University Press, [1990] 2008). On leisure time in the WPA, see Currell, *The March of Spare Time,* 49–51.

52. Curdo Williams, "Unit News: Unit F," *Keyhole,* May 19, 1937, p. 3.

53. "They 'Took' It," *Keyhole,* December 23, 1936, p. 5. See also "Ex-CCC Enrollees to Join in Forming Chicago Club," *Keyhole,* April 14, 1937, p. 1.

54. Theodore J. Bell, "Dame Nature and Us," *Trojan,* October 9, 1936, p. 8.

55. Report after report noted that Chicago was the primary market for the commodities raised on Illinois farmland. See, for instance, George T. Latimer, "Completion Report A-13-Ma," Box 2. Illinois. Camp D-2—Gilman, Drainage Project Initial and Completion Reports, 1936–1938, RG 114, NACP. On northern Michigan's forests, see chapter 4 in William Cronon, *Nature's Metropolis: Chicago and the Great West* (New York: W. W. Norton, 1992); and Joseph John Jones, "The Making of a National Forest: The Contest over the West Michigan Cutover, 1888–1943" (Ph.D. diss., Michigan State University, 2007). On African American work in forests in the South, see Johnson and McDaniel, "Turpentine Negro," 51–62.

56. Clarence Collins, "Back to Nature," *Gilman Gabber,* July 31, 1936.

57. Forest Preserve District of Cook County, "Skokie Lagoons," Series V, Box 19, Folder 289, FPDCC.

58. A. E. Rose, "One Year's Progress," *Camp Carroll Volcano,* August 7, 1936, p. 3.

59. "Forestry News," *The Trojan,* June 15, 1939, p. 9.

60. On African American enrollment in Skokie Lagoons companies and Harold Ickes's instrumental role in the project, see Boxes 2 and 3, Station and Strength Reports, 1933–1942, RG 35, NACP; "Largest CCC Camp Plans Celebration"; and Phoebe Cutler, *The Public Landscape of the New Deal* (New Haven, CT: Yale University Press, 1985), 58.

61. Forest Preserve District of Cook County, "Skokie Lagoons," FPDCC.

62. Forest Preserve District of Cook County, Engineering Dept., "The Skokie Development," Series V, Box 19, Folder 289, FPDCC. On the project's rela-

tive success in meeting these objectives, see Forest Preserve District of Cook County, "Skokie Lagoons," FPDCC.

63. Forest Preserve District of Cook County, "Skokie Lagoons," FPDCC. On broader aesthetic trends with respect to nature, see Paul Sutter, *Driven Wild: How the Fight against Automobiles Launched the Modern Wilderness Movement* (Seattle: University of Washington Press, 2002).

64. Forest Preserve District of Cook County, Engineering Dept., "The Skokie Development," FPDCC.

65. Roy S. Corey, "Narrative Report of S.P. 16 (Company 699 and Company 2667, Colored) for the Months of August and September, 1935," Box 27 SP 13-SP16, Folder Skokie Lagoons State Park, Illinois. SP 16, Project Reports on Civilian Conservation Corps Projects in State and Local Parks, 1933–1937, RG 79, NACP.

66. On African American companies' work of excavating channels and constructing dikes, see F. E. Wilson, "Narrative Report for the Month of January of the Work Accomplished by S.P. 16 (Company 610, Colored)" (January 1935), Box 27 SP 13-SP16, Folder Skokie Lagoons State Park, Illinois. SP 16, Project Reports on Civilian Conservation Corps Projects in State and Local Parks, 1933–1937, RG 79, NACP; Roy S. Corey, "Narrative Report of CCC Accomplishments (Camp S.P. 16, Company 699)" (March 31, 1936), Box 27 SP 13-SP16, Folder Skokie Lagoons State Park, Illinois. SP 16, Project Reports on Civilian Conservation Corps Projects in State and Local Parks, 1933–1937, RG 79, NACP; Boxes 1–10, Station and Strength Reports, 1933–1942, RG 35, NACP; W. J. Swisher, "Narrative Report for the Month of September of the Work Accomplished by S.P. 27 (Company 609, Colored)" (September 1934), Box 29 SP 24-SP29, Folder Skokie Lagoons State Park Report for SP-27—Illinois. Winnetka, Illinois, Project Reports on Civilian Conservation Corps Projects in State and Local Parks, 1933–1937, RG 79, NACP; and W. J. Swisher, "Narrative Report for the Month of April, 1935 of the Work Accomplished by S.P. 27 (Company 609, Colored)," Box 25 SP 12-SP16, SP 25-SP29, Folder Department of the Interior, National Park Service, State Park Conservation Work, Skokie Lagoons State Park, Project Reports on Civilian Conservation Corps Projects in State and Local Parks, 1933–1937, RG 79, NACP.

67. "How the Enrollee Spends His Time."

68. Quote in "CCC Camp Work Program Explained," *Legionnaire Times,* March 1941. See also Frank H. Nelson, "Deer Grove State Park #38, Company 605, C.C.C., Palatine, Cook County, Ill." (March 31, 1936), Box 35 SP 38, Folder Deer Grove State Park. Camp 36. Palatine, Illinois, Project Reports on Civilian Conservation Corps Projects in State and Local Parks, 1933–1937, RG 79, NACP; "1936 Marches On: 14 Things to Remember," *Deer Grove Ledger,* November 29, 1936, p. 2.

69. Eugene W. McGaan, "A Slant on Soil Conservation," *Gilman Gabber,* February 27, 1937. See also "Initial Report, Project A-7, Camp D-6, Ill." (January 15, 1937), Box 6. Illinois. Camp D-6—Annawan, Drainage Project

Initial and Completion Reports, 1936–1938, RG 114, NACP. On drainage projects nationwide, see Sutton, "First Anniversary."

70. Sutton, "First Anniversary." See also George T. Latimer, "Final Reports, Project A-16-F-b, Spring Creek Drainage Dist., Iroquois County, Illinois" (January 17, 1937), Box 2. Illinois. Camp D-2—Gilman, Drainage Project Initial and Completion Reports, 1936–1938, RG 114, NACP; and George T. Latimer, "Completion Report, Project A-17-P-a" (July 22, 1936), Box 2. Illinois. Camp D-2—Gilman, Drainage Project Initial and Completion Reports, 1936–1938, RG 114, NACP.

71. "Special Report for Mr. William P. Hannon" (March 30, 1937), Box 61, Folder Illinois SCS-7 Stockton Co. 610, Camp Inspection Reports, 1933–1942, RG 35, NACP. See also "S.C.S. News," *Keyhole*, August 3, 1936, p. 5.

72. George T. Latimer, "Completion Report for Project no. A-12-La," Box 2 Illinois. Camp D-2—Gilman, Drainage Project Initial and Completion Reports, 1936–1938, RG 114, NACP; Walker, *The CCC through the Eyes of 272 Boys*, 32; "Initial Report, Project A-7, Camp D-6, Ill.," RG 114, NACP; W. A. Keene, "Initial Report, Project A-8, Camp D-6-Ill" (October 23, 1936), Box 6. Illinois. Camp D-6—Annawan, Drainage Project Initial and Completion Reports, 1936–1938, RG 114, NACP; "Drainage Camps Embark on Hydraulic Research Program," *Gilman Gabber*, October 31, 1936. On the modernizing but fairly static nature of Southern farming methods (the mechanical cotton picker did not revolutionize the industry until after World War II, for example, and mules were still in widespread use even as tractors proliferated), see chapters 5 and 8 in James C. Cobb, *The Most Southern Place on Earth: The Mississippi Delta and the Roots of Regional Identity* (New York: Oxford University Press, 1992); Charles Spurgeon Johnson, *Shadow of the Plantation* (Chicago: University of Chicago Press, 1934), 23; chapter 6 in Powdermaker, *After Freedom;* and Nate Shaw and Theodore Rosengarten, *All God's Dangers: The Life of Nate Shaw* (New York: Random House, 1974), 177–187, 462–466.

73. George T. Latimer, "Completion Report, Project C-6-Fa" (March 23, 1936), Box 2. Illinois. Camp D-2—Gilman, Drainage Project Initial and Completion Reports, 1936–1938, RG 114, NACP.

74. "Unit News," *Keyhole*, January 20, 1937, p. 6; "Unit News," *Keyhole*, February 24, 1937, p. 3; "Unit News," *Keyhole*, April 14, 1937, p. 6.

75. These estimates were based on Sam Cline, "Work Program CCC 13th and 14th Periods," *Trojan*, April 15, 1939, p. 10; Alfred Gay, "Planting Season Underway," *Trojan*, October 15, 1938; Lowe to John Dancy, DUL; "Deer Season Opens," *Trojan*, November 15, 1938; "News Releases," *Trojan*, November 1939, p. 11; "How the Enrollee Spends His Time"; "Enrollees Collect Forest Tree Seed," *Trojan*, October–November 1940, p. 11; "Forestry News: Farm Woodlot Demonstration Cutting," *Trojan*, April 15, 1939, p. 9; "Planting Season Opens," *Trojan*, September 1939, p. 14; and "Forestry News: Planting," *Trojan*, May 15, 1938.

76. W. A. Keene, "Drainage Camp D-6-Ill., Completion Report on Project A-42" (September 13, 1937), Box 6. Illinois. Camp D-6—Annawan, Drainage Project Initial and Completion Reports, 1936–1938, RG 114, NACP. See also "Initial Report, Project A-7, Camp D-6, Ill.," RG 114, NACP; Silas Hoagland to Mr. John G. Sutton, District Engineer (March 26, 1936), Box 2. Illinois. Camp D-2—Gilman, Drainage Project Initial and Completion Reports, 1936–1938, RG 114, NACP; Latimer, "Completion Report, Project A-17-P-a," RG 114, NACP. To elaborate on just one striking example: in approximately two and a half years of operation, the estimated "commercial value" of the work accomplished by a single African American drainage company in a single Illinois county—where nearly 90 percent of cropland relied on artificial drainage—was $775,000 in 1930s dollars (nearly $12 million in 2011 dollars). By April 1938, African American enrollees in that company had already excavated nearly two million cubic yards of soil, cleared more than 5.5 million square yards of brush and trees, and laid 43,000 feet of tile lines. After that assessment, the company operated another four full years—until the CCC itself ceased operations in 1942. George T. Latimer, "Bureau of Agricultural Engineering News," *Gilman Gabber*, April 26, 1938.

77. On the longevity of this work, see, for example Latimer, "Final Reports, Project A-16-F-b, Spring Creek Drainage Dist., Iroquois County, Illinois," RG 114, NACP; and George T. Latimer, "Completion Report, Joe Benes Drainage Dist.—Projects A-65-WW-a and Sup #1 A-65-WW-a Tile Relay" (January 16, 1937), Box 2. Illinois. Camp D-2—Gilman, Drainage Project Initial and Completion Reports, 1936–1938, RG 114, NACP.

78. McGaan, "A Slant on Soil Conservation."

79. "Iroquois Farmer Plans Land Use Program," *Legionnaire Times*, March 1941; "Unit News," *Keyhole*, March 24, 1937, p. 3.

80. Charles G. Sauers to Mr. Stanley O'Carroll (April 20, 1937), Series V, Box 3, Folder 29, FPDCC.

81. Richard Wright, *12 Million Black Voices* (1941; New York: Thunder's Mouth Press, 1988), 64. On the seasonal cycle of Southern agriculture, see Charles Spurgeon Johnson, *Growing Up in the Black Belt: Negro Youth in the Rural South* (Washington, DC: American Council on Education, 1941), 170; Neil R. McMillen, *Dark Journey: Black Mississippians in the Age of Jim Crow* (Urbana: University of Illinois Press, 1989), 128; Powdermaker, *After Freedom*, 77–78; Sara Brooks and Thordis Simonsen, *You May Plow Here: The Narrative of Sara Brooks* (New York: Norton, 1986), 143–152; Shaw and Rosengarten, *All God's Dangers*, 178–184; and Gottlieb, *Making Their Own Way*, 17–19.

82. Drake and Cayton, *Black Metropolis*, 523. See also chapter 7 in Grossman, *Land of Hope*.

83. United States Department of Labor, "A Chance to Work in the Forests," DUL. See also Walker, *The CCC through the Eyes of 272 Boys*, 27.

84. Swisher, "Narrative Report for the Month of April, 1935," RG 79, NACP.

85. W. J. Swisher, "Narrative Report for the Month of February, 1935 of the Work Accomplished by S.P. 27 (Company 609, Colored)," Box 25 SP12-SP16, SP25-SP29, Folder Department of the Interior, National Park Service, State Park Conservation Work, Skokie Lagoons State Park, Project Reports on Civilian Conservation Corps Projects in State and Local Parks, 1933–1937, RG 79, NACP. See also Swisher, "Narrative Report for the Month of September," RG 79, NACP.

86. "Planting Season Opens." See also "Planting Season," *Trojan*, September 1939, p. 13.

87. "Planting Season Opens."

88. Jernberg and Caraman, *My Brush Monkeys*, 201. See also pages 27–30.

89. "Staying on Top," *Trojan*, September 15, 1938. See also Jernberg and Caraman, *My Brush Monkeys*, 173.

90. W. J. Swisher, "Narrative Report for the Month of August, of the Work Accomplished by S.P. 27 (Company 609—Colored)" (August 1934), Box 29 SP 24-SP29, Folder Skokie Lagoons State Park Report for SP-27—Illinois. Winnetka, Illinois, Project Reports on Civilian Conservation Corps Projects in State and Local Parks, 1933–1937, RG 79, NACP; W. J. Swisher, "Narrative Report for the Month of July, of the Work Accomplished by S.P. 27 (Company 609) (Colored)" (July 1934), Box 29 SP 24-SP29, Folder Skokie Lagoons State Park Report for SP-27—Illinois. Winnetka, Illinois, Project Reports on Civilian Conservation Corps Projects in State and Local Parks, 1933–1937, RG 79, NACP.

91. Swisher, "Narrative Report for the Month of August," RG 79, NACP.

92. "The Weather," *Gilman Gabber*, July 31, 1936.

93. "S.C.S. News"; Lowe to John Dancy, DUL.

94. "Forestry News: Moss Procurement." See also "Forestry News," *Trojan*, May 15, 1939, p. 1; Lowe to John Dancy, DUL.

95. John L. Hobbs, "Chicago Rookies Can't Take It," *Trojan*, August 1939, p. 19.

96. Wilson, "Narrative Report for the Month of January," RG 79, NACP.

97. Roy S. Corey, "Narrative Report for the Month of January of the Work Accomplished by S.P. 16 (Company 699, Colored)" (January 1935), Box 27 SP 13-SP16, Folder Skokie Lagoons State Park, Illinois. SP 16, Project Reports on Civilian Conservation Corps Projects in State and Local Parks, 1933–1937, RG 79, NACP. On similar conditions across the state that also spurred African American enrollees' refusal to work, see Harold G. Chafey to Mr. Charles H. Kenlan, Assistant to the Director, CCC (March 9, 1939), Box 61, Folder Illinois P-85 Pekin, Camp Inspection Reports, 1933–1942, RG 35, NACP; William P. Hannon, "Camp Report" (March 29–30, 1937), Box 61, Folder Illinois SCS-9, Camp Inspection Reports, 1933–1942, RG 35, NACP; William C. Graham, "Statement" (May 9, 1939), Box 62, Folder Illinois SCS-15 Carroll Co., Camp Inspection Reports, 1933–1942, RG 35, NACP; JB Bellinger to William P. Hannon, Special Investigator (February 25, 1936),

Box 62, Folder Illinois SCS-15 Carroll Co., Camp Inspection Reports, 1933–1942, RG 35, NACP; E. Mortimer Harris, "For Your Atten.," *Camp Carroll Volcano*, December 7, 1936, p. 1; Harold G. Chafey to Mr. Charles H. Kenlan, Assistant to the Director, CCC (February 17, 1939), Box 61, Folder Illinois SCS-12 Mercer Co., Camp Inspection Reports, 1933–1942, RG 35, NACP; Camp Gilman V3678 to Charles H. Kenlan, Assistant to the Director, CCC (December 28, 1938), Box 63, Folder Illinois SCS-44 Gilman formerly D-2 Gilman, Ill, Camp Inspection Reports, 1933–1942, RG 35, NACP.

98. Richard Wright, *Black Boy* draft, p. 487, Series I, Box 9, Folder 206, RW.

99. Swisher, "Narrative Report for the Month of February," RG 79, NACP.

100. F. E. Wilson, "Narrative Report for the Month of February, 1935 of the Work Accomplished by S.P. 16 (Company 610) (Colored)," Box 25 SP 12-SP16, SP 25-SP29, Folder Department of the Interior, National Park Service, State Park Conservation Work, Skokie Lagoons State Park, Project Reports on Civilian Conservation Corps Projects in State and Local Parks, 1933–1937, RG 79, NACP.

101. CR Logan, "Camp SCS 7 Stockton, Ill" (January 31, 1936), Box 61, Folder Illinois SCS-7 Stockton Co. 610, Camp Inspection Reports, 1933–1942, RG 35, NACP.

102. Cline, "Work Program CCC 13th and 14th Periods."

103. "Unit News," *Keyhole*, March 24, 1937, p. 3. See also Bell, "Dame Nature and Us." At the same time, however, enrollees at the same camp singled out one man for ridicule for having something of an ecological consciousness, saying that he "earned the name of 'nature' by preaching everything comes from nature and sooner or later returns to nature. We wonder if he will join a nudist colony trying to return to nature himself." Dotries Mason, "Barrack no. 2," *Deer Grove Ledger*, February 9, 1937, p. 4.

104. "Birth of Camp Aledo"; "First Year Ends at Camp Aledo."

105. "Camp Deer Grove Scene of Many Achievements."

106. "Unit News," *Keyhole*, February 24, 1937, p. 3. On the long African American tradition of hunting in the South, see Scott Giltner, "Slave Hunting and Fishing in the Antebellum South," in *To Love the Wind and the Rain*, ed. Glave and Stoll, 21–36.

107. "Mosquitoes Attack Camp Deer Grove; Casualties Heavy," *Deer Grove Ledger*, November 15, 1936, p. 1. See also Carr, "My First Day"; and "Mosquito Nets Turned in as the Season Ends," *Trojan*, September 1939, p. 4.

108. The explicit policy of one Michigan African American camp newspaper was to "print news from an optimistic point of view" to avoid "endangering the feelings and morale of its readers," which speaks to a positive bias in company newspapers that is balanced in part by internal reports and investigations. Alfred Gay, "To Our Readers," *Trojan*, August 1939, p. 2.

109. Henry 'Red' Ballard, "Limestone," *Camp Carroll Volcano*, August 21, 1936, p. 3.

110. Williams, "Unit News: Unit F." Other enrollees, meanwhile, felt this was "the most menial and back-breaking of tasks." Kifer, "The Negro under the New Deal," 24.

111. Curdo Williams, "Unit News: Station R-O-C-K Quarry—Unit F," *Keyhole,* January 20, 1937, p. 6. See also Curdo Williams, "Unit News: Unit F," *Keyhole,* April 14, 1937, p. 6.

112. Jernberg and Caraman, *My Brush Monkeys,* 178.

113. John Roundtree, "The Civilian Conservation Corps and the Benefit that It Has Been to Me," *Trojan,* August 1940, p. 16.

114. Ibid., 16–17.

115. Stanley W. Banks, "Saga of the C's," *Trojan,* October 15, 1938.

116. "Race Workers Play Important Part in Skokie Lagoon Project," *Chicago Defender (National Edition),* October 6, 1934, p. 20.

117. Quote in Adam Green, *Selling the Race: Culture, Community, and Black Chicago, 1940–1955* (Chicago: University of Chicago Press, 2007), 20. See also "2,000 to Take Part in CCC Day Aug. 2nd," *Chicago Defender (National Edition),* August 3, 1940, p. 9; Box 9, Folder War Department Special Personnel Reports 1940, Statistical Reports on Enrollees, 1933–1942, RG 35, NACP.

118. Corey, "Narrative Report for the Month of August," RG 79, NACP.

119. Grace, "Idlewild is Ideal!" *Pittsburgh Courier,* August 31, 1929, p. 7.

120. "Boys Brand CCC Camp as Peonage Farm," *Chicago Defender (National Edition),* December 11, 1937, p. 1.

121. Allonia W. Underwood, "Statement of Investigation" (December 21, 1937), Box 59, Folder Illinois F-2 Pomona Co. 620, Camp Inspection Reports, 1933–1942, RG 35, NACP; Melvin P. Twerdal, Jr., "Statement of Investigation" (December 21, 1937), Box 59, Folder Illinois F-2 Pomona Co. 620, Camp Inspection Reports, 1933–1942, RG 35, NACP; "Report of the Proceedings of a Board of Officers in the Case of the Investigation and Report on the Administration of the 620th Company, CCC, Camp Pomona, F-2 (Ill), Alto Pass, Illinois, since November 5, 1937," Box 59, Folder Illinois F-2 Pomona Co. 620, Camp Inspection Reports, 1933–1942, RG 35, NACP.

122. "Statement from MF Amen, Commanding," Box 59, Folder Illinois F-2 Pomona Co. 620, Camp Inspection Reports, 1933–1942, RG 35, NACP. Twenty-one enrollees were discharged as a result of the conflict; eight were from Chicago, four from Detroit, and the rest from small Illinois cities. Half of the Chicago enrollees were from the South Side, and the apparent "ringleader" lived just six blocks west of Washington Park. "Subject: Report of Investigation Relative Alleged Condition at Camp Pomona F-2 (Illinois). to: The Adjutant General, Washington, DC" (January 25, 1938), Box 59, Folder Illinois F-2 Pomona Co. 620, Camp Inspection Reports, 1933–1942, RG 35, NACP. For hints of similar discord from "Chicago boys" enrolled in a Skokie Lagoons company who were then transferred to a camp near Danville, Illinois, in 1942, see Harold G. Chafey, "Supplemental Report Camp SCS-48, Company 2603, Danville,

Illinois" (March 23, 1942), Box 64, Folder Illinois SCS-48 Danville, Camp Inspection Reports, 1933–1942, RG 35, NACP. On a remarkably similar conflict in an Ohio African American CCC camp, see Walker, *The CCC through the Eyes of 272 Boys*, 51–53.

123. "Report of the Proceedings of a Board of Officers," 30, RG 35, NACP; Claybourne H. Norris, "Letter to Editor, Chicago Defender" (December 21, 1937), Box 59, Folder Illinois F-2 Pomona Co. 620, Camp Inspection Reports, 1933–1942, RG 35, NACP.

124. "Report of the Proceedings of a Board of Officers," 33, RG 35, NACP.

125. "Statement from MF Amen, Commanding," RG 35, NACP.

126. "Report of the Proceedings of a Board of Officers," 18, 23, RG 35, NACP.

127. Ibid., 30.

128. Harry Collier, "Mr. Kenlan. the Following are My Notes Taken from Enrollees of Camp F-2, Alto Pass, Ill.," Box 59, Folder Illinois F-2 Pomona Co. 620, Camp Inspection Reports, 1933–1942, RG 35, NACP.

129. Harry Collier to Mr. Charles H. Kenlan, Assistant to the Director, CCC (December 24, 1937), Box 59, Folder Illinois F-2 Pomona Co. 620, Camp Inspection Reports, 1933–1942, RG 35, NACP.

130. The commander's worldview echoed that of a working-class Irish Catholic Chicagoan in James T. Farrell's novel *Young Lonigan*, who says (in a narrative set a generation earlier, in 1916, on Chicago's South Side), "Some niggers are all right. These southern ones know their place," but the "northern bucks are dangerous." James T. Farrell, *Studs Lonigan: A Trilogy* (New York: Library of America, [1932] 2004), 90.

131. Chafey, "Supplemental Report," RG 35, NACP. For similar racial prejudice voiced by a white CWA official in Chicago, see *Final Report: CWA Project 1340, a Consolidation of Projects* (1934), CPD.

132. Lieutenant Colonel AGD to the Director, Civilian Conservation Corps (December 22, 1941), Box 64, Folder Illinois SCS-48 Danville, Camp Inspection Reports, 1933–1942, RG 35, NACP.

133. On this longer tradition, see especially chapter 1 in Robin D. G. Kelley, *Race Rebels: Culture, Politics, and the Black Working Class* (New York: Free Press, 1994).

134. "Camp Inspection Report" (May 9, 1939), Box 61, Folder Illinois SCS-7 Stockton Co. 610, Camp Inspection Reports, 1933–1942, RG 35, NACP; "Supplementary Report. Company 610, SCS-7, Stockton, Illinois" (May 10, 1939), Box 61, Folder Illinois SCS-7 Stockton Co. 610, Camp Inspection Reports, 1933–1942, RG 35, NACP.

135. Harold G. Chafey, "Supplemental Report. Camp SCS-15, Company 2664, Mt. Carroll, Ill" (June 7, 1940), Box 62, Folder Illinois SCS-15 Carroll Co., Camp Inspection Reports, 1933–1942, RG 35, NACP.

136. CCC Camp Carroll to Mr. Harold G. Chafey (November 26, 1940), Box 62, Folder Illinois SCS-15 Carroll Co., Camp Inspection Reports, 1933–1942, RG 35, NACP.

137. On Parchman Farm and widespread convict leasing practices in the South, see David M. Oshinsky, *"Worse than Slavery": Parchman Farm and the Ordeal of Jim Crow Justice* (New York: Free Press, 1996); and Douglas A. Blackmon, *Slavery by Another Name: The Re-Enslavement of Black People in America from the Civil War to World War II* (New York: Doubleday, 2008).

138. "Narrative Report, Deer Grove Camp, State Park no.-38, Palatine, Illinois" (January 1935), Box 35 SP 38, Folder Deer Grove State Park. Camp 36. Palatine, Illinois., Project Reports on Civilian Conservation Corps Projects in State and Local Parks, 1933–1937, RG 79, NACP.

139. Corey, "Narrative Report for the Month of January," RG 79, NACP.

140. Roy S. Corey, "State Park #16, Company 699, Colored" (December 1935 & January 1936), Box 27 SP 13-SP16, Folder Skokie Lagoons State Park, Illinois. SP 16., Project Reports on Civilian Conservation Corps Projects in State and Local Parks, 1933–1937, RG 79, NACP.

141. Statistics covering more than three years of CCC enrollment in Illinois (1938–1941) indicate that the attrition rate for both African American and white enrollees hovered around 10 percent. In fact, African American enrollees appear to have been more likely to reenroll in the CCC for an additional six-month period, which was perhaps suggestive of how much more difficult it was for African Americans—last hired, first fired—to find employment outside the CCC. Box 9, Folder War Department Special Personnel Reports 1940, Statistical Reports on Enrollees, 1933–1942, RG 35, NACP. A study of Cleveland African American enrollees corroborates this assertion. Walker, *The CCC through the Eyes of 272 Boys*, 66.

142. Swisher, "Narrative Report for the Month of September," RG 79, NACP.

143. F. E. Wilson, "Narrative Report of S.P. 27 (Company 609, Colored) for the Months of August and September, 1935," Box 29 SP 24-SP29, Folder Skokie Lagoons State Park Report for SP-27—Illinois. Winnetka, Illinois, Project Reports on Civilian Conservation Corps Projects in State and Local Parks, 1933–1937, RG 79, NACP.

144. W. J. Swisher, "Narrative Report of S.P. 27 (Company 609, Colored) for the Months of June and July, 1935," Box 25 SP12-SP16, SP25-SP29, Folder Department of the Interior, National Park Service, State Park Conservation Work, Skokie Lagoons State Park, Project Reports on Civilian Conservation Corps Projects in State and Local Parks, 1933–1937, RG 79, NACP.

145. On African American work songs and urban migration, see chapter 4 in Lawrence W. Levine, *Black Culture and Black Consciousness: Afro-American Folk Thought from Slavery to Freedom* (New York: Oxford University Press, 1977).

146. Jernberg and Caraman, *My Brush Monkeys*, 33. For the African American stereotypes, complete with dialect, see especially pages 23–60. Although the names and places have been changed, the officer was almost certainly employed at either Camps Baldwin or Bitely, both near Idlewild. It seems likely the officer chose "Green Pastures" as the fictionalized name

to also reference the Detroit Urban League summer camp in Michigan, by then a well-known youth camp. Mention of "an East Indian" who "talks to the boys on the subject of psychology" almost certainly refers to Joseph A. Downing, also known as Joveddah De Rajah. See Stephens, *Idlewild*, 94–109.

147. Jernberg and Caraman, *My Brush Monkeys*, 35.

Epilogue

1. Richard Wright, "The Shame of Chicago," *Ebony* 7, no. 2 (December 1951), 26–27.

2. Ibid., 24; Richard Wright, *Black Boy (American Hunger): A Record of Childhood and Youth* (New York: HarperPerennial Modern Classics, [1945] 2006), 262.

3. Wright, "The Shame of Chicago," 28.

4. Ibid., 32.

5. Mayor's Commission on Human Relations, *Recreation for All: A Manual for Supervisors and Workers in Recreation* (1946), Box 171, Folder 5, WC.

6. W. E. B. Du Bois, "Postscript," *Crisis* 41, no. 6 (June 1934), 182.

7. See chapters 3 and 4 in Ronald J. Stephens, *Idlewild: The Rise, Decline, and Rebirth of a Unique African American Resort Town* (Ann Arbor: University of Michigan Press, 2013).

8. "George Arthur, Chicago 'Y' Secretary, Dies," *Chicago Defender (National Edition)* June 7, 1941, 12; William J. Parker to Albert W. Harris (May 2, 1945), Box 19, Folder 16, YMCAM; "Minutes of the Board of Directors of the Wabash Avenue Department YMCA" (June 17, 1947), Box 6, Folder 67, YMCAW.

9. "Southside Community Committee Bulletin" 1, no. 4 (September 1947), 3, Box 98, Folder 4, CAP; South Side Community Committee, "Journal" (1942), 29, Box 98, Folder 1, CAP; Southside Community Committee, "Report," Box 98, Folder 1, CAP; "Digest Report for 1945 of the Southside Community Committee" (1945), 3, Box 98, Folder 3, CAP; Southside Community Committee, *Bright Shadows in Bronzetown: The Story of the Southside Community Committee* (Chicago, 1949).

10. Clinton Harrell, Jr. to Myrtle Sengstacke (July 20, 1950), Box 236, Folder 24, ASF. Married to *Defender* publisher John Sengstacke, Myrtle Sengstacke was an active supporter of the Girl Scouts as well as the YMCA in this period.

11. "Minutes from the Wabash YMCA 1948 Annual Staff Conference" (September 21, 1948), Box 6, Folder 67, YMCAW; "Camp" (September 21, 1948), Box 6, Folder 67, YMCAW; "Board of Directors Meeting" (February 18, 1958), Box 6, Folder 68, YMCAW; Roi Ottley, "Neighborhood Y.M.C.A. Spells End to Slum," *Chicago Daily Tribune*, April 10, 1960, p. NA1.

12. See the Introduction in Jeffrey Helgeson, "Striving in Black Chicago: Migration, Work, and the Politics of Neighborhood Change 1935–1965" (Ph.D. diss., University of Illinois at Chicago, 2008); and Edward Glaeser, Jacob Vigdor, and the Manhattan Institute, "The End of the Segregated Century: Racial Separation in America's Neighborhoods, 1890–2010," *Civic Report* 66 (January 2012), 6. For broader trends in this second wave of migration, see James N. Gregory, *The Southern Diaspora: How the Great Migrations of Black and White Southerners Transformed America* (Chapel Hill: University of North Carolina Press, 2005).

13. Excellent studies of these postwar trends in Chicago include Arnold R. Hirsch, *Making the Second Ghetto: Race and Housing in Chicago, 1940–1960* (New York: Cambridge University Press, 1983); Nicholas Lemann, *The Promised Land: The Great Black Migration and How it Changed America* (New York: A. A. Knopf, 1991); Sudhir Alladi Venkatesh, *American Project: The Rise and Fall of a Modern Ghetto* (Cambridge, MA: Harvard University Press, 2000); Amanda I. Seligman, *Block by Block: Neighborhoods and Public Policy on Chicago's West Side* (Chicago: University of Chicago Press, 2005); Mary E. Pattillo, *Black on the Block: The Politics of Race and Class in the City* (Chicago: University of Chicago Press, 2007); D. Bradford Hunt, *Blueprint for Disaster: The Unraveling of Chicago Public Housing* (Chicago: University of Chicago Press, 2009); and Jeffrey Helgeson, *Crucibles of Black Empowerment: Chicago's Neighborhood Politics from the New Deal to Harold Washington* (Chicago: University of Chicago Press, 2014). More generally on the urban crisis and postwar trends in Great Migration destinations, see Thomas J. Sugrue, *The Origins of the Urban Crisis: Race and Inequality in Postwar Detroit* (Princeton, NJ: Princeton University Press, 1996); Robert O. Self, *American Babylon: Race and the Struggle for Postwar Oakland* (Princeton, NJ: Princeton University Press, 2003); Thomas J. Sugrue, *Sweet Land of Liberty: The Forgotten Struggle for Civil Rights in the North* (New York: Random House, 2008); and Douglas S. Massey, *American Apartheid: Segregation and the Making of the Underclass* (Cambridge, MA: Harvard University Press, 1993).

14. Glen E. Holt, Dominic A. Pacyga, and Chicago Historical Society, *Chicago, a Historical Guide to the Neighborhoods: The Loop and South Side* (Chicago: Chicago Historical Society, 1979), 87–99; "Smash Cobra Gang's Attempt to Mar Event," *Chicago Defender (National Edition)*, August 8, 1960, p. 1; "Five Teens Assault Girl, 16," *Chicago Defender (National Edition)*, July 13, 1961, p. 1; "3 Chicago Parks Listed in U.S. Dangerous Dozen," *Chicago Tribune*, September 20, 1963, p. C10; "Arrest 63, Stop Gang War," *Chicago Defender (National Edition)*, August 10, 1964, p. 1; "Rip Shoddy Conditions in Washington Park," *Chicago Defender (National Edition)*, July 17, 1975, p. 4; Timuel Black, interview with the author, January 21, 2010.

15. On Idlewild in this period, see chapter 6 in Stephens, *Idlewild;* and chapter 5 in Lewis Walker and Benjamin C. Wilson, *Black Eden: The Idlewild Community* (East Lansing: Michigan State University Press, 2002). On these more

general trends nationwide, see chapter 7 in Andrew Kahrl, *The Land Was Ours: African American Beaches from Jim Crow to the Sunbelt South* (Cambridge, MA: Harvard University Press, 2012).

16. "Board of Directors Wabash Avenue YMCA" (January 19, 1960), Box 6, Folder 68, YMCAW.

17. "An Address by: Dr. Martin Luther King, Jr., Chicago Freedom Festival, the Amphitheatre, Chicago, Illinois, Saturday, March 12, 1966," 2–3, Series III, Box 278, Folder 2934, CUL.

18. "Rights Hecklers Burn Cars," *Chicago Tribune,* August 1, 1966, p. 1; "Dr. King Is Felled by Rock," *Chicago Tribune,* August 6, 1966, p. 1. For a much more nuanced and in-depth treatment of the Chicago Freedom Movement and the violence that confronted protestors in Marquette Park, see especially Mary Lou Finley et al., *The Chicago Freedom Movement: Martin Luther King Jr. and Civil Rights Activism in the North* (Lexington: University Press of Kentucky, 2015), 51–59; chapter 30 in Taylor Branch, *At Canaan's Edge: America in the King Years, 1965–68* (New York: Simon & Schuster, 2006); and James R. Ralph, *Northern Protest: Martin Luther King, Jr., Chicago, and the Civil Rights Movement* (Cambridge, MA: Harvard University Press, 1993).

19. Martin Luther King and Clayborne Carson, *The Autobiography of Martin Luther King, Jr.* (New York: Warner Books, 1998), 305.

20. National Advisory Commission on Civil Disorders, *Report of the National Advisory Commission on Civil Disorders* (Washington, DC: U.S. Government Printing Office, 1968), 1.

21. "Many Stores Looted; Firemen Face Snipers," *Chicago Tribune,* April 6, 1968, p. N1; "Troops Find New Homes in Jackson Park," *Chicago Tribune,* April 8, 1968, p. 14.

22. Quoted in Peter B. Slevin, *Michelle Obama: A Life* (New York: Alfred A. Knopf, 2015), 53. For a much more in-depth account of Michelle Obama's Great Migration roots, see Part I in Rachel L. Swarns, *American Tapestry: The Story of the Black, White, and Multiracial Ancestors of Michelle Obama* (New York: Amistad, 2012).

23. Barack Obama, *Dreams from My Father: A Story of Race and Inheritance* (New York: Three Rivers Press, 2004; 1995), 145.

24. Michelle Obama, *American Grown: The Story of the White House Kitchen Garden and Gardens across America* (New York: Crown Publishers, 2012), 15.

25. "Police Clash with Whites on Rainbow Beach; Nab 11," *Chicago Tribune,* July 17, 1961, p. 3; "Race Waders Back; 9 Seized," *Chicago Tribune,* July 10, 1961, p. B12; "10 are Seized at 'Freedom' Trek to Beach," *Chicago Tribune,* July 9, 1961, p. 28.

26. See, among many others, chapters 5, 6, and 16 in Robert J. Sampson, *Great American City: Chicago and the Enduring Neighborhood Effect* (Chicago: University of Chicago Press, 2012).

Acknowledgments

From its earliest stages, this book was shaped in countless ways by Harvard University's History of American Civilization Program, and it would not exist without the wisdom, guidance, and support of my advisors there, Evelyn Brooks Higginbotham, Lawrence Buell, Andrew Kahrl, and Davarian Baldwin. Evelyn and Larry were integral to the project from the very beginning, and Andrew and Davarian have been immensely helpful as it matured; I cannot say enough about how much they have meant to me both professionally and personally, and I will be forever grateful to them all. In its latter stages, the project also greatly benefited from the insight and vision of two anonymous readers as well as Harvard University Press's editorial team—especially my editor, Andrew Kinney. Any and all shortcomings are mine, not theirs.

The vast majority of my archival research took place in Chicago, and research funding from Harvard's History of American Civilization Program and the Charles Warren Center for Studies in American History helped make those trips possible. The Dean of Faculty at Lake Forest College generously granted financial support to publish the many images in this text that were discovered on those archival trips over the course of many years. My debt to many people in Chicago is deep, and there is no one I am more grateful to than Julia Bachrach, formerly of the Chicago Park District Special Collections, who consistently went above and beyond what any researcher can reasonably expect from an archivist. Timuel Black, Margaret Burroughs, Carl Davis, Charles Davis, Clarice Durham, Jimmy Ellis, and Ben Gaines were all unfailingly generous with their time, kindly answering questions from (and often welcoming into their homes) a scholar they did not know from Adam—but whom Michael Flug, the legendary former archivist for the Vivian G. Harsh Research Collection at the Carter G. Woodson branch of the Chicago Public Library, had been kind enough to introduce. This book is richer for their stories, and I have tried my best to represent their memories faithfully; I hope the black Chicago in these pages is one they and many other South Siders recognize. Thanks are also due to archivists and staff in Chicago and beyond, including Dan Harper at the University of Illinois at Chicago Special Collections, the Chicago History Museum, the University of Chicago Special Collections, the Carter G. Woodson and Harold Washington branches of the Chicago Public Library, the National Archives at College Park, Yale's Beinecke Library, and the New York Public Library's Schomburg Center. Fellow panelists, commenters, and audience members at various venues where I have presented this research helped improve the project in numerous ways: these venues include Williams College's Log Lunch; the Massachusetts Historical Society Environmental History Seminar; the W. E. B. Du Bois Institute Colloquium; the Yale Northeast Environmental History Conference; Harvard's History of American Civilization colloquia and workshops; Harvard's American Literature Colloquium; and annual meetings of the American Historical Association, American Studies Association, the Association for the Study of Literature and the Environment, the Social Science History Association, and the American Society for Environmental History, where Colin Fisher's support and insight have been especially welcome.

Countless people have shaped me intellectually over the course of nearly twenty years in academia, and whether or not we talked about this project directly, they influenced it. At Purdue University, Ryan Schneider, Susan Curtis, and Leigh Raymond all pushed my scholarly boundaries, and while making the sometimes difficult transition from engineer to humanist I enjoyed the friendship and support of Chris Abreu, Tom Hertweck, Mark Bousquet, Lee Bebout, Charles Park, Delayne Graham, and many others. If there are better teachers than Bob Lamb and Kip Robisch, I have not met them. Bob has been my academic godfather since my freshman year and was almost singlehandedly responsible for my transition from engineering to American Studies; Kip let me recite Bob Dylan lyrics as poetry and, arguably more importantly, turned me on to the environmental humanities. Bob and Kip have been my most important and beloved mentors for nearly two decades now, and I am still striving to live up to their examples—I could not be happier that they have since become good friends. At Harvard, many people shaped the project in ways large and small, and I want to thank, in particular, John Stauffer, Arthur Patton-Hock, Christine McFadden, Mary Anne Adams, Jeanne Follansbee, Mo Moulton, and the Widener Library staff. At Harvard's W. E. B. Du Bois Institute, I enjoyed a rewarding fellowship year in the company of, among others, Fred Opie, Peniel Joseph, Diane McWhorter, Ed Pavlic, Tahir Hemphill, Krishna Lewis, and, of course, Henry Louis Gates. I remain immensely thankful that Ralph Bradburd and Jennifer French gave me the opportunity to teach the environmental humanities at Williams

College; one could not ask for better students than I had there, as well as in Harvard's History and Literature Department. Nick Howe, Sarah Gardner, Pia Kohler, Drew Jones, James Manigault-Bryant, Natalie Bump Vena, Karen Merrill, Mea Cook, and DeeDee Lewis all made my two years at Williams rewarding ones both professionally and personally. I have only just begun what I hope will be a long tenure at Lake Forest College, but already it feels like home thanks to the wonderful Environmental Studies students there and Glenn Adelson (who read the entirety of this manuscript with his keen eye), Ben Goluboff, Jeff Sundberg, Miguel de Baca, Todd Beer, Holly Swyers, Rebecca Graff, Alex Blanchard, and many others in the wider community.

Last but not least, deep thanks are due to numerous friends and family. Harvard University's Winthrop House gave my wife and me friends that became a family: Gregg Peeples, Michele Gauger and all of Team Awesome, Joanna Miller, David Simms, Enoch Kyerematen, Heather Grant, Isabel Barbosa, and too many students to name turned a dormitory into a home. The ways in which friends from Harvard's American Civilization Program made my years in Cambridge some of the best of my life are too many to count; many of them read pieces of this project at various stages, and the book in your hands is undoubtedly better for it. But most of the best memories from those graduate and postgraduate years have absolutely nothing to do with academia, thank goodness. I will always miss long afternoons at the Lesley basketball courts, happy hour beers on Shays patio, and truffle fries at the Cellar with Tim McGrath and Tenley Archer, Brian and Hillary Hochman, Jack Hamilton, Pete L'Official, Nick Donofrio, George Blaustein, Maggie Gram, Eva Payne and Evan Kingsley, Eli Cook, Derek Etkin, Katherine Stevens, Erin Dwyer, Clinton Williams, David Kim, Jamie Jones, and Scott Poulson-Bryant. Long live the ACBL and PSD. Friends and family near and far—Dan and Betsy McDowell, Ryan Gates and Serena Oaks, Megan and Jertez Hunter, Brian Anderson and Laura Gleason, Joey Sample and Andrew Hall, Jason Gromski, Eleni and Scott Drake, Courtney Parker, Jayson Cooley, Joe Monical and Anna Lee, Nathan Shipley and Rhea Myerscough, Craig and Ariel Ferguson, and the Up North Vincent clan among many others—were always supportive even when they wondered out loud why this book still was not done.

Most of all, thanks are due to my Indiana and Chicago families. They are small, but their support has been enormous. My mother-in-law, Kate Vincent, and sister-in-law Meg Vincent provided a home away from home on my research trips to Chicago; I probably still owe them some wine. Marilyn and Jim, my mom and dad, have always been there for me. I do not know exactly what they did or how they did it, but from a very early age they—along with my grandparents, Louise, Owen, Helen, and Wilfred—instilled in me the values that have allowed me to succeed. Without them I would not have a bachelor's degree, much less a doctorate and a published book. Mom and Dad: thanks will never be enough. I love you, and I can only hope I become the sort of parent you have both been to me. My biggest supporters of all have been my immediate family: my wife, Laura, and our good dogs, Tippy, Buddy, and Crispin. From Indianapolis to Cambridge to Chicago, Laura has been by my side since well before this book was even a glimmer of an idea. I would not have wanted it any other way. Laura, this book is for you and our brand-new daughter, Catherine Louise: I love you, I love you, I love you both.

Index